INTERNATIONAL SURVEY OF FAMILY

Published on behalf of the International Society of Family Law

INTERNATIONAL
SOCIETY OF FAMILY
LAW

INTERNATIONAL SURVEY OF FAMILY LAW

2023 Edition

Edited by
Robin Fretwell WILSON
June CARBONE

In collaboration with
Emma KRUGER

INTERSENTIA

Cambridge – Antwerp – Chicago

Intersentia Ltd
8 Wellington Mews
Wellington Street | Cambridge
CB1 1HW | United Kingdom
Tel: +44 1223 736 170
Email: contact@larcier-intersentia.com
www.larcier-intersentia.com

Distribution for the UK and
Rest of the World (incl. Eastern Europe)
NBN International
1 Deltic Avenue, Rooksley
Milton Keynes MK13 8LD
United Kingdom
Tel: +44 1752 202 301 | Fax: +44 1752 202 331
Email: orders@nbninternational.com

Distribution for Europe
Lefebvre Sarrut Belgium NV
Hoogstraat 139/6
1000 Brussels
Belgium
Tel: +32 (0)2 548 07 13
Email: contact@larcier-intersentia.com

Distribution for the USA and Canada
Independent Publishers Group
Order Department
814 North Franklin Street
Chicago, IL 60610
USA
Tel: +1 800 888 4741 (toll free) | Fax: +1 312 337 5985
Email: orders@ipgbook.com

International Survey of Family Law. 2023 Edition
© The editors and contributors severally 2023

Artwork on cover: © Cienpies Design – Shutterstock

ISBN 978-1-83970-401-7
D/2023/7849/153
NUR 828

British Library Cataloguing in Publication Data. A catalogue record for this book is available from the British Library.

PREFACE

The 2023 edition of the International Survey of Family Law celebrates the International Society of Family Law's (ISFL) fiftieth anniversary. This first of two Jubilee editions begins with fascinating memoirs recounting the discussions that led to ISFL's creation, a conference in Opatija, Yugoslavia with tanks rumbling nearby on the eve of the Balkan War, the ISFL's expansion with meetings in Australia, Japan, and South Africa, and the role of the Society in anticipating and creating a foundation for family law reform.

This first Jubilee edition complements the more personal memoirs with retrospectives on long-term changes in family law across the globe. The chapters describe 'a revolution in family law' over the last half century as much of the world shifted from a unifocal emphasis on marriage to much more inclusive systems of family regulation. Individual chapters recount how, in Portugal, the democratic governments that followed the overthrow of Portugal's dictatorship embraced family law liberation, the transformation in Belgium in the legal definition of parenthood, and the Scottish developments broadening recognition of different family relationships. Other chapters consider the parallel developments in Japan and China, with the Japanese shifting from a patriarchal system of family regulation to greater recognition of gender equality, and from multigenerational families to nuclear families to individual expression, while the Chinese have reformed family law and procedure as part of the 'rejuvenation of the Chinese nation'.

The chapters focused on more recent developments, in turn, report on the continuing process of family law reform and retrenchment. This first Jubilee edition reviews the incorporation of artificial intelligence into family law techniques, with a particularly trenchant comparison of the success in doing so with online platforms in Australia and the much greater resistance from practitioners in the Netherlands. Another chapter examines the evolution of the relationship between civil and Shari'a courts in Israel, as Muslim litigants obtained the ability to choose between civil and religious tribunals. It describes the result as the 'Islamisation of Israeli law', with civil courts applying relatively conservative interpretations of shari'a law and the 'Israelisation of shari'a law', as the Islamic tribunals adopted relatively more liberal interpretations of the same religious principles. Other chapters consider the continuing controversies over the recognition of same-sex relationships in the island nations of the Southern Pacific and Brazil, the reconciliation of legal recognition of modern informal families with the customary law of Kenya, the need for reforms in the legal treatment of the elderly in Poland, inheritance law reforms in China, and a comparison of the right to privacy in the United States and Israel, after the US Supreme Court overturned a half century of protection of abortion access under the privacy rubric.

We are especially grateful for the French translation of abstracts. The translation continues to be done by the Family Law Centre of the University Jean Moulin Lyon 3 under Christine Bidaud's direction. This year's volume was produced in collaboration with Emma Kruger. We are also grateful to Pamela Melton for her assistance with the preparation of the Survey. We would also like to thank Piotr Fiedorczy for his valuable work in assembling the Reflections, which provide an oral history of the ISFL.

The next Jubilee edition of the Survey will continue the celebration of the ISFL's fiftieth anniversary.

June Carbone, Minnesota
Robin Fretwell Wilson, Illinois
July 2023

CONTENTS

LIST OF CONTRIBUTORS

Elisabeth Alofs
Professor of Family (Property) Law, Head of the Department of Private & Economic Law and Director of the Master in Notarial Studies, Vrije Universiteit Brussel/Free University Brussels, Belgium

Masha Antokolskaia
Professor of Private and Family, Vrije University Amsterdam, the Netherlands

Bill Atkin
Professor of Law, Te Herenga Waka, Victoria University of Wellington, New Zealand

Małgorzata Balwicka-Szczyrba
Associate Professor of Law, Faculty of Law and Administration, Department of Commercial Law, University of Gdańsk, Poland

June Carbone
Robina Chair of Law, Science and Technology, University of Minnesota, United States of America

Aurélie Cassiers
Teaching Assistant in Family and Matrimonial Law and PhD Student, Hasselt University, Belgium

Chen Wei
Professor of Law, Former Director of the Foreign Family Law and Women Theories Institute, Civil and Commercial Law School, Southwest University of Political Science and Law, Chongqing, China; Vice Chairman, Marriage and Family Law Research Institute, China Law Society, Beijing, China

Jennifer Corrin
Professor Emerita, The University of Queensland, Australia

Ruth Deech, Baroness Deech of Cumnor, DBE, KC (Hon)
Member of the House of Lords, United Kingdom

John Eekelaar
Emeritus Fellow, Pembroke College, University of Oxford, United Kingdom

Hugues Fulchiron
Professor, Co-Director of the Family Law Center, Research Team Louis Josserand, Université Jean Moulin Lyon 3, France; Judge at the Cour de cassation

Marsha Garrison
1901 Distinguished Research Professor of Law, Brooklyn Law School, New York, United States of America

Marco Giacalone
Postdoctoral Researcher, Co-Director of the Digitalisation and Access to Justice Research Group (DIKE), Department of Private & Economic Law, Vrije Universiteit Brussel/Free University Brussels, Belgium

Mary Ann Glendon
Learned Hand Professor of Law, Emerita, Harvard University, United States of America

Ayako Harada
Professor, Graduate School of Law, Nagoya University, Japan

He Haiyan
Doctor of Law and Lecturer, Law School, Chengdu University; Scientific Researcher, Sichuan Anti-Domestic Violence Knowledge Popularization Base, Chengdu, China

Mark Henaghan
Professor of Law, University of Auckland, New Zealand

Emilie Hermans
PhD Student, Hasselt University and Namur University, Belgium

Nishat Hyder-Rahman
Postdoctoral Researcher, Department of Private & Economic Law, Vrije Universiteit Brussel/Free University Brussels, Belgium; Lecturer, Department of Private, Business & Labour Law, Tilburg University, the Netherlands

Sanford N. Katz
Darald & Juliet Libby Emeritus Professor, Boston College Law School, United States of America

Pamela Laufer-Ukeles
Professor of Law and Public Health, Academic College of Law and Science, Hod Hasharon, Israel

Nigel Lowe KC (Hon)
Emeritus Professor of Law, Cardiff University, United Kingdom

Lu Xiaobei
Paralegal, Jincheng Tongda & Neal Law Firm, Shenzhen, China

Géraldine Mathieu
Professor of Family Law and Youth Law, Namur University, Belgium

Patrick Parkinson AM
Emeritus Professor of Law, University of Queensland, Australia

Antonio Jorge Pereira Júnior
Professor of the Law Postgraduate Program, University of Fortaleza, Brazil

Jamil Ddamulira Mujuzi
Professor of Law, Faculty of Law, University of the Western Cape, South Africa

Ido Shahar
Senior Lecturer of Middle Eastern and Islamic Studies, University of Haifa, Israel

Elaine E. Sutherland
Professor Emerita, Stirling Law School, University of Stirling, Scotland, United Kingdom; Distinguished Professor of Law Emerita, Lewis and Clark Law School, Portland, Oregon, United States of America

Anna Sylwestrzak
Associate Professor of Law, Faculty of Law and Administration, Department of Civil Law, University of Gdańsk, Poland

Hazel Thompson-Ahye
Independent Senator, Republic of Trinidad and Tobago Parliament; Former Family Law Course Director, Council of Legal Education, Hugh Wooding Law School, Republic of Trinidad and Tobago

Paula Távora Vítor
Professor, Faculty of Law and Researcher, Family Law Center and Institute for Legal Research (IJ | UCILeR), University of Coimbra, Portugal

Paul Vlaardingerbroek
Emeritus Professor, Faculty of Law, Tilburg University; Deputy Judge, Court of Rotterdam, the Netherlands

Robin Fretwell Wilson
Mildred Van Voorhis Chair in Law, University of Illinois College of Law, University of Illinois System, United States of America

Karin Carmit Yefet
Senior Lecturer, Faculty of Law, University of Haifa, Israel; Member of the Global Young Academy

Zhu Fan
Associate Professor of Law, Civil and Commercial Law, Southwest University of Political Science and Law, Chongqing, China

PART I

REFLECTIONS ON 50 YEARS
OF THE INTERNATIONAL SOCIETY
OF FAMILY LAW

REFLECTIONS ON THE INTERNATIONAL SURVEY OF FAMILY LAW

Bill Atkin*

1. INTRODUCTION

During the period of my involvement with the *Survey*, which started in 1981, I saw it go from an informal internal publication to an official, smart-looking and professional vehicle for the dissemination of ideas and developments on a global basis. During the period from 2007 to 2016, I had the privilege of being the General Editor of the *International Survey*. I inherited a going concern, and was glad to pass it on in much the same state. Although very time-consuming, it was a great enterprise to be involved with. It enabled me to reinforce existing networks, but also to build new friendships and intellectual relationships. Every year there was a definite 'product' in the form of a handsome volume. It was a very positive experience for me.

I was no doubt seen as a likely prospect to edit the *Survey* because I had contributed to the *Survey* every year since 1981, writing about my home country New Zealand. That contribution began early in my career, and helped cement my

---

* Professor of Law, Te Herenga Waka/Victoria University of Wellington, New Zealand.

own development as an academic. When I was asked to take over the editorship, I felt daunted, but at least I knew roughly what was entailed. I shall comment more specifically on my experiences later on, but first let us explore some of the history of the *Survey*, with some key moments in its life.

2. HISTORY

2.1. FROM MODEST BEGINNINGS TO A REGULAR PUBLICATION OUTLET

The precise beginnings of the *Survey* I have found to be murky. The earliest copy I have on my shelves was published in 1979, and is the 'No. 4' issue. The first copies were in the form of an annual newsletter, published under the Society's auspices. Frank Bates, then a reader at the University of Tasmania, and now emeritus professor at the University of Newcastle, New South Wales, had just become editor in time for the 1979 issue, and in his Preface he stated: 'I have taken the liberty of changing its title to that of the Annual Survey of Family Law, as that name seems better to describe the aims of the publication.'[1] The wording suggested that it was a unilateral decision, but it stuck, apparently without opposition, and the name continued until 1984.

The 1979 volume contained chapters on Australia, England, Greece, Japan, Puerto Rico, South Africa, Spain and the United States. They were basically summaries of what had happened in the family law area during the relevant year. This pattern continued for some time, with yearly updates from a small range of jurisdictions. The 1980 volume added India, Ireland and Yugoslavia, but omitted Japan. The 1981 *Survey*, No. 6, was the third under Bates' editorship. It was not actually published until 1982, with eight chapters, including Canada and New Zealand.

The seventh issue foreshadowed changes. Michael Freeman, Professor at University College London, took over the editorship after a hiatus. The 1982 issue was the seventh, but was not published until 1984. As Freeman said in the Introduction: '[the] considerable lapse of time since the last volume' was largely because of abortive attempts to secure the services of a publisher to put the *Survey* 'on a more professional basis'.[2] He flagged that the next volume, covering 1983–1984, would be 'the most comprehensive' so far, with contributions solicited from over 20 authors.

The really big change did not occur, though, until issue No. 9. This 1985 *Survey* was published in 1986 by the University of Louisville School of Law's

---

[1] F. BATES, *Annual Survey of Family Law 1979* (no official publisher), p. v.

[2] M. FREEMAN, *Annual Survey of Family Law 1982* (no official publisher), p, i.

Journal of Family Law. It contained 29 chapters, including Michael Freeman's discussion of the recently decided landmark case on children's rights of *Gillick*;[3] a chapter on Iranian 'Family Law After the Islamic Revolution'; and another on the Soviet Union, 'The Transition to the Gorbachev Era', all very contemporary. The extensive coverage in this issue certainly reflects Freeman's wish that the *Survey* be more comprehensive: all continents are represented, and many chapters carefully analyse discrete topics rather than simply giving an annual update.

President John Eekelaar, in his 'President's Remarks' said, in relation to the Journal of Family Law, that 'we believe ... we have found a way to make available much useful information both to members of the Society and other interested persons. We hope that this arrangement will promote the objectives of the Journal as much as of the Society.'[4] The deal with the University of Louisville may be seen, in hindsight, as a coup for the Society and the *Survey*. The earliest versions of the *Survey* were internally produced, and designed primarily for consumption by Society members. The form of publication was not sophisticated but, at least for the copies in my possession, had proper soft bound covers, with different colours for different years. From the 1985 *Survey*, the publication took the form of a proper journal. Moreover, it was no longer purely for internal consumption, but was instead available to all who subscribed to the Journal, or had access to it. In other words, the *Survey* was available much more widely than before.

An innovation in volume 10 of the *Survey* was the inclusion of five book reviews.[5] The books were on adoption (by Philip Bean), Scandinavian law relating to unmarried cohabitation[6] (one book by Anders Agell, and another by Helge Thue), divorce (Leonore Weitzman), sexual divisions (Katherine O'Donovan), and Michael Freeman's own *State, Law and the Family*.[7] These names will ring bells, as will the reviewers: Jean Seglow, Svend Danielson, Carol Smart, Regina Graycar and Leonore Weitzman (not reviewing her own book, I hasten to add). Book reviews continued for only a couple of years, none appearing after volume 13 (1989). There were no reviews in my time as editor. I wonder whether publishers are sending out fewer books for review these days, and hence fewer reviews are published generally. I am trying to think when I last received a book to review.

Volume 10 saw a further innovation. For the first time, there were French résumés for each chapter. These appeared at the end of each chapter rather than the beginning, as they now do. Michael Freeman thanked Felicity Carby-Hall for her assistance with the abstracts. Later on, the *Survey* itself was published in French for several years. This would have been a mammoth task, and it

---

3   *Gillick v. West Norfolk Area Health Authority* [1986] AC 112 (HL).
4   J. EEKELAAR, 'President's Remarks' (1986) 25 *J. Fam L.* x.
5   'Annual Survey of Family Law 1986' (1987) 26 *J. Fam L.* 255 ff.
6   In Australasia, we use the phrase 'de facto relationship'.
7   M.D.A. FREEMAN, *State, Law and the Family*, Tavistock, 1984.

became unmanageable. Apparently, the Executive Council discussed how best to provide for French-speaking members of the Society and decided on French abstracts. Andrew Bainham states that this happened for the first time with the 2004 edition, but in fact it had occurred earlier.[8] In my time as General Editor, ensuring that we had French résumés was an important part of the production process. Some authors wrote their own English abstracts, but often I did so as part of the editing work. I can read French, but I was not able to translate the abstracts. Thus, I was extremely grateful that Dominique Goubau from Montreal did this task. He had help, a bit later on, from Hugues Fulchiron and his team at Lyon. The 2021 edition includes thanks to Dominique, and Christine Bidaud, Professor at Lyon 3 University.

While on the question of translation, some chapters arrived in a foreign language: Spanish, French and, occasionally, Portuguese. For many years, Peter Schofield offered his translation services. Unfortunately, by the time I took over Peter was very unwell, and thus could not continue. I recall having to pay (through my university) for a translation from a Spanish text. The translation retained many of its Spanish origins and a former student fluent in Spanish agreed to do further work on it for free (though I bought him a good lunch!). Subsequently, I required submissions to be in English. Even so, I had to work hard turning some manuscripts into readable English.

2.2. A STAND-ALONE PUBLICATION

Major developments occurred in 1994. The Executive Council of the Society decided that the time for change had come. It wanted to establish the *Survey* as its own independent publication, and so cut the long and successful ties with the University of Louisville. An agreement was reached with Martinus Nijhoff Publishers. A name change was also part of the new deal: the *Annual Survey* became the *International Survey*. There was even a new editor: Andrew Bainham, then of Christ's College Cambridge, took over from Michael Freeman. The first book version of the *Survey* was thus published in The Hague, both in hardback and paperback versions, although the 1994 *Survey* did not actually get published until 1996. Of Michael Freeman, Bainham said that, without his efforts, 'there would in my view be no Survey – at least not one recognisable as the one we see today. During his ten years as editor, a staggering eighty countries were surveyed worldwide.'[9] Bainham was delighted that Freeman agreed to write on England, in

---

[8]   I refer to Andrew Bainham's nine-page report to the Society's general meeting in Salt Lake City, July 2005.

[9]   A. BAINHAM (ed.), *The International Survey of Family Law 1994*, Martinus Nijhoff Publishers, 1996, p. xx.

'his inimitable style'. For example, commenting on a United Nations committee report, Freeman said, '[g]iven that Mrs Thatcher gave a "solemn undertaking" at the World Summit on children in 1990 to give high priority to the rights of children, this report demonstrates a huge chasm between pious words and real actions.'[10] And, later, '[t]he Minister's statement oozes complacency',[11] when commenting on what Britain had done in the Year of the Family.

Andrew Bainham commented on the variety of approaches taken by authors of chapters.[12] In relation to countries where there were regular contributions, the chapters corresponded more or less to the year in question. Others covered the time period since the last contribution. If the country was covered for the first time, more background information was appropriate (for example, Bulgaria and Malta, in 1994). The *Survey* was now truly deserving of the epithet 'international', but it was also less of a pure report on family law events in the relevant countries. Perhaps we could say it was a survey, but more than a survey. It was certainly an opportunity for authors to feature their own countries, but also to analyse and critique the ways in which their countries had tackled particular issues. We thus saw more of policy arguments and family jurisprudence.

2.3. NEW PUBLISHERS

The new millennium saw another change in publisher. Jordan Publishing Ltd. of Bristol in England took over the task, with the Family Law imprint. The title of the publication also changed so that it reflected the year of publication. The previous version was published in 1999, but called *The International Survey of Family Law 1997*. This must have appeared curious to the uninitiated, especially with the move away from a strict 'annual' summary of events in the respective jurisdictions. Now we found the title *The International Survey of Family Law 2000 Edition*, actually published in 2000. This practice continues to this day.

Jordans continued as the publisher throughout my time as General Editor. However, towards the end of the period, it was felt that the Society should go through an exercise of seeing whether a change would be sensible. The decision was eventually made to offer the role to Intersentia, which had a solid base in Cambridge, England. Intersentia has, in recent times, established itself as a leading publisher of family law titles in Europe (and do we now have to add post-Brexit Britain?). Even though Jordans has recently come under the LexisNexis world-wide umbrella, Intersentia has been a presence at International Society

---

[10]   Ibid., p. 200.
[11]   Ibid., p. 202.
[12]   Ibid., p. xix.

events, and has gained wide respect. Professor Margaret Brinig – known to many of us as Peg – the Fritz Duda Family Professor of Law at the University of Notre Dame in the United States, took over from me, and edited the final edition that Jordans published: the 2017 edition. The 2018 edition was Intersentia's first, with thanks recorded to Ann-Christin Maak-Scherpe and Rebecca Moffat. Jordans had a neat cover design, conveying all the necessary information. It was a standard formula with the colour-coding changing each year. Intersentia has continued this approach, with a standard design, and colours varying with each edition, but it includes more than words. It has what could be described as a flash graphic with a large globe covered and surrounded by stylised figures. In these contemporary and diverse days, it is not always easy to capture the idea of 'family' without leaving someone out. The current cover reflects amazingly well the diversity of 'family' – of differing ages (young and old), ethnicities from all continents, and multiple forms of relationships. It is paperback, not hardback, as with earlier issues of the *Survey*, but stands up well. With the move to Intersentia, we now find an index for each issue, something that was raised in my time but put into the 'too-hard basket'. The Society ought to be proud of the current production of the *Survey*.

Peg Brinig has now handed over the reins to June Carbone of the University of Minnesota and Robin Wilson of the University of Illinois. Job-sharing sounds like a very sensible idea!

2.4. DIGITAL PUBLICATION

One final point needs to be made on the history of the *Survey*. During my time as General Editor, one of the looming questions was digitisation. While many of us still like to hold a book in our hands, the reality is that so much is now done online. Many of our students know little else. The delivery of knowledge and ideas has undergone a revolution, and the *Survey* needed to catch up with this. In a broad sense, the publication had to be made widely available if it was to have the desired impact. In a narrower sense, authors also wanted to get wide recognition, and that comes mostly these days via the internet.

In 2012, Jordans made the *Survey* available for purchase as an e-book. At the same time, it began talks with Hein Online. The latter proved successful, as I noted in my report to the Executive Council in April 2015. We can find editions of the *Survey* going back to 1994 on Hein Online. This continues with Intersentia. Apart from the print copies, the *Survey* can also be bought in e-book formats (PDF and EPUB), and a copy is provided to Hein Online.[13]

---

[13] Thanks to Rebecca Moffat of Intersentia for confirming these points.

3. PERSONAL EXPERIENCES

3.1. THE CHAPTERS

As part of my preparation for this short chapter, I decided that it would be useful to do a mini-analysis of the volumes published during my time. In some ways, choosing only my years as editor is a bit random. However, ten years gives a reasonable sample, and shows something of the impact that the *Survey* has had. Besides, being self-indulgent in this way brought back fond memories of my time as editor – 'oh, I remember that piece now'; 'that one was fascinating'; 'phew, that took a lot of editing'; 'we have not had that country before', and so on.

What emerged, then, from my examination of the years 2007 to 2016? The shortest volume was my first, in 2007, with 17 chapters. I found that first year challenging. How was I going to round up authors and contributions? Andrew Bainham had given me a number of contacts, but they did not seem enough, nor did they all come through. Somehow or another we got there, and I breathed a sigh of relief. The next year turned out to be one of the biggest volumes, with 28 chapters, as authors came out of the woodwork. In my time, 2008 was beaten only by 2014, with 29 chapters. The other smallest years were 2010 and 2015, both with 21 chapters. In total, 239 chapters were published in the ten years under consideration. That represents a great wealth of information, analysis, legal development and stimulating ideas. Great thanks are due to all the authors who wrote and shared their experience, research and local knowledge.

Where did these chapters come from? They were from all corners of the globe. My slightly rough and ready calculations produced the following results in terms of countries represented:

- Europe 27
- Africa 16
- Asia and the Middle East 10
- Oceania 9
- North America, including the Caribbean 4
- Latin America (Mexico counted here) 4

In addition, there were chapters on International Family Law and European Law, and, more recently, two on Africa, in 2018 (children and informal justice systems, and sentencing primary caregivers, respectively), and one in 2021, where the focus was on the African Charter on the Rights and Welfare of the Child. International Family Law covered the United Nations, including, naturally, the Convention on the Rights of the Child, European documents and jurisprudence, and Hague Conventions on private international law. In 2009, a chapter covered the 'South Pacific', and examined custody of children in several small Pacific states. In other words, some chapters covered a region, rather than a specific country.

There are discrepancies in the above list, most notably in the paucity of countries represented from Latin America. That has continued in the most recent *Surveys*, except for Brazil. The figures for some of the zones reflect the number of nations actually within them, for example North America (although there have been quite a few Caribbean nations; Trinidad and Tobago was in the 2021 edition). Europe dominates, and there are very few European nations that have not appeared at all, with most appearing more than once. Even the Faroe Islands have turned up, in 2019. Oceania is reasonably well-represented because it includes Australia and New Zealand, and because Jennifer Corrin has done a wonderful job in writing up some of the smaller Pacific nations, often co-authoring with a local academic. The same is also true in part of Africa, where Julia Sloth-Nielsen has used her extraordinarily wide knowledge to discuss nations that might not otherwise have been represented. Africa was also represented by the work of Fareda Banda, of the School of Oriental and African Studies, London. Indeed, she acted as 'Associate Editor (Africa)' for several years.[14]

Unsurprisingly, some countries appeared only once in my time, while others had chapters in every *Survey*. In the first group we find the following: Angola, the Bahamas, Botswana, Fiji, Finland, Greece, the Gulf States, Hong Kong, Iran, Kazakhstan, Kenya, Lesotho, Lithuania, Mauritius, Mexico, Mozambique, Namibia, Papua New Guinea, Sierra Leone, Tonga, Turkey, Uganda, Vanuatu, Zambia and Zanzibar. This is not to say that they were not represented in years other than during my editorship.

Another group of countries appeared just about every time: for example, England, Australia, New Zealand, South Africa, the United States, Japan, Korea, India, Serbia and Canada. In some instances, the same author wrote every time, such as Mary Welstead from England, Olga Cvejić Jančić from Serbia, and Martha Bailey from Canada. Frank Bates wrote on Australia until he 'retired' from doing so with his 2011 contribution. Frank was always on time. Deadlines do not always mean much to academics. To Frank they were immutable dates, and he would be very apologetic if he was a few days over. I must say, however, that I did not have to hassle people too much to get their pieces in to me, although inevitably some never surfaced. While the *Survey* has had some writers of long standing, several countries had a revolving door. Japan, Korea, South Africa, and the United States are examples. My practice in these cases was usually to ask a senior professor, most likely on the Executive Council, to nominate someone to undertake the report for the country concerned.

---

[14] In earlier years, Bart Rwezaura, Tanzania, fulfilled this role.

Of course, there was also a middle group of countries that featured on a regular two- or three-yearly cycle. Often it depended on who was available to write, or whether there had been a turn of events in the country that deserved a write-up.

3.2. THE AUTHORS

One may well ask how I secured authors and their chapters. The answer to this is multifaceted. As just noted, some were nominated locally. Others wrote every time, or often enough to be called regulars. It was easy enough to find out whether they could write in any particular year or not. Sometimes, a regular would recommend someone else. It was always encouraging when this was a new academic or a current doctoral student. The *Survey* is a place where leaders of the family law academia, and sometimes practitioners, can share their wisdom. It is also a vehicle for the younger scholar to obtain a publication and see their research in print. Sometimes these people wrote to me directly, out of the blue. They were not the only ones to do so, but usually their contributions were reliably of a high standard. Another way in which I was able to commission chapters on new countries, or by new authors, was to meet potential contributors at Society conferences. Living in New Zealand, on the other side of the world, meant that it was not always easy for me to attend conferences that involved long-haul flights, often at times when we were teaching, during the southern hemisphere academic year. I thus made a point of arranging my commitments so that I could get to World Conferences, and combine them with some other visits, plus some holidaying. World Conferences were also the venue of two Executive Council meetings – the *Survey* Editor is *ex officio* on the Council. It was thus important to get to those particular conferences. In between them, I missed out on Council meetings in some wonderful places, like Italy, Paris, New York, Uppsala and London, but, because it was in a teaching break, I did get to a meeting in Girona, Catalonia, with some stopover time in Barcelona.

I suspect that some authors wrote out of a sense of duty, but were happy to support the enterprise. Others doubtless wrote because they saw it as a good opportunity to get their name and credentials before their international peers. Several did it to get academic credit. This occasionally meant that they required their piece to be blind referee-ed. The quality control of the *Survey* rests largely with the General Editor, but this will not satisfy all national agencies. South Africa is a prime example. Accordingly, I arranged for a review process to take place. I could not afford for this to take a long time (sometimes, one of the deficiencies of refereeing is that the referee does not keep to schedule). For this purpose, I had some reliable people whom I knew would turn the job round quickly.

3.3. THE CONTENT

What about the content of the *Survey*? It was a great privilege to receive such a variety of submissions on so many topics. Just about anything you can think of to do with family law has featured. Family law has been volatile over the years, which is good for scholars, and makes it ripe for analysis in a forum such as the *Survey*. This volatility is not uniform, which is unsurprising, but it means that the matter of the moment will be different in different countries. Perhaps one of the most obvious examples is marriage equality. The rapid change in the law – by legislatures, courts, and through referendums – was hard to predict, but was certainly momentous. It was primarily a Western phenomenon, including a surprising number of Catholic countries. It remains well off the agenda in Islamic nations, plus Asian, Pacific and African ones. In my Preface to the 2016 edition, I said that family law was in a state of flux: 'The exact nature of the topical issues varies because of different histories, cultures, values, and religions and the nature of social change … One of the great benefits of this annual survey of family law is the opportunity to see the panorama of challenges across the globe.'[15]

Two of the many themes worth highlighting briefly are science and cultural diversity. Science affects humankind in many ways, but at the personal level no more so than assisted human reproduction. The ability to create a human embryo outside the body has changed the ground rules for a number of areas, not least legal parenthood and parentage. Beyond this, though, we have things like stem-cell research, cloning, and the possibility of artificial wombs. *Survey* writers picked up on these topics, and will doubtless do so in years to come. Watch this space.

Cultural diversity is a broad topic that is especially pertinent in colonised parts of the world, but, with immigration, poses big challenges for the old colonising nations as well. Pluralism and family law go together in a way that we would not have appreciated 50 years ago. This may be seen in relation to religion, shari'a law, groups such as Roma, and especially indigenous culture. The latter is sometimes the reawakening of the history and mores of the local peoples, who have been swamped by the law and practices of the settler population. Increasingly, custom clashes with the British or European models of family life, parenting and decision-making. Western formulae of human rights, for all their great worth in protecting the individual, might not quite fit into the collective model typically found in indigenous cultures. *Survey* writers have explored the tensions here, and will continue to do so.

---

[15]   B. ATKIN (ed.), *The International Survey of Family Law 2016 Edition*, Jordans, 2016, p. xxix.

4.   CONCLUDING REMARKS

I have not mentioned money. This was not my brief as General Editor. In fact, the cost of the publication comes from Society membership fees, and every member receives an annual copy as a result. My job was to ensure that the manuscript was prepared for editing each year. I received excellent service from the publishers,[16] and, apart from the very occasional glitch on my part, I was proud of the end product. The same is true of the editions that I have subsequently received, not to mention the preceding versions.

In writing this piece, I have gone back to earlier issues. In my Preface to the 2010 Survey, I said a couple of things that serve as a good summing up.[17] I noted the enthusiasm of my students for family law, and suggested this was because it is about the human condition, where they can make a difference. So often the rest of us are absorbed in our own legal world and what comes across our desk. The *Survey* gives us the opportunity to study family law around the globe: 'Reading what is happening in another jurisdiction takes us out of our own corner and exposes us to thinking and developments in other places. It helps us examine our own country's laws from a broader perspective and to see what different pressures and solutions apply elsewhere'. It was an honour to serve as General Editor, and I am extremely grateful to all who contributed to the publication process. The Society and the *Survey* both have an important future.

---

[16]   I record my thanks to Greg Woodgate and Cheryl Prophett (who lived on a barge!) of Jordans. I managed to have a valuable in-person meeting with them in Bristol in 2008, early in my time as General Editor.

[17]   B. ATKIN (ed.), *The International Survey of Family Law 2016 Edition*, Jordans, 2010, p xiii.

MEMORIES OF THE INTERNATIONAL SOCIETY OF FAMILY LAW

Baroness Ruth DEECH DBE KC (Hon)

The Society has made four outstanding contributions to legal scholarship. First, it was one of the earliest organisations to welcome women scholars on an equal footing, take them seriously, and give them leadership positions and the prominence that they deserved. Second, it helped to establish family law as an academic subject. It may be hard to believe for our younger members, but there was a time when family law was not on any university syllabuses, and practitioners were expected to learn it as they went along. Third, the Society has been a force for progressive reform of family law, with an influence on international organisations, governments and scholars outside family law. Fourth, it was, and still is, a superb network for people from across all continents to share their insights into family law, and to forge strong friendships. I shall always be grateful for the intellectual and personal incentives that it afforded me.

Times have changed so much, but the older members will recall that there were very few top women law professors in the 1970s. Dr Claire Palley OBE (coincidentally my predecessor as Principal of St Anne's College Oxford University, which she headed from 1984 to 1991)[1] was a human rights specialist, and the first woman to hold a chair in law in the UK. Ivy Williams was the first woman to teach law in the UK – again, at my college.[2] Her speciality was the Swiss Civil Code, although I surmise that she must have had to teach a wide range of legal subjects to the women of Oxford, at a time when family law was not on the syllabus. It is thought that the first professor of family law, and certainly the first author of a textbook on the subject, was Professor Peter Bromley.[3] In the same year as the publication of his book, 1957, which was the centenary of the Act permitting civil divorce in England and Wales for the first time (Matrimonial Causes Act 1857, UK), a book appeared commemorating this.[4] Also published

---

[1]   https://first100years.org.uk/claire-palley-the-u-k-s-first-female-law-professor/.
[2]   http://www.oxforddnb.com/view/10.1093/ref:odnb/9780198614128.001.0001/odnb-9780198614128-e-36924.
[3]   https://www.familylaw.co.uk/news_and_comment/obituary-professor-peter-mann-bromley.
[4]   R.H. GRAVESON and F.R. CRANE (eds.), *A Century of Family Law*, Sweet & Maxwell, 1957.

in 1957 was Oliver McGregor's *Divorce in England*, one of the earliest books to view family law from a social science perspective. The history of fledgling family law is covered by Frances Burton in *Family Law* (Routledge, 2012). By the mid 1960s, Olive Stone, although not a professor (undeservedly), was teaching at the LSE, and was a force in the early ISFL. I was persuaded to start teaching family law in Oxford in 1970 by John Eekelaar – the moving spirit of English family law – who was very insistent that I do it, and I am so grateful that he was! He, in turn, told me that he had been taught by Otto Kahn-Freund at graduate level. Other early influencers were Professor Hugh Bevan and Philip Lewis, who took on child law.

I had sampled family law briefly when I studied in 1967 for the examination that was then called 'Bar Finals', the black-letter law examination that qualified one academically for practice at the Bar. My recollection is that it was only concerned with memorising the procedural rules and identifying the right forms to fill in. More excitingly, I had participated, albeit as the most junior of assistants, in the drawing-up of divorce reform proposals at the Law Commission from 1966–1968. The project, headed up by Professor L.C.B. Gower, culminated in a paper outlining a new law based on 'irretrievable breakdown', and entitled *The Field of Choice*.[5] After some compromises it was accepted by the government of the day, and became the Divorce Reform Act 1969.

Those were exciting times for family law. It was, however, lonely, as there were so few other colleagues with whom to interact. I had heard about the establishment of the ISFL at the very start, but it was not until 1979 that I attended my first conference, Uppsala. This was because my daughter was born in 1974, and it would have been hard to leave her before that date. Uppsala (theme – 'Family Living in a Changing Society') was a revelation. The world was full of family lawyers! And on the Swedish campus they were putting the study of relationships into practice. The most significant moment for me was the reception of my paper on cohabitation (very controversial then as it is now), putting forward the case as to why it should not become the subject of a legal regime. I realised that I had discovered an important subject on which reasonable people could hold differing views, and could do so in a most scholarly and stimulating way. I have not stopped writing about it for the last 40 years, and it still is the subject of debate and disagreement.

Women attendees at early conferences included Brenda Hoggett, as she was then, now Baroness Hale, President of the UK Supreme Court until her retirement in 2020, and the very embodiment of the importance of family law;

---

[5]   https://s3-eu-west-2.amazonaws.com/lawcom-prod-storage-11jsxou24uy7q/uploads/
2016/08/LC.-006-REFORM-OF-THE-GROUNDS-OF-DIVORCE-THE-FIELD-OF-
CHOICE-REPORT-ON-A-REFERENCE-UNDER-SECTION-3le-OF-THE-LAW-
COMMISSIONS-ACT-1965.pdf.

Professor Yukiko Matsushima of Tokyo; Professor June Sinclair, Vice Principal of the University of the Witwatersrand; Professor Linda Nielsen, who was appointed Rector of the University of Copenhagen; Professor Margaret Hughes of Saskatchewan; Professor Bea Verschraegen; Olive Stone (I recall she insisted that the ISFL logo be gender-neutral); Professor Gillian Douglas; the Hon. Claire l'Heureux-Dube of the Canadian Supreme Court; Mary-Ann Glendon (subsequently US Ambassador to the Holy See); Professor Marsha Garrison; Marie-Thérèse Meulders-Klein of the Catholic University of Louvain, who was awarded the Crown Order of Belgium; Professor Carol Bruch of the University of California, Davis; and Professor Lenore Weitzman, a sociologist, whose controversial works on the economics of divorce and the contract of marriage brought a new dimension to our deliberations. At the Brussels conference in 1985 there was a very public disagreement between Professor Bruch and Professor Weitzman over the ownership of data.

Almost from the start, papers delivered at ISFL conferences melded sociological observations with legal accounts, bringing influential new perspectives to the study of family law. This approach was especially marked amongst participants from the US, Canada, the UK and Australasia. I must admit that I did not profit much from the conference papers delivered by some delegates from further afield, typically entitled along the lines 'The Law of Ruritania on Adoption'; that is, straightforward accounts of the law in their countries, without contextual comment. I understood that some delegates from more repressive countries (and this was in the days before the Soviet Union came to an end) could only enjoy the privilege of travel to a conference if they gave a paper, and for this reason they were embraced. Indeed, we had first-rate and very active Russian members from the earliest days. Now we have members from 50 countries. I mention these outstanding women professors because such women were rare then, and I believe that their leadership in the Society bolstered their eminence in their home universities.

The Society also helped to cement the position of family law as a popular academic subject in universities. The wealth of research generated by the Society, for example in the annual surveys of developments in family law (for which Andrew Bainham took much responsibility), and the books that resulted from conferences, added to the varied and stimulating scholarship essential for such university study. In my early days as a member of the Inner Temple, one of the four ancient Inns of Court for barristers in London, I was sometimes asked by senior judges what I taught. Disappointingly, their response to the topic of family law was often to say, 'how can that be an academic subject? One picks it up on the job.' Certainly, the international influence of the ISFL, its reaching out to all quarters of the world, and its partnering with other international institutions in the same field, gave credibility to the study of family law. The ISFL sparked regional conferences, which kept up the momentum between World Conferences, and also served to give a platform that was more local and affordable for lawyers in the region in question. The ISFL always made an effort to give financial assistance to members from poorer parts of the world, to ensure that they could participate in conferences; nevertheless, those of us with only very small travel budgets from our universities looked with envy at the well-endowed US professors.

As one gets older, one notices that the same topics appear again and again at ISFL conferences: ageing, new forms of family, domestic abuse, child welfare, divorce, cohabitation, same-sex couples, assisted reproduction. It is good to note that newer, younger members from different parts of the world have their own fresh opinions on these issues. At the same time, the prolific publications and publicity engendered by the Society's activities, and the influence of some of its members on government, must certainly have advanced reform of these issues. After 50 years of the ISFL's existence, we find, for example, that divorce is moving more towards no-fault; that the legal differences between children born in and out of wedlock are vanishing; that traditional marriage is no more popular or privileged than other forms of union, whether heterosexual or same-sex; that the law places more emphasis on the welfare of children; that empirical research is regarded as a prerequisite to reform; that international comparisons are essential perspectives in national reform; that the importance of the genetic revolution is acknowledged; and that gender equality, in and out of marriage, is progressing. None of these topics has yet reached a perfect utopia, but they are all on the march, in no small part due to the work of ISFL members and the liberal atmosphere they advanced. There is no danger that conferences will run out of topics to discuss and changes in the law to analyse.

Networking and cooperation between members were important from the start, and even more so for members of the Executive Council, of which I was one for some years, since we had the motive to meet between World Conferences. There were members whom one admired and with whom one formed strong friendships. I include Professor Sanford Katz, Professor Lynn Wardle, the late lamented Professor Petar Sarcevic, and the Society officers from the Netherlands who carried out much of the administrative work so efficiently. I also miss very much Dieter Giesen, David Rosettenstein, Anders Agell and Petar Lodrup (once acting justice of the Supreme Court of Norway). To be able to write to colleagues (and now, of course, email) across the world to consult on an area of law was an inestimable advantage in research.

One could also learn a great deal from travelling to the venues of conferences. In May 1991 the World Conference was scheduled in Opatija, Yugoslavia, now part of Croatia. The war that led to the break-up of Yugoslavia started in June 1991, but by May we knew that war was imminent, as Croatia sought independence, resisted by the Serbs. Croatia declared its independence in June, and war broke out over the summer of that year. Many of the American delegates to the conference cancelled their attendance. I anxiously consulted my family and was somewhat belittled by their indifference to my safety, as they encouraged me to attend! Very early one morning as I set out from Oxford for the airport, I was much cheered to find at the bus station that John Eekelaar had also decided that the risk was worth taking, and we travelled to Opatija for a good, if rather thinly attended conference. There was an air of unrest in the town, with national songs being sung and independence excitedly debated, but it made for an unforgettable experience, and one that I was glad to have enjoyed, as tourists did not return to the former Yugoslavia for some years after that. The holding of a conference in Durban allowed us to go on safari and to Sun City; and Brisbane in 2000 was the gateway to the Gold Coast and the Barrier Reef. That conference was organised by my one-time pupil, Professor John Dewar. Salt Lake City in 2005 was an introduction to another way of life, as we observed the Mormon restrictions on alcohol, tea and coffee, and enjoyed the courtesy of the polite young students on the Provo campus. I have to admit that a few days without coffee and alcohol were trying, and we discovered a way to get around the laws. As well as the conferences mentioned above, I also attended the conferences in Cardiff (1994), Vienna (2008), Lyon (2011), Amsterdam (2017) and Antwerp (2023), which I suspect will be my last.

Together with Professor Meulders-Klein, I organised a regional conference in Oxford in 1999, on 'Biomedicine, the Family and Human Rights', to mark the 25th anniversary of the establishment of the ISFL, and it resulted in a book edited by the organisers and Paul Vlaardingerbroek. It was the first conference I had ever organised, and although it was very enjoyable and productive, it was immensely difficult. I had not counted on the expense and complications of the requirements of simultaneous translation, the complexity of the forms required to obtain funding from the EU, the reams of paper required, and the personal preferences of the delegates. It was the time of the 'mad cow disease' (bovine spongiform encephalopathy), which a few years earlier had rendered British beef on the bone unsafe to eat, and caused the EU to impose a worldwide ban on British beef from 1996. Many of the Americans coming to my regional conference insisted that there be no beef on the menu – constructing meals for several days without beef, which by then was considered safe in the UK, was quite a challenge! The French delegates wanted to know if there were bidets in the rooms (bidets in Oxford college bathrooms, can you imagine?), and the Scandinavian delegates were quite demanding about with whom they wanted to share rooms. This regional conference, like all World Conferences, started with despair over the financing, and ended in triumph.

One of the proudest moments of my life was the award, by the Society to me, of the Exceptional Service Award 2011. The Society did much more for me and my legal career than I did for it. It has been a force for good, and I sincerely wish it continues to be so for the next 50 years.

THE ORIGINS AND DEVELOPMENT OF THE SOCIETY

John Eekelaar

I was fortunate to be among those who attended a meeting at the University of Birmingham, England, in April 1973, at which the ISFL was conceived. There is an account of it by Harry D. Krause in the *American Journal of Comparative Law*, vol. 22 (1) 216–7 (1974). I am not sure whose idea it originally was, but the meeting's hosts must have been significantly involved. They were J. Neville Turner and Anthony H. Manchester. Anthony became the ISFL's first Treasurer. His later academic interests turned towards legal history. Neville was the first General Secretary; he later went to Australia (Monash University), where he developed a wide range of interests, including in sports law, law and literature, history and jazz. There was an affectionate obituary, accessible at https://oztypewriter. blogspot.com/2018/04/death-of-gentleman-and-scholar.html, published after he passed away in 2018. It is extraordinary to think that his role in the early stages of a successful international organisation can be counted among the many fruits of his varied interests.

Other names mentioned by Krause were obviously important in the formation of the society, and most went on to play significant parts in it. Ze'ev Falk's quiet yet insistent determination to bring about the ISFL's objectives made him an obvious first President. Of the others Krause mentions (Olive Stone, Frank Bates, Alastair Bissett-Johnson, Mauricette Craffe, Henry Finlay, Dieter Giesen, Aidan Gough, Sanford Katz, Julien Payne, Jennifer Temkin and Ray Watson), I later got to know particularly well Bates, Finlay, Giesen, Katz and Krause himself. Frank and Henry were wonderful hosts when I later visited Australia, and each did important work for the ISFL. I maintained contact with Henry's wife, Leah, for many years after he died.

Dieter Giesen later spent time as a Visiting Fellow of my college (Pembroke, Oxford), mixing in enthusiastically with the other Fellows, and the then Master, with whom he shared a taste for good malt whisky, as part of his almost obsessive drive to engage with the English-speaking (and common law) world. He hosted the ISFL's first World Conference in (the then) West Berlin in 1975, in the shadow of the wall, and Frank Bates edited the publication of its proceedings as *The Child and the Law* (Oceana, 1976), the first of many such collections of

ISFL conference proceedings. Dieter maintained his dynamic role in the ISFL after that, even though his academic interests had now included medical law. I will not forget the visit Dieter arranged for me to go to Bonn to speak about women's rights to a committee of the (then) West German Parliament – not so much because of that meeting, but because of the hospitality afterwards (warning: do not mix too much weissbier with Riesling!). His early death came as a shock to all of us. Sanford Katz has also spent much time in England, some of it as a Visiting Fellow at my college, and also at All Souls College in Oxford, and I have enjoyed his and his wife Joan's hospitality in Boston on a number of occasions, and their frequent visits to Oxford over the years. Sanford and I have collaborated on many family law projects, including producing edited volumes of the proceedings of three ISFL World Conferences.

I succeeded Neville as General Secretary, which continued until my spell as President of the ISFL from 1985–1988, and this provided more opportunities for friendships with, and inspiration from, many other people. In all, I have been to 13 ISFL World Conferences, and a few regional ones (including in the Bahamas and Chongqing), and all were memorable in their own way. The second World Conference was convened by the great South African lawyer Bobby Hahlo, in Montreal in 1977 (shortly after the Olympics had been held in that city). I still have his wife Hannah's lovely drawing of a family group hanging on my dining-room wall. This, for a short time, became something like a logo for the ISFL, but was discontinued because some objected that the figure of the mother has her head bowed, and two children are depicted, projecting a stereotype. Perhaps this could be a theme for a future conference! The conference in Uppsala in 1979, convened by Anders Agell, which considered the current trends in marriage and cohabitation, was particularly memorable for me as it doubled as (part of) my honeymoon (I am not sure if my wife has forgiven me!). Marie-Thérèse Meulders-Klein hosted a wonderful conference in Brussels in 1985, and Ichiro Shimazu one in Tokyo in 1988, giving me and many others an opportunity for our first visit to Japan, happily at cherry blossom time.

The conference in Opatija, Croatia, in 1991, held shortly before the Balkan War broke out, when tensions were rising, and tanks were to be seen on country roads, was hosted by our devoted member Petar Sarcevic, another friend whom we lost too young. My wonderful former doctoral supervisee Thandabantu Nhlapo hosted the conference in Durban, South Africa, in 1997, shortly after that country emerged from the apartheid era, in 1994. Thandabantu later (among many other things) became Deputy Ambassador at the South African Embassy in the US, and Deputy Vice-Chancellor of the University of Cape Town. This conference introduced many members to the lands of my origin, in Southern Africa. The opening address was given by the great Justice Albie Sachs, a veteran fighter against the apartheid regime, one arm lost as a result of an attack by the regime's agents, who spoke of the tensions between universality and particularism, and uniformity and pluralism, when there are rights to be the same and to be different, in the diversity of the new South Africa, and which is reproduced in the conference proceedings, *The Changing Family: Family Forms and Family Law* (Hart Publishing, 1998), edited by Thandabantu and myself.

In the early days of the ISFL, we were conscious that we were primarily an organisation of lawyers. But we wanted to open up exploration of relationships between the law and other areas of study relevant to family law, and so we sought to recruit a distinguished figure from some such area to give a keynote speech at the beginning of the conference. Thus, for the 1977 Montreal conference (on family violence – then a relatively new topic for family lawyers, and sadly still very important), we invited the noted psychoanalyst Anthony Storr, whom I knew from Oxford. The 1979 Uppsala conference, dealing with marriage and cohabitation, was started off by the well-known family sociologist William J. Goode, and the 1982 Harvard conference, convened by Sanford Katz on the resolution of family disputes, by the pioneer in the field of alternate dispute resolution Frank E. Sander. The renowned economist and philosopher Amartya Sen gave the keynote address at the 1985 Brussels conference on family, state and individual economic security, and the distinguished social and population historian Peter Laslett initiated the 1988 Tokyo conference on ageing in a modern society. Later conferences have moved away from this, perhaps because extralegal studies have become more integrated into the discipline of family law itself.

Looking at the topics dealt with in its conferences, it is evident that the ISFL has often anticipated issues that only became highly topical later. This may have been aided by its engagement with non-legal disciplines. But while it must welcome the free presentation of opinion, the ISFL should not promote any ideology, and nor should it be perceived to be doing so. This can, in my experience, give rise to difficult issues for the ISFL, and may present new challenges for the future as, as is to be hoped, it expands the diversity of its membership. It must always be remembered that the ISFL is a 'scientific' society dedicated to the advancement of knowledge about, and understanding of, a fundamental aspect of human social behaviour.

AN INTERNATIONAL SOCIETY OF FAMILY LAW REMEMBRANCE

Marsha GARRISON

I no longer remember what sort of notice I received, in 1982, announcing an International Society of Family Law World Conference that would take place at Harvard Law School in June. I had never heard of the International Society of Family Law. Even the subject of family law was new to me. I am pretty sure that the Spring 1982 semester was the first time I had ever taught the course, and I was still learning the basics. It was a period of tremendous upheaval in the field: no-fault divorce was gaining ground, gender-based roles and rules were disappearing, and both women and children were gaining new rights and entitlements. It was an exciting time in family law – that was a major reason why I had volunteered to teach a subject I had deemed too dull to study when in law school. The prospect of a conference bringing together family law scholars from around the world was immensely exciting. I sent in my registration form.

The conference was packed and immensely interesting. At this remove, I can no longer remember details, but I do recall meeting many fascinating people, and the constant sense of learning something new. Various presentations about the move to no-fault divorce also gave me an idea for an empirical research project that ultimately consumed years of my time, but I do not think I can blame the ISFL for that!

That exciting 1982 conference was my last ISFL experience for more than a decade. During those early days, there were no regional conferences – or at least there were none in North America – and other 1980s World Conferences took place in venues (Brussels, Tokyo, the former Yugoslavia) far more distant than Boston. By this point, I had young children and wanted to stay closer to home.

Sometime in, when? – 1993 or 1994 – a bright gold notice turned up in the mail. Its top border was decorated with an abstract design of peaks, and it announced a North American regional ISFL conference to take place at the Jackson Lake Lodge in the Tetons, in June. There were then no regular American events devoted to family law scholarship, other than the annual meeting of the Family Law section at the American Association of Law Schools. The section meeting typically consisted of one panel of presentations, and it offered little opportunity to learn about new work in the field. The prospect of a two-day family law event was, thus, immensely attractive, and the distance was reasonable. The venue even offered the opportunity for a brief family vacation. Remembering the 1982 event, I was also sure that the conference would be worthwhile.

This first North American regional conference more than met my expectations, even though it was quite different from the bustling World Conference of 1982. Although close to 100 family law specialists came, the spectacular, spacious setting invited leisurely, informal conversation. I recall many of these conversations, with moose in the distance. I met a number of individuals who became real friends in family law. I remember making a presentation about the final piece of the empirical research project that the 1982 conference had suggested to me. My presentation was scheduled in the last set of panels. There were perhaps five people who came. But the conference had been such a pleasure that I did not care.

A year or two later, there was another wonderfully interesting regional conference, in Quebec City. Even though I continued to skip World Conferences, I was definitely hooked on the ISFL, and began to play a role in planning these regional events.

Sometime in early 2000, I received a note from Professor Lynn Wardle, then ISFL Secretary General, asking if I would be interested in running for the ISFL executive council. I told Lynn that I would not be able to attend the World Conference at which the election would take place (Australia); he said that was unnecessary. I talked with my dean about the travel that would be necessary should I be elected, but assured her that this was most unlikely, given that I knew very few ISFL members outside the United States. The dean agreed to my candidacy, and, to my surprise, I was elected.

The following January or February, I attended my first ISFL Executive Council meeting at the Hotel Burgundy in Paris. I am sure that fellow Americans Barbara Woodhouse and Peg Brinig joined the Council the same year that I did. I remember meeting thoughtful colleagues from at least a dozen different countries, sensing that the ISFL was in excellent hands, hoping I had something to contribute, and feeling confident that my ExCo membership would offer many wonderful opportunities.

My next Council meeting, which took place at the same venue, was very different, as it followed the September 2001 attacks on the World Trade Center and Pentagon. It was a sober time. Few people were travelling during that period; my round-trip ticket from Boston to Paris cost $79. On the return journey, my flight was endlessly delayed due to a blizzard that was pummelling the entire East Coast. The plane finally took off with almost no passengers – so few that I was upgraded to business class despite my bargain ticket.

As these recollections of my first two Council meetings suggest, I remember the people who attended the Executive Council meetings, and the places where they took place, far more sharply than I remember the specific topics of discussion. I am confident that we discussed how the September 2001 attacks might affect the 2002 World Conference in Copenhagen and Oslo, at that Paris meeting. But most meeting content is now a blur. Over 20 years of ExCo meetings, there have been many discussions of by-law changes, the development of a new website and membership management system – and then a newer website and management system – as well as the ongoing issues of producing the International Survey, collecting dues and planning conferences. Much work was done, and many very special people have generously given their time and talents to doing it.

I am confident that, since 2000, I have attended all World Conferences and North American regional conferences. Each has offered not only ample opportunity to learn about the most recent scholarship in family law, but also to meet colleagues from around the world and learn from their experiences and diverse perspectives. I have made many friends. I have grown as a family law scholar. And I have had so many enjoyable experiences that I cannot begin to count them all.

I remain immensely grateful to the ISFL for all the professional and personal opportunities it has given me. Its first 50 years have been a grand success, and there is every reason to expect equal success of the next 50. Certainly, every young scholar in family law should be a member. There is no other organisation that offers the depth, breadth and wealth of opportunities to contribute to family law's development and participate in the global family law community.

MARIE-THÉRÈSE MEULDERS-KLEIN, IN MEMORIAM

Mary Ann GLENDON*

With the demise of Marie-Thérèse Meulders-Klein, the International Society of Family Law has lost one of its most beloved and distinguished members. She will be long remembered for her path-breaking contributions to family law, comparative law and bioethics, as well as for her outstanding service to law reform as a member of, and advisor to, national and international commissions. Those of us fortunate enough to have known her will treasure the memory of her gracious personality, her generosity to colleagues, and her exemplary intellectual integrity. Her immense learning, intellectual curiosity, scientific rigour, graceful writing style, and civility in argument have set a high standard for all who work in the areas of family law and comparative legal studies.

To fully appreciate her contributions, it is important to recall that she began her academic career in the 1960s, just when Western nations were on the brink of a massive revolution in ideas and behaviour concerning sexuality, marriage and family life. Those changes were so sudden and so profound that not even professional demographers saw them coming. At an international conference organised by Professor Meulders-Klein in 1985, French demographer Louis Roussel spelled out just how dramatic the developments of the preceding two decades had been:

> What we have seen between 1965 and the present, among the billion or so people who inhabit the industrialized nations, is … a general upheaval across the whole set of demographic indicators, a phenomenon rare in the history of populations. In barely twenty years, the birth rate and the marriage rate have tumbled, while divorces and illegitimate births have increased rapidly. All these changes have been substantial, with increases or decreases of more than fifty percent. They have also been sudden, since the processof change has only lasted about fifteen years. And they have been general, because all industrialized countries have been affected beginning around 1965.[1]

---

*   Learned Hand Professor of Law, Emerita, Harvard University.
[1]   L. ROUSSEL, 'Démographie: deux décennies de mutations dans les pays industrialisés' in M.-T. MEULDERS-KLEIN and J. EEKELAAR (eds.), *Family, State and Individual Economic Security*, vol. I, Story Scientia, 1988, pp. 27–28.

Marie-Thérèse Meulders-Klein was one of the first to explore the legal implications of that massive social experiment that brought new opportunities and liberties to many adults, but exposed children and other dependents to new risks.

By the end of the century, family law had become a major battleground in a war of ideas. That development, Meulders-Klein realised, required attention to very serious questions:

> How can this body of law be constructed upon the dust and powder of divided opinions, scattered elements, and ephemeral sentiments? And how can justice be grounded in a law that is neither intelligible nor widely respected? ... The absence of shared values – apart from liberty identified with happiness – leaves in suspense the questions of meaning and of justice. The triumph of Desire over Law would bring less liberation than disarray and anguish if the 'other' becomes the very image of possible danger and if principled justice gives way to the unsustainable lightness of an existence without attachments, sufficient unto itself.[2]

The most important of her works wrestling with those questions are collected in *La Personne, la Famille et le Droit*, published in 1999. It was characteristic of Meulders-Klein, with her determination to get to the root of things, that she approached her subjects by emphasising the concept of the 'person', which she described as 'the most precious word in the legal vocabulary'.[3] She insisted that it was essential to get the notion of legal personhood right if one hoped to steer safely between the twin dangers of hyper-individualism and collectivism: 'Between the solitary individual and the State, brothers and enemies, perhaps the only coherent principle possible for a humane democracy is respect for the person, each unique in his human dignity but each belonging to the human family.'[4]

She proceeded, in the first half of the book, to deal with family law in flux. These perceptive essays on marriage, cohabitation, divorce, filiation, children's rights, parental responsibilities, grandparents, and reconstituted families display an unusual combination of legal erudition with a sophisticated grasp of modern biology and genetics. It is clear that the author benefited greatly, not only from her experience as a member of several blue-ribbon national commissions, but also from her long and happy marriage to the great author-physician Michel Meulders, with whom she raised four sons.

One of the major themes in those family law essays is the tension between individual rights and family protection policies, and the ongoing search for

---

[2]   M.-T. MEULDERS-KLEIN, *La Personne, La Famille et le Droit: Trois décennies de mutations en Occident 1968–98*, Bruylant, 1999, p. 525.

[3]   Ibid., at p. 1.

[4]   Ibid., at p. 6.

a just equilibrium between them. Meulders-Klein called attention to the different weights accorded to those competing values in civil law and common law systems. She warned her fellow continental Europeans of the unintended consequences that might follow from an uncritical reception of certain aspects of Anglo-American law. At the same time, she provided common law lawyers with a fresh and challenging perspective on their legal arrangements. She correctly identified tendencies in the common law systems towards an extreme form of libertarianism. Those tendencies, she pointed out, could thwart efforts to establish a healthy relationship between individual freedom and the social structures that, paradoxically, both support and constrain individual liberty.

Though trained as a private law specialist, Meulders-Klein brushed aside the curtain between public and private law early in her career, in order to deal comprehensively with her subject. That led her into the sociology of law, and prompted her to write one of the most perceptive essays in the 1999 volume, an analysis of the shifting roles of the family, market work and the State as determinants of an individual's social standing and economic security.

In the second half of her book, under the heading 'The Individual, the Family, the State', Meulders-Klein treated public and international law as they bear on the family. She was one of the first scholars to recognise the potentially far-reaching implications of international developments for what used to be considered the quintessentially local subject-matter of family law. She pointed out, for example, the subtle erosion of the role of parents, and the concomitant expansion of the role of the State, in the widely acclaimed 1989 UN Convention on the Rights of the Child.

As time passed, she came to see the international arena as a major launching pad for extreme forms of individualism and libertarianism, which led her to issue a prescient warning, in her essay on 'Internationalization of Human Rights and the Evolution of Family Law: Voyage without Destination?' Then, in 'Private Life, Family Life and Human Rights', she traced the advance of these ideologies in the case law of the European Court of Human Rights.

She was careful to specify that her cautionary observations were not intended to deny the 'supreme value of human rights'.[5] On the contrary, she said, they expressed her fear of the impoverishment of human rights 'through over-investment in the subject'. With scrupulous fairness, she noted that, just as hyper-individualistic rights can undercut systems of family protection, claims of 'protecting the family' can be used to excuse violations of the human rights of women and children.

She also noted that the problem of how to achieve a proper balance between individual rights and family protection principles is bound up with another

---

5   Ibid., at p. 525.

equally thorny problem: different nations and cultures take differing approaches to the values at stake, weigh them differently, and arrive at different solutions. What is the scope and what are the limits of legitimate pluralism in these matters? Who decides?

Meulders-Klein did not offer simple answers. Rather, like the great teacher she was, she emphasised the importance of framing the right questions. Human rights and the family cannot be sharply opposed, she pointed out, because human freedom and dignity can only be protected if there are sufficient numbers of men and women who support those principles, and healthy families where children have the best chance of becoming such men and women. As the drafters of the French Civil Code put it, in words she quoted with approval, '[t]he family is the source and basis of civil society as a whole ... the cradle of the state and of the virtues of all the citizens.'[6]

That ancient political understanding, reflected in Article 16 of the Universal Declaration of Human Rights, was one of the most valuable contributions of the civil law tradition to the universal human rights project. Thanks to the seminal writings of Marie-Thérèse Meulders-Klein, it may yet have a role to play in shaping responses to the current dilemma of how to hold together the twin ideals of individual freedom and a community where all share in a common responsibility.

---

[6] M.-T. MEULDERS-KLEIN, 'The Individual, the Family, and the State: Dependence, Independence, or Inter-dependence?' in *Festkrift till Anders Agell*, Iustus Forlag, 1996, pp. 413, 416.

REMEMBRANCE OF THINGS PAST

Sanford N. KATZ

It was certainly serendipity that I should be an Associate at Clare Hall, University of Cambridge in the spring of 1973, when I received a letter from Ze'ev Falk, which was forwarded to me from my home institution, Boston College Law School. In the letter Ze'ev proposed a meeting of family law scholars in Birmingham, England. Since I was in England, a trip to Birmingham, a city I had never visited, sounded interesting. I had no idea what to expect, nor who would be in attendance. My wife Joan, and my two young sons, drove to Birmingham, never realising that the meeting would have an enormous impact on me, both professionally and personally. Indeed, the meeting would change my life.

It also changed the course of family law. One of the consequences of the meeting was the decision to create a society – the International Society of Family Law (ISFL) – that would hold an annual meeting and bring together family law scholars on a global basis. Of the scholars present at the meeting, Ze'ev Falk, J. Neville Turner, Tony Manchester, Frank Bates, Alastair Bissett-Johnson, Aidan Gough and John Eekelaar stand out in my memory. Little did I realise at that time that John Eekelaar would become not only a co-author in a number of publications, but a very close friend. What is so interesting about the meeting was the fact that all of us, mostly young scholars, were seriously interested in family law as an area for research and teaching. That is particularly noteworthy because in the United States, at that time, family law was not considered an important part of a law school curriculum, even though it was, and is, a subject found in most American bar examinations, and is a major area for law practice. That has changed, and family law now takes its place with contracts, torts, property, business associations, constitutional law and procedure in the teaching of fundamental principles of law. Indeed, it encompasses contemporary social issues in American society, like same-sex marriage, reproductive technologies and abortion.

Through the years, I have met and became personal friends with a number of ISFL members, including John Eekelaar, Bobby Hahlo, Olive Stone, Dieter Giesen, Marie-Thérèse Meulders-Klein, Petar Sarcevic, Peter Lodrup, Anders Agell, Reiner Frank, Nigel Lowe, Linda Nielsen, Bea Verschraegen, Claire l'Heureux-Dube, Paul Vlaardingerbroek, Lynn Wardle, Ruth Deech and Stephen

Cretney. I have vivid memories of touring the cities where our conferences were held, with Petar Sarcevic and Ruth Deech. It was a memorable experience to accompany Marian Wardle to great museums and hear her commentaries on some of the famous paintings, and to learn how to appreciate great art. My wife and I were the guests of Peter Lodrup and his wife Greta, in Oslo. The sites for our World Conferences also provided me and my wife with the opportunity to travel to places that I do not believe I ever would have visited. While in West Berlin in 1975, we visited East Berlin and received some insight into the plight of East Berlin Germans. In Opatija in 1991, we just missed the war that broke out in the Balkans. I remember investigating whether a boat was available to take me and my wife to Venice should air transportation out of the country become dangerous or even impossible. Durban in 1997 was particularly interesting because of the country's having abandoned apartheid a few years earlier. It was the first time I had visited the continent of Africa, and the visit left an indelible mark on me. Never before had I experienced anything like the safari a group of us joined before the conference.

International conferences in Opatija, Croatia, Durban, South Africa, West Berlin, Uppsala, Sweden and Queensland, Australia provided me and those who attended with opportunities to meet scholars who shared our deep interest in family law. Over the years, the ISFL Executive Council has had the uncanny ability to choose themes for a conference three years ahead that proved to be timely. For example, the theme of the Society's first International Conference, held in West Berlin in April 1975, dealt with children and the law, a subject that had just begun to be of concern to scholars and legislators. In 1977, the theme was violence in the family. Once again, domestic violence had not yet caught the attention of family law scholars. Child abuse and neglect were recognised as social issues of concern to social workers, but not necessarily as legal issues and matters for the attention of lawyers. Also, in American law, the family was considered an enclosure that should be free from governmental interference, and thus a great deal of leeway was given to husbands and wives in conducting their relations with each other and with their children. For example, in almost all American states, a husband could not rape his wife, because of the idea that a wife was under his control, and should be obedient. That has since changed. Corporal punishment of children was justified under the doctrine of parental immunity. That, too, has changed. Family violence was viewed as assault and battery, and thought to be a part of tort law. Now the area is safely included as an issue to be studied in family law.

In 1979, the third World Conference was held in Uppsala, Sweden, and the theme was family living in a changing society, a topic that opened up a variety of topics relating to social change. In particular, marriage and cohabitation were discussed. Little did we know then that, by the law's recognition of an alternative to marriage, it was, to a certain extent, paving the way for an alternative definition of marriage – one that would include same-sex couples.

In 1982, I was elected President of the Society. It was in that year that I hosted the conference in Cambridge, Massachusetts, where the theme was alternative conflict resolution. Perhaps it was the attraction of a conference in the United States that attracted over 180 participants from 23 countries. But the topic opened up a whole new approach to resolving disputes, not in a court with its procedural rules, but in an informal setting. It was thought that family disputes required a more relaxed approach. Thus, mediation in divorce was born.

In 1985, the International Conference was held in Brussels, Belgium, hosted by Marie-Therese Meulders-Klein. The theme concerned individual security, an area of major concern even today, when politicians discuss the role of the individual and the State in protecting individual security. It was at this conference that my wife and I were formally introduced to Her Majesty Queen Fabiola of Belgium. That was a memorable event, to be sure.

In 1988, the International Conference was held in Tokyo, where the theme was ageing in modern society. I did not attend that conference, but the theme introduced a whole new area of inquiry: the impact of an ageing population on family law issues. Now, elder law is an area of family law research and, indeed, a speciality in family law practice.

The Croatia International Conference in 1991 focused on parenthood. Presentations examined the roles of motherhood and fatherhood in the new decade. No longer were those roles separate and distinct; they were interchangeable, with mothers and fathers often employed outside of the home, and with fathers assuming responsibilities that had traditionally been part of the mother's role. A wife's economic contribution to the marital enterprise was recognised and, in divorce, a monetary figure was attached to it. Also in divorce, it was no longer presumed that mothers gained custody of children over fathers. Both mothers and fathers had equal opportunity to gain custody. The maternal preference rule, long applied in American courts, was no longer automatic.

Since 1991, I have attended International Conferences held in Cardiff, Wales; Durban, South Africa; Queensland, Australia; Copenhagen and Oslo; Salt Lake City, Utah; Vienna, Austria; and Lyon, France. Each conference was meticulously planned and hugely successful in terms of attendance and the presentation of papers. The regional conferences that have been held from time to time have also been extraordinarily successful. I attended a wonderful regional conference in the Bahamas in 2014, hosted by Hazel Thompson-Ahye, that not only had scholarly presentations, but was memorable for its featuring Bahamian music at a special event, and providing a tour of historic sites.

One can both see and appreciate the foresight the Executive Council displayed in choosing conference topics. They were open to comparative analysis from a legal perspective, and also provided insight into the cultures of countries. What was so surprising was the discovery that often there were few major differences in either the rules of law or the approach to the issues. Some countries were ahead of others in recognising the issues and making changes in their laws. Many of our members were, and are, active in legislative reform in their own countries, and bring to their roles insights gained through discussions with members of the Society, as well as through material presented at conferences.

What is extraordinary is how scholars from different countries – from different cultures, languages and mindsets – got along so well. Disputes did arise: the most prominent one concerned the language to be used at each international conference, and whether there would be simultaneous translation if English was chosen as the language of the conference, which it was. Mostly, it was the cost of the simultaneous translation that caused concern, and whether individual conference budgets could cover the expense, not whether there should or should not be the translation.

John Eekelaar and I have co-edited three of the books that have been produced from the International Conferences: *Family Violence* (1978), *Marriage and Cohabitation in Contemporary Societies* (1980) and *Resolution of Family Conflict: Comparative Legal Perspectives* (1984). From time to time, I have contributed to the Society's annual publication, providing an American perspective on certain family law issues. It was a great honour for me to receive the Distinguished Service Award from the Society.

I have been enriched by the intellectual stimulation gained from the exchange of ideas and perspectives of scholars, both men and women, from practically all over the world. I have tried to encourage young American family law scholars, especially women, to join the Society, and I am happy to say that they have done so, some reaching leadership positions in the Society. Who would have thought that a small group of relatively unknown family law scholars meeting in Birmingham, England in 1973 would have established a society that would have gained the recognition and respect of other international societies and international institutions, as well as having had a profound impact on family law worldwide?

EXPERIENCES OF THE INTERNATIONAL SOCIETY OF FAMILY LAW

Personal Reflections

Nigel Lowe KC (Hon)*

1. UPPSALA 1979

My first experience of the International Society of Family Law (ISFL) was the third World Conference, held in Uppsala, Sweden in 1979, which I attended together with my colleague at the University of Bristol, Gillian Douglas. I had never been to an ISFL World Conference before, and I was excited by the prospect – and I was not disappointed. For me, it remains one of the best and most stimulating international conferences I have attended. The theme of the conference was 'Cohabitation', which in those days was regarded as being very 'avant-garde', but then, this was Sweden after all. Indeed, I recall one of the sociological papers was on 'deviant behaviour', and examined, in particular, jurisdictions in which, because of its incidence, cohabitation had become

---

* N.V. Lowe KC (Hon), Emeritus Professor of Law, Cardiff University, UK. He joined the Society in 1978/79, was co-opted onto the Executive Council in 1992, became an elected member in 1994 at the Cardiff conference, of which he was the Convenor, was elected as a Vice President in 2008, and in 2014 received the Society's Distinguished Service Award.

'normative' as opposed to 'deviant' behaviour. Another memorable paper was one given by Eric Clive, who argued that marriage could be jettisoned as a legal concept (*aliter* a religious one) in favour of one based on cohabitation. Food for thought indeed!

I remember, too, being impressed and not a little overwhelmed by a scholarly paper presented by a German academic examining English common law. I was clearly going to have to 'up my game' if I was to perform on the world stage.

Amongst the myriad of stars that attended and presented at Uppsala, one stood out above the rest – Mary Ann Glendon. Not only did she give a fascinating paper, but on one occasion she considered the English simultaneous translation of a paper given in French to be inadequate. She offered to take those who wanted to to a separate room, where she gave a seminar on what the speaker was trying to say. Sadly, that was the only occasion that I came across Mary Ann.

The conference, of course, was not without incident – I remember one in particular. After a German scholar had made his presentation in English, he was asked a question, to which he turned to the German-speaking Chair and answered in German. The Chair translated his answer into English. At this point, all the French-speaking delegates walked out, complaining that the Chair should also have translated the response into French! This was not the only sharp exchange that I witnessed, including another between two English academics. All this, however, kept us on our toes. On a lighter note, I recall some sessions being accompanied by loud bangs. These turned out to be cannon shots at a degree ceremony being conducted outside – the cannon being fired in celebration of any graduand whose degree was *cum laude*!

The conference was well-organised and, especially at the breakout sessions, there was ample time for discussion. One innovation of the conference was the establishment of a conference 'pub', to which many of us, particularly the young academics, repaired in the evenings when there were no other conference events. That proved a great success and I, for one, participated in many earnest conversations, including one quite heated debate on how family law should be taught at universities. Youthful enthusiasm, and perhaps exuberance, were to the fore.

The conference was blessed with the most fantastic weather (weather, as you will see, is one of the recurring themes of this reminiscence – after all, I am a Brit) and, of course, the sun and the heat were exacerbated by the extreme length of the Scandinavian summer evenings (the conference was held in June). I often arrived back at the hall of residence in the dying light, around midnight, only to be confronted by the birds' dawn chorus just beginning. It was just as well that the weather was so brilliant, for my recollection is that it was quite a walk from the hall of residence to the Law Faculty. But I have a clear memory of walking in the glorious mornings towards the silhouetted cathedral on the distant horizon. Incidentally, I wonder whether many delegates appreciated that, hanging on the walls of the Law Faculty building, were *original* Breughels (long since stashed safely away).

Of course, the conference put on a number of events. We enjoyed a boat trip, inter alia, to the royal theatre, Drottningholms Slottsteatr, where a special dancing event was put on for the delegates. Especially memorable was the conference banquet at Uppsala Castle. The main dish was elk, which was ceremoniously brought in, held high by numerous waiters and waitresses. That was very much to be enjoyed, and even the second helping was welcome, but by the time a third helping was offered many delegates were defeated. After the meal, there was some spectacular singing from the galleries high above. There followed dancing, but I will draw a veil over that. Suffice to say that it was not my finest hour (more of dancing later!).

I met a galaxy of leading academics for the first time at the Uppsala conference, and with many I have had a continuing relationship ever since. Although, of course, I met many from outside the UK – not least Anders Agell, William Duncan, Sanford Katz, Henry Finlay, Peter Lødrup, Marie-Thérèse Meulders-Klein, Michael Olmsdahl, Judge Pedersen and Pauline Tapp – ironically, it was also the first time that I met a host of UK family law academics, including David Bradley, Alistair Bissett-Johnson, Eric Clive, Stephen Cretney (who was later to become a colleague at Bristol), Ruth Deech, Michael Freeman, Ann Halpern, Brenda Hoggett (as she was then known), Susan Maidment, Judith Masson, David Pearl and Olive Stone.

Uppsala opened my eyes to the world. It was a great, stimulating, well-organised conference which was blessed with fabulous weather, and had a magic and – for some – a romantic atmosphere: it was Sweden, after all!

2.   BRUSSELS 1985

I did not attend the 1982 Conference held in Boston, because of the cost, so the next conference I went to was the fifth World Conference, held in Brussels in 1985. Again, I did not offer a paper, and attended only as a participant. My recollection of this conference is sketchy, but undoubtedly *the* incident of the conference was the accusation of plagiarism by one US delegate against another, just when she was about to deliver her paper. In fact, I was not present when this cause célèbre took place, but news of it rapidly went round the conference. But I will not dwell on that incident, but instead move on to the next conference, held in Tokyo in 1988, about which I have vivid memories.

3.   TOKYO 1988

Appropriately, the theme of the sixth World Conference was 'Ageing', and my colleague, Gillian Douglas and I decided we would present a paper on the legal position of grandparents, making the assumption that grandparents were 'old'.

In fact, our sample of grandparents comprised one aged 36, and the overall average age was 58. I should add that, now I am a grandparent myself, I would not make too many assumptions about age! Of course, it was expensive to travel to Japan, and unfortunately Gillian was unable to find funding. I went without her. I was fortunate to obtain a conference travel grant from the British Council (that was conditional on giving a lecture at a Japanese University – but more of that later), and I was also given some support by the Japanese organisers.

I duly set off from Bristol in good heart, armed, as I was, with a good paper, in part based upon empirical research, which was my first direct experience of that type of scholarship. Soon after arriving at London Heathrow, I met John Eekelaar, David Pearl and, for the first time, Andrew Bainham. We had a drink and a chat before checking in together, but, to my and everyone else's astonishment, I alone was upgraded to business class! This puzzled David in particular, the more so as the seat next to mine was empty. But for me, at any rate, the Tokyo conference had got off to an excellent start. Not quite so good, however, was the four-hour coach ride from Narita Airport to the centre of Tokyo (in those days there was no Narita Express, which now takes less than hour).

We were staying in a hotel in Shinjuku, which is an astonishingly busy part of the city. The sheer size and bustle of central Tokyo took a little time to adjust to. Day or night it was incredibly crowded. The one plus, from the British point of view, was that the Japanese drive on the left; that is, in our view, the 'right' way!

The conference venue was situated some distance from our hotel, and required us to take the Metro, another truly amazing experience for Westerners, particularly as we had to use Shinjuku station – one of the busiest, if not the busiest, station in the world, and one which took some getting used to; but, of course, we did.

The scientific programme began with papers on the demography of ageing. The first of these was by the world-renowned demographer Peter Laslett, of Cambridge. Looking at it again it still makes salutary reading. Indeed, the whole topic of the elderly might be worth revisiting at a future World Conference. The point that Peter and a number of other speakers were making was that, in developed countries at least, we were living (as we still are) in an increasingly ageing society, which puts pressure on communities, and has implications for the legal response. We learned that there are different 'ages' of being old, as we descend, with varying degrees of rapidity, from physical and mental health, and economic independence, to physical frailty, mental instability and economic dependence. Indeed, I well remember chairing a session involving presentations by the then Brenda Hoggett (then of the English Law Commission, now Baroness Hale) and Margaret Shone (Institute of Law Research and Reform, Alberta, Canada), and commenting afterwards that it was the most depressing session I had had the privilege of chairing. It was not because of the quality of their papers – they were, of course, excellent – it was because of their message of what we had to look forward to – the descent into decrepitude, dependence and death! Thirty-one years on, this message is not lost on me!

As already mentioned, my presentation was about the rights of grandparents. It was memorable because we woke up on the morning of my paper to find that there had been heavy snowfall. This was a rare event – possibly the first time in the century – for there to be snow in April in Tokyo. My presentation was scheduled as the first of the day. Being cold, everyone was heavily dressed, which meant everyone was bulkier, and that only added to the crowding on the Metro. There were crowd-packers on the platforms, and we were duly pushed in. David Pearl kindly accompanied me, and though we are not the tallest of fellows, as against the fellow Japanese travellers we were able to see where we were going.

I duly arrived in time, only to be met by my Chair, the well-known Canadian academic Don MacDougall, who thought the vast conference hall would be empty. After all, who would travel through the snow to hear, inter alia, me? He was wrong. The Japanese delegates turned up in force, and the hall was quite full. As a matter of fact, though its content was good enough, it was perhaps not the finest example of delivery by me, and was not helped by some inaccurate translations into Japanese, as I was told afterwards.

Naturally, I met a lot of Japanese delegates. One of the first was Professor Taeko Miki from Waseda University, whose opening words to me, in perfect English, were that she did not like the new format of the *Guardian* newspaper. She had a formidable knowledge of Western law and culture. I met her again two years later, when she invited me to give a talk at Waseda. I met others, through the good offices of both Satoshi Minamikata and David Pearl, including Professor Matsoshima, Professor Ohara and Professor and Mrs Isono. These Japanese contacts were to prove useful with regard to the funding of the Cardiff conference, six years on. Of course, I met other delegates, including Sally (later Baroness) Greengross of Age Concern (UK), Robert Levy and Lynn Wardle from the US (who, on one occasion, was practising his kanji ahead of his forthcoming stay in Japan), Rainer Frank and Bea Verschraegen. I also met some Canadians who, one night, invited me to go to dinner with them. They were staying at a different hotel, some distance away from mine, and this involved me in travelling by Metro, which I now seemed to be able to negotiate on my own. They were great fun and, on this occasion, not only did they obtain a recommended restaurant from their hotel, but commandeered a staff member to accompany us to the restaurant and order the food for us! They later organised another dinner, this time in the Ginza (a vibrant quarter of Tokyo with particularly bright lights), to which a number of delegates came. As is the Japanese tradition, we all had to sit on the floor, which was something I could do in those days. It was an entertaining finale to the Tokyo conference.

Among the other social highlights, for me, were a coach tour of the city, including a visit to a Zen garden and to Tokyo Tower, and a post-conference tour supposedly to see Mt. Fuji. In fact, it was wet and misty, and far from seeing Mt. Fuji you could barely see your hands in front of you. Still, we did have the pleasure of seeing the Great Buddha at Kamakura (which featured in a scene in the James Bond film *You Only Live Twice*).

That was not the end of my Japanese visit, for, as I have said, my British Council travel grant was conditional on my giving a lecture (in fact, my paper was on sale of goods) at a Japanese university. If it had not been for my friend Satoshi, this condition would have been a formidable hurdle. As it was, he arranged for me to visit the University of Niigata, which is about 200 miles north-west of Tokyo, and to which one could travel, at breakneck speed, by 'bullet train'. That trip was highly successful, and led to further trips to Japan, but that is another story.

The Japanese conference introduced me to a totally different culture, and to different ways of thinking. In 1988 it was an exotic place to visit and, particularly in Niigata, Westerners were still sufficiently unusual as to be stared at. Furthermore, there were few signs in English, and on my last night in Tokyo, I took some photos of what I thought were particularly pretty lights, only to be told by a Japanese colleague on my return to Bristol that what I had photographed was a sign saying 'live sex show'!

4. OPATIJA 1991

The next World Conference was held in Opatija, in what was then Yugoslavia. By that time, I had moved to Cardiff University, and indeed it was one of the conditions of my appointment that the Law School would pay for me to attend the conference. The School also paid for Gillian, who had moved to Cardiff a year before me. Once again, we decided to collaborate to produce a paper for the conference, whose general theme was 'Parenthood in Modern Society'. Our paper, entitled 'Becoming a Parent in English Law', explored the varying degrees of control that English law imposes on the acquisition of parental status, and argued that there was a need for a full-scale review of parenthood, to complement that undertaken for children under the Children Act 1989.

But well-prepared though our paper may have been, we very nearly did not deliver it. That was because of the impending political troubles that were clearly developing in Yugoslavia, which everyone was aware could blow up at any time, though the trigger was likely to be the push for independence by Slovenia, which was set for June, a few weeks after the conference. A number of potential delegates dropped out. Gillian rang up the UK Foreign and Commonwealth Office and asked if they thought it would be safe to travel to Opatija. 'Opatija?', they responded, 'Never heard of the place. Therefore, it must be safe'! On the strength of this less than convincing advice, we decided to go.

We flew via Zurich to Ljubljana, now the capital of Slovenia. There was a lot of building going on. We did not dwell on this, after all there is always building going at airports, but within six weeks all that construction had been destroyed in the opening skirmish of the break-up of Yugoslavia! We went to Opatija, in what is now Croatia, by coach. Opatija is an interesting but slightly strange place. It had wide, elegant boulevards next to the Adriatic Sea, and some of the architecture was similarly elegant, and had a 'spa' feel to it, but there were also 'communist-style' concrete buildings, of which our hotel and conference centre was one. I had the impression that most events passed Opatija by, and I somehow doubt that it suffered too much direct damage during the troubles of the 1990s, but I do not know, because I have not been back there since. In fact, Rijeka is close by, and that certainly did suffer some damage. All that said, there was a 'heavy' atmosphere. Everyone knew war was coming, and seeing the odd convoy of tanks only added to the sense of foreboding. I imagine that many must have had similar sense of foreboding in 1939. What a nightmare it must have been for Petar Šarcević, the Convenor, and Marie-Thérèse Meulders-Klein, the President. Not surprisingly, they agonised about whether to call the conference off. That they did not is a tribute to their nerve and faith, which, as it turned out, was fully rewarded, for the conference essentially passed without incident, and produced a rich and diverse crop of papers.

I say that the conference passed without incident in its widest sense, but, of course, there were memorable 'conference-type incidents'. For example, one of the first presentations was by Michael King. He turned up but his luggage did not, and in his luggage was his paper: a salutary lesson for any travelling academic – keep your paper/presentation with you at all times! Of course, Michael carried off his slot with admirable skill. Another 'incident' involved the perennial problem at conferences: what do you do with a speaker who overruns? This was a problem faced by Ruth Deech when chairing one of the sessions. One of her speakers was wildly overrunning and, despite numerous warnings, would not stop. In the end, Ruth physically carried her off the stage with the speaker still talking while being carried off! Admittedly, delivering a meaningful ten-minute paper requires discipline and skill (there ought to be training for this). In the case of our presentation, Gillian and I could see that we couldn't both speak, given our allotted ten minutes, so we agreed that she would make the presentation. I appeared on the podium, and was silent but ready to answer any questions. But there were none, so my net contribution from the podium was total silence. Sometime later in the conference, an Australian academic congratulated me on my 'masterly performance', adding that it was a whole lot better than some of those (not necessarily in our session) who did speak!

One of the reasons that no questions were put to us is that we were 'upstaged' by the speaker that followed us, namely Olga Dyuzheva. This was the first time many of us had met anyone from Russia, and naturally all the questions at the end were directed to her. Olga was not the only Russian presence at the conference, for another was Olga Khazova. Apparently, Petar had helped to fund the two Russians' attendance. It proved a wise investment for the Society, for not only were they a big hit in Yugoslavia, but each of them later became members of the Executive Council.

The two Olgas were two of a number of persons I met for the first time in Opatija: they included Stephen Parker and Patrick Parkinson (both of whom had been at Cardiff in the past), Mark Henaghan, Maarit Jänterä-Jareborg, Anna Singer, Margareta Brattström, Carol Bruch, Christine Davies, Paul Vlaardingerbroek and Hans van Loon. Of course, there were also lots of friends there from previous conferences as well.

There was a varied social programme, including dinner on a boat, and a memorable closing banquet with the inevitable dancing, to the haunting and rather prophetic song 'It's Over Now'! But the outstanding event was a visit to Slovenia, as a guest of Miroslava Gec-Korošec, and to the giant caves at Postojna, complete with their own double-tracked underground railway to transport us from the top to some way below. The visit to the caves turned out to be an inspired choice, for the weather had turned decidedly cold and very wet. Of course, it was damp inside the cave, but we were protected from the elements. I seem to recall some speeches at the bottom and a choir. That evening, we had a dinner at which our President, Marie-Thérèse, pledged the Society's undying support for the peace-loving people of Slovenia, which, given the circumstances and the fact that the main conference was taking place in Croatia, was perhaps a little risky.

For me, Opatija had another significance, for it occurred to me during the conference that we could host the next one at my new university in Cardiff. I had long thought that international family law would make a good and, at that stage, innovative, conference theme. I thought that Cardiff would be fully supportive, and that it would 'up' the profile of the Law School and the University. I mentioned this to one other person, and in no time the rumour went all round the conference that the next one would be at Cardiff. People I had never properly spoken to before came up to me and asked if it was true, and what were the facilities like. I recall being interrogated at the bottom of the cave. I had absolutely no formal authority to say that Cardiff would host such an event on, but, as things came to pass, I did convene the next conference.

So the conference came to an end. Some of us made our way back to Ljubljana, and off we flew back to Zurich. There was a sense of relief, and some delegates even clapped as we took off, but, as I said to my immediate passengers, it is more customary to applaud after one has safely landed! Sadly for Yugoslavia, all our forebodings came to pass, and it was not long before there was civil war. But Petar had, in the end, been lucky. He had successfully convened the seventh World Conference, and helped edit the conference book, which is a lasting testimony to his memory. As a matter of fact, when Croatia became independent, Petar became its ambassador, first to Switzerland and then to the US.

5.   CARDIFF 1994

For me, preparations for the Cardiff conference began almost as soon as I returned from Opatija. Over the summer of 1991, Gillian and I put together our bid (costed, I recall, at £30,000) and, in doing so, we were aided by Cardiff City Council. As it turned out, ours was not the only bid; another was from Brazil. I was asked to present the Cardiff bid, as was the Brazilian representative with their bid, at an Executive Council meeting held in London in the autumn of 1991. Although ours was the better put together bid, with a coherent and innovative theme (the international aspects of family law, neatly encapsulated by the title 'Families Across Frontiers', a title dreamt up by Gillian's husband, Hugh), the Council hesitated. Of course, Rio de Janeiro and Copacabana beach seemed much more alluring than Cardiff, which one English member of the Council rudely dubbed 'Leeds by the sea' (that jibe actually increased support for our bid), but a real consideration was holding successive World Conferences in Europe. But against that, Cardiff was seen as a 'safe bet', which was a big consideration after Opatija. The Council deferred its decision and, in the meantime, asked me if I would consider convening the conference in Brazil, a request that I refused. Subsequently, at an Executive Council meeting in Leiden, in Spring 1992, which I did not attend, it was decided to accept the Cardiff bid. Round one was complete.

Over the next year, we secured our venues (though, later, they all had to be changed by one week), negotiated some preferential rates, and secured help from Cardiff University, and further help from Cardiff City Council. I began also to acquire sponsorship, not least from Japan. One foundation provided ¥ 5 million (about £30,000); another private Japanese sponsor provided $US 5,000. The EU agreed to give €30,000, and a French-based organisation agreed to provide £10,000 to pay for simultaneous English/French translation services. Once I had such money, I found I could pressurise other institutions into giving money. One of these was what was then the Welsh Office. When they refused my initial request, I wrote to the Minister (John Redwood MP) at Westminster, and said that, in the light of the international sponsorship, it was simply not an option to offer nothing. I said that, as a gesture of goodwill, I would accept £1,000. I received a cheque for £1,000 in the following day's post! This gave me a personal insight into life of the rich – to those that have, more will be given!

In short, then, from an early stage, finances were not a problem. On the contrary, Cardiff was a well-resourced conference. As more money came in, we were able to expand and improve the programme, offer financial support to a wide range of speakers, hire student helpers, and produce quality conference material. Some of the money went on appointing a conference organiser, Glenda Bland, who was worth her weight in gold. My wife is called Brenda, and I often muddled my 'Brendas' with my 'Glendas'. In any event, I bored my family silly with my increasing obsession with the conference.

Apart from the money, I had another stroke of luck. Quite unknown to me when making the proposal, 1994 was the UN International Year of the Family, and through the good offices of Henryk Sokalski (the UN Coordinator of the Programme), whom I met in Vienna at an Executive Council meeting, our conference was designated as one of the UN's official events. Henryk gave one of the opening addresses.

Many of the venues we used spoke for themselves. The National Museum of Wales, with its world-class collection of Impressionist paintings, was where we held the opening reception, complete with a Harpist, who played downstairs, and an impressive school-student quartet, who played in the galleries among the aforementioned paintings. We held a wine-tasting event at Cardiff Castle, and the closing banquet at the City Hall. All these venues were in easy walking distance of the conference hotel. We also held a dinner dance under a huge marquee in Duffryn Gardens, to which we laid on coach transport. The real problem was where to hold the plenary sessions. The best lecture theatre, the Reardon Smith, had no coffee facilities, while the venue that had the best drink facilities, the Sherman Theatre, had an inadequate lecture theatre for our purposes. However, outside the Reardon Smith was an open space of grass, and I had the idea that we could put a marquee on it. Apparently, no one had previously thought of doing this, but when we sought permission to do it, we were told that we needed planning permission! That, of course, required time and money to obtain, but Glenda managed to do it. Furthermore, the hotel agreed to provide and serve the refreshments. It proved to be a wonderful general facility for the conference, and a very handy meeting place.

While the securing of venues and finances took obvious priority, no less important, of course, was the scientific programme. There were various facets to this. First, there was the question of lead speakers. Of course, I took advice, not least from Permanent Bureau of the Hague Conference on Private International Law, which readily lent its full support to the conference. I visited the Bureau sometime in 1992, specifically to meet Adair Dyer and Hans van Loon (Deputy Secretary General and Secretary General of the Hague Conference, respectively), who both gave papers at the conference, and, with their help, contacted Gonzalo Parra-Aranguren, who had written the Explanatory Report to the newly concluded 1993 Hague Convention on Intercountry Adoption. Another important speaker was Margaret Killerby, who was the Head of the Private and International Law Division at the Council of Europe. I was also pleased that Dieter Henrich (Regensburg) and Helge Thue (Oslo) agreed to speak. As time went on, I realised that I was in a powerful position to invite speakers. For example, I met and was impressed by Geraldine Van Bueren, at the Third Meeting of the Special Commission to Review the Operation of the 1980 Hague Abduction Convention, at The Hague, and encouraged her to present at Cardiff, and she duly gave an impressive closing Paper on 'Crossing the Frontier'.

Similarly, I attended a conference in Washington, for example, and enjoyed a presentation by Geoffrey Greiff, and invited him to Cardiff.

But, in a sense, engaging lead speakers was relatively easy. What, at any rate, I found difficult was handling the vast array of submissions based on abstracts. This involved initially accepting and rejecting applications. That was time-consuming enough, but even more challenging was putting them all together in a coherent programme. It was here that I received invaluable and timely help, first from Patrick Parkinson, who happened to be visiting Cardiff in the summer of 1993. It was he who sorted all the acceptances into a themed order. I shall forever be grateful to Patrick for that unsolicited service. The next problem was how to arrange all the potential papers in a timed conference, and here I had inspired help from Anders Agell and, particularly, from Peter Lødrup. Mind you, that did not come without a price. It was originally arranged that I would meet Anders and Peter in Copenhagen, where they were attending a meeting of Baltic lawyers, but after arriving I discovered that Anders had had to return home because of family illness. On that occasion, I was rescued by Linda Nielsen, who kindly invited me to her house for dinner, where, incidentally, we discussed the possibility of holding a future World Conference in Denmark. On leaving Linda's, I discovered it had snowed! I should just add here that Linda gave one of the closing papers at the Cardiff Conference, 'Procreative Tourism, Genetic Testing and the Law' – a tour de force, and prophetic too.

The meeting was rearranged, and we met in Oslo in December 1993 (where, of course, there was snow – lots of it!). At first, the three of us worked at the University, but when Anders left, the two of us repaired to Peter's house. What emerged from that meeting (and I have to acknowledge it was Peter's creation) was to have a detailed grid of plenary slots and breakout slots. At that stage, we filled in the slots with the known speakers, but thereafter it was relatively simple to slot new people in, or take them out if they later withdrew. It was a brilliant system, which worked! What a brilliant man Peter was.

To complete the story of the scientific programme, mention should be made of the great support given to the conference by the British judiciary and family law practitioners. Lord Mackay, the Lord Chancellor, agreed to open the conference, and in early May I went to 'brief' him about the event and the Society. On my way there, I read a newspaper headline that the Leader of the Opposition, John Smith, had suddenly died. As a mark of respect, Parliament was suspended for the day. That gave unexpected time to Lord Mackay, so instead of my allotted five to ten minutes, I had a 45-minute meeting with him! I had been quite nervous ahead of my meeting, but he quickly put me at my ease. One of the closing papers was given by Lord Justice Mathew Thorpe; interestingly, on the 'The Influence of Strasbourg on English Family Law'. He was not the only representative of the Court of Appeal. Dame Elizabeth Butler-Sloss participated in the conference, and chaired one of the sessions. Lord Justice Balcombe also attended. While I valued this support, I should put on record that the conference was fully supported by British academic family lawyers and, indeed, by those from across the world.

The scientific programme was not the only aspect of the conference that was meticulously prepared. Each of the venues was vetted and personally visited. Gillian and I even had a practice banquet, as a result of which we made changes to the menu to make it more Welsh. Perhaps most amusing was the practice wine tasting, after which I, for one, emerged completely sozzled!

Soon the time approached when the conference would begin. I became more and more obsessed, first to the bemusement of my family, but later to their boredom with me. One obsession was what the weather would be like, but I need not have worried: the weather was glorious throughout the conference. The refreshment marquee was used as a shield against the blazing sun. I even had a delegate from Angola complaining about the heat! In fact, I realised afterwards how weather-dependent the conference arrangements had been – walking from venue to venue was a pleasure rather than ordeal; Duffryn Gardens were wonderful in the evening sunshine, and the marquee exceedingly pleasant.

Not that the Conference went off without any incident. For me, it started dramatically, when a colleague suddenly announced that he would not drive (in the conference car – I told you the conference was well resourced!) to meet the Lord Chancellor, so I had to go instead. As the Lord Chancellor was a member of the Cabinet, the local MPs had to be informed of his arrival, as well as the police, and he had to be met by the station master in his formal dress. In other words, it was a big deal. My problem was twofold: I had never driven the car before, and I was not sure of the route! I managed to arrive at the station (on time), and found that a space had been reserved for me, which was being patrolled by a policeman. I explained who I was, but asked if the space could be extended, as I did not know how to reverse the car. He was most obliging. I duly met Lord Mackay and his entourage (not all of whom could be accommodated in the car), but I had to explain that I was not sure how to navigate the one-way system to get to the hotel. He just roared with laughter. Although I had visions of headlines saying 'Law don crashes car with Lord Chancellor', we did eventually get to the hotel in one piece.

Another amusing incident occurred a little way into the conference. We were supporting a number of delegates, and I held £5,000 cash in the hotel safe. We determined to give this in a brown envelope to each of the beneficiaries. But this meant sorting it out, and one afternoon, with the help of the husband of one of the speakers, we went to my hotel room and opened up the cash. Unfortunately, we forgot that the room fan was on (remember it was a hot week), and suddenly all these bank notes were flying around the room, and there we were scrambling around trying to retrieve them! But everyone duly got paid.

Actually, the conference went pretty smoothly. Both the scientific and social programmes went well. The wine tasting, which was an optional event, took place in Cardiff Castle, but because it could only accommodate roughly 180 people, the event had to be arranged in two separate sessions – although I was sure I saw some delegates at both! The beauty of wine tasting is that people think they have drunk more than they have, so it is relatively cheap to put on. It was a great success; so, too, was the dinner dance at Duffryn Gardens. The only problem for me was at the end of the dinner, when Dame Elizabeth 'demanded' that I lead her onto the dance floor to begin the dancing. I was horrified, for, as I have previously hinted, dancing is not my forte. Fortunately, Peter Nygh, an Australian judge who knew Elizabeth well, whisked her off to the dance floor, and the pair waltzed immaculately. The final social event was the conference banquet, which we held in Cardiff City Hall. After the meal, in what many recall was the *pièce de résistance* event, we had a full Welsh male-voice choir (led by a female conductor). As an encore, they sang 'Land of my Fathers', thereby providing a fitting cultural climax to the conference. Mind you, I was shocked to see many of the choir smoking in the bar afterwards.

The conference was well attended, with representatives from all around the world, and, if I recollect correctly, some 90 papers were given. Among the debutant paper-givers at an ISFL conference were Masha Antokolskaia, who was the Convener of the 2018 Amsterdam Conference, and Robbie Robertson, of South Africa, who has been a stalwart member of the Executive Council. Another ISFL debutant was the now Hazel Thompson-Ahye, who turned up without preregistering. Luckily for her, I could accommodate her at a discount rate. That proved a good investment from an ISFL point of view, as she later became an Executive Council member (and was to have been the Convenor of the 2020 World Conference in Barbados, had not COVID-19 intervened). Another delegate was Thandabantu Nhlapo, who became the Convenor at the next World Conference, in 1997, in Durban.

I found that being a Convenor was an immensely rewarding experience, but an all-time-consuming and draining one. At the end of each day, I returned to my hotel room utterly exhausted. I must say I was mighty pleased and relieved to pass the baton on.

One final postscript – Gillian and I edited the conference book. That took a long time, but the outcome was a fitting legacy of the conference. I had assumed that copies would be posted to each contributor, but instead one day I returned to my room at the University to find about 96 copies there. We ended up having to post them on!

6.   SUBSEQUENT CONFERENCES

From now on I will be brief, as this recollection has already become lengthy.

6.1.   DURBAN 1997

The next conference after Cardiff was at Durban, in 1997. The theme of the conference was 'The Changing Family – Family Forms and Family Law'. I gave a paper on adoption, building on research that I had been conducting together with my colleague at Cardiff, Mervyn Murch (I called this 'Murch research'). The basic tenet of the paper was that, rather than regarding adoption as the finite end of a process, as the practice had developed in England and Wales, where it had become more common to adopt older children out of care, it was better to regard it as part of an ongoing and often complex process of family development.

The ISFL's first venture to Africa proved highly successful.

6.2.   BRISBANE 2000

From Africa, the ISFL moved to Australia, and to Brisbane in particular. This was my first visit to Australasia. The build-up to this conference was not without incident. A row had developed at an Executive Council meeting held in Modena in March 2000, the nub of which was who should carry the risk of a loss: the Convenors, in this case John Dewar and Stephen Parker? Stephen, naturally, argued that any loss should not be the Convenors' risk. The Council responded by saying that they could not give carte blanche to Convenors to run up indeterminate losses. The matter was not resolved (and nor has it been since?). Stephen effectively walked out of the meeting, and for a time communications between the Council and the Convenors were lost. It was even suggested that I might go to Brisbane to act as a go-between. Happily, that proved unnecessary. The conference went ahead. It did not incur a loss, and was a great success. But both John and Stephen subsequently withdrew from the Society, which was a great pity, and a loss to the ISFL.

In fact, I hugely enjoyed the conference, and on top of that I was elected as a Vice President of the Society. The overall theme of the Conference was 'Practice, Process and Procedure'. My paper, co-authored with Mervyn Murch, looked at children's participation in the family justice system, building on the findings from two empirical research projects conducted at Cardiff Law School concerning children's experience of adoption and divorce.

I recall one amusing incident when I was chairing a particular session. The speaker asked me to look after her overheads while she was speaking, and in the course of doing this I tripped over the wire. The speaker took absolutely no notice of my predicament and simply carried on asking for the 'next slide'! Fortunately, I was not hurt, but Stephen was not that amused when I said I might have had to sue him!

Towards the end of the conference, my daughter joined me, and we had a memorable fortnight looking round the magnificent country, or at least parts of it.

6.3. COPENHAGEN/OSLO 2002

The next conference, the only twin-centred conference I have ever attended, was held in Copenhagen and Oslo, in 2002. The co-Convenors were Linda Nielsen and Peter Lødrup. The conference was blessed with the most fantastic weather. Indeed, the first person I met on arrival at the hotel in Copenhagen was complaining about the lack of air conditioning. The glorious weather continued throughout the conference; that is, both in Copenhagen and Oslo. The good weather meant that we had the smoothest of crossings on an enormous ferry, and undoubtedly one of the memorable highlights was sailing up the fjord towards Oslo in the early morning. It is the only way to arrive in style at the Norwegian capital.

Actually, accommodating everyone on the ferry was an administrative nightmare, especially as most cabins (we sailed overnight) were double berths. That posed no problem for married couples, but most delegates were unaccompanied. The herculean task of matching people to appropriate cabins fell to a Danish judge, Judge Svend Danielsen. He undertook this task with cheerful efficiency. But he made one error, matching one Japanese lady (whose gender was not easy to determine by her first name) with an Italian gentleman! Fortunately, she was accommodated in a single-berth cabin which had been held in reserve to cover such eventualities. But allocating berths was not the only problem. Another was ensuring no one missed the ferry. The organisers' task was not helped by one delegate flying to Oslo, and a couple driving all the way round, and, in both cases, not telling anyone of their plans to do so. But, somehow, we all duly arrived in Oslo.

Although that ferry journey had a lasting memory for me, there was, of course, a scientific conference going on. As ever, there were a variety of excellent papers delivered under the general conference theme, 'Family Life and Human Rights', 62 of which can be found in the book of the conference, edited by Peter Lødrup and Eva Modvar. But one paper not included in the book was delivered early on, in Copenhagen, by Göran Lambertz, then the Swedish Chancellor of Justice, on a topic that was new to me, namely 'Honour Killing', which was a developing issue in Sweden. Since then, this issue has assumed more general prominence. Another non-published presentation was my own. I was not originally intending to give a paper, but Katharina Boele-Woelki asked me to step in for her and talk about the early work of what was then a fledgling organisation: the Commission on European Family Law (CEFL), which was then working on its first field of study – divorce and post-divorce spousal support. I must confess that I did not take this brief seriously enough, and had totally underestimated the interest it. In fact, when this interest dawned on me, I started to sketch out my presentation in my bunk bed on the overnight ferry. This was indeed leaving it late, as the session I was in was the first of the Oslo part of the conference, which took place in the afternoon following a morning tour, in sweltering heat, of Oslo (what a contrast to my Tokyo experience) on arrival. The session was packed with delegates, sitting on the floor and behind the speakers. Our Chair, June Sinclair, said she was going to be strict and allow speakers 15 minutes. Fifteen minutes, I thought – how can I spin out my notes for that long? I spoke for twelve-and-a-half minutes, and was congratulated on my timing. But I faced some tough questions afterwards.

6.4. VIENNA 2008

Sadly, I missed the Salt Lake City conference because of illness, so the next conference I attended was in Vienna, in 2008. If the Scandinavian conferences were lucky with the weather, the Vienna conference was unlucky in the extreme. In fact, the week before the ISFL conference, when I was attending another conference, the weather had been glorious. But the heatwave broke over the weekend, and the following week was wet, cold and miserable.

The Convenor for this conference was Bea Verschraegen, whom I had first met in Tokyo. The theme of the conference, 'Family Finances', plugged a glaring gap in the issues previously covered by the ISFL World Conferences. This meant a change of focus, from my point of view, and I presented a paper on prenuptial agreements, which at that stage was a hot issue in the UK. As it happened, Roger Kay of Chester produced a paper on the same topic, so afterwards we got together and produced a joint article, which we entitled 'The Status of Prenuptial Agreements in English Law – Eccentricity or Sensible Pragmatism?', and which was published in the book of the conference, which Bea produced in remarkably quick time the following year.

7. SOME FINAL THOUGHTS

The Vienna conference is the last of the World Conferences, to date, that I have attended. A variety of reasons conspired to prevent my attendance at subsequent conferences – prior commitments, cost and health – but I was delighted to attend the eighteenth World Conference in Antwerp. It was like old times!

My 40 years, and counting, of involvement with the ISFL have been richly rewarding, and I have a lot to thank the Society for. The World Conferences, in particular, have opened my eyes to the world, exposed me to new ideas, and enabled me to meet a whole host of talented people, many of whom have subsequently become friends (though some, sadly, have died). The varied themes of the conferences have, respectively, stimulated work in new directions, and given me the opportunity to present the results of completed research on a world stage.

Inevitably, when writing a retrospective such as this, places, events and people come to the fore, and it would be easy for an outsider to consider that all this has been a monumental world junket. But that would be a mistake. The importance of sharing experiences across the world cannot be underestimated. At a minimum, it opens one's eyes to the fact that many of legal issues discussed at the conferences are faced by a multiplicity of jurisdictions across the world, and that sometimes another jurisdiction offers a good solution. On a grander scale, the Society helps to promote a wide international understanding, which, at a time of growing nationalism and introspection, is something to be valued, treasured and preserved. Long may the ISFL prosper!

REMEMBERING THE INTERNATIONAL SOCIETY OF FAMILY LAW

The Recent Past

Patrick PARKINSON AM

Compared with some others who have written of their memories of the ISFL for this volume, I represent a slightly younger generation of family law scholars who joined ISFL, not in its infancy, but when it was already well-established.

Although I was born and educated in Britain, I was, by the stage of joining the ISFL, a young academic in Australia, one of several British family lawyers who left Britain in the mid1980s when prospects in Australia were so much brighter (and the weather so much better). Two of them, Stephen Parker and John Dewar, together organised the World Conference in Brisbane in 2000. Both went on to distinguished careers in university leadership, as Vice-Chancellors of the University of Canberra and La Trobe University, respectively.

1. MY EARLY INVOLVEMENT WITH THE ISFL

My first World Conference was in Opatija, Croatia in 1991, a conference to remember, not least for being held in the shadow of war between Croatia and Serbia. The war did not finally break out until a few weeks later, but it was in my mind, like everyone else's, when deciding whether it would be safe to travel there. Pictures in the newspapers of tanks on the street were a little confronting, but I was reassured enough by the press accounts that the road to Opatija would not be laden with mines, and so I made the journey.

The conference itself, ably organised by Petar Šarcević, was an immensely enriching experience. I reconnected with my family law tutor at Oxford, Ruth Deech, and John Eekelaar, both of whom played such an important role in the work of the ISFL in those years. I also met others from many different parts of the world. Predominantly, at that stage, the members came from Europe and North America, but even in a conference which had a reduced attendance due to the political situation, there was an impressive enough representation from other parts of the world to make it evident that this was truly an international society. The previous World Conference had been held in Tokyo.

As it happens, I gave a paper in the same session as Nigel Lowe and Gillian Douglas, an account of which is given in Nigel's recollections in this volume. There were to be six presentations in a 90-minute session, and we were told that we would strictly have only ten minutes each, in order to allow half an hour for questions and discussion. Ruth Deech was the polite but firm chairperson. She had the challenge of what to do when a speaker, whose first language was not English, ignored repeated warnings that she had far exceeded her allotted time, and refused to stop. This was a good introduction to the diplomatic challenges of leading the ISFL. Those of us who have the good fortune to be native English-speakers do not find the same difficulties in conveying complex ideas in a short time-frame as those who have had to translate their work painstakingly from their native language to a foreign tongue.

After Opatija, I did not miss a World Conference. It was a priority for me to attend, even though the distance from Australia to almost anywhere else in the world is vast. Just to get to one of our nearest neighbours, Indonesia, is an eight-hour flight from Sydney. To Europe is a journey of more than 20 flying hours, and to the East Coast of the US about the same. However, the travel was always worthwhile. Through the ISFL, I made friends across the world, and was able to listen to, and learn from, some of the world's finest family law scholars. It was the ISFL that introduced me to the great benefits of comparative family law scholarship, and also to the importance of listening to the insights of scholars from other disciplines. The conferences always had excellent social events and optional excursions, and attendance also provided an opportunity to visit countries that I might not otherwise have had reason to visit.

2. HOLDING OFFICE IN THE ISFL

After a few years, I joined the Executive Council, which gave me further opportunities to get to know scholars from different parts of the world. I was immensely surprised and honoured, in 2011, to be asked to become President, not least because I had not held other offices in the Society or organised a World Conference.

The way Presidents and other office holders are chosen in the ISFL may seem, to those not closely involved, to be somewhat opaque. The tradition is for the President for the time being to consult all the previous Presidents who remain active in the Society about who should be nominated as the next President. The nomination thereby reflects the consensus of those who have previously held that office. The Secretary General is selected in the same way, as are the Vice Presidents, who are chosen to achieve good regional representation from different parts of the world. For practical reasons, the Treasurer, at least in recent years, has been Dutch, because our bank accounts are situated there.

Nominations go to the General Meeting held during each World Conference. I can only recall there being one contested election for the Presidency, and the office-holders are, likewise, typically elected unopposed. There is usually some competition for positions on the Executive Council, which is healthy, but the Council has the power to co-opt members. This power has been used wisely, if sparingly, in the past, to ensure that no region of the world lacks representation, and to involve younger members in the work of the Society, as a form of succession planning. I first became a member of Council by co-option, no doubt with these rationales in mind.

I recall that, after I was elected as President, a member of Council raised the question of how Presidents are chosen, and in particular, whether it was in accordance with the Constitution. With characteristic tact, the member emphasised that the issue was not being raised out of any dissatisfaction with the choices that had been made. Rather, the lack of transparency was the issue.

I agreed, and we set up a sub-committee to consider what would be the best way of electing office-holders in the future. Somewhat to my surprise, the sub-committee came back with the recommendation to maintain the status quo. The method that had been used was entirely constitutional, as the former Presidents were simply a group of members who satisfied the requirement of a minimum number of people to nominate candidates. It was, and is, of course, open to any member to stand for the Presidency, with the requisite number of nominators. The system, the sub-committee concluded, had served the Society well. It ensured some degree of continuity from one Executive Council to the next, because each new President typically has a lot of prior experience as a member of the Council, but also allows for some diversity of geography, gender and primary language. Lynn Wardle (USA), Marsha Garrison (USA) and I are native English speakers, but I can also recall Presidents since I joined the Society from Norway, Croatia, Germany, France and the Netherlands.

3.   2011–2014

My time as President, from 2011–2014, was a period of change in terms of the running of the Society, greatly assisted by Marsha Garrison, who continued for a second term in the office of Secretary General. Our Treasurer when I commenced, Adriaan van der Linden, had done an outstanding job in keeping track of the members, sending out reminders to renew when their paid terms of membership were coming to an end. However, this was laborious and time-consuming work, and I thought it would be sensible to automate the process. Furthermore, the Council had agreed to build a new website. Until that time, our website had been hosted by Brigham Young University in the US, and was built through the sterling efforts of Lynn Wardle, who served as Secretary General and then President, in the previous decade. The consensus was that, with changes in the available technologies, the website needed to be refreshed, and in any event should be free-standing rather than a site housed at a particular university.

Thus, we began to build a new website and membership management system, and at the same time designed a new logo. The system allowed for credit card payments and automated reminders. We could also do much more with the website in terms of search capacities and other enhancements. There were teething problems, with a few members reporting that they had not been able to complete payment. It was surprisingly difficult, at that time, to get a reliable payment gateway to deal with credit card payments from so many different countries of the world! However, for most members, the system worked smoothly, and it saved a great deal of manual work for the Treasurer.

We also had our first World Conference in South America in 2014. It was convened by Prof. Giselle Groeninga, and took place in Recife, Brazil. We were warmly hosted by our Brazilian colleagues, and formally welcomed by the local legal profession. The conference was a great success. We introduced a scholarship scheme for that conference, to allow scholars from poorer countries, particularly in Africa, to attend.

Also during this period, Adriaan's successor as Treasurer, Prof. Masha Antokolskaia, who became the President, did much to assist the ISFL to become properly registered in the Netherlands – a somewhat complex, but necessary, process that required changes to be made to the ISFL Constitution.

4. THE CHALLENGE OF IMPROVISATION

One of the most interesting experiences during my time as President was to attend a conference in South Korea. This was organised jointly as a regional conference of the ISFL, and of the Seoul Family Court. Marsha Garrison attended, as did former President Rainer Frank of Germany. The ISFL organiser was our colleague on the Executive Council, Prof. Jinsu Yune of the Seoul National University. The conference was to celebrate the fiftieth anniversary of the Seoul Family Court. As visitors to Seoul, we experienced the most wonderful hospitality from our Korean hosts.

There was, however, a catch. I had come prepared to give my paper, and to say something as ISFL President at the opening event. That, however, was only the beginning. I found myself being asked to make speeches at the commencement of proceedings on subsequent days, and at other events as well. I think I counted six occasions in all. I had definitely run out of sensible things to say by the third occasion, but it did not seem to matter.

5. THE CONTINUING SUCCESS OF THE ISFL

It has been good to see the Society continue to flourish under succeeding Presidents, Marsha Garrison, Hugues Fulchiron and Masha Antokolskaia, and the various Executive Council members. The COVID-19 pandemic put a pause on our face-to-face activities, but the Society found other ways to connect and to function. It continues to be renewed with the input of new generations of outstanding family law scholars.

The fiftieth anniversary is a great milestone. Long may the ISFL continue to bring the world together in family law scholarship.

REMEMBERING AND CELEBRATING THE INTERNATIONAL SOCIETY OF FAMILY LAW AT OUR GOLDEN JUBILEE

Hazel THOMPSON-AHYE*

In 1973, in Birmingham the International Society of Family Law was born.
Professor Falk was the one in whose brain this brilliant idea took form.
The objective of the Society was the study and discussion of Family Law
Furtherance of international research, dissemination of ideas and much more.
The **first ISFL World Conference** was held in West Berlin, in 1975.
Its theme, *The Child and the Law*, is still so very much alive.
The **second World Conference** in Montreal, Canada, in 1977
Was on *Violence in the Family*, an ever-present painful cry to heaven.
Family Living in a Changing Society was theme of **World Conference three**
In 1979, in Sweden, new knowledge gained, we didn't leave ignorantly.
Come 1982 at Harvard Law School, the **fourth World Conference** was held.
The first in the USA, but the theme, I do not know, and no one could tell.
Belgium in 1985 was the **fifth**, on *The Family, the State and Individual Security*.
Still so relevant and concerning to all, whether you live in the country or
the city.
The **sixth World Conference** in 1988, in Tokyo, Japan, was the first in Asia.
Issues of the Ageing in Modern Society was the theme chosen for us to hear.
The **seventh World Conference** in 1991, in Croatia, had longest title you'd see:
*Parenthood, The Legal Significance of Motherhood and Fatherhood in a
Changing Society.*
The **eighth World Conference,** in 1994, in Cardiff, Wales, was my first.
Families Across Frontiers, an intellectual fare, birthed in me an insatiable thirst.

---

*   Senator Hazel Thompson-Ahye, H.B.M., Vice President ISFL.

For the **ninth World Conference** in 1997, I went to Durban, South Africa,
to dine.

One of the conference presentations later published in the *Survey* was mine.

Changing Family Forms: World Themes and African Issues was the topic.

*The Relationship Between Social Change and the Law – The Concept of 'Family'
and the Child Born Out of Wedlock*, was my pick.

The **tenth World Conference** was held in 2000, in Queensland, Australia.

The theme, *Family Law Processes, Practices and Pressures* was good to hear.

The **eleventh World Conference** was held in Copenhagen and Oslo

On the theme, *Family Law and Human Rights*, one that we all know.

The **twelfth World Conference** in Utah, organised in 2005 by Lynn Wardle

On *Family Law, Balancing Interests and Pursuing Priorities* was a good model.

My paper on *The Law and the Cohabitant* and the law we had recently passed

Was published in the conference book and West Indian Law Journal superfast.

The **thirteenth World Conference** was held in Vienna, Austria in 2008.

Family Finances was the theme and the planned social events were great.

The **fourteenth** was in Lyon, France, on *Solidarities between Generations*.

I presented on our problems of the aged that were similar to all nations.

In the midst of my research, I discovered the UN classified me as old.

An idea on which, despite my children's concurrence, I was not sold.

The **fifteenth World Conference** in Recife, Brazil, in 2011, was a joy

To interact with the students, who were so enthusiastic, both girls and boys.

The topic was *Family Law: Universalities and Singularities*.

And we learnt that each country has its own peculiarities.

I presented on *Corporal Punishment: A Painful Blow to Children's Rights*.

A solution to which, despite commitment to child rights, no end is in sight.

The **sixteenth World Conference** 2017, on *Family Law and Family Realities*.

In Amsterdam, the Netherlands, revealed many situations of families.

The **seventeenth**, *Family Law and Crisis Going through Pandemics*.

Conducted online, showed Secretary Ursula's resourcefulness and work ethic.

For our **eighteenth**, we explored *Rethinking Law's Families and Family Law?*

It was our **Golden Jubilee**, a grand reunion in Belgium and so much more.

SOME NOTIONS OF A FORMER TREASURER AND PRESIDENT OF THE INTERNATIONAL SOCIETY OF FAMILY LAW

Paul Vlaardingerbroek

1. MY EARLY AND LATER YEARS OF ENGAGEMENT WITH ISFL

I got acquainted with ISFL when I started my work as a lecturer at the university in Tilburg. My former boss and promoter was Prof. Dr Madzy Rood-de Boer, who had been nominated professor of family law at Tilburg University[1] and the University of Utrecht. She was one of the founding mothers (and fathers) of ISFL, in 1973. The other promoter from me was Prof. Dr. Jan Vranken. Madzy Rood-de Boer invited me to become a member of this society, and introduced me at my first ISFL conference, in Louvain-la Neuve (very close to Brussels) in 1985. Actually, this was the fifth ISFL World Conference, which was held in July 1985, on the theme 'The Family, the State and Individual Security'. At that time Prof. John Eekelaar from Pembroke College in Oxford (UK) was the president of ISFL. The lectures gave me a good insight into the different law systems with regard to financial family support, alimony and social security. Brussels is not far away from Tilburg, and for me it was a very good opportunity to meet the officers of ISFL, and many ISFL members and other scientists (like psychologists and sociologists). It was a great experience to learn so much about other family law systems in our world. During the different international family law lectures, I also learned about aspects of animosity between several legal experts, and

---

[1] In 1984, the name of the university was Katholieke Hogeschool Tilburg. Later on, this name changed several times: from Katholieke Hogeschool Tilburg to Katholieke Universiteit Brabant, and later to Universiteit van Tilburg. For several years now, it has been called Tilburg University.

about professional jealousy between them. Nevertheless, it was a very interesting and inspiring conference, which was perfectly organised. The convenor of the conference was Professor Marie-Thérèse Meulders-Klein, who did a perfect job, together with her staff at the University of Louvain-la-Neuve. For me, it felt like joining a society with many other interested scientists in the field of family and child law. Later on, I not only felt I was a member of a society, but also a member of a second family. I will come back to this later.

At the conference in Brussels, it was announced that the next World Conference was going to be held in Tokyo, Japan, from 6–12 April 1988. The theme would be 'Issues of Ageing in Modern Society'. Of course, this was not only a very good theme, given the growing number of elderly in many countries, but also convenient for me to combine the conference with a holiday in Japan. The only problem was that our family had planned to move to another house, construction of which was set to be completed in April of 1988. My wife Aletta and our three young children had to move without my help, but fortunately our family members and friends were there to assist her. I returned from Tokyo (and from my holiday) when (almost) everything was settled in our new home. I still look back at a wonderful and relaxing experience! We had an excellent experience, particularly since it snowed on the first day of the conference, just as the cherry blossoms were beginning to bloom.

After the sixth World Conference in Tokyo, with more than 450 participants, new World Conferences were held. I still remember the very special ISFL meeting in 1991. That conference was held in Opatija, a nice tourist village in the Istria peninsula, by the Mediterranean Sea, in the former Yugoslavia. This conference, which had been organised by Petar Sarcevic, who later became president of ISFL, took place on the eve of the Balkan war between former parts of Yugoslavia. Due to the threat of war, many ISFL members skipped their trip to Opatija, and only 187 participants attended the conference. Because there was infighting between the parts of the former Yugoslavia (Croatia, Bosnia–Herzegovina, Serbia and Slovenia), and the threat of conflict between their 'civil' armies, many members and registered participants for this conference cancelled their registrations, and did not attend. Of course, this was a tragedy for the convenor(s) of the conference. Given the 'hard words' in the region between the former provinces, the hotels in Opatija – which is now part of Croatia – were only a about a third full. Fortunately, the conference was a great success. The theme of this conference was 'Parenthood: The Legal Significance'. We had a very good meeting, but the circumstances were, to put it mildly, far from ideal. Only a few weeks after the closing of the conference in Opatija, and shortly after the departure of the ISFL participants, Ljubljana Airport was attacked. Fortunately, none of the participants in the conference were harmed or involved in any incidents in the airport. Actually, the day after the conference, we had a guided tour in Istria. From our small bus we saw many beautiful villages, beaches and mountains. It was a very nice trip, but we also felt immense tensions between the Croats and Serbs, which had their origins in World War II, and perhaps also long before that. After this war, which lasted from 1991 to 1995, the Bosnian Serb leaders Radovan Karadzic and General Ratko Mladic were condemned as war criminals.

At the Opatija conference, I was nominated at the ISFL Council meeting to become Treasurer of the organisation. I succeeded Professor William Duncan (Dublin, Ireland) a few months later. After a meeting with him in The Hague (where he lived, and worked as an expert for the Hague Conference of Private International Law), I started to reorganise the administration of the Society. In 1988, ISFL had over 600 members in 43 countries. Unfortunately, I found out that ISFL had many non-paying members, who had once been members, but had forgotten to pay their subscription fees in later years. Financially, this was a considerable problem, because we had to pay for the publishing of the annual *Surveys of Family Law*, the annual meetings of the Executive Council (EXCO), and the reduction in fees for members coming from developing countries. Thus, with the officers of the Council (Anders Agell, President, and Peter Lødrup, Secretary-General),[2] we decided to clean up the membership list. We decided to send letters to all members by post (email addresses were not common in those days!). With the help of my wife and children, we folded more than 600 letters, put them in envelopes, and took them to the post office. However, the disappointment was great when we discovered that fewer than half of the addressed members reacted with a renewal of their membership and a new payment. Thus, we tried to trace the addresses of our 'lost members', which resulted in some 100 further replies. Some mentioned their new addresses, others started repaying their subscription fees, and others replied that they had changed jobs (and/or interests) or retired from their universities. Although ISFL lost many members through this (necessary) clear-out operation, we did save money by lowering the costs of the annual *Surveys*, and by not sending any more mailings (surveys, bulletins and newsletters) to non-existent members. The EXCO also started negotiations with publishers, to find one who could publish our annual *Surveys* and send them to our members at a moderate price. As a result of this pruning of the membership, we started with an updated membership list, cut costs, and increased subscription revenue. We put that money in a (Robeco) bank account that I had opened. With this new account, we had success because of the rising exchange rates, especially in the years till 2020. Meanwhile, we continued publishing the annual *Surveys* through the Law School of the University of Louisville. The executive editor of many of these volumes was Prof. M.D.A. Freeman from University College, London.[3] I served ISFL as

---

2   Both officers were good colleagues and friends. Anders was a professor at the University of Uppsala (Sweden), and Peter was a professor at the University of Oslo (Norway).

3   See the chapter 'Reflections on the International Survey of Family Law', in this book, by Bill Atkin, Professor of Law, Te Herenga Waka/Victoria University of Wellington, New Zealand.

Treasurer from 1 May 1991 till 1 September 2006, when Dr Adriaan van der Linden (Utrecht University) succeeded me. In the years preceding this, we had a growing number of members, although not everyone paid their subscription fees in due course. In 2005, I was appointed as President of the Society, and I served until the World Conference in 2008.

2. SOME REMARKS ABOUT THE PAST AND THE FUTURE OF ISFL

In the years that I was an officer of the Executive Council, I had many meetings with the other officers. The officers of the ECXO are the President, the Secretary-General, the Treasurer and the Immediate Past President. They are also frequently in contact with each other. Working as an officer, or as a member of the Council, takes up a lot of time – time that cannot be invested in other business, or in private life. However, I never felt that working for ISFL was a waste of time. Actually, it enriched my life to have so many 'family members' all around the world. Indeed, it gave me the feeling that I was member of a great family of colleagues and friends. It is always a plus if you can ask your colleagues elsewhere about developments in the law in their country, or in the country you live and work in, and be able to compare your legal context with other colleagues, especially when they live abroad. Of course, it was and is much easier to contact a foreign colleague if you know them because you have met them at a regional or international conference. This was the case at the meetings of the Executive Council, but also when it was necessary to meet between these meetings. We also often used the phone, and later on, we sent emails to each other. From May 1991 till September 2008, I was in the heart of ISFL, and I really enjoyed and loved working for our Society, and with so many famous academics in family law. I will never forget the people I worked with in our ISFL community: academics like Agell, Bainham, Brinig, Baroness Deech, Dethloff, Eekelaar, Fulchiron, Frank, Freeman, Groeninga da Almeida, Katz, Lødrup, Lowe, Matsushima, Minamikata, Meulders-Klein, Panforti, Parkinson, Robinson, Rubellin-Devichi, Sarcevic, Thompson, Wardle, Verschraegen, Fretwell Wilson, and many more. Unfortunately, it is impossible to show my gratitude and respect to all colleagues with whom I worked in our ISFL, because the list would become too long.

However, I look forward to meeting many ISFL members at our next World Conference, in Antwerp, in July 2023. In 2019/20 I had intended to come to the World Conference in Barbados, and I had even booked my flights and a hotel room, but unfortunately COVID-19 prevented us from going there. It would have been great to have seen my family of academic colleagues on a tropical island. I still have deep respect for Hazel Thompson, who had to decide to cancel this conference in 2020, and to postpone this conference to 2023.

The next World Conference in Antwerp, convened by Frederik Swennen, will probably be the last ISFL conference that I will attend, but I really look forward to meeting all ISFL members. For the future of ISFL, I sincerely hope that many young scholars and other academics will find interest in joining our Society, and that all members pay their subscription fees, because otherwise the Society is doomed to shrink, and to lose its status in the academic world. Also, young academics should be recruited to build a better world for families and children. Combining national and international perspectives is important for that effort, and young scholars should be encouraged and supported to invest part of their careers working for our Society.

Unfortunately, some of my former colleagues and friends have died, but I will never forget them. Old soldiers never die, they just fade away!

Or, should I say, old officers never die, they just fade away!

PART II

50-YEAR RETROSPECTIVES
ON FAMILY LAW

GLOBAL PERSPECTIVES

50 YEARS OF DEVELOPMENTS IN FAMILY LAW IN THE WESTERNISED WORLD

The Long and Winding Road

Masha ANTOKOLSKAIA

Résumé

En 2023, l'ISFL célébrera son jubilé d'or des 50 ans d'existence. Si l'on considère la période allant de 1973 à 2023, il apparaît clairement qu'aucune autre période de l'histoire du droit de la famille n'a connu autant de changements profonds presque simultanés dans autant de pays. Le grand ensemble, que l'on pourrait appeler schématiquement le « monde occidental » (Europe, Amérique du Nord, Australie et Nouvelle-Zélande), mais aussi l'Amérique du Sud et le Japon ont connu à cette époque une véritable révolution dans le domaine du droit de la famille. Il est difficile de résumer les transformations les plus importantes qui ont eu lieu dans ce laps de temps relativement court. Le mouvement pour les droits des femmes a réussi à surmonter la domination séculaire de l'homme au sein de la famille. L'égalité au moins formelle entre les hommes et les femmes est désormais une réalité dans l'ensemble du monde occidental. Avant cette période, les pays occidentaux ne reconnaissaient qu'une seule forme de relations personnelles : le mariage légal. En revanche, aujourd'hui, une variété de relations personnelles sont légalement reconnues : le mariage hétérosexuel et homosexuel, le partenariat enregistré et la cohabitation non institutionnalisée. Au début de cette période, seule une poignée de pays autorisait le divorce sans faute. À partir des années 70', la révolution du divorce sans faute a gagné le monde occidental, de sorte qu'aujourd'hui, quasiment aucun pays ne maintient la faute comme seul motif de divorce. À la veille de cette période, les enfants illégitimes étaient partout fortement désavantagés. Aujourd'hui, le statut juridique des enfants nés de parents non mariés est fondamentalement égal à celui des enfants dont les parents sont mariés. L'enfant a été perçu comme une personne en pleine croissance, dotée de ses propres droits et de sa propre voix, plutôt que comme un sujet passif devant être protégé et éduqué par les adultes. Dans le domaine de la protection des personnes handicapées, cette période a été marquée par un véritable changement de paradigme, passant de la traditionnelle protection au nouveau modèle du renforcement de l'autonomie.

Le moteur du changement était le même partout : la deuxième transition démographique, l'émancipation économique, sociale et juridique des femmes et l'émergence de l'État-providence se sont combinés pour créer les conditions socio-économiques qui ont rendu possible la mise en œuvre des idées des Lumières dans le droit de la famille. Les changements de cette période ont affecté l'ensemble du monde occidental, mais le rythme et la profondeur des transformations ont différé d'un pays à l'autre. Plusieurs éminents chercheurs ont attribué ces différences à l'influence des cultures nationales. Dans mes travaux antérieurs, j'ai suggéré que, parmi tous les facteurs sociétaux que l'on peut considérer, ce sont surtout les différences dans l'équilibre du pouvoir politique entre les camps « progressiste » et « conservateur » qui font varier le rythme de la modernisation du droit de la famille dans les divers pays occidentaux. La période du dernier demi-siècle a été une période généralement progressiste de l'histoire de la plupart des régions du monde. Cependant, même dans ce climat généralement tourné vers le progrès, chacun n'était pas également satisfait de ces changements. Les camps conservateurs de chaque pays ont résisté au processus de transformation dans la mesure de leur influence politique, mais n'ont pas pu empêcher les changements à venir.

L'évolution rapide et sans précédent du droit de la famille des pays occidentaux dans la même direction pourrait faire rêver [ou cauchemarder] qu'un « point final » de l'évolution du droit de la famille – une sorte de « fin de l'histoire » – est proche. Les événements de ces dernières années pourraient nous aider à sortir de cette illusion. Si nous examinons la situation actuelle, il semble que la période généralement progressiste, qui a débuté à la fin des années 60', touche maintenant à sa fin. Le pouvoir politique des forces conservatrices et ultraconservatrices s'accroît dans de nombreux pays occidentaux et dans d'autres parties du monde. Cette tendance se répercute immédiatement sur la famille, car le droit de la famille devient souvent l'un des premiers champs de bataille des nouvelles guerres culturelles. Les régimes conservateurs et les camps conservateurs font de la défense des valeurs familiales traditionnelles leur cri de guerre. Ainsi, le régime de l'extrême conservateur Poutine s'emploie à renverser la tradition de longue date progressiste du droit de la famille en Russie sous le mot d'ordre de la défense des valeurs familiales traditionnelles contre les parades homosexuelles. Les partisans de l'extrême-conservateur Trump lancent une attaque similaire contre les éléments progressistes du droit de la famille aux États-Unis. La même tendance se manifeste en Pologne et en Hongrie et – dans une moindre mesure – dans d'autres pays d'Europe de l'Est.

1. INTRODUCTION: 50 YEARS OF FAMILY REVOLUTION

In 2023 the International Society of Family Law (ISFL) celebrates its golden jubilee. If we look back at the past half-century, stretching from 1973 till 2023, it becomes clear that there has hardly been any other phase in the history of family law that has witnessed so many momentous changes in so many countries. Various scholars admit that a large area, which could be roughly dubbed the 'Westernised world'[1] (Europe, North America, and Australia and New Zealand), but also South America, South Africa, Japan and many other countries – has experienced, over this time, a real revolution in the field of family law. Throughout this turbulent period, the ISFL has united family law scholars and practitioners with different, sometimes even opposing, views, and has promoted respect and tolerance for each other values and convictions.

As a result of 50 years of these unparalleled developments, the traditional family, based on marriage as a lifelong union, which seemed to be so universal and stable, has all but vanished. The previously existing largely homogeneous

---

[1]   This term is used to cover the jurisdictions which generally follow the patterns of European history, and whose ideas on family law are directly – or indirectly, through later reception – profoundly influenced by the Enlightenment: Western and Eastern Europe (including Turkey), Canada and the United States, as well as Australia and New Zealand, and Latin American Countries. I use this term rather than the term 'industrialised countries', as industrialised countries also include East and Southern Asian countries much less influenced by the European patterns.

society has given way to a pluralistic society, in which different family forms and different sets of family values co-exist alongside each other. Due to the general atmosphere of tolerance, men and women became more and more free to choose between marriage or some other form of intimate relationship. At the beginning of the period, the Westernised countries recognised only one form of intimate relationship: a lawful marriage. In contrast, today a whole range of varieties of intimate relationships are legally recognised and/or socially accepted: heterosexual and homosexual marriage, various types of registered partnerships, and, last but not least, non-institutionalised cohabitation. Extramarital sex, non-marital cohabitation, and birth outside wedlock have lost their stigmatic character. Same-sex relationships first became decriminalised, then legalised, and next – in some countries – incorporated into marriage. Due to the fact that more and more children were being born outside marriage, it became increasingly unacceptable for the legal status of these children to differ from that of the children born in a marriage. Thus, eventually, 'illegitimate' children were granted a truly equal place alongside their 'legitimate' brothers and sisters. The women's rights movement managed to overcome the centuries-long dominance of men within the family. At least formal equality between men and women is now the fact throughout the whole of the Westernised world. At the beginning of this period, only a handful of countries allowed for no-fault divorce. From the 1970s onwards, a no-fault divorce revolution swept through the Westernised world, so that now hardly any country there maintains fault as the only divorce ground. Divorce and serial monogamy are now largely considered normal. During this period, children's rights have grown into one of the main issues of family law. A child came to be perceived as a growing personality, with its own rights and voice, rather than as a passive subject of protection and education by adults. In the field of legal support and representation of persons with disabilities, this period has witnessed a genuine paradigm shift from the old protection paradigm to the modern empowerment paradigm.

As we look at the results of all these almost simultaneous revolutionary changes, it is interesting to contemplate their historical roots, their driving forces and their political and societal actors. It is also rather interesting to consider where family law stands right now, and what challenges lie in front of it. Are we at the end of a historical period? Has the family revolution achieved its goals and thus ended? Have family law issues become less controversial, and the tolerance for each other's family values and practices greater? Of course, one cannot even try to touch upon all these issues in a single piece. In this chapter, I will briefly sketch the historical roots, as well as the ideological and political background, of these unprecedented revolutionary transformations (section 2), and briefly outline the main developments of family law in the field of marriage and divorce (section 3). I will conclude by trying to look at the current state of family law from the perspective of the developments of the past five decades.

2. IDEOLOGICAL ROOTS OF THE FAMILY REVOLUTION

The evolution of the family law of the whole of the Westernised world was driven directly – or indirectly, through later reception – by more or less the same ideological incentives. Ever since the French Revolution, Europe, North America and other Westernised countries have been split into two camps: a progressive one, inspired by the ideology of the Enlightenment, and a conservative one, aspiring to preserve or restore traditional family forms and values.[2] The proponents of Enlightenment ideology believed that there was one universally valid system of values, and that the objective of law was to emancipate men and to improve human life[3] in accordance with those values. The French philosophers perceived marriage as an asset for an individual: a means to achieving personal happiness,[4] rather than a duty, and 'a conventional social and economic relationship.'[5] The right to dissolve an unhappy marriage was a logical end to the vision of a marriage as 'one of the avenues open to man in his pursuit of happiness.'[6] Other ideas put forward in the time of the Enlightenment concerned the limitation of parental and male power, and (albeit hesitantly) the promotion of gender equality.[7]

Conservatives were equally certain of the universal validity of the traditional family values, sanctified by religion and convention. They saw the objectives of family law as being to preserve the sanctity of marriage and the stability of the family. Thus, the clash between two systems of values, both claiming to be universally valid, caused a discord between the conservative and progressive camps, and has ideologically divided each European country. Family law became a battleground in the clashes between these camps. From the seventeenth century up to the 1970s, all Westernised countries underwent more or less the same transformations. Until the 1970s, the development of family law was generally typified by a great deal of stability and the slow passage of reforms. The changes – save for some temporarily sweeping breakthroughs following the French (1789), Portuguese (1910) and Russian (1917) Revolutions, and a few other instances – were, for the most part, a steady evolutional development.

---

2   For more details, see M. Antokolskaia, *Harmonisation of Family Law in Europe: A Historical Perspective: A Tale of Two Millennia*, Intersentia, 2006.

3   L. Tomesen, 'Ideeënstelsels die ten grondslag liggen aan het Europese cultuurdebat' in L. Tomesen and G. Vossen (eds.), *Denken over cultuur in Europa*, Bohn Stafleu, p. 6.

4   J. Traer, *Marriage and the Family in Eighteenth-Century France*, Cornell Univ. Press, 1980, pp. 70–71.

5   Ibid., p. 49.

6   M. Rheinstein, *Marriage Stability, Divorce, and the Law*, Univ. of Chicago Press, 1972, p. 25.

7   Women's equality was, however, only a marginal and hesitant theme in the palette of the Enlightenment: D. Williams, *The Enlightenment*, CUP, 1999, pp. 38–40.

The general similarity of the development of family law, along with the overall similarity of the European history of ideas, predetermined the steady similarity in the agendas of the ideological debates between the proponents and the opponents of the modernisation of family law in the whole of the Westernised world. Each of the periods of gradual modernisation of family law was typified by its own ideology: the ideology of Enlightenment, nineteenth-century liberalism, feminism, children rights, emancipation of sexual minorities, etc. All these ideological trends generated their own sets of values with regard to family and its legal regulation. Each new ideological trend met resistance from conservative opponents, and therefore aggravated the ideological divide between the conservative and progressive camps.

The value differences in family law do not usually lie along state borders, but are present within every Westernised country. The population in each particular country is split into various different 'cultures', based on different values. The 'culture' and 'values' of an urban family of highly educated young professionals differs significantly from the 'culture' and 'values' of a rural family of middle-aged traditional farmers in any country, be it Ireland, Australia, Sweden or Canada. Friedman spoke in this respect of 'a dizzying array of cultures'[8] within a single legal culture. The modernity of family patterns and family values adhered to by different groups differs greatly from one social environment to another. In spite of the presence of ever-competitive value systems, each country has a predominant culture and values that are generally those of the majority of the population, or of the *élites dirigeantes*.[9] Therefore, the pertinent family law is either a reflection of the predominant values or a compromise between the values of the various groups. Thus, it is possible to suggest the existence of conservative and progressive pan-Western legal ideologies and legal cultures in respect to family law, in the sense that each of those ideologies has its own rank and file in each Westernised country (and in other countries of the world as well): sometimes this is a majority; sometimes a tiny stratum. The countries with more modern family laws also have population groups with conservative family values, and the countries with conservative family laws always have population groups that represent the most modern views on family life. The understanding within the progressive groups reaches across borders; they often look abroad to support their ideas, and they repeatedly call on federal or international courts and commissions dealing with human rights issues, in order to adjudicate their confrontations with their opponents from their own countries, states or jurisdictions.[10]

---

[8]   L. FRIEDMANN, *The Republic of Choice: Law, Authority and Culture,* Harvard Univ. Press, 1990, p. 213.

[9]   I am indebted to E. ÖRÜCÜ for this term. See her *Critical Comparative Law: Considering Paradoxes for Legal Systems in Transition,* Preadvies voor de Nederlandse Vereniging voor Rechtsvergelijking, Kluwer, 1999, p. 86.

[10] See on this issue, for instance, M. FREEMAN, 'Is a Political Science of Human Rights Possible?' (2001) 2 *NQHR* 134 ff.

3. THE COURSE OF REFORMS

In the last 50 years, two distinct periods of family law developments have been seen. The first of these stretched from around 1970 till around 2000. During this period, marriage and divorce underwent revolutionary modification and liberalisation, in line with the ideas of personal freedom to enter into and dissolve marriages, as well as equality of spouses and parents. These ideas have already existed since the Enlightenment, and nineteenth-century feminism.

The second period began around the turn of the millennium. During this period, marriage and family have been undergoing a truly revolutionary transformation, based on new ideas of inclusiveness and the equal rights of sexual minorities. It started with opening up marriage to persons of the same sex, and is still evolving in search for the most adequate solutions for the legal accommodation of LGBT+ parentage. Another hallmark of this period is legal emancipation of persons with impaired decision-making capacities, in line with the requirements of the 2006 UN Convention on the Rights of Persons with Disabilities (UNCRPD).

3.1. 1970–2000: REVOLUTIONARY MODIFICATION OF TRADITIONAL FAMILY

If we look closely at the family law revolution that swept through the Westernised world from 1970 till 2000, we can see that the motor and the ideological background of the changes were the same everywhere. The combined influence of the second demographic transition, the economic, social and legal emancipation of women, and the emergence of the welfare state created socio-economic conditions that finally made massive implementation of Enlightenment ideas into family law possible.

3.1.1. Marriage

Regarding this period of the reforms, Mary Ann Glendon rightly emphasises that 'the reforms that began in the 1960s did not destroy the traditional family. What these reforms mainly did was to consolidate and sometimes increase the power of several movements that were already going forward.'[11] After almost two centuries of cultural and ideological clashes, and steady societal and legal developments, Westernised societies were more or less prepared to accept the reforms of marriage law in line with Enlightenment and feminist ideals. The importance of the procreative function of marriage diminished drastically, as

---

[11]   M.A. GLENDON, *The Transformation of Family Law*, Univ. of Chicago Press, 1989, p. 311.

marriage ceased to be the only union through which children were bestowed full legal rights in respect of the parents and their families.[12] Spousal relationships were evolving from the man as breadwinner, and the woman as housekeeper and childcarer, to the modern family of two breadwinners sharing parental and household responsibilities on a more or less equal basis. Although analysis of this evolution has focused primarily on the emancipation of women, the changes in the roles of men and the concept of fatherhood have been almost equally significant. More and more fathers started to play a central role in nurturing and bringing up their children.[13] Due to women's emancipation, increasing female employment, and the progress of social welfare, the function of the family as provider of financial means and security has diminished, and the role of marriage has generally shifted from a production unit to a consumption unit.[14] This development has contributed to an attitudinal shift in the emphasis of marriage, from communitarian to individualistic.[15] In line with the Enlightenment ideal, the main function of marriage became to provide spouses and children with companionship, personal fulfilment, love and happiness.[16]

However, this new 'hedonistic' function of marriage appeared to have its downsides. Marriage based on affection and free commitment, rather than on economic necessity and duty, proved to be less stable and durable.[17] Seeing the justification of marriage continuation in the emotional satisfaction of partners, rather in obligations towards their children,[18] leads to negative effects of divorce on children, and problems of post-divorce parenting. The other side of love-based marriage is that love often comes to an end only in one of the spouses, rather than both of them, leaving the 'abandoned' spouse with bitterness and anger. As the hedonistic function of marriage came more to the fore, the

---

[12]   F. SWENNEN, *Het huwelijk afschaffen?* Intersentia, 2003, p. 1; H. WILLEKENS, 'Explaining Two Hundred Years of Family Law in Western Europe' in H. WILLEKENS, (ed.), *Het gezinsrecht in de sociale wetenschappen*, Vuga, 1997, p. 69.

[13]   Statistically speaking, the modern role division is typical for only a minority of families, as a survey of American, European and Australian literature reveals that, in absolute terms, fathers still spend less time with their children than mothers do: E. DERMOTT, 'Intimate Fatherhood: A sociological analysis', Routledge, 2008, pp. 43 ff.

[14]   M. GARRISON, *Family Life, Family Law, and Family Justice: Tying the Knot,* Routledge, 2023, pp. 21–24.

[15]   In other words, 'the passage from family to individual'. C. MARTIN and I. THÉRY, 'The PACS and Marriage and Cohabitation in France' (2001) 15 *IJLPF* 154.

[16]   According to Alan Bénabent, the new concept of marriage involves that marriage as a means to the fullest possible development of a person: A. BÉNABENT, 'Le Liberté individuelle et le mariage' (1973) *RTD civ.* 480.

[17]   Mary Ann Glendon notes that modern marriage law simultaneously expresses the closeness and intensity, as well as the instability, of the modern marriage, based on emotional rather than economic ties: M.A. GLENDON, *The New Family and the New Property*, Butterworth, 1981, p. 29.

[18]   G. DOUGLAS, *Obligation and Commitment in Family Law*, Hart Publishing, 2018, p. 69.

partners' expectations as to the quality of their relationship grew higher and higher. Under the influence of these transformations, the modus of marriage has generally shifted from life-long monogamy to serial monogamy.

3.1.2. Cohabitation

Although the prevalence of extramarital cohabitation has grown without precedent in the period under discussion, it turned out to be much less a threat to marriage than its conservative adversaries claimed. At the turn of the millennium, in Europe, around 30 per cent of all couples under 30 years old were cohabiting.[19] This expansion of non-marital cohabitation proceeded in stages. Drawing on the experience of Sweden, Kathleen Kiernan has divided the recent developments of non-marital cohabitation into four stages.[20] During the first stage, cohabitation was no more than 'a deviant avant-garde phenomenon practiced by a small group' of progressive intellectuals.[21] In the second stage, it became 'a prelude or a probationary period', after which the partners marry and have children. In the third stage, cohabitation became socially 'acceptable as an alternative to marriage', and the birth of a child was no longer seen as a reason to marry.[22] During the fourth stage, cohabitation and marriage became 'indistinguishable' in respect to child-rearing and social acceptance.[23] In the period between 1970 and 2000, most Westernised countries evolved from the first to the second or third stage,[24] and only a few reached the fourth one.[25] However, unmarried cohabitants, even if one focuses only on heterosexual couples, are very diverse.[26] They can be roughly divided into three groups:[27] (1) cohabitation

---

[19]   H. TONER, *Partnership Rights, Free Movement, and EU Law*, Hart Publishing, 2004, p. 31.

[20]   K. KIERNAN, 'The Rise of Cohabitation and Childbearing Outside Marriage in Western Europe' (2001) 15 *IJLPF* 3.

[21]   Ibid.

[22]   Ibid.

[23]   Ibid.

[24]   Germany, the UK, the Netherlands, Belgium, Austria and other countries with relatively high levels of cohabitation find themselves at the third stage. In Southern European countries, such as Greece, Italy, Spain and Portugal, as well as Ireland and Eastern Europe, cohabitation is still a rather marginal phenomenon: ibid., at 58.

[25]   The vanguard countries, like Sweden and Denmark, have already reached the fourth stage; cohabitation is about to eclipse marriage there. Countries like Finland and France are catching up with them: K. KIERNAN, 'The State of European Unions: an Analysis of Partnership Formation and Dissolution' in M. MACURA and G. BEETS (eds.), *Dynamics of fertility and partnership in Europe: insights and lessons from comparative research*, vol. 1, United Nations, 2002, p. 75.

[26]   C. SMART and P. STEVENS, *Cohabitation Breakdown*, Family Policy Studies Centre, 2000.

[27]   For an analysis of the various social forms of cohabitation, see W. SCHRAMA in *De niet-huwelijkse samenleving in het Nederlandse en Duitse recht*, Kluwer, 2004, pp. 95–98 and further writing, e.g. 'The Dutch Approach to Informal Lifestyles: Family Function over Family Form?' (2008) 22 *IJLPF* 314–315. This author classifies cohabitation into premarital, long-term and post-marital cohabitation.

as trial marriage; (2) cohabitation instead of marriage; and (3) cohabitation after marriage. By far the largest proportion of unmarried cohabitants are young people in trial marriages: a relatively unbound experimental stage of their relationship in which the partners want to find out whether they are suited to each other, without committing themselves to marriage. In many Western countries, trial marriage has become a standard prelude to marriage. The second group consists of a much less sizeable, albeit steadily growing, number of individuals who choose cohabitation as a permanent relationship form. This group consists of partners who remain cohabiting even after having children. The size of this group varies significantly from country to country, and can be estimated on the basis of the number of children born outside marriage. Only this relatively small group can be seen as a social equivalent – an alternative or a 'threat' – to marriage. The third, also relatively small, group of unmarried heterosexual cohabitants consists of late-middle-aged individuals who, after terminating previous relationships, prefer cohabitation to marriage, in order to avoid any legal consequences that could disadvantage the children of previous relationships.

3.1.3. Divorce

The negative side effects of liberalisation of marriage law gave conservatives justified cause for concern, and have allowed them to slow down the pace of divorce liberalisation in most Westernised jurisdictions. Countries traditionally adhering to the Catholic doctrine of indissolubility of marriage – Spain, Italy, Ireland[28] and Malta[29] – have introduced divorce after furious fights, often involving several referendums. Despite the fact that, after the 1970s, the advocates of the liberalisation of divorce law have led the way, non-compromise divorce reforms, like those in California,[30] Sweden or Spain, have remained rather infrequent. In most jurisdictions, the main policy challenge was to find a compromise between two opposing paradigms. The first paradigm was the liberal belief in the right of the spouses to decide for themselves whether, and when, their marriage had to come to an end. The second paradigm was the belief that divorce should not be made too easy, as the primary purpose of divorce law was to buttress the institution of marriage and protect the weaker spouse and children. As the balance of political power of conservative and progressive forces differs significantly from one jurisdiction to another, these compromises, and consequently the national divorce laws, appear to be rather dissimilar.

---

[28] Family Law (Divorce) Act, 1996, Part II.
[29] See Art. 66B, Civil Code of Malta.
[30] GARRISON, above n. 14, pp. 31–34.

3.1.4.   To Sum Up

The reforms described above have, in fact, 'saved' marriage, by bringing its legal regulation into accordance with its new social function and ideological connotation. At the turn of the millennium, marriage and family were different from their traditional precursors, but not radically so. Marriage was still the same monogamous heterosexual marriage, just more equal, more individualistic, and more easily dissoluble.

3.2.   AFTER THE TURN OF THE MILLENNIUM: THE TIME OF REAL REVOLUTIONARY CHANGE

Referring to the overall progressive ideological tendency on the eve of the new millennium, Van Hoecke and Warrington suggested that there were no more paradigmatical differences in Europe on the level of legal ideology.[31] However, around the turn of the millennium, same-sex marriage, LGBT+ rights, multiple parentage, and – in some countries – reconsidering the right to abortion, gave rise to new paradigmatic ideological controversies. Contrary to what was expected, in many countries tolerance of each other's family values and practices has not increased further, but has instead declined.

This time, the main ideological battle started in the US. There has always been a notable difference between the US, on the one hand, and Europe and Canada, on the other. Western European and Canadian societies remained fairly homogenous throughout the whole of the half-century period.[32] In the most other Westernised countries, family law reform had its contentious points – like during introduction of same-sex marriage in Spain, in 2005 – but did not tend to lead to a lasting increase of polarisation within society. In contrast, in the US, the period of relative uniformity of society at the beginning of the family revolution in the 1970s was followed by a period of 'Great Divergence'.[33] During that contentious period, economic, cultural and political disparity was continuing to

---

[31]   M. VAN HOECKE and M. WARRINGTON, 'Legal Cultures, Legal Paradigms and Legal Doctrine: Towards a New Model for Comparative Law' (1998) *47 Int'l & Comp. LQ* 535.

[32]   In Western Europe and Canada, according to the Gini coefficient (after taxes and transfers), income inequality between the 1970s/80s and late 2000s has decreased in Belgium, Greece, France, Ireland and Portugal, and has increased only slightly in Canada and the rest of Western Europe. In contrast, in the US and the UK, the same period witnessed a significant increase in income inequality. *Income distribution – Inequality –* OECD Stats, available at: https://data.oecd.org/inequality/income-inequality.htm.

[33]   T. NOAH, 'The United States of Inequality: Introducing the Great Divergence', *Slate.com.*, 3 September 2010, cited in J. CARBONE and N. CAHN, 'Red v. Blue Marriage' in M. GARRISON and E. SCOTT (eds.), *Marriage at the Crossroads: Law, Policy, and the Brave New World of Twenty-First-Century Families*, CUP, 2012, on p. 4 of the electronic copy, available at: http://ssrn.com/abstract=1995822.

grow in the US.[34] As Naomi Cahn and June Carbone explain in their seminal book *Red Families v. Blue Families*, during this period the old conservative/progressive divide between the proponents of liberal and conservative family values started to coincide with the political divide between the two main US political parties: the Republicans ('red') and the Democrats ('blue').[35] This change is associated with the transition from an industrial to a post-industrial information economy. In the US, with its relatively weak welfare state, this transition produced a sharp shift in well-paid jobs, favouring the college-educated members of the middle class – males as well as females —[36] which resulted not only in a growing economic disparity between two-breadwinner middle-class ('blue') families and the more traditional working-class ('red') families, but also distinctly different family patterns and opposing ideological responses to family change.[37] Blue families are characterised by late marriages, the first-career-then-children attitude, equal parenting, greater reliance on contraception, and low birth rates. This so-called 'middle-class strategy' leads to a lower divorce rate. Red elites, who tend to be more religious, find this strategy anathema, because it involves non-marital sex, unmarried cohabitation, and birth control. Red families in general are typified by more children (often due to early unplanned pregnancies),[38] higher marriage rates, and earlier marriages (sometimes triggered by unplanned pregnancy), but blue-collar, poor, red families are characterised by declining marriages and high divorce rates.[39] This conflates the class divide produced by a changing economy and the ideological divide that responds to it. Marriage became increasingly selective, rarer and more stable – enjoying a more elite status[40] – than was the case in the past,[41] and thus it became reserved merely for the blue families. The persistent decline in the divorce rate among blue families is in stark contrast with the simultaneous trend, over-represented among red families, towards more cohabitation and less stability within cohabiting couples.[42] Ideologically,[43] the difference between the red and blue families has reached the point of 'cultural war' in relation to 'dominant forms of family life and the meaning of marriage within it'.[44] The presidency of Donald Trump has only exacerbated this war,

---

[34]   J. CARBONE and N. CAHN, *Red Families v. Blue Families: Legal Polarization and the Creation of Culture*, OUP, 2010, p. 5.

[35]   Ibid.

[36]   Ibid., p. 1.

[37]   Ibid., p. 6.

[38]   GARRISON, above n. 14, pp. 56–67.

[39]   Ibid.

[40]   Ibid., p. 25.

[41]   P.N. COHEN, 'The Coming Divorce Decline' (2019) 5 *Socius: Sociological Research for a Dynamic World* 1–6.

[42]   Ibid.

[43]   Ideological divide is greater at the elite level, but working-class families are more likely to marry, divorce and remarry in red states, and more likely to cohabit in blue states.

[44]   CARBONE and CAHN, above n. 34, p. 3.

most of which is being waged about the recognition of same-sex relationships, abortion[45] and contraception.

Initially confined to the US, growing intolerance to each other views started to spread to Europe and other Westernised countries in the late 2010s. In Europe, the extreme spectrum of the new cultural divide is now represented by Russian and Belarusian dictatorial regimes.

3.2.1. Marriage

A really revolutionary transformation in the field of marriage was the emergence, and then widespread prevalence, of same-sex marriage. In 2001, the Netherlands became the first country in the world to open up marriage for same-sex couples. In 2023, same-sex marriage exists in 34 countries,[46] most of them Westernised. The majority of these countries have legalised same-sex marriage through legislation, however in several countries, including Austria, Brazil, Canada, South Africa and the US, the opening-up of marriage for same-sex couples resulted from judicial intervention through constitutional rights provisions.[47] In Europe in 2023, 18 of the Council of Europe's 46 Member States have opened up marriage to same-sex couples. The European Court of Human Rights has recently established a clear ongoing trend within Member States, in the direction of legal recognition of same-sex couples.[48] In a series of decisions since 2015,[49] the Court has ruled that Member States have a positive obligation to provide for some form of formal relationship for same-sex couples, and that failing to comply with this obligation violates Articles 8 and 14 of the European Convention on Human Rights. However, in several decisions,[50] the Court has stressed that the decision to open marriage up to same-sex couples still remains within the margins of appreciation of the Member States.

---

[45]   On 24 June 2022, the US Supreme Court overruled *Roe v. Wade*.

[46]   Andorra, Argentina, Australia, Austria, Belgium, Brazil, Canada, Chile, Colombia, Costa Rica, Cuba, Denmark, Ecuador, Finland, France, Germany, Iceland, Ireland, Luxembourg, Malta, Mexico, the Netherlands, New Zealand, Norway, Portugal, Slovenia, South Africa, Spain, Sweden, Switzerland, Taiwan, the United Kingdom, the United States of America and Uruguay: Human Rights Campaign, 'Marriage Equality Around the World', https://www.hrc. org/resources/marriage-equality-around-the-world.

[47]   Human Rights Campaign, 'Marriage Equality Around the World', https://www.hrc.org/ resources/marriage-equality-around-the-world.

[48]   EHRM [GC] 17 January 2023, 40792/10, 30538/14 and 43439/14 (*Fedotova and others v. Russia*), §§175–176.

[49]   EHRM 25 July 2015, 18766/11 and 36030/11 (*Oliari and Others v. Italy*); EHRM 14 December 2017, 26431/12 and 3 others (*Orlandi and Others v. Italy*).

[50]   EHRM 24 June 2010, 30141/04 24 (*Schalk and Kopf v. Austria*), §§101 and 108; EHRM 2012, 25951/07 (*Gas and Dubois v. France*), §66; §37; EHRM 9 June 2016, 40183/07 (*Chapin and Charpentier v. France*), §48; EHRM [GC] 17 January 2023, 40792/10, 30538/14 and 43439/14 (*Fedotova and others v. Russia*).

Recognition of same-sex marriage was such a radical departure from the traditional concept of monogamous heterosexual marriage that its conservative opponents have expressed doubt whether same sex-marriage still can be called 'marriage',[51] and have started another round of complaints about it 'threatening' the institution of marriage.[52] In most Westernised countries, the step towards recognition of same-sex relationships as equal, and the introduction of registered partnership and/or same-sex marriage, once made, became widely accepted, and did not lead to lasting polarisation.

Despite this evident trend, same-sex marriage remains controversial in many parts of the world, and among certain populations. Out of 33 countries around the world that prohibit same-sex marriage on a national level, 15 are European countries.[53] Several of these do not provide for any other form of formal relationship for same-sex couples. Resistance to such recognition exists not only in obscure dictatorships, like Russia and Belarus, where defending the traditional family against gay parades became an essential part of a cultural and political crusade against 'perverse' Western values, but also in some democratic countries, like Latvia, Poland, Hungary, the US and, recently, also in Italy and Israel.

3.2.2. Cohabitation

After the turn of the millennium, cohabitation became a true alternative to marriage, in many parts of the Westernised world. Some progressive Dutch and Belgian[54] scholars even proposed to abolish civil marriage, leaving parties free to agree on the legal effect of their relationship.[55] Unmarried cohabitation became socially accepted in almost all Westernised countries, and its prevalence has grown, albeit unevenly, everywhere.[56] The number of couples choosing a cohabitating relationship as a permanent relationship form, and not marrying, even after giving birth to children, has also increased significantly. Nonetheless, the majority of countries were reluctant to pass specific regulation with respect to heterosexual non-marital cohabitation.[57] Their reluctance was not a reflection of conservative attitudes alone, but, rather, was grounded in objections coming from

---

51   GARRISON, above n. 14, p. 70.
52   M. STRASSER, 'Family, same-sex unions and the law' in J. EEKELAAR and R. GEORGE (eds.), *Routledge Handbook of Family Law and Policy*, Routledge, 2021, pp. 54–56.
53   Armenia, Belarus, Bulgaria, Croatia, Georgia, Hungary, Latvia, Lithuania, Moldova, Montenegro, Poland, Russia, Serbia, Slovakia and Ukraine.
54   F. SWENNEN, *Het huwelijk afschaffen?*, Intersentia, 2003.
55   W. SCHRAMA, 'Marriage and Alternative Status Relationships in the Netherlands' in J. EEKELAAR and R. GEORGE (eds.), *Routledge Handbook of Family Law and Policy*, Routledge, 2021, p. 22.
56   E. SUTHERLAND, 'Unmarried Cohabitation' in EEKELAAR and GEORGE, ibid., p. 65.
57   See M. ANTOKOLSKAIA, 'Economic Consequences of Informal Heterosexual Cohabitation From A Comparative Perspective: Respect Parties' Autonomy or Protection of the Weaker Party?' in A. VERBEKE, et al. (eds.), *Confronting the frontiers of family and succession law: liber amicorum Walter Pintens*, Intersentia, 2012, pp. 41–64.

opposing sides of the political spectrum.[58] A blend of these arguments composed the doctrine of 'law-free space' or non-regulation. One of the ideas behind this doctrine was the conservative fear that the legal regulation of cohabitation would weaken the institution of marriage.[59] Other reasons for the reluctance to regulate cohabitation had to do with the liberal concern for personal autonomy, and the feminist fear that cohabitation regulation modelled on marriage would reinforce traditional gender-role divisions, resulting in women's dependency on men.[60] In addition, the multiplicity of different patterns of cohabitation[61] gave rise to the expectation that it would be impossible to design any general rules that were able to cover all those forms.[62] For a long time, it has successfully been argued that if cohabitants voluntarily choose to avoid the legal regulation attributed to marriage, the State should respect their choice and not try to impose another form of legal regulation on them.[63] There is growing evidence that partners often do not take the required steps to formalise their relationships, not because they do not want legal protection,[64] but because they do not think about the legal implications of their relationships,[65] are ignorant regarding the applicable rules and legal consequences of unmarried cohabitation,[66] or one of the partners does not wish to formalise the relationship.[67]

After the turn of the millennium, the attitude toward regulation of unmarried cohabitation started to change. The legislatures of more and more countries became aware that cohabitation – particularly when children are born into the relationship – needs at least some default legal protection. A growing minority

---

[58] For a recent overview of this debate, see E. SUTHERLAND, 'Unmarried Cohabitation' in EEKELAAR and GEORGE, above n. 55, pp. 65–69.

[59] For a short account of the situation at the turn of millennium, see C. FORDER, 'Civil Law Aspects of Emerging Forms of Registered Partnerships', paper to Fifth European Conference on Family Law, *Civil Law Aspects of Emerging Forms of Registered Partnerships. Legally Regulate Forms of Non-Marital Cohabitation and Registered Partnerships*, The Hague, 1999, p. 7. On the undesirability of creating 'two competing systems', see A. AGELL 'The Legal Status of Same-Sex Couples in Europe – A Critical Analysis' in K. BOELE-WOELKI and A. FUCHS (eds.), *Legal Recognition of Same-Sex Couples in Europe*, Intersentia, 2003, p. 131. For an account of the situation in 2020, see E. SUTHERLAND, 'Unmarried Cohabitation' in EEKELAAR and GEORGE, above n. 55, pp. 64–72.

[60] R. DEECH, 'What's a woman worth? The maintenance law', Gresham Lecture, 2009, https://www.gresham.ac.uk/watch-now/whats-woman-worth-maintenance-law.

[61] M.-T. MEULDERS-KLEIN, 'Les concubinages: diversités et symboliques' in J. RUBBELIN-DEVICHI, *Des concubinages: droit interne, droit international, droit compare*, Litec, 2002, pp. 604–610.

[62] FORDER, above n. 59, p. 7.

[63] W. SCHRAMA, 'Een redelijk en billijk relatievermogensrecht' (2010) 4 *TPR* 1722–1723.

[64] SCHRAMA, *De niet-huwelijkse samenleving*, above n. 27, pp. 394–395.

[65] J. SCHERPE, 'The Legal Status of Cohabitants – Requirements for Legal Recognition' in K. BOELE-WOELKI (ed.), *Common Core and Better Law in European Family Law*, Intersentia, 2005, pp. 287–291; SCHRAMA, *De niet-huwelijkse*, above n. 27, pp. 552 ff.

[66] A. BARLOW, et al., *Cohabitation, Marriage and the Law*, Hart Publishing, 2005, pp. 28 ff.

[67] C. FORDER, 'European Models of Domestic Partnership Laws: The Field of Choice' (2000) 17 *Can. J. Fam. L.* 381.

of Western countries provide, or are preparing to provide, for some kind of default regulation for the economic consequences of termination of unmarried/ unregistered heterosexual cohabitation. The solutions chosen in these counties represent a whole scale of remedies,[68] stretching from providing a minimum level of protection (Sweden), to complete equalisation with marriage (Slovenia). Furthermore, in some countries the protection covers property law, partner maintenance and inheritance law, while in others the protection is limited to only one or two of these fields.

3.2.3. Divorce

Since the turn of the millennium, the main policy challenge has shifted from the grounds of divorce[69] to the role of the State in dealing with uncontested divorce, for example the choice between judicial and administrative procedure, and private or summary procedure;[70] and to dealing with contested divorce with minor children, for example preventing escalation of conflict between the parents by introducing mediation and other alternative dispute resolution schemes.[71] The most notable example of the success of the latter is represented by the 2006 Australian reform. Several European jurisdictions with relatively restrictive divorce laws, such as (at least in theory) England and Wales (2020),[72] France and Italy, where liberalisation of divorce used to be a big issue, have suddenly introduced sweeping liberalisation. In the recent years, two major reforms, for example in France (2016)[73] and Italy (2014–2015),[74] took place

---

[68] For an attempt to systematise these responses, see M. ANTOKOLSKAIA, 'Economic Consequences of Informal Heterosexual Cohabitation From A Comparative Perspective: Respect Parties' Autonomy or Protection of the Weaker Party?' in VERBEKE, et al. (eds.) above n. 57, pp. 41–64. For a recent overview of responses, see E. SUTHERLAND, 'Unmarried Cohabitation' in EEKELAAR and GEORGE, above n. 55, pp. 69–72.

[69] H. KRAUSE, 'Comparative Family Law' in M. REIMANN and R. ZIMMERMANN (eds.), *The Oxford Handbook of Comparative Law*, OUP, 2006, p. 1113.

[70] For more background information on the history of administrative divorce in Europe, see M. ANTOKOLSKAIA, 'Divorce Law From a European Perspective' in J. SCHERPE (ed.), *Research Handbook on European Family Law*, Edward Elgar Publishing, 2013.

[71] For an overview, see M. ANTOKOLSKAIA, 'Dissolution of Marriage in Westernized Countries' in EEKELAAR and GEORGE, above n. 55, pp. 75–106.

[72] Divorce, Dissolution and Separation Act 2020, https://www.legislation.gov.uk/ukpga/2020/11/ contents/ enacted. See also L. TRINDER, et al., *Finding Fault?: Divorce Law and Practice in England and Wales*, Nuffield Foundation, 2017; L. TRINDER and M. SEFTON, *No Contest: Defended Divorce in England and Wales*, Nuffield Foundation, 2018, and other reports.

[73] Law no. 2016-1547 of 18 November 2016 de modernisation de la justice du XXIe siècle. See also F. FERRAND, 'Non-Judicial Divorce in France – Progress or a Mess?' in G. DOUGLAS, M. MURCH and V. STEPHENS (eds.), *International and National Perspectives on Child and Family Law: Essays in Honour of Nigel Lowe*, Intersentia, 2018; C. BIDAUT-GARON, H. FULCHIRON, et al., 'A Chronicle of French Family Law' in M. BRINING (ed.), *The International Survey of Family Law*, LexisNexis, 2017.

[74] Decree of 12 September 2014 No. 132, converted into Law of 10 November 2014 No. 162 and Law of 6 May 2015 No. 55. See also C. VALENTE, 'An Overview on the Italian

without much preparation and ideological debate, under the guise of the pragmatic argument of diminishing the caseload of the judiciary by providing for private or administrative procedures for uncontested cases. Meanwhile, several jurisdictions with longstanding traditions of liberal divorce, like Denmark[75] and the Netherlands,[76] have focused their attention on the prevention and resolution of parental conflicts, and the minimisation of the negative effects of divorce for children, through diminishing the adversarial nature of the divorce procedure by promoting agreements, employing mediation, and endorsing collaborative divorce.

4. CONCLUSION

The unprecedented rapid and collective movement of family law in Westernised countries could mean that the dream (or nightmare) of a 'final point' of family law evolution – a kind of 'end of history' – is near. However, the events of the past decade could snap us out of this illusion. Once reform of family law moves on, and the old controversies cease to exist, or become less prominent, new controversies will emerge. For instance, the formal equality of women and the equal status of children born from unmarried parents have become self-evident and commonly held beliefs. Despite a steady decline in the number of marriages, a high incidence of divorce, and an increase in cohabitation instead of marriage, marriage has not lost its standing and importance. Marriage is no longer seen by the majority of the populations of Westernised countries as the gateway to a loving sexual relationship, and living together and having children, but rather as the 'crown' on an affective relationship.[77] Grounds of divorce are no longer the subject of heated debates. At the same time, the issues of same-sex marriage, multiple parentage, abortion, high-conflict divorce, domestic violence, the right to change one's gender (especially in relation to minors), and the new modes of protection of vulnerable adults without affecting their legal capacity, have all remained problematic and/or polarising in many Westernised countries.

If we look at our present situation, it seems that the generally progressive period that started at the end of the 1970s is now losing its vigour. Although

---

Panorama: Family Law Faces Social Changes' in B. Atkin (ed.), *The International Survey of Family Law*, LexisNexis, 2016.

[75] A. Kronborg and C. Jeppesen de Boer, 'Co-operation: The Glue that Unites the Danish Family Justice System' in M. Maclean, R. Treloar and B. Dijksterhuis, *What Is a Family Justice System For?*, Hart Publishing, 2022, pp. 37–57.

[76] M. Antokolskaia, M. Buddenbaum and L. Coenraad, 'Experimenting with a Non-Adversarial Procedure for Child-related Parental Disputes in the Netherlands' in Maclean, Treloar and Dijksterhuis, above n. 75, pp. 155–171.

[77] Schrama, *De niet-huwelijkse samenleving*, above n. 27, p. 39. In the same sense, see Garrison, above n. 14, pp. 50–51.

modernisation of family law remains the main trend, and progressive reforms are occurring in many countries, the opposing conservative tendency is becoming stronger. The polarisation and intolerance to each other's views and values that has already been afflicting the US for some time is now affecting other Westernised countries. Terms such as 'cancel culture', 'woke' and *'le wokisme'* have various connotations in different countries and circles, however they always indicate political and cultural polarisation and intolerance. Extreme demands for political correctness and associated language purism annoy some people, and undermine the unity and credibility of the progressive camp. The political power of conservative and ultraconservative forces is growing in many Westernised countries, and in other parts of the world. This trend has an immediate effect on family law, as family law often becomes one of the first battlefields of new cultural wars. There is an alarming correlation between extreme conservatism in family law and a disdain for democracy, individual freedom and the rule of law. For example, the totalitarian regime in Russia is currently busy reversing the longstanding tradition of progressive family law in Russia, and tolerates no opposing views. The extreme conservative Trump supporters launch similar attacks on the progressive elements of US family law. The same tendency, but to a lesser extent, is manifested in Poland and Hungary, and in some other Eastern European countries. In 2023, newly elected extreme-right conservative coalitional governments in Israel and Italy integrated rolling back progressive family laws into their programmes.

In this climate of growing polarisation, it is increasingly important for the ISFL to stay true to its mission of uniting instead of dividing – promoting tolerance, respect and dialogue between family law experts from all around the world, irrespective of their views, cultures or situations.

GLOBAL PERSPECTIVES

50 YEARS OF CONTRIBUTIONS TO FAMILY LAW BY LEADING ISFL MEMBERS

Mark Henaghan

Résumé

Cet article est consacré aux développements majeurs du droit de la famille au cours des 50 dernières années à travers le prisme des contributions clés de membres de l'ISFL, tels que John Eekelaar, Michael Freeman, June Carbone, Robin Fretwell Wilson et d'autres, sur les changements du droit de la famille dans le monde. Le présent texte examine les changements intervenus dans des domaines tels que le mariage, les enfants, le patrimoine, le financement et l'implication de l'État pour la protection des membres vulnérables de la famille.

L'article présentera les modifications majeures dans les domaines susmentionnés et montrera comment les écrits et les publications scientifiques des membres de l'ISFL, passés et présents, ont généralement été à la pointe de ces transformations. Ces changements ont un effet d'entraînement dans tous les pays du monde. L'article mettra également en évidence les domaines dans lesquels de nouvelles évolutions du droit de la famille sont nécessaires et sur lesquels les membres de l'ISFL écrivent actuellement.

1. INTRODUCTION

Fifty years, or half a century, is a long time in a fast-moving subject like family law. I was a second-year law student in 1973, when the youth of the world were very much in awe of the hippie movement, and we all had long hair to prove our credentials. It was a time of challenging the ideas of the past; a time when the feminist movement was in full swing, the civil rights movement was booming, and the anti-war movement was on the march. The concept of rights was at the centre of the challenges for change, and recognition of the diverse groups that exist in our societies.

It was a great time for the ISFL to begin its mission – to bring family law on to an international stage, so that ideas surrounding family law can be shared and worked on around the globe. It is significant that the first conference held by the ISFL was on the child and the law.[1] Children are the most vulnerable members of family life, and have not always been treated well by family law. A leading figure in the development of the common law, Blackstone, said that children need correction. It was most appropriate that the long-time dedicated family law scholar Frank Bates was the first editor of the book that came from the conference.[2] Bates was a prolific writer on all areas of family law, and dedicated his life to making sure that family law was well-understood by the profession, academics, students and the public.[3]

2. THE DEVELOPMENT OF CHILDREN'S RIGHTS: MICHAEL FREEMAN

The one and only Michael Freeman, a long-time member of the ISFL and speaker at ISFL conferences, went on to lead the world with his research and writing on children's rights. His seminal work, *The Rights and Wrongs of Children*, published in 1983, provided a detailed justification for why children should have rights and discussed the establishment of a framework to ensure their rights are taken seriously.[4]

From the beginning, Michael Freeman was concerned about the trite nature of children's rights discourse. He observed that talk of children's rights had been 'struck by the intemperate nature of some of the proposals and by the lack of a coherent structure.'[5] The major difficulty faced by those who advocated

---

[1]   F. Bates (ed.), *The Child and the Law: The Proceedings of the First World Conference of the International Society on Family Law Held in Berlin, April 1975*, Oceana Publications, 1976.

[2]   Ibid.

[3]   See, e.g. F. Bates, *An Introduction to Family Law*, Gaunt Inc., 1987; F. Bates, 'Redefining the Parent/Child Relationship: A Blueprint' (1975–76) 12 *University of Western Australia Law Review* 518; F. Bates, 'Cohabitation and Separation in the Law of Desertion' (1970) 21 *Northern Ireland Legal Quarterly* 111.

[4]   M.D.A. Freeman, *The Rights and Wrongs of Children*, Francis Pinter, 1983. See M. Henaghan, 'Michael Freeman's Contribution to Childhood Rights' in A. Diduck, N. Peleg and H. Reece (eds.), *Law in Society: Reflections on Children, Family, Culture and Philosophy – Essays in Honour of Michael Freeman*, Brill, 2015.

[5]   Ibid., p. i.

for children's rights was H.L.A. Hart's 'will theory' of children's rights, which identifies rights-holders only by their ability to enforce or waive the right in question.[6] This would make it very difficult for children to have any rights, because the argument would be that they lack competence to enforce them. Early writing on rights had focused on trying to fit children's rights into the will theory, arguing that 'even quite young children are capable of competent thought and of making informed choices'.[7] Michael Freeman separated himself from liberationists as early as 1983 – they were 'politically naïve, philosophically faulty and plainly ignoring psychological evidence'.[8]

Michael Freeman based his theory of children's rights on the tension between protecting children and giving them autonomy to make their own decisions – a dichotomy he described as the distinction between 'protecting children and protecting their rights'.[9] His theory aims to encompass both positions as a theory of liberal paternalism. At the centre of Michael Freeman's theory is the necessity of society to provide 'a childhood for every child'.[10] Michael Freeman's version is based on the reality that the very notion of childhood is constructed by adults, who 'impose their conceptions of childishness on beings whom they consider to be children'.[11] His book traces the history of childhood, giving examples such as the fact that, in Dickens' time, children could be married and controlling households by age 13 or 14, and young children worked for a living, whereas now we expect children to learn and play at those ages.[12]

The bottom line of Freeman's theory is that children are fundamentally distinct from adults, with different needs, claims and interests.[13] An essential feature of the difference between children and adults is that children are dependent.[14] Freeman uses the work of social scientists to make it clear that older children think differently from both younger children and adults.[15] Thus, Freeman worked from the reality of the continuum of children's lives rather than the ideal of children.

The core principle in Freeman's analysis of children's rights is that it provides a basis for the most precious of all human goods: the freedom to develop one's own freedom and personality. This is important not only for children but for society, as for each child that comes into the world, society adapts itself, because each new child brings their own unique personality and character to

---

6   M.D.A. Freeman, 'Taking Children's Rights More Seriously' in P. Alston, S. Parker and
     J. Seymour (eds.), *Children, Rights, and the Law*, Clarendon Press, 1995, p. 58.
7   J. Fortin, *Children's Rights and the Developing Law*, CUP, 3rd ed., 2009, p. 6.
8   M.D.A. Freeman, above n. 4, pp. 2–3.
9   Ibid., p. 5.
10   Ibid., p. 3.
11   Ibid., p. 7.
12   Ibid., p. 10.
13   Ibid., p. 12.
14   Ibid., p. 120.
15   Ibid., p. 12.

the commonweal. Freeman's theory is antithetical to the position that children are simply a means to society's ends, and must be moulded in certain ways to meet society's expectations. This form of predetermination of children's lives kills the diversity of human nature that is so vital for survival. Freeman's theory, if adopted universally, would eliminate many of the psychological and emotional problems caused by controlling children and imposing society's expectations on them, rather than accepting children for who they are.

The ultimate goal of Freeman's theory is for children to develop rational independence.[16] This is not possible at a young age, and we cannot expect children to do it themselves, or we would be abandoning children to their rights. An example of abandoning children to their rights would be to permit a young child to decide their own diet, which would likely lead to health problems. Alternatively, when designing a playground for young children, to ignore the needs of three- and four-year-olds (for whom the playground is intended) would make the playground unfit for its purpose. On the protective freedom for children, Freeman prepares children for their independence by placing duties on parents:

> We must ask ourselves the question: from what actions and decisions would we wish, as children, to be protected, on the assumption that we would in due course desire to be rationally autonomous, capable of planning our lives and deciding on our own system or ends as rational beings?[17]

Freeman's application of children's rights would centre not on age, but on the activity in question, and indeed on the particular child. For instance, the freedom of children to walk to school alone may differ between small towns with little traffic and large cities where there are high volumes of traffic.

Freeman's theory is, ultimately, political. Its aim is that, once children's rights are accepted as a feature of the political landscape, they will ideally feature in policy decisions at a governmental level. This would make governments accountable to children's interests, as an important limitation on their powers. Freeman reinforces this idea by encouraging the phenomena of children's rights to be regularly scrutinised and updated to match the society.[18] An example is the United Nations Convention on the Rights of Child, which includes many rights, but not the right to nourishment, whether that be food or love and care.

Ultimately, Freeman is a person of action, and he calls for all academics in this field to make sure that children's rights are taken seriously:

> If children's rights are to be more than a political slogan, then children must demand them and must be encouraged and educated to do so. Access to people, lawyers and

---

[16]   Ibid., p. i.
[17]   Ibid.
[18]   Ibid., p. 33.

others, with an expertise and a commitment will enable the young to develop the sort of claims consciousness which is a part of a rational autonomy.[19]

The ISFL has a lot to thank Freeman for. The ISFL is eternally grateful for him being one of its most powerful and original thinkers. He will always have a major influence on children's rights.

3. TWO TOWERING FIGURES: JOHN EEKELAAR AND SANFORD KATZ

The conference book of the second conference was edited by two towering figures: John Eekelaar and Sanford Katz. The topic for the conference, family violence, is one that still looms over family law like a cloud. Here in Aotearoa New Zealand, a desirable country to live, we still have major issues with family violence.

Katz has been a leading figure in writing about evolving models for marriage alternatives, such as his contribution to the 1999 Family Law Quarterly, where he looked at cohabitation, same-sex marriage and domestic partnerships.[20] Back in 1999, these were new and emerging areas, rather than commonly accepted, as they are today. ISFL academics continue to write about developing issues before they reach the mainstream.

Eekelaar and Katz went on to edit the next two conference booklets. The first was on marriage and cohabitation, at a time when cohabitation was beginning to be more accepted and recognised in family law. This acceptance and recognition has been an advantage of the ISFL being able to encourage discussion and research of emerging issues, in order to identify the tensions and issues underlying reform efforts, and to deal with these issues. The next topic the ISFL took on, led by Eekelaar and Katz as editors, lies below all family law matters – namely how to resolve conflict. We know that the adversarial system can be brutal and hurtful for all those involved in it, and mediation, at times, has been seen as an important counter to this, as a way to resolve disputes. But we also know that mediation can be used to push people into decisions they are not happy with.

Eekelaar has done a great deal of work in this area. The book he wrote with Mavis Maclean on family justice gives a very thorough and comprehensive view of all the studies that identify the potential problems with moving away

---

[19]   Ibid., p. 281.
[20]   S.N. KATZ, 'Emerging Models for Alternatives to Marriage' (1999) 33 *FLQ* (*Family Law Quarterly*) 663.

from a system of justice, to a system where people are left to resolve their own disputes.[21] Eekelaar and Maclean make the distinction between behaviour-focused approaches to family law, where the emphasis is on modifying people's expectations and behaviour, and outcome-focused approaches to family justice, where the emphasis is on fairness and impartiality in the application of the law.[22] They point out the risk that if we focus only on behaviour, then there is no litmus test for what behaviour is appropriate or not. There is no setting of general standards, but rather outcomes would depend on who is involved in the behaviour-modification process. As Katherine O'Donovan said, the law of the jungle begins to prevail.[23] A family justice system needs clear signals to society about what its expectations are, as expressed in statutes and court decisions that regulate behaviour. These expectations are tested and adapted over time, as society changes, but they provide stability that is not present when the system is totally private, and nobody knows what is truly happening. It is not that the law is perfect, as Eekelaar has written over many articles critiquing the principles and application of family law. The law is always to be improved, and there has been no better person who has provided frameworks to understand the role of family law in the history of the common law than Eekelaar. He has been driven to improve the world's understanding of family law in the hope that it achieves better families.

Eekelaar went on to edit four more major conference books for the ISFL. First, on family law and individual economic security (in two volumes with Marie-Thérèse Meulders-Klein).[24] Second, an important work that looked at the State's responsibilities for providing family security for families: *An Aging World: Dilemmas and Challenges for Law and Social Policy* (with David Pearl).[25] This was way back in 1989, and it is now of even more immediate importance, as the world continues to age, that we understand how family law has an impact on those who are ageing, such as grandparents. It is, again, evidence of how important the ISFL has been in allowing issues to be picked apart and given thoughtful analysis. And, in 1993, Eekelaar joined with Petar Šarčević to edit the book on parenthood and modern society.[26] This book stemmed from the first family law conference that I attended. Petar did a great job organising it before the war broke out in the Balkans – one could feel the tension in the air and the sadness

---

21   J. Eekelaar and M. Maclean, *Family Justice: The Work of Family Judges in Uncertain Times*, Hart Publishing, 2013.

22   Ibid., ch. 2.

23   K. O'Donovan, *Sexual Divisions in Law*, Weidenfeld and Nicolson, 1986, p. 198.

24   J. Eekelaar and M.T. Meulders-klein (eds.), *Family, State and Individual Economic Security*, Kluwer, 1988.

25   J. Eekelaar and D. Pearl (eds.), *An Aging World: Dilemmas and Challenges for Law and Social Policy*, Clarendon Press, 1989.

26   J. Eekelaar and P. Šarčević (eds.), *Parenthood in Modern Society: Legal and Social Issues for the Twenty-First Century*, Kluwer, 1993.

of the people, who could sense what was to come. The final conference Eekelaar played a major role in was *The Changing Family: International Perspectives on the Family and Family Law*.[27] This topic is very close to what we are looking at in the 50th anniversary year of the ISFL: fixing families in a changing world. It shows how far ahead the ISFL has been in predicting and trying to resolve problems. Family law academics and practitioners need to be forward-looking when determining what will work best to resolve family situations.

Eekelaar, with his conceptual thinking and detailed, careful research, has done a great deal to influence how family law can be thought about. His major work, *Family Law and Social Policy*, opened the door for family law to be seen in a much broader context than merely the rules and obligations between families.[28] His more recent book, *Family Law and Personal Life*, now in its second edition, developed a number of different theories of how family life can be seen through the lens of significant philosophical principles.[29] There are many enduring thoughts from this book. The one that has stuck with me the most is the idea that we should not fix family law in such a way that it cannot change for the future. One thing about family law that Eekelaar always emphasises is that society is changing, and family law must adapt to these changes.

4. INTERNATIONAL FAMILY LAW: NIGEL LOWE

We have also been fortunate to have wonderful world-leading academics in the field of family law, such as Nigel Lowe, who has dedicated his life to tracking the implementation of the Hague Convention on International Child Abduction. Lowe, along with Gillian Douglas, edited the 1996 conference book *Families Across Frontiers*.[30]

Nigel Lowe's contribution to international family law has been immense. He can truly be described as the father of international family law.[31] His contribution is not only important for family law practitioners and academics around the world; it is also essential for the development and improvement of international family law itself. The theme of Lowe's work is that there is a need for cooperation and consistency between different countries, which is why the

---

27 J. EEKELAAR and T. NHLAPO (eds.), *The Changing Family: International Perspectives on the Family and Family Law*, Hart Publishing, 1998.

28 J. EEKELAAR, *Family Law and Social Policy*, Weidenfeld and Nicolson, 1978.

29 J. EEKELAAR, *Family Law and Personal Life*, OUP, 2nd ed., 2017.

30 N. LOWE and G. DOUGLAS (eds.), *Families Across Frontiers*, Kluwer, 1996.

31 See M. HENAGHAN and R. BALLANTYNE, 'Nigel Lowe and International Family Law: An Immense Contribution' in G. DOUGLAS, M. MURCH and V. STEPHENS (eds.), *International and National Perspectives on Child and Family Law: Essays in Honour of Nigel Lowe*, Intersentia, 2018, p. 247.

ISFL is so important. There is also a need for robust administrative processes and, most importantly, clear empirical data about how international family laws are actually working. One of the important trends that Lowe noted from his statistical analysis is that there is a growing number of Hague Convention cases where a parent removes a child from their habitual residence to escape a violent relationship, or returns to their country of origin to access familiar support networks. It has also been picked up in the statistics that there need to be more effective ways to incorporate children's views in child abduction cases.

5.   WE ARE NOT UNIVERSAL IN THE WAY WE SEE FAMILY LAW

In 1998, the theme of the conference was 'The Changing Family'.[32] Family law will always face the challenge of keeping up with the pace of society. The ISFL, in its conferences, has always been able to provide a rich array of papers on what society's changes mean. In later conference books, such as *Family Law Processes, Practices and Pressures*,[33] *Family Life and Human Rights*,[34] and *Balancing Interests and Pursuing Priorities*,[35] the ISFL has always been aware that there are many views of family law.

One of the great strengths of family law is that we do not all see the changes and the principles of family law in the same way, in the Society. A rights lens is not the only lens we look through. Wonderful writers and thinkers, such as June Carbone and Robin Fretwell Wilson, do not always see family law through the lens of rights, because this can break families up into individual units contesting with one another. Their work is in the same orbit as Mary Ann Glendon, who argued that rights talk has impoverished American legal discourse by substituting rights for the care of the community.[36] In her view, family law discourse 'treats families as a collection of individuals rather than organic units'.[37]

We cannot forget Margo Melli, who made a massive contribution to our understanding of child support. She was the first to put forward guideline formulas for child support, to lessen the discretion that had been involved.[38]

---

[32]   J. Eekelaar and T. Nhlapo, above n. 27.
[33]   J. Dewar and S. Parker (eds.), *Family Law Processes, Practices and Pressures: Proceedings of the Tenth World Conference of the International Society of Family Law, July 2000, Brisbane, Australia*, Hart Publishing, 2003.
[34]   P. Lødrup and E. Modvar (eds.), *Family Life and Human Rights: Papers Presented at the 11th World Conference of the International Society of Family Law*, Gyldendal, 2004.
[35]   L.D. Wardle and C.S. Williams (eds.), *Family Law: Balancing Interests and Pursuing Priorities*, William S. Hein & Co., 2007.
[36]   M.A. Glendon, *Rights Talk: The Impoverishment of Political Discourse*, Free Press, 1991.
[37]   J.T. Oldham and P.M. Kurtz (eds.), 'Tributes to Family Law Scholars Who Helped Us Find Our Path' (2022) 55 *FLQ* 341, 355, referring to ibid., 123.
[38]   J.T. Oldham and P.M. Kurtz, ibid., 368–369.

She also contributed to the American Legal Institute, where she played a large part in the *Principles of the Law of Family Dissolution*.[39]

In Robin Fretwell Wilson and Shaakirrah R. Sanders' chapter 'By Faith Alone', they make the point that the law must reach into communities and understand them from the inside, rather than ignore them from the outside.[40] To do this, the law must gain the insight of communities, to see that a child is in need in the first place.

Lynn Wardle, who led the conference in Utah,[41] opened us up to a very different way of seeing family law. It is crucially important that the ISFL remains open to all points of view, because incorporating differing perspectives is how the law will remain alive. Wardle was clear that family law should be based on strong Christian values, and that traditional marriage is at the centre of family law.

Vienna was the perfect venue for the conference on family finances, and the ISFL owes a great deal to its European members who take a very different view of families. Europeans are, generally, more community-based, and emphasise the State's support of families rather than families fending for themselves. They have a strong sense of community property jointly owned by both partners in a relationship. Finances are crucial to families; families cannot always thrive on their own. I am very proud to have grown up in Aotearoa New Zealand, which introduced the welfare state in the 1930s, to try to ensure that all families have opportunities.[42] Scandinavia has led the world in this respect by providing families with strong support. It is crucial that every child and every family gets a fair chance, so Vienna, by bringing together scholars from the countries with the strongest welfare states, and those with the greatest neo-liberal orientation, provided an ideal venue to host this exchange of perspectives on family finances.

The next conference, again hosted in Europe, namely Lyon, was hosted by Hugues Fulchiron.[43] It looked at families between generations, and the pressures and changes on the traditional family structure. Many ideas emerged for how to ensure the well-being of families, in a world where there is more potential for isolation, and greater need for community support.

It was most appropriate to have the fifteenth World Conference in Brazil.[44] The Latin America region faces many challenges of poverty that are not always seen on such a scale in 'Western' countries, but also their history, approach to life, and the ways families endure through adversity, are quite different from

---

[39]   Ibid., 369.
[40]   R.F. WILSON and S.R. SANDERS, 'By Faith Alone: When Religious Beliefs and Child Welfare Collide' in R.F. WILSON (ed.), *The Contested Place of Religion in Family Law*, CUP, 2018.
[41]   L.D. WARDLE and C.S. WILLIAMS, above n. 35.
[42]   Social Security Act 1938 (N.Z.), enacted by New Zealand's first Labour government.
[43]   H. FULCHIRON (ed.), *Solidarities between Generations*, Bruylant, 2013.
[44]   M.F. BRINIG (ed.), *Selections from the Recife Congress*, International Society of Family Law.

Western countries. In the future, I hope we do much more in these countries, which require support to ensure their voices are heard.

It was sad that the conference organised by Hazel Thompson-Ahye was affected by COVID-19. Hazel managed to later organise a regional conference that was superb. It focused attention on the many family law issues that arise in countries that had been colonised, and which face difficulties in applying conflicting cultural norms and values to family law. Coming from Aotearoa New Zealand, I can well identify with these countries, as we, too, had Indigenous people colonised, and continue to struggle with the difficult process of addressing the consequences. Only now are their rights starting to be recognised and their family structures acknowledged, when it was not too long ago that their structures, such as customary adoptions, were rejected by family law.

The last in-person conference for the Society was again held in Europe, namely Amsterdam, and concerned family law realities. This is a crucial theme for the future because, for a long time, legislators and policy-makers, especially in Western countries, believed that family law was made for perfect families. In reality, this never happens. Family law must deal with the realities of life. This theme runs through many ISFL conferences.

Not surprisingly, the last conference was hosted online, and it looked at families going through crises and the pandemic. The pandemic has put families through immense psychological and financial stress. Family violence becomes more prevalent when families are stuck at home. This conference raised vital issues in family law when people face restrictions to their freedom of movement.

6. THE FUTURE

In the future, it is important that the ISFL reaches communities not reached before, either because they have been suppressed through colonisation and have only begun to emerge, or because they are economically suppressed and do not have the resources to have their voices heard. Indigenous communities have a great deal to offer, as they have survived a world much tougher than today's world. They have a collective mentality to look after one another, and for everyone to be part of the whole. No society is ever perfect, but it is important for Indigenous people to have their voices and histories heard so that we can understand the future. A wonderful Māori whakataukī (proverb) is 'ka mua, ka muri': I walk backwards into the future with my eyes fixed on my past. We must be humble about our limitations. We must be careful not to let Western perspectives over-dominate. We must make sure that voices we have not heard before are brought to our presence, because it will only be in the diversity of voices that we will understand what 'family' means across the globe.

It is important for the ISFL to remain relevant and strong that the focus of future conferences is on countries we need to hear more from. Africa is a large part of the world, and we have some outstanding speakers from Africa, so it would be important to have a conference dedicated to African countries that amplifies voices we do not often hear. With the Ukraine–Russia war, there should also be an emphasis on the harm that disruption can cause to children, and how this disruption can best be alleviated to ensure the best for children and their families.

We should also focus on a problem we have not often focused on: the solo parent. These parents are often mothers, but can also be fathers. Family law is often focused on the couple, but children can be raised in a variety of different circumstances, including where one parent is doing a Herculean job.

We must realise that much of the family law we have discussed and created is based on colonial ideas. Indigenous peoples often have their own family structures and systems, and distinctive viewpoints about families and family law. These structures have often been neglected or destroyed. Thankfully, in Aotearoa New Zealand, there has been a re-emergence of Māori whānau (family).[45] Māori see families as being much wider than the typical European or Pākehā family. For Māori, the concept of whānau incorporates wider family members, such as tūpuna (grandparents). There is a much more collective approach to family law, with an emphasis on whanaungatanga (kinship lines), whakapapa (ancestry) and mana tamaiti (the intrinsic value derived from children belonging to a family). For example, in te ao Māori (the Māori world), the concept of closed adoptions, where adopted children are cut from their birth parents, is an alien concept. Māori employ whāngai adoptions, where children are brought up by people other than their birth parents, but they do not lose that vital connection to their whakapapa. Grandparents often play a very crucial role in children's lives in te ao Māori.

There also needs to be an understanding and incorporation of relationships that are seen as sitting outside the traditional family structures, such as polyamorous relationships. Members of such relationships should be recognised and treated fairly by the family law system.

Finally, we need to consider that family law is deeply connected to societal values. We have a responsibility to ensure that those values emphasise inclusiveness, understanding, tolerance, and compassion for the way families choose to live their lives. Provided no harm is done, these practices should be celebrated.

---

[45] See J. RURU, 'Kua tutu te puehu, kia mau: Māori aspirations and family law policy' in M. HENAGHAN and B. ATKIN (eds.), *Family Law Policy in New Zealand*, LexisNexis, 5th ed., 2020.

BELGIUM

50 YEARS OF BELGIAN PARENTAGE LAW

Time to Celebrate or Contemplate?

Aurélie Cassiers, Emilie Hermans and Géraldine Mathieu

Résumé

Cet article retrace l'évolution du droit de la filiation en Belgique au cours des 50 dernières années. Sera mis en lumière, le glissement d'une législation fondée sur le mariage vers une législation qui s'appuie également sur des liens biologiques ou sociétaux, qui est ouverte aux couples de femmes et qui fait de l'intérêt supérieur de l'enfant une considération primordiale. Cette évolution législative, à travers trois importantes réformes (1987, 2006, 2014), est principalement le résultat de jurisprudences de la Cour européenne des droits de l'homme et de la Cour constitutionnelle. Les conséquences de certaines des plus importantes jurisprudences en la matière seront donc analysées. La conclusion s'attachera à envisager quelques évolutions possibles pour l'avenir, par exemple en ce qui concerne un droit de la filiation plus neutre sur le plan du genre.

1. INTRODUCTION

Belgian parentage legislation has evolved significantly over the past half-century, in response to a series of social as well as scientific changes. Crucial trends, such as the ever-increasing social equality between women and men, the social acceptance of children born out of wedlock, the consecration of the child's best interests standard, medically assisted reproductive technologies, the opening of marriage to same-sex couples, and the (legal) recognition of transgender persons, have put pressure on Belgian parentage law to evolve in line with these developments. What follows will provide a concise overview of the most important changes that characterise the history of Belgian parentage law, both in terms of the creation and contestation of a parentage bond, and the specific foundations of parentage law.

2. BEFORE 1987

Before 1987, Belgian family law, enshrined in the Belgian Civil Code,[1] was characterised by an indissoluble connection between marriage, natural procreation and the subsequent establishment of a parentage bond.[2] The law of filiation granted parenthood to two parents: the mother and father, who were married, and had created a biological blood bond with their born child.[3] The nineteenth-century legislator put forward an undeniable connection between sexual intercourse, and the biophysiological bond and genetic bond, as well as the social bond, between the parents and their child.[4] If a child was born within a matrimonial context, the inclusion of the mother's name on the birth certificate perpetuated a legal parentage bond. Moreover, the Civil Code offered no possibility of contesting parentage on the mother's side.[5] The mother's husband was the child's father by virtue of the presumption of paternity. This implied that there was a presumption that the mother had sexual relations with her husband exclusively. The husband's paternity could only be contested in

---

[1]   The Belgian Civil Code, which has its origins in the 1804 Code Napoleon, contains the basic principles of parentage law. The Act of 13 April 2019 established a new Civil Code, which entered into force on 1 November 2020. Since then, the Civil Code of 21 March 1804 has been referred to as the 'Old Civil Code' (Art. 2 of the Act of 13 April 2019, *Belgian Official Journal*, 14 May 2019). At the time of writing (September 2022), the provisions of family law in the old Civil Code are still in force.

[2]   Y.H. LELEU, *Droit des personnes et des familles*, Bruylant, 2020, p. 545; P. SENAEVE and C. DECLERCK, *Compendium van het personen- en familierecht*, Acco, 2022, p. 238.

[3]   G. VERSCHELDEN, *Origineel ouderschap herdacht*, die Keure, 2005, p. 55.

[4]   P. SENAEVE and C. DECLERCK, *Compendium van het personen- en familierecht*, Acco, 2022, p. 238; T. WUYTS, *Ouderlijk gezag*, Intersentia, 2013, pp. 30–31.

[5]   N. DOPCHIE, 'Le droit de garde de l'enfant au père ou à la mère ? Point de vue médicopsychologique' (1979) *Rev. trim. dr. fam. (Revue trimestrielle de droit familial)* 355.

very limited circumstances,[6] and the presumption of paternity was, therefore, a quasi-absolute principle.[7] By protecting marriage in this way, the Civil Code created much more certainty about paternity, and supported the husband. This system aimed to put female reproduction completely under the control of the husband, so that he could be sure that his wife would only bear his children, and that his assets remained within the family.[8]

Nevertheless, the rules regarding the establishment of a parentage bond were less favourable with regard to non-marital children. Children born outside of a matrimonial context had to depend on the decision of their parents, who could acknowledge their child in the birth certificate or any other authentic act.[9] Using this distinction, the legislature wanted to perpetuate family peace and devalue extramarital cohabitation forms, so that children could grow up in a stable, legitimate nuclear family.[10]

The *Marckx v. Belgium* judgment, pronounced on 13 June 1979 by the European Court of Human Rights, marked a turning point, by calling into question the established distinction between marital and non-marital children.[11] On the one hand, the Court condemned the Belgian State for violating Article 8 of the European Convention of Human Rights (ECHR), which includes respect for family life, both towards the child and the mother, given that, under Belgian law, the mother had to take action and acknowledge her child in order to express her maternity with respect to non-marital children.[12] The Court considered that, from the moment of birth, family life is established between the woman

---

[6]   Only the husband himself could contest his paternity, within the short term of one or two months after the birth, based on limited grounds of contestation: the physical removal or an accident during the period of conception or the moral impossibility because of adultery by the wife around the time of conception, and this only if he knew nothing about the birth. See old Arts. 313 and 316, old Civil Code.

[7]   N. GALLUS, *Le droit de la filiation. Rôle de la vérité socio-affective et de la volonté en droit Belge*, Larcier, 2009, p. 16; P. SENAEVE and C. DECLERCK, *Compendium van het personen- en familierecht*, Acco, 2022, p. 238; A.C. VAN GYSEL, *Traité de droit civil belge, I, Les personnes, Volume I, Personnalité juridique, Relations familiales*, Bruylant, 2015, pp. 568–569.

[8]   A. HEYVAERT, *Het personen- en familierecht ont(k)leed*, Mys en Breesch, 2001, p. 166; F. SWENNEN, *Het personen- en familierecht (zevende, herziene uitgave)*, Intersentia, 2021, p. 8.

[9]   Y.H. LELEU, *Droit des personnes et des familles*, Bruylant, 2020, p. 545; P. SENAEVE and C. DECLERCK, *Compendium van het personen- en familierecht*, Acco, 2022, p. 238; F. SWENNEN, *Het personen- en familierecht (zevende, herziene uitgave)*, Intersentia, 2021, p. 440; A.C. VAN GYSEL, *La famille*, Anthemis, 2018, p. 56.

[10]   J. GERLO, 'Hiërarchie der afstammingen of gelijkheid van statuten' (1972–1973) *R.W. (Rechtskundig Weekblad)* 1908; T. WUYTS, *Ouderlijk gezag*, Intersentia, 2013, p. 30.

[11]   ECtHR, 13 June 1979, nr. 6833/74, *Marckx v. Belgium*; Y.H. LELEU, *Droit des personnes et des familles*, Bruylant, 2020, p. 546; G. MATHIEU, *Droit de la famille*, Larcier, 2022, p. 265; F. SWENNEN, *Het personen- en familierecht (zevende, herziene uitgave)*, Intersentia, 2021, pp. 9 and 441; A.C. VAN GYSEL, *La famille*, Anthemis, 2018, p. 60; T. WUYTS, *Ouderlijk gezag*, Intersentia, 2013, p. 111.

[12]   G. VERSCHELDEN, *Handboek Belgisch Personen-, familie- en relatievermogensrecht*, die Keure/la Charte, 2021, p. 17.

who gave birth and the child. Given that Belgian parentage law prevented the establishment of a legal parentage bond with respect to the mother from the moment of birth, a violation of Article 8 of the ECHR was found.[13] On the other hand, in connection with Article 8 of the ECHR, a violation of Article 14 of the ECHR, i.e. the general prohibition of discrimination, was determined, given that no objective and reasonable justification could legitimise a distinction between marital and non-marital children in the context of establishing maternal filiation.[14] The judgment, therefore, had a huge impact in the context of establishing a legal parentage bond and its consequences. It strengthened the position of the mother, and sought to provide a unitary system, so that maternity was established regardless of whether the child had been born within or outside marriage.

3. THE ACT OF 31 MARCH 1987

The condemnation of the Belgian State in *Marckx v. Belgium* resulted in a reform of parentage law, enshrined in the Act of 31 March 1987.[15] In legal doctrine, the main aspects of this reform were brought together under three specific headings.[16]

First of all, there was a tendency towards *equalisation*, as the unequal treatment of marital and non-marital children was largely eliminated. As regards the establishment of filiation regarding the mother, the legislature relied on the principle *mater semper certa est*.[17] The inclusion of the mother's name on the birth certificate thus indiscriminately perpetuates a fixed maternal parentage for all children, whether born within or outside marriage.[18] In this way, the

---

13   ECtHR, 13 June 1979, nr. 6833/74, *Marckx v. Belgium*, para. 31.
14   G. VERSCHELDEN, *Handboek Belgisch Personen-, familie- en relatievermogensrecht*, die Keure/ la Charte, 2021, p. 17.
15   Act of 31 March 1987 amending a number of provisions relating to parentage, *Belgian Official Journal*, 27 May 1987, hereinafter 'Act of 31 March 1987'.
16   Y.H. LELEU, *Droit des personnes et des familles*, Bruylant, 2020, p. 546; P. SENAEVE and C. DECLERCK, *Compendium van het personen- en familierecht*, Acco, 2022, p. 239; T. WUYTS, *Ouderlijk gezag*, Intersentia, 2013, p. 113.
17   L. VAN SLYCKEN, 'Het nieuwe afstammings- en adoptierecht: een evolutie of revolutie' (1987–88) *R.W.* 346; E. VIEUJEAN, 'Le nouveau droit de la filiation' (1987) *Ann. Fac. Dr. Liège (Annales de la faculté de droit de Liège)* 105.
18   Old Art. 312, para. 1, old Civil Code. In the exceptional situation that the mother's name does not appear on the birth certificate, or if there is no such certificate, the mother may, alternatively, acknowledge her child (old Art. 313, old Civil Code). In the absence of both preceding means of establishing maternal parentage, it can be done judicially, provided it is proved that the child is the same as that to whom the alleged mother gave birth (old Art. 314, old Civil Code). See Proposition of law amending a number of provisions relating parentage and adoption, *Parl. St.* Senate, 1977–78, nr. 305/1, p. 38; L. VAN SLYCKEN, 'Het nieuwe afstammings- en adoptierecht: een evolutie of revolutie' (1987–88) *R.W.* 346; E. VIEUJEAN, 'Le nouveau droit de la filiation' (1987) *Ann. Fac. Dr. Liège* 105.

aforementioned connection between marriage, procreation and parentage was no longer strictly indissoluble, given the disconnection of two important components of the family, being the relationship between the biological parents and the establishment of a parentage bond.[19] Next, a trend of *liberalisation* was noted, since outdated restrictions on the establishment, as well as the contestation, of the parentage bond were removed or made more lenient. Finally, there was also a tendency towards *modernisation*, as parentage law was adjusted for the first time in light of new sociological and biotechnological developments.[20] After all, from the 1970s onwards, Belgium made use of medically assisted reproductive techniques in an organised manner, with the result that there is no longer an automatic connection between sexual intercourse, the biophysiological bond, the genetic bond and the social bond.[21] The Act of 31 March 1987 took these social and medical developments into account by providing a first, but limited, legal basis for medically assisted reproduction, in Article 318, para. 4 of the old Civil Code.[22] This Article states that the mother's husband is considered to be the legal father if he expressly consents to the act whose purpose was procreation. For a long time, the aforementioned Article was the only legal basis for medically assisted reproduction, until, in 2007, the legislator drafted a special law on the matter (see section 5.2).[23]

As for the establishment of paternity, a distinction was still made depending on whether the child was born within or outside marriage, given that the presumption of paternity applied only to children within a marital context (*pater is est quem nuptiae demonstrant*).[24] Legislators stressed that this should be interpreted as broadly as possible.[25] Based on this line of thought, the text of Article 315 established the following presumption: 'the child born during the marriage or within not more than 300 days after the dissolution or annulment of the marriage has the husband as father'.[26] In addition, the father could

---

[19] F. SWENNEN, 'Wat is ouderschap?' (2016) *T.P.R.* (*Tijdschrift voor Privaatrecht*) 21; T. WUYTS, *Ouderlijk gezag*, Intersentia, 2013, p. 112.

[20] X. DIJON, 'La filiation paternelle de l'enfant né par insémination artificielle avec donneur' (1990) *R.G.D.C.* (*Revue Générale de Droit Civil*) 95; M.T. MEULDERS-KLEIN, 'Le droit de l'enfant face au droit à l'enfant et les procréations médicalement assistées' (1988) *Rev. trim. dr. civ.* (*Revue trimestrielle de droit civil*) 645.

[21] T. WUYTS, *Ouderlijk gezag*, Intersentia, 2013, p. 25.

[22] A.C. VAN GYSEL, *La famille*, Anthemis, 2018, p. 110; L. VAN SLYCKEN, 'Het nieuwe afstammings- en adoptierecht: een evolutie of revolutie' (1987–88) *R.W.* 349; E. VIEUJEAN, 'Le nouveau droit de la filiation' (1987) *Ann. Fac. Dr. Liège* 112.

[23] Act of 6 July 2007 on Medically Assisted Reproduction and the Disposition of Supernumerary Embryos and Gametes, *Belgian Official Journal*, 17 July 2007, hereinafter 'Act on MAR'.

[24] A.C. VAN GYSEL, *La famille*, Anthemis, 2018, p. 71; L. VAN SLYCKEN, 'Het nieuwe afstammings- en adoptierecht: een evolutie of revolutie' (1987–88) *R.W.* 346; E. VIEUJEAN, 'Le nouveau droit de la filiation' (1987) *Ann. Fac. Dr. Liège* 101.

[25] *Parl. St.* Senate, 1977–78, nr. 305-1, p. 11; *Parl. St.*, Senate, 1984–85, nr. 904/2, p. 45.

[26] Old Art. 315 old Civil Code; *Parl. St.* Senate, 1984–85, nr. 904/2, p. 45.

acknowledge[27] his child outside of the marriage context, but only with the mother's consent, or through the court considering the child's best interests.[28] If paternity was not established based on the presumption of paternity or acknowledgement, the legal parentage bond could be judicially established.[29] The possibility of judicial establishment of paternity was opened widely,[30] in order to avoid discrimination between men and women.[31]

In the parliamentary preparations, it was, furthermore, stated as an objective that the biological truth should be approximated as much as possible when it comes to the establishment of the parentage bond. However, it was added that a socio-affective bond deserved a place in the legal system as well, and that it was by no means intended that biological truth should take complete precedence over socio-affective parenthood.[32] The legislator thus considered that it might be in the child's best interests not to break an already established and socio-affectively experienced parentage bond, and therefore attached importance to the principle of 'possession of state' *(bezit van staat/possession d'état).*[33] This term indicates a whole set of pre-existing, continuous and outwardly observable facts which indicate that a person is acting as a parent of a child, with the outside world seeing and perceiving it that way.[34] Accordingly, a claim to contest maternal parentage was excluded if the child has possession of state corresponding to the birth certificate, even if the name of the mother mentioned in the birth certificate did not correspond to biological maternity.[35] Likewise,

---

[27] An acknowledgment is an authentic instrument by which a person gives notice that a bond of paternity (or maternity, above n. 18; or co-maternity, below n. 96) exists between themself and a child. The acknowledgement procedure is carried out by the municipality's civil registrar. Acknowledging a child establishes parentage between the child and the person acknowledging the child, retroactively to the time of the child's birth.

[28] Old Art. 319, old Civil Code.

[29] Old Art. 322 ff, old Civil Code.

[30] Previously, the claim to investigate paternity could only be brought by the child.

[31] 'Any restriction in the investigation of paternity would be unjust, not only with regard to the child but also to his or her mother, in a system where maternal parentage is established from birth' (authors' own translation): see Proposition of law amending a number of provisions relating parentage and adoption, *Parl. St.* Senate, 1977–78, nr. 305/1, p. 14.

[32] *Parl. St.* Senate, 1977–78, nr. 305/1, pp. 3–4.

[33] L. VAN SLYCKEN, 'Het nieuwe afstammings- en adoptierecht: een evolutie of revolutie' (1987–88) *R.W.* 348.

[34] Art. 331*nonies*, al. 3, old Civil Code provides a non-exhaustive enumeration of facts that can prove the parentage bond: the child has always borne the name of the person from whom they are said to be descended; the latter has treated him or her as their child; that person has provided for the child's maintenance and upbringing; the child has treated that person as his or her father, mother or co-mother; the child is acknowledged as such by the family, and in society; the public authorities consider him or her as such.

[35] Old Art. 312, para. 2, old Civil Code; J. GERLO, 'De vaststelling van de afstamming' (1987) *T.P.R.* 1055.

the application to contest an acknowledgement was to be rejected if the child had 'possession of state' against the acknowledging person, even if the latter was proven not to be the child's biological father or mother.[36] Moreover, in certain situations of judicial acknowledgement or establishment of paternal parentage, the legislature granted the court discretion over the child's best interests. In such situations, if the mother or child opposed a biological parent's effort to establish legal parentage, the judge could, thus, give priority to the child's best interests, and deviate from the attempt to establish a biological parentage bond.[37] In addition, biological and socio-affective reality were complemented by the expression of will as the basis for so-called intentional parenting. This was reflected in the aforementioned Article 318, para. 4 of the old Civil Code, which confirmed that the paternity of the mother's husband could not be disputed if he had consented to medically assisted reproduction or any other acts with procreation as a purpose.[38] From the Act of 31 March 1987, it thus became clear that there were three distinct bases of parentage law (biology, socio-affective reality, and intention), which could be weighed against each other, with the child's best interests being a further connecting factor cutting across the three bases.

The work of the 1987 legislature was considerable but rather imperfect. Subsequent to the entry into force of the Act of 31 March 1987, a number of incompatibilities of the new parentage provisions with the principles of equality and non-discrimination, enshrined in Articles 10 and 11 of the Belgian Constitution, were addressed in legal doctrine.[39] In particular, the discriminatory nature of paternal acknowledgement subject to the mother's consent (old Article 319, para. 3, old Civil Code) was unanimously rejected by legal doctrine, given that no form of control for the father was provided, for an establishment of maternal filiation in general, and for the rather exceptional maternal acknowledgement in particular. In line with these concerns, the Court of Arbitration[40] considered that the dependence of paternal acknowledgment on prior consent by the mother constituted a violation of Articles 10 and 11

---

[36] Old Art. 330, para. 2, al. 2, old Civil Code.

[37] Old Art. 319, para. 3, al. 4, old Civil Code; old Art. 322, al. 1, old Civil Code; J. GERLO, 'De vaststelling van de afstamming' (1987) *T.P.R.* 1075; L. VAN SLYCKEN, 'Het nieuwe afstammings- en adoptierecht: een evolutie of revolutie' (1987–88) *R.W.* 348.

[38] S. DE MEUTER, 'Het kind en zijn moeder(s): Het moederschap na medisch begeleide voortplanting, inzonderheid draagmoederschap' (1990) *T.P.R.* 658.

[39] J. DE GRAVE, 'Le principe d'égalité dans le droit de filiation: limites, exceptions et contrôle' (1990) *Revue de droit*, 11–36; F. RIGAUX, 'Le nouveau droit de la filiation à l'épreuve des droits de l'homme' (1987) *A.D.L. (Annales de droit de Louvain)*, 379–415; P. SENAEVE, 'De vaderlijke erkenning van een buitenhuwelijks kind en het gelijkheidsbeginsel' (1990–1991) 36 *R.W.* 1212; E. VIEUJEAN, 'Le nouveau droit de la filiation' (1987) *Ann. Fac. Dr. Liège* 115.

[40] In 1980, the Constitutional Court was established, under the name Court of Arbitration. On 7 May 2007, the name was changed to the Constitutional Court.

of the Constitution.[41] The Court confirmed this ruling on several occasions,[42] also underlining that the absence of any possibility for the court to exercise control over the best interests of the child under 15 years, in the case of the establishment of paternal parentage through acknowledgement, was contrary to Articles 10 and 11 of the Constitution.[43]

4. THE ACT OF 1 JULY 2006

Some 20 years after the Act of 31 March 1987, the Act of 1 July 2006 carried out a thorough revision of the entire parentage law.[44] This reform was deemed necessary in light of the discriminatory provisions identified by the Court of Arbitration with regard to the regulations as they applied under the Act of 31 March 1987. Rather than simply remedying the above-mentioned discriminatory provisions bit by bit, the legislature opted for a comprehensive overhaul of parentage law. The objectives of this reform were, to some extent, similar to those of the Act of 31 March 1987 mentioned above.[45]

On the one hand, there was, once again, an *equalisation* trend. First, greater equality was to be achieved by making the establishment and contestation of maternal and paternal parentage largely subject to the same rules.[46] In doing so, the legislature, for instance, added Article 329*bis* to the old Civil Code, which stipulated that the acknowledgement of a parent was only admissible if the parent whose parentage bond had already been established gave his or

---

[41] On the one hand, the Court held that the above distinction indisputably created an unjustifiable difference in treatment between the mother and the father of an extramarital child. Furthermore, the Court of Arbitration held that old Article 319, para. 3 of the old Civil Code also created a difference in treatment between children born within and outside a marital context. After all, the presumption of paternity applied to children born within the marriage, whereas with regard to non-marital children, paternal filiation needed to be established, in the first instance, on the basis of a legal action emanating from the man who wished to establish a parentage bond towards the child. In addition, as already addressed, the latter was dependent on a 'volatile factor', being the mother's consent: see Court of Arbitration, 21 December 1990, nr. 39/90.

[42] Court of Arbitration, 8 October 1992, nr. 63/92; Court of Arbitration, 14 July 1994, nr. 62/94; Court of Arbitration, 14 May 2003, nr. 66/2003.

[43] Court of Arbitration, 14 May 2003, nr. 66/2003, B.8.8.

[44] Act of 1 July 2006 amending the provisions of the Civil Code relating to the establishment of parentage and its consequences, *Belgian Official Journal*, 29 December 2006; G. Mathieu, 'La réforme du droit de la filiation: une refonte en profondeur' (2007) *Rev. trim. dr. fam.* 334–335; J. Sosson, 'Le droit de la filiation nouveau est arrivé' (2007) *J.T. (Journal des Tribunaux)* 365 and 391.

[45] M. Demaret, 'La réforme du droit de la filiation' in Y.H. Leleu (ed.), *Chroniques notariales. Faculté de droit de l'Université de Liège*, Larcier, 2006, pp. 309–311.

[46] P. Senaeve, 'De nieuwe afstammingswet van 1 juli 2006' (2007) *T. Fam.(Tijdschrift voor Familierecht)* 15–16.

her prior consent. In this way, the legislator no longer disadvantaged the father in a discriminatory manner, by using the word 'parent', and by requiring the prior consent of the other parent in both situations (see section 3).[47] Second, the various ways of establishing and contesting parentage were made, as far as possible, consistent with one another, as regards their fundamental and formal conditions. Lastly, the establishment and contestation of marital paternal filiation, on the one hand, and non-marital paternal filiation, on the other, were regulated more uniformly.[48] The latter unification came at the expense of protecting marital stability in the law of filiation.[49] In terms of *liberalisation* and *modernisation*, the aim was to adapt the legal text to the new priorities of modern society.[50] Accordingly, the presumption of paternity was drastically reduced in a number of situations where there was doubt about the actual existence of a family nucleus. Moreover, the biological non-marital father became the holder of the claim to contest the established marital paternity, in that way reducing the protection of the legitimate family.[51] Thus, there had become a gradually increasing reluctance to protect the family nucleus and the child born within a marital context, at least in so far as no social reality had developed.

It should also be noted that the importance of the child's best interests in establishing or maintaining a parentage bond was repeatedly emphasised during the parliamentary preparations.[52] In addition, the ongoing search for a delicate balance between the different bases of the law of filiation was highlighted.[53] On the one hand, in establishing paternity, the role of biological reality was strengthened, due to the aforementioned restriction of the scope of application of the presumption of paternity, and by opening up the action to contest the

---

47 Art. 13 of the proposition of law amending the provisions of the Civil Code relating to the establishment of parentage and its consequences, *Parl. St.* Chamber of Representatives, 2003–04, nr. 51-0597/001.

48 T. WUYTS, *Ouderlijk gezag*, Intersentia, 2013, p. 114.

49 F. SWENNEN, *Het personen- en familierecht (zevende, herziene uitgave)*, Intersentia, 2021, p. 442.

50 M. DEMARET, 'Le droit de la filiation réformé' (2007) *Rev. not. b. (Revue du notariat belge)* 117–118.

51 G. VERSCHELDEN, 'Het hervormde afstammingsrecht: een nieuw compromis tussen biologisch en sociaal ouderschap' (2007–08) *R.W.* 339; T. WUYTS, *Ouderlijk gezag*, Intersentia, 2013, p. 114.

52 Report, *Parl. St.* Chamber of Representatives, 2004–05, nr. 51-597/24, pp. 5–8, 11, 12, 16, 26, 42, 43, 48, 49, 55–57, 62 and 68; Proposition of law amending the provisions of the Civil Code relating to the establishment of parentage and its consequences, Report, *Parl. St.* Chamber of Representatives, 2004–05, nr. 51K597/32, pp. 5, 24–28, 42, 45; Proposition of law amending the provisions of the Civil Code relating to the establishment of parentage and its consequences, Report, *Parl. St.* Senate, 2005–06, nr. 3-1402/7, pp. 3, 9, 12, 13, 15-18, 25, 41, 42, 47, 48 and 58.

53 Y.H. LELEU, *Droit des personnes et des familles*, Bruylant, 2020, p. 547; G. VERSCHELDEN, 'Het hervormde afstammingsrecht: een nieuw compromis tussen biologisch en sociaal ouderschap' (2007–08) *R.W.* 338.

---

established marital paternity to the non-spouse claiming to be the biological father. At the same time, but completely contradictory to the tendency towards biologisation, 'possession of state' had become a ground of inadmissibility for any claim to contest the paternity of the husband.[54] For this reason, legal doctrine argued that the closer connection to biological reality was, in fact, overshadowed by the socio-affective reality embodied by the principle of 'possession of state'.[55]

5. FROM 2006 TO THE PRESENT DAY

5.1. THE CONSECRATION OF THE BEST INTERESTS OF THE CHILD

Unlike other areas of family law, such as parental authority, custody right or adoption, it can be seen from the previous section that parentage law was not built from the outset around the child's best interests, but was instead based on choices made upstream by the legislature, following a subtle combination of the different values that have evolved over time: family stability; equality; socio-affective bond; biological bond; and equality between parents, and between married and unmarried couples, and children.

Today, however, under the influence of the case law of the Constitutional Court,[56] the child's best interests[57] have become the central pillar of our new parentage law.[58]

---

[54] A. Rasson-Roland and J. Sosson, 'Coups de tonnerre constitutionnels dans la filiation: l'article 318 du Code civil dans la tourmente …' (2011) *Rev. trim. dr. fam.* 582; F. Swennen, *Het personen- en familierecht (zevende, herziene uitgave)*, Intersentia, 2021, p. 442.

[55] G. Verschelden, 'Het hervormde afstammingsrecht: een nieuw compromis tussen biologisch en sociaal ouderschap' (2007–08) *R.W.* 358; T. Wuyts, *Ouderlijk gezag*, Intersentia, 2013, p. 115.

[56] It should be pointed out that, in matters of filiation, most of the judgments were given on preliminary questions. This means that '[t]he question put to the Court is always contextualised and limited to a specific aspect of the legislation. The same is true for the European Court of Human Rights, which always rules in the context of a particular situation. This characteristic explains the differences that may appear between the assessments of the two courts in cases that are rarely exactly similar, which makes attempts at systematisation perilous' (own translation) (A. Rasson-Roland and B. Renauld, 'L'influence du droit constitutionnel sur le droit de la famille' (2015) 75 *A.D.L.* 324).

[57] The consideration of the child's best interests, in any decision concerning him or her, has been proclaimed since 2008, in Article 22*bis*, para. 4 of the Constitution. The control of compliance with this provision by the legislative norms is, therefore, the responsibility of the Constitutional Court, by virtue of Art. 142 of the Constitution and Art. 1, 2° of the special Act of 6 January 1989 on the Constitutional Court.

[58] See N. Massager, *Le droit de la filiation après la loi du 21 décembre 2018: l'intérêt de l'enfant redéployé*, Larcier, 2019, pp. 97–101; G. Mathieu and A.C. Rasson, 'Le droit de la famille à l'aune du respect de l'intérêt supérieur de l'enfant' (2021) 6–7 *Act. dr. fam. (Actualités du droit de la famille)* 167 ff.

First of all, while the 2006 legislator had put in place, in the context of an action for acknowledgement or judicial establishment of filiation, a *marginal* control of the child's interest, only triggered if the child was older than one year, the Court imposed a systematic and complete control of the child's interest, irrespective of age.[59] In order to comply with the Court's case law, the Act of 21 December 2018[60] amended Articles 329*bis* and 332*quinquies* of the old Civil Code, to remove the marginal nature of the control of the child's interest and the reference to the child's age.

Furthermore, in the context of the judicial establishment of paternity, the Court considered that Article 332*quinquies* of the old Civil Code, interpreted in the sense that it did not allow the judge to take into consideration the child's interest when the child's mother brought the action against the biological father, in the event of the latter's opposition, violated Articles 10, 11, 22 and 22*bis* of the Constitution, read in conjunction with Article 8 of the ECHR. However, according to the Court, Article 22*bis* of the Constitution allowed the judge to control the child's best interests, even if the Article did not foresee such control; in this case, it did not violate the Constitution and the ECHR.[61]

In matters of incestuous filiation, the Constitutional Court condemned Article 325 of the old Civil Code, in so far as it absolutely prevented the judge from granting a judicial establishment of paternity, even if they found that the establishment of parentage corresponded to the child's best interests. The impossibility of taking this best interests into account in an effective and efficient manner could not be justified by the objective of prohibiting incestuous relationships.[62] In order to comply with this judgment, the Act of 21 December 2018

---

[59] Constitutional Court, 16 December 2010, nr. 144/2010 and Constitutional Court, 3 May 2012, nr. 61/2012 (one-year lead time); Constitutional Court, 7 March 2013, nr. 30/2013, and Constitutional Court, 2 July 2015, nr. 101/2015 and nr. 102/2015 (marginal control). For a study of the judicial jurisprudence on this issue, see T. Wuyts, 'Biologisch ouderschap en de rol van het belang van het kind bij de vestiging van een afstammingsband' (2021) 1 *T.J.K. (Tijdschrift Jeugd- en Kinderrechten)* 78–80.

[60] Act of 21 December 2018 containing various provisions on justice, *Belgian Official Journal* 31 December 2018, hereinafter 'Act of 21 December 2018'.

[61] Constitutional Court, 28 November 2019, nr. 190/2019; Constitutional Court, 18 June 2020, nr. 92/2020. See M. Beague, 'L'intérêt de l'enfant dans le cadre d'une action en recherche de paternité introduite par la mère à l'encontre d'un homme qui ne veut pas être père' (2020) *Rev. trim. dr. fam.* 988 ff; I. Boone, 'De gerechtelijke vaststelling van het vaderschap getoetst aan de Grondwet' (2019–2020) *R.W.* 1529 ff; I. Boone, 'Recente ontwikkelingen in het afstammingsrecht en het naamrecht (2017–2019)' in I. Boone and C. Declerck (eds.), *Themis 111 - Personen- en familierecht*, die Keure, 2020, pp. 27 ff; M. Coune, 'La place du projet parental et de l'intérêt de l'enfant dans les affaires de paternité imposée' (2021) *Rev. trim. dr. fam.* 249 ff; B. Lambersy and C. Vergauwen, 'De biologische vader hoeft zich niet in de steek gelaten te voelen' (2020) 16 *R.A.B.G. (Rechtspraak Antwerpen Brussel Gent)* 1311 ff; N. Massager, 'De l'intérêt pour l'enfant de n'avoir pas de père' (2020) *Act. dr. fam.* 16 ff; T. Wuyts, 'Biologisch ouderschap en de rol van het belang van het kind bij de vestiging van een afstammingsband' (2021) 1 *T.J.K.* 71 ff.

[62] Constitutional Court, 9 August 2012, nr. 103/2012.

---

amended Article 325 of the old Civil Code (action to establish paternity), as well as Articles 314 (action to establish maternity) and 325/10 (action to establish co-maternity) of the same Code: the prohibition of the establishment of a dual parent–child relationship of a child born of absolute incest[63] remains the principle, but the judge is now authorised to make an exception to it if such establishment does not conflict with the child's best interests. More recently, the Constitutional Court has also held that Article 321 of the old Civil Code – stating that paternal acknowledgement is not allowed when it creates a relationship between the mother and the candidate father which reveals a marriage impediment that cannot be waived by the family court (absolute incest) – violates Articles 10 and 11 of the Constitution, read in conjunction with Articles 8 and 14 of the ECHR and Articles 3.1 and 7.1 of the International Convention on the Rights of the Child (CRC). The father had acknowledged the child without knowing the incestuous character of his relationship with the child's mother, and, once this was known, the public prosecutor filed an application to annul the paternal acknowledgement. The Court declared Article 321 of the old Civil Code unconstitutional, because it did not allow the maintenance of the dual parentage bond in the case of absolute incest, even if it corresponded to the child's best interests.[64]

In the matter of fraudulent acknowledgement,[65] the Court considered that the procedure, as organised by the Act of 19 September 2017[66] (absence of appeal against the refusal of the civil registrar to record an acknowledgement he or she considers fraudulent), did not allow the judge to assess *in concreto* the interests of the various persons concerned, and, in particular, the primary interest of the children.[67] Following this ruling, the Act of 31 July 2020[68]

---

[63] Absolute incest refers to a relationship between two persons between whom there is an impediment to marriage which the family court cannot dispense with (ascendants and descendants, on the one hand, and brothers and sisters, on the other).

[64] Constitutional Court, 14 July 2022, nr. 99/2022.

[65] An acknowledgement is said to be fraudulent, within the meaning of Article 330/1 of the old Civil Code, when it appears from a combination of circumstances that the intention of the person recognising the child is manifestly only to obtain an advantage in terms of residence, linked to the establishment of a parent–child relationship, for him or herself, for the child, or for the person required to give his or her prior consent to the acknowledgement.

[66] Act of 19 September 2017 amending the Civil Code, the Judicial Code, the Act of 15 December 1980 on access to the territory, residence, settlement and expulsion of foreigners and the Consular Code, with a view to combating fraudulent acknowledgement and containing various provisions on the search for paternity, maternity and co-maternity, as well as on marriage of convenience and legal cohabitation of convenience, *Belgian Official Journal*, 4 October 2017. By adopting this law, the legislator wished to tackle the phenomenon of acknowledgement of children made with the sole aim of circumventing the legal provisions on residence, known as 'fraudulent' acknowledgement, after having committed to the fight against marriages and legal cohabitations of convenience.

[67] Constitutional Court, 7 May 2020, nr. 58/2020, B.27.4.

[68] Act of 31 July 2020 on various urgent provisions relating to justice, *Belgian Official Journal*, 7 August 2020.

modified Article 330/2 of the old Civil Code, which now stipulates that the refusal of the civil registrar to establish the act of acknowledgement may be appealed against by the person who wishes to acknowledge the child before the family court; that the persons whose consent to the acknowledgement is required are called to the case; and that the court determines whether it is a fraudulent acknowledgement, taking into account the interests involved and, in particular, those of the child.

The Court also found that Article 332*quinquies*, para. 3 of the old Civil Code, by making it impossible to establish a paternal parentage bond in the absence of a biological link, in the context of heterologous medically assisted reproduction that led to the child's birth, disproportionately infringed the child's right to respect for his or her private and family life, and to have his or her best interests considered (see section 5.2).[69]

In the context of actions to contest filiation, the Court has overturned the absolute nature of the exception of inadmissibility based on the existence of 'possession of state',[70] thus opening the door to a balance of rights and interests to be carried out by the judge *in concreto*, with the child's interest taking on greater weight in the balance than the interests of the other protagonists.[71]

Since its judgment nr. 30/2013 of 7 March 2013, the Court has consistently reiterated that, when drawing up a legal regime in parentage matters, the legislator must allow the competent authorities to balance the interests of the various persons concerned *in concreto*:[72] otherwise, the measure would not be

---

[69]   Constitutional Court, 7 February 2019, nr. 19/2019.

[70]   Constitutional Court, 3 February 2011, nr. 20/2011; Constitutional Court, 7 March 2013, nr. 29/2013; Constitutional Court, 9 July 2013, nr. 96/2013; Constitutional Court, 9 July 2013, nr. 105/2013; Constitutional Court, 7 November 2013, nr. 147/2013; Constitutional Court, 19 September 2014, nr. 127/2014; Constitutional Court, 25 September 2014, nr. 139/2014; Constitutional Court, 12 March 2015, nr. 35/2015; Constitutional Court, 26 November 2015, nr. 168/2015; Constitutional Court, 3 February 2016, nr. 18/2016. For a critique of this consistent case law of the Court with regard to the protection of the interests of the child, see N. GALLUS, 'L'apport de la jurisprudence de la Cour constitutionnelle au droit de la filiation' (2021) *Le Pli juridique* 24–26.

[71]   It should be noted in this context that the child's interest is expressed, in particular, through the emergence of his or her right to know his or her origins. This right now plays a fundamental role in the balancing of the various interests at stake, and its preservation may directly affect the outcome of an action to contest parentage brought by the person claiming paternity, sometimes implying the coincidence of biological parentage and legal parentage, to the detriment of the socio-affective truth, and sometimes the maintenance of legal parentage corresponding to the socio-affective bond, to the detriment of the biological truth, once the child is made aware of his or her history.

[72]   The concrete examination of the child's interest, in matters of filiation, had already been required since Judgment nr. 66/2003, in which the Court stated that, although, as a general rule, it may be considered to be in the child's interest to have his or her double filiation established, there can be no irrebuttable presumption that this is always the case (Constitutional Court, 14 May 2003, nr. 66/2003, B.5).

proportionate to the legitimate objectives pursued.[73] In this balance, the child's interest is of primary importance, without, however, being absolute, because the child represents the weakest party in the family relationship.[74]

If the Court sometimes adopts a certain ambivalence and deviates from its line of conduct,[75] the general trend in its case law relating to parentage law, and more broadly to family law, seems very clear, and one can only be delighted: each judge is required to consider, in as a primary consideration, the child's best interests, in a balance of interests carried out *in concreto*. The law to be applied by the court cannot be a shield in this respect, and must be interpreted in accordance with Article 22*bis*, al. 4 of the Constitution, combined with Article 3.1 of the CRC. If the law directly contradicts this Article, it is up to the court to ask the Constitutional Court for a preliminary ruling.[76]

5.2. PARENTAGE AFTER MEDICALLY ASSISTED REPRODUCTION

Medically assisted reproduction is regulated in Belgium by the Act on MAR of 2007. This Act sets up the parentage rules applicable to medically assisted reproduction, including when donor gametes or embryos are used (heterologous assisted reproduction). In this case, there is a clear switch from legal parentage based mainly on the genetic and biological bonds between the child and their parents, to legal parentage based on the parents' intentions.

Regarding donorship, there are two main rules. The first is that the donor is excluded from the child's parentage,[77] and no legal actions can be initiated by or

---

[73] Constitutional Court, 7 March 2013, nr. 30/2013, B.7. See also Constitutional Court, 19 March 2015, nr. 38/2015, B.4.3; Constitutional Court, 2 July 2015, nr. 101/2015 and nr. 102/2015, B.8; Constitutional Court, 24 September 2015, nr. 126/2015, B.4.3; Constitutional Court, 25 May 2016, nr. 77/2016, B.5; Constitutional Court, 16 February 2017, nr. 24/2017, B.5; Constitutional Court, 1 February 2018, nr. 11/2018, B.7. It should be noted, however, that in Judgment nr. 48/2014 of 20 March 2014, the Constitutional Court was able to consider that the principle of taking into account, in a balance carried out *in concreto*, the interests of all the parties concerned, was not absolute, and did not apply, in particular, to the action for judicial establishment of paternity brought by a child of full age, with regard to his or her biological father (in this case deceased). In the Court's view, the legislature was reasonably entitled to consider, within the limits of the aforementioned margin of appreciation, that, in judicial proceedings to establish filiation, the right of each person to have his or her filiation established must take precedence, in general, over the interests of the peace of families and the legal security of family relationships, and, in particular, over the right of persons related to the biological father not to have their private and family lives infringed (Constitutional Court, 20 March 2014, nr. 48/2014, B.10).

[74] Constitutional Court, 7 March 2013, nr. 30/2013, B.10.

[75] See G. Mathieu and A.C. Rasson, 'Le droit de la famille à l'aune du respect de l'intérêt supérieur de l'enfant' (2021) *Act. dr. fam.* 186 ff.

[76] See Art. 26 of the special Act of 6 January 1989.

[77] Art. 2, (i)–(j) and (p)–(q), Act on MAR.

against the donor.[78] The second rule is that, from the moment of implantation of the donated embryos or insemination of the donated gametes, the parentage rules as set out in the Civil Code operate in favour of the intended parent(s).[79] These rules only apply when the donors and the intended parents go through a recognised fertility centre.

For the establishment and contestation of maternity, the rules did not change, because they remained based on the principle of *mater semper certa est*. The mother still becomes the mother through the delivery of the child, and the inscription of her name on the child's birth certificate, irrespective of which woman the egg cell originated from.[80] This also means that a surrogate mother will become the child's legal mother.[81]

Regarding paternity, there is no difference from natural procreation, if the partner's sperm is used. The only difficulty concerns post-mortem insemination with the sperm, or with embryos made out of the sperm of the deceased partner:[82] in these circumstances, judicial establishment of paternity is only possible at the request of the mother or the child.[83]

Further, the presumption of paternity[84] applies if the parents are married to each other, even if the couple has used a donor's sperm. As already mentioned, if the spouse has consented, this presumption of paternity cannot be disputed (see above section 3).

When an unmarried woman gives birth to a child, the parentage bond with regard to the intended father can only be established by acknowledgement, or

---

78   Art. 27, al. 2 and Art. 56, al. 2, Act on MAR.
79   Art. 27, al. 1 and Art. 56, al. 1, Act on MAR.
80   Proposition of law on medically assisted reproduction, *Parl. St.* Senate, 2005–06, nr. 3-1440/1, p. 12.
81   To date, there has been no legal framework about surrogacy. To become a parent of the child, the intended father has to acknowledge or adopt the child (depending on whether or not the surrogate mother is married), and the intended mother has to adopt the child. See, for more details, G. MATHIEU, *Droit de la famille*, Larcier, 2022, pp. 406–409; L. PLUYM, *Een familierechtelijk statuut voor draagmoederschap*, Wolters Kluwer, 2015, pp. 75–87. Since 2003, statutory reforms have been proposed regarding surrogacy, but none of them have been enacted. See, for an overview of the proposals up until 2014, L. PLUYM, *Een familierechtelijk statuut voor draagmoederschap*, Wolters Kluwer, 2015, pp. 6–10; G. SCHAMPS and J. SOSSON, *La gestation pour autrui: vers un encadrement?*, Bruylant, 2013. The last proposal is from 2019 (Proposition of law organising centres for surrogacy, *Parl. St.* Chamber of representatives, 2019–20, nr. 55-0855/001).
82   Post-mortem insemination is only possible between six months and two years after the death of the person who asked for the cryoconservation of the gametes or embryos (Arts. 16 and 45, Act on MAR). Thus, the presumption of paternity or co-maternity is no longer applicable, because the child will be born more than 300 days after the dissolution of the marriage through the death of that person (Arts. 315 and 325/2, old Civil Code).
83   N. GALLUS, *Bioéthique et droit*, Anthemis, 2013, pp. 119–122; L. OPLINUS, *Medische hulp bij voortplanting*, Intersentia, 2022, pp. 360–363; G. VERSCHELDEN, *Handboek Belgisch Personen-, familie- en relatievermogensrecht*, die Keure, 2021, p. 103.
84   Art. 315, old Civil Code.

by judicial establishment of paternity. There is disagreement in the doctrinal field as to how far the Civil Code protects the intended father.[85] On the one hand, some authors believe that the parentage rules in the Civil Code that refer to the biological-genetic basis should actually be read as referring to intentional parentage.[86] On the other hand, some other authors state that the second rule[87] of the MAR Act does not allow deviation from the parentage rules formulated in the Civil Code, as these are a matter of public order.[88]

In the context of the above-mentioned issues, the Constitutional Court ruled, in a recent judgment of 7 February 2019,[89] that Article 332*quinquies*, para. 3 of the old Civil Code violates Articles 10 and 11 of the Constitution, in so far as it prevents the judicial establishment of the paternity of the man whose desired parenthood has led to the birth of a child through medically assisted reproduction with donated gametes. If the Constitutional Court receives a prejudicial question regarding a situation where a man agreed to a medically assisted reproduction, and would like to acknowledge the child, but the mother has refused to give her consent, the Court may have similar reasoning, and also conclude that there has been a violation of Articles 10 and 11 of the Constitution.[90]

Furthermore, it has been discussed whether the donor can acknowledge the child voluntarily, with the mother's consent. As indicated, Article 2 of the Act on MAR states that no parentage bonds can be established between the donor

---

85   See also Report to the Commission, *Parl. St.* Senate 2005–06, nr. 3-1440/9, pp. 123–124.

86   See E. DECORTE, 'Afstamming langs vaderszijde: over de (on)mogelijkheden na medisch begeleide voortplanting met donorzaad' (2019) 3 *T.J.K.* 272; L. OPLINUS, *Medische hulp bij voortplanting*, Intersentia, 2022, pp. 374–375; P. SENAEVE and C. DECLERCK, *Compendium van het personen- en familierecht*, Acco, 2020, p. 287; P. SENAEVE, 'Medische begeleide voortplanting met donorsperma en onderzoek naar het vaderschap' (2019) 5 *T. Fam.* 141; T. WUYTS, 'De afstamming na medisch begeleide voortplanting' in P. SENAEVE, F. SWENNEN and G. VERSCHELDEN (eds.), *De hervorming van het afstammingsrecht: commentaar op de wetten van 1 juli 2006, 27 december 2006 en 6 juli 2007*, Intersentia, 2007, pp. 329–331; G. VERSCHELDEN, *Handboek Belgisch Personen-, familie- en relatievermogensrecht*, die Keure, 2021, p. 104.

87   Cf. above n. 79.

88   See M. DERÈSE and G. WILLEMS, 'La loi du 6 juillet 2007 relative à la procréation médicalement assistée et à la destination des embryons surnuméraires et des gamètes' (2008) *Rev. trim. dr. fam.* 353–355; N. GALLUS, *Bioéthique et droit*, Anthemis, 2013, pp. 119 and 122–125; G. GÉNICOT, 'Le secret des origines biologiques dans les procréations assistées faisant appel à un tiers: un dispositif à questionner' in N. GALLUS and N. MASSAGER (eds.), *Procréation médicalement assistée et gestation pour autrui. Regards croisés du droit et de la pratique médicale*, Anthemis, 2017, pp. 85–86; G. MATHIEU, *Droit de la famille*, Larcier, 2022, p. 399; J. SOSSON, 'Filiation après procréation médicalement assistée et comaternité: principes et pièges' in N. GALLUS and N. MASSAGER (eds.), *Procréation médicalement assistée et gestation pour autrui. Regards croisés du droit et de la pratique médicale*, Anthemis, 2017, pp. 132–135; G. WILLEMS, 'La filiation après PMA à l'épreuve du contrôle de constitutionnalité: vers une consécration législative de la parenté intentionnelle' (2019) *J.T.* 455–456.

89   Constitutional Court, 7 February 2019, nr. 19/2019.

90   G. MATHIEU, *Droit de la famille*, Larcier, 2022, p. 400.

and the unborn child. However, Articles 27 and 56 of the same Act prohibit only a legal action relating to parentage. In the case of an acknowledgement, no legal action is required if the mother agrees with the assertion of paternity. Therefore, acknowledgement by the donor should be possible, until somebody (child, candidate father) contests it.[91]

5.3. THE POSITION OF THE CO-MOTHER IN BELGIAN PARENTAGE LAW

Since the 1980s, at least at some fertilisation centres, lesbian couples have had access to medically assisted reproduction.[92] Nevertheless, the mother's partner did not have a legal parentage status in relation to the child, even if she was the child's genetic mother. According to the Constitutional Court, this situation was problematic (no inheritance rights, no parental responsibilities, etc.) for these children. However, it was the legislature's task to find a solution to extend parental responsibilities to people who did not have a parentage bond with the child.[93]

With the Act on the establishment of co-maternity of 5 May 2014,[94] the legislature allowed the establishment of filiation at birth, between the child and the mother's female partner. This Act sets up the establishment of co-maternity as parallel to the establishment of paternity, by replacing the biological bond between the child and the father with the agreement of the co-mother to medically assisted reproduction. Thus, the intention of the intended parents becomes the key to establishing co-maternity. In summary, there are three ways to set up a parentage bond between a child and his or her co-mother: the presumption of co-maternity, as a result of the marriage between the mother and the co-mother of the child;[95] acknowledgement;[96] and the judicial establishment

---

[91] See L. OPLINUS, *Medische hulp bij voortplanting*, Intersentia, 2022, pp. 371–372; P. SENAEVE and C. DECLERCK, *Compendium van het personen- en familierecht*, Acco, 2020, pp. 287–288; V. VANDERHULST, 'Medisch begeleide voortplanting' in F. DEWALLENS and T. VANSEEVELT (eds.), *Handboek gezondheidsrecht vol. II*, Intersentia, 2014, pp. 106–107; T. WUYTS, 'De afstamming na medisch begeleide voortplanting' in P. SENAEVE, F. SWENNEN and G. VERSCHELDEN (eds.), *De hervorming van het afstammingsrecht: commentaar op de wetten van 1 juli 2006, 27 december 2006 en 6 juli 2007*, Intersentia, 2007, pp. 316 and 329.

[92] L. OPLINUS, *Medische hulp bij voortplanting*, Intersentia, 2022, p. 379.

[93] Constitutional Court, 8 October 2003, nr. 134/2003, B.7.

[94] *Belgian Official Journal*, 7 July 2014. See Arts. 325/1–325/10, old Civil Code.

[95] Art. 325/2, old Civil Code.

[96] Art. 325/4, old Civil Code. In the case where the child's mother does not agree with the acknowledgement, the judge will have to see whether there was agreement to the medically assisted reproduction from which the child resulted, instead of a biological bond (Art. 325/4, al. 2 old Civil Code).

of co-maternity.[97] The parentage bond of the co-mother can also be contested[98] where it is proven that the co-mother is not the woman who agreed to the medically assisted reproduction (or, in the case of marriage, with any act having the purpose of procreation), or that the child is not the result of this agreement. These protection rules are only applicable if the mother and the co-mother utilised the 'official way', i.e. a recognised fertilisation centre for reproduction, and did not choose an 'at-home solution' – except in the case of marriage.

5.4. THE POSITION OF TRANSGENDER PERSONS IN BELGIAN PARENTAGE LAW

The status of transgender persons and specific rules regarding parentage have evolved since 2007. Before 2007, a legal change of sex was complicated. Transgender people had to request a modification of their birth certificate, or their status, from the court, because of a 'mistake' regarding their sex. The sexual conversion had to be complete and definitive, through hormonal and surgical treatment.[99] After a sexual conversion, it was, therefore, not possible to beget children. The Act of 10 May 2007[100] kept the requirement of the impossibility of conceiving children in accordance with the person's previous sex.[101] In other words, candidates for a legal modification of sex had to become infertile. The Act provided specific parentage provisions relating to transgender persons: the legal sex change did not affect the existing parental ties between transgender persons and their children.[102] However, as soon as a document indicating the new sex was drawn up, the law seemed to exclude the establishment of paternal filiation with regard to transwomen.[103] For a transman, there was no similar provision, because sterilisation implied that this person could not give birth any more, and he could still proceed to paternal acknowledgement of a child given birth to by his female partner after the legal sex reassignment.[104]

There was a lot of criticism[105] regarding the conditions imposed by the Act of 2007, such as the necessity of sterilisation, which was condemned (in relation

---

[97] Arts. 325/8–325/10, old Civil Code.
[98] Arts. 325/3 and 325/7, old Civil Code.
[99] See N. GALLUS, *Actualités du droit des personnes et des familles. Le point en 2018*, Anthemis, 2018, pp. 16–17.
[100] Act of 10 May 2007 on transsexuality, *Belgian Official Journal*, 11 July 2007.
[101] N. GALLUS, *Actualités du droit des personnes et des familles. Le point en 2018*, Anthemis, 2018, p. 18.
[102] Old Art. 62*bis*, para. 8, al. 1, old Civil Code.
[103] Old Art. 62*bis*, para. 8, al. 2, old Civil Code.
[104] N. GALLUS, *Actualités du droit des personnes et des familles. Le point en 2018*, Anthemis, 2018, p. 19.
[105] Ibid.; M. PETERS, 'La loi de 2017 et le principe d'autodétermination de l'individu' (2020) 6 *T.B.B.R. (Tijdschrift voor Belgisch Burgerlijk recht)/R.G.D.C. (Revue Générale de Droit)* 358.

to other member states) by the ECtHR.[106] These concerns led to reform of the legal aspects of transgender people, and resulted in the Act of 25 June 2017, 'reforming the regimes relating to transgender persons as regards the mention of a change of sex registration in civil status records and its effects'.[107] This new legislation no longer requires the sterilisation of transgender people. Therefore, the rules regarding parentage have become more complex, because it is possible to become a parent before and after a change of sex.

As under the previous legislation, sex modification does not change the parental bonds of children already born.[108] Such a disposition ensures the stability of the parentage for those children.[109]

As for children born after the adjustment of registration of sex, there exists a set of specific rules. If a transman gives birth to a child, he will be the child's mother, according to the *mater semper certa est* principle, since the legislature considered it necessary to avoid changing the entire Belgian parentage law.[110] If a transman gives birth to a child, and is in a relationship with a woman, his spouse/partner will become the child's co-mother. If a transman who gives birth is married to a man, it is necessary to look at the marriage date. If they were married after the modification of the sex, Article 143 of the old Civil Code stipulates that, if the marriage was entered into between persons of the same sex, Article 315 of the old Civil Code would not apply.[111] This means that the legal establishment of parentage based on the presumption of paternity of the (male) partner, regarding the child, is problematic, or, according to some,[112] impossible.[113] Nevertheless, acknowledgement or judicial establishment of paternity is still possible.[114] If a couple were married before the change of the sex, the presumption of paternity will apply, and the transman's spouse will be the father.

---

[106] See ECtHR, 10 March 2015, nr. 14793/08, *Y. Y. v. Turkey*; ECtHR, 6 April 2017, nr. 79885/12, 52471/13 and 52596/13, *A. P., Garçon et Nicot v. France*.

[107] *Belgian Official Journal*, 10 July 2017 (old Arts. 45, 62*bis*–62*ter*, old Civil Code). The Act of 18 June 2018 changed the numbering of the Articles (62*bis*–62*ter* became Art. 135/1 and 135/2, old Civil Code), and adapted the procedure to the new rules of the Civil Code, without changing the substantive requirements.

[108] Art. 135/2, para. 1, al. 1, old Civil Code.

[109] E. Bribosia, N. Gallus and I. Rorive, 'Une nouvelle loi pour les personnes transgenres en Belgique' (2018) *J.T.* 265.

[110] Art. 135/2, para. 2, al. 1, old Civil Code; Art. 312, old Civil Code; Proposition of law reforming the regime relating to transgender people regarding the sex's change in civil acts and its effect, *Parl. St.* Chamber of Representatives, 2016–2017, nr. 54-2403/1, pp. 23–24.

[111] Art. 143, al. 2, old Civil Code.

[112] J.L. Renchon, 'Le nouveau régime juridique du changement de sexe' (2018) 2 *Rev. trim. dr. fam.* 246–247.

[113] G. Verschelden and J. Motmans, *De rechtspositie van transgender personen in België*, Intersentia, 2020, p. 96.

[114] J.L. Renchon, 'Le nouveau régime juridique du changement de sexe' (2018) 2 *Rev. trim. dr. fam.* 247.

If a transwoman has procreated naturally with her partner, or has consented to medically assisted reproduction, the provisions concerning the legal establishment of paternity will apply. Nevertheless, she will not be registered as the father on the child's birth certificate, but as the co-mother.[115] The fact that a transwoman can and must be mentioned as a co-mother, but a transman cannot be mentioned as a co-father, results from the absence of status of the 'co-father' in Belgian parentage law.[116]

Finally, the old Civil Code states that parentage is based on the new sex, for other cases than those mentioned above.[117] This means that a transman who has a child with his partner through medically assisted reproduction will be the child's father. In the future, if a transwoman (with an artificial uterus) gives birth to a child, she will be the mother.[118]

Notwithstanding the achievements of the Act of 25 June 2017, the Constitutional Court pronounced the partial annulment of this Act shortly after its publication. The Constitutional Court stated that, due to the absence of any possibility of modifying sex registration to any option other than 'male' or 'female', the law discriminated against persons with non-binary gender identity. The Court invited the legislature to revise the law by adding a third category, or even more categories, to the existing binary categories, or by suppressing the registration of sex or gender as part of the civil state.[119]

6. CONCLUSION

The history of Belgian parentage law illustrates the abandonment of the patriarchal model, in which marriage and natural procreation were the pivotal starting points, in favour of a gradual opening up to a variety of families built around equal individuals, with a primary focus on the child's best interests.

However, while numerous evolutions have taken place over the years, the interests of all individuals have not been addressed, leaving a series of potential inequalities still at play in contemporary Belgian parentage law. This includes the situation of male homosexual couples who desire to have children, but who currently cannot both establish a legal parentage bond at birth with a child, and must rely on surrogacy, which does not have a legal framework in

---

[115] Art. 135/2, para. 2, al. 2–3, old Civil Code.
[116] J.L. RENCHON, 'Le nouveau régime juridique du changement de sexe' (2018) 2 *Rev. trim. dr. fam.* 248.
[117] Art. 135/2, para. 2, al. 4, old Civil Code.
[118] Proposition of law reforming the regime relating to transgender people regarding the sex's change in civil acts and its effect, *Parl. St.*, Chamber of Representatives, 2016–2017, nr. 54-2403/1, p. 26.
[119] Constitutional Court, 19 June 2019, nr. 99/2019, B.7.3.

Belgium, or a lengthy and costly adoption procedure. Also, more clarity would be appreciated regarding the situation of the intended father when donor sperm is used. Furthermore, although a specific legal framework was developed for transgender persons, this contains a series of inconsistencies and potential inequalities, mainly in situations where a transman gives birth to a child, and where a transwoman conceives a child. Finally, the Constitutional Court's ruling of 19 June 2019 calls into question the tenability of a parentage law drafted on a binary basis, as the ruling essentially prompts us to screen different branches of law, including parentage law, for gendered inequalities. In legal doctrine, as well as in political and public opinion, there are various viewpoints concerning a gender-neutral adaptation of parentage law in the Belgian Civil Code. These views range from a social reluctance to change long-established approaches to parentage, to sensitivity to the families created by nontraditional couples, and the need to make adjustments to accommodate them, and to strong support for the total abolition of gender-based distinctions in parentage.[120]

In the present authors' opinion, past evolutions and achievements can certainly be celebrated, as they have impacted significantly on what Belgian parentage law looks like today. Nevertheless, actions to address the potential inequalities described above need to be contemplated thoroughly, meaning that crucial reflection exercises will have to take place regarding the position of the above-mentioned individuals in our parentage law.

---

[120] Y.H. LELEU, *Droit des personnes et des familles*, Larcier, 2020, p. 544; J.L. RENCHON, 'Une filiation monosexuée?' in J. SOSSON and H. FULCHIRON (eds.), *Parenté, Filiation, Origine. Le droit et l'engendrement à plusieurs*, Bruylant, 2013, p. 257; F. SWENNEN, 'Wat is ouderschap?' (2016) *T.P.R* 2016 63–65; G. VERSCHELDEN, 'Nieuwe transgenderwetgeving: knopen doorhakken' (2015) 10 *T. Fam.* 242.

CHINA

50-YEAR RETROSPECTIVE

Divorce Law Practice under Chinese-Characteristic Judicial Philosophy

Zhu Fan and Lu Xiaobei

Résumé

Issue du système politique et juridique chinois, la philosophie judiciaire chinoise est une composante de la culture nationale. Au cœur du mode judiciaire de gouvernance sociale, la philosophie judiciaire chinoise cherche à servir l'ensemble de la société par une justice dynamique et à donner au peuple un sentiment d'équité et de justice à travers le processus judiciaire.

L'étude de la pratique du droit du divorce au cours du dernier demi-siècle montre que la philosophie judiciaire chinoise a eu une influence sur celle-ci à tous les niveaux : tant du point de vue macro que micro, du général au point particulier et aussi bien quant à la révision et à l'interprétation du droit du divorce que quant à la procédure de divorce.

La pratique du droit est guidée par les politiques judiciaires, ces dernières faisant écho à l'opinion politique et publique et remédiant aux lacunes de la législation dans la gouvernance sociale.

Grâce à l'orientation et à l'influence des politiques judiciaires, la pratique judiciaire chinoise en matière de divorce a permis de concrétiser la liberté matrimoniale, d'atténuer la contradiction entre la volonté du peuple et le concept dit de « l'idéal » et de réaliser une unification harmonieuse des fonctions d'orientation de la loi et de gouvernance sociale.

Simply going through the text of The Marriage Law or The Civil Code of the PRC is not enough to understand the Chinese divorce legal system. It can even be said that divorce legal practice, especially judicial practice, is the main body of the Chinese divorce legal system. By reviewing more than half a century of Chinese divorce law practice, this chapter not only shows readers the changes in the Chinese divorce legal system, but also the judicial philosophy with Chinese characteristics, and the unique rule-of-law mode.

1. DIVORCE LEGAL PRACTICE FROM THE ESTABLISHMENT OF NEW CHINA TO 1980

1.1. LEGISLATIVE CHARACTERISTICS AND DIVORCE SYSTEM OF THE MARRIAGE LAW 1950

With the establishment of New China in 1949, the existing laws in the Republic of China were repealed,[1] and The Marriage Law of the People's Republic of

---

[1]   Before the establishment of New China, the CPC Central Committee published '关于废除国民党的〈六法全书〉和确定解放区司法原则的指示' ('Instructions on Abolishing the Kuomintang's Six Laws and Determining the Principles of Justice in the Liberated Areas'), on 22 February 1949.

China 1950 (hereinafter referred to as the Marriage Law 1950) was drafted and published, totalling 27 articles. The law, influenced by revolutionary base legislation[2] and the former Soviet Union's marriage and family legislation, featured a simplicity of language and convenience in implementation that made it easy for people who were not trained as lawyers to learn and use the law. The main content of the divorce system included the following:

1. The way of divorce: the dichotomy between administrative registered divorce and litigious divorce has continued to this day. By registering divorce with the people's government, the former requires the husband and the wife to both agree to divorce, and to properly deal with their children and property; the latter also applies to cases where one of the parties requests a divorce by filing for divorce with the people's court.

2. The procedure and requirements of litigious divorce: if a party requests a divorce, it may only be done through ordinary civil trial procedures (China has never had specific family proceedings to deal with marriage and family cases). There was no civil procedure law at the time of the Marriage Law 1950, and the people's court handled cases in accordance with the requirements of the Supreme People's Court's judicial interpretation documents.[3] Paragraph 1 of Article 17 of the Marriage Law 1950 stipulated that, '[i]f a man or woman firmly requests a divorce, the divorce will be granted when mediation by the district people's government and judicial organs is ineffective'. Paragraph 2 stipulated that, '[i]f a man or woman firmly requests a divorce … if mediation fails, judgment will be rendered'. Mediation in divorce cases is a mandatory procedure under the law, which is one of the characteristics of Chinese divorce legislation.

3. Special protection of divorce: marriage of revolutionary soldiers or women who are pregnant is under special protection.

4. Legal consequences of divorce: in the event of divorce and if the mother is breastfeeding, the child shall live with the mother, and the people's court decides according to the interests of the child, in cases of competition for physical custody of the child between parents. In the division of property in divorce, more protection is given to the woman.[4]

---

2   '中华苏维埃共和国婚姻条例' ('Marriage Regulations of the Soviet Republic of China') in 1931, '中华苏维埃共和国婚姻法' ('Marriage Law of the Soviet Republic of China') in 1934, '陕甘宁边区婚姻条例' ('Marriage Regulations of Shaanxi-Gansu-Ningxia Border Region') in 1939, '晋冀鲁豫边区婚姻暂行条例' ('Provisional Regulations on Marriage in the Shanxi-Hebei-Shandong-Henan Border Region') in 1942, '晋察冀边区婚姻条例' ('Marriage Regulations of Jinchaji Border Region') in 1943, etc.

3   See the Supreme People's Court, '各级人民法院刑、民事案件审判程序总结' ('Summary of Trial Procedures for Criminal and Civil Cases in People's Courts at All Levels'); China's first Civil Procedure Law (Trial) was promulgated in 1982.

4   The law stipulated that the woman's premarital property belongs to the woman, and that joint debts incurred during the marriage are to be paid by the man, in the event that the joint

1.2. THE CONTRADICTION BETWEEN LEGISLATIVE GOALS AND BACKWARD REALITY

The Marriage Law 1950 continued the principles and tasks of marriage legislation in the revolutionary base areas, namely abolishing the feudalist marriage system and implementing the new democratic marriage system of 'freedom of marriage, monogamy, equal rights for men and women, and protection of the legitimate rights and interests of women and children'. The implementation of freedom of divorce, with revolutionary romanticism, stipulated that if one of the parties insists on divorce, the divorce will be granted if mediation fails.

With the very low social and domestic status of women at that time, it was difficult to extend the implementation of the laws of the revolutionary base areas to the whole of China, and most of the people, and even some cadres, had difficulty in accepting such divorce laws. In particular, it was usually women who unilaterally filed for divorce, leading some people to believe that marriage law is divorce law, which protects women and persecutes men. In some areas

> [b]ecause the leading organs and cadres lacked a correct and comprehensive understanding of the marriage law, they failed to seriously and correctly promote the marriage law and handle marriage disputes, and some cadres even adopted a resistant attitude toward the implementation of the marriage law, supporting the old feudal vices and interfering with freedom of marriage. As a result, arranged marriages are still popular in these areas, and women continue to be oppressed, abused, and even commit suicide or be killed because of the lack of freedom of marriage.[5]

According to *Xinhua Monthly*, between 1950 and 1952, tens of thousands of women committed suicide or were killed because they were unable to choose their own marriages, or were abused.[6]

---

property is insufficient to pay them. In addition, the financial assistance system, whereby the other party shall assist in the event of hardship of one party after divorce, is usually to the woman's benefit as well.

[5]   See '中央人民政府政务院关于贯彻婚姻法的指示' ('Instructions of the State Council of the Central People's Government on the Implementation of the Marriage Law'), 1 February 1953.

[6]   Incomplete statistics: from May 1950 to September 1951, there were 1,245 such people in Shandong Province; 119 people in the nine counties of Huaiyin Special Zone in North Jiangsu Province, from May to August 1950; and more than 10,000 people in the six provinces of the Central and South China Region, from May 1950 to September 1951. In the first half of 1952, a total of 429 people committed suicide, or were killed, due to marriage problems in North China, among which the largest number was in Chahar Province, with 70 cases and more than 100 deaths in total. In Eastern China, from the promulgation of the Marriage Law to the end of 1952, more than 11,500 women committed suicide, or were killed because of marriage and family problems. See XIAO AISHU, '建国初期妇女因婚姻问题自杀和被杀现象研究' ('A Study on the Phenomenon of Women's Suicide and Murder due to Marital Problems in the Early Founding Period of the People's Republic of China') (2005) 2, 齐鲁学刊 (Qilu Journal) 64–65.

1.3. INSTRUCTIONS OF JUDICIAL POLICY FOR THE PEOPLE'S COURTS TO HANDLE DIVORCE CASES

The CPC Central Committee and the State Council of the Central People's Government have repeatedly issued instructions to inspect the implementation of the Marriage Law.[7] March 1953 was designated as the month of the campaign to implement the marriage law, and the CPC Central Committee put forward the policy of insisting on education for divorce cases. This is because marriage and family disputes are internal conflicts within the people, and are mainly a matter of ideology: therefore, the understanding and support of the people are sought through propagation and education. Instruction of the State Council of the Central People's Government on the Implementation of the Marriage Law required that,

> [f]or a large number of resisting arranged marriages and family discord caused by the lack of freedom of marriage, basically we should adopt the approach of criticism and education, raising awareness, improving and consolidating the relationship between the couple; for a very small number of couples that are seriously violating the Marriage Law and are in really bad relationships that can not continue, divorce should be granted, but must be carefully mediated and the existence of grounds for divorce must be convincing for the general public.

In fact, the Report on the Drafting Process and Reasons of the Marriage Law of the People's Republic of China, made by the Legal Affairs Commission of the Central People's Government to the Central People's Government Committee in April 1950, Certain Questions and Answers on the Implementation of the Marriage Law by the Legal Affairs Commission of the Central People's Government, in June 1950, and Answers on Marriage Issues by the Legal Affairs Commission of the Central People's Government, in 1953, all denied the above-mentioned text, and expressly stated that divorce may not be decreed according to 'specific circumstances' after mediation has failed.

The implementation of the marriage law by means of a mass movement demonstrated the determination of the CPC Central Committee to break up the

---

[7]   '中共中央关于保证执行婚姻法给全党的通知' ('Notice from the Central Committee of the Communist Party of China to the Whole Party on Guaranteeing the Implementation of the Marriage Law'), 30 April 1950; '中央人民政府政务院关于检查婚姻法执行情况的指示' ('Instruction of the State Council of the Central People's Government on Inspection of the Implementation of the Marriage Law'), 26 September 1951; '中央人民政府政务院关于贯彻婚姻法的指示' ('Instruction of the State Council of the Central People's Government on the Implementation of the Marriage Law'), 1 February 1953; '中共中央关于贯彻婚姻法运动月工作的补充指示' ('Additional instructions from the Central Committee of the Communist Party of China on the implementation of the Marriage Law Campaign Month'), 18 February 1953, etc.

feudal family system and liberate women. The liberation of women facilitated women's participation in social activities, especially production activities, and laid a solid foundation for the socialist transformation and construction of a new China. The mission of the Marriage Law and the judicial objectives of the People's Courts are centred on socialist construction. China's political and legal work line is that political and legal work obeys the leadership of the Party, implements the mass line, combines with productive labour, and serves the central work of the Party and the State. A People's Court inspection report, published in 1960, stated that the Party's policy on marriage issues should be firmly implemented:

> it is necessary to start from the points of view that are beneficial to the complete liberation of women, the development of the social productive forces, the socialist revolution and socialist construction, and the unity and progress within the people, to advocate mutual love and respect between couples, to help each other, to put the interests of the socialist cause in the first place and to cultivate and develop the moral qualities of socialism and communism in the spirit of putting the public before the private.[8]

It is a unique Chinese political and legal tradition and judicial philosophy that judicial work serves the overall situation. Only by placing China's divorce law practice in such a context can we truly understand the purpose and working methods of the People's Courts.

1.4. THE TRIAL APPROACH OF MASS LINE AND THE HANDLING OF DIVORCE CASES

The mass line in the trial work means that the trial work should rely on the people, contact the people and facilitate the people.[9] The People's Court's work policy in civil trials is 'relying on the people, conducting investigation and research, settling problems on the spot and mainly using mediation', which is the famous Ma Xiwu Way of Trial.[10] The mediation-based judicial policy has

---

8   '青岛市台西区人民法院检查五年来处理离婚案件情况的报告（草稿）' ('Report of the Primary People's Court of Taixi District of Qingdao City Examining the Handling of Divorce Cases in the Past Five Years (Draft)') (1960) 20, 人民司法 (The People's Judicature) 11.

9   Ma Xiwu, '马锡五副院长在全国公安、检察、司法先进工作者大会的书面讲话' ('Written speech by Vice President Ma Xiwu at the National Conference of Advanced Workers in Public Security Organs, the People's Procuratorates and the People's Courts') (1959) 10, 人民司法 (The People's Judicature) 36.

10   The Ma Xiwu Way of Trial is the abbreviated name for a set of judicial concepts and trial systems implemented in the Shaanxi-Gansu-Ningxia Border Region during the Anti-Japanese War, which emphasise investigation and research, facilitate mass litigation, and resolve disputes on the spot. In recent years, the Supreme People's Court has repeatedly revisited the Ma Xiwu Way of Trial, and requested that its spiritual core and contemporary value be

a great impact on the handling of divorce cases. With judges carrying the case files to the countryside and relying on the masses and research, the vast majority of cases were solved on the spot, based on clarification of the facts and the use of grassroots cadres and the masses to conduct the mediation.[11] According to Huang Zongzhi's case study, the People's Courts, at that time, had developed a set of methods, procedures and practices to mediate divorce disputes. The judges went into the village community, visited the neighbours and local party organisations, understood the background and status of the marriage, analysed the root causes of the conflict, and actively used means, including political education, organisational pressure and material stimulation, to try to save the marriage between the parties.[12]

Facilitating people in justice is also derived from the judicial tradition of the revolutionary base. This was evident from the very simplified and convenient judicial procedures in the Shaanxi-Gansu-Ningxia Border Region, such as cancelling litigation fees; the fact the filing of a civil action could be oral or written (without unified format, clarity was the only requirement); the fact that a trial could be conducted on any occasion, and in any location and form, including trial in the field; that judgments were simple and easy to understand, etc.[13] Around 1943, the High Court of the Shaanxi-Gansu-Ningxia Border Region carried out a judicial reform, mainly emphasising the standardisation of judicial trials and the professionalisation of personnel, which ended with the resignation of the acting president, Mr. Li Mu'an. Among the many reasons for the failure of the reform, one of the criticisms of the reform idea of standardising the procedure was that it was at odds with the design of the judicial system for the convenience of the people in the border region.[14] In 1951, the Supreme People's Court specifically instructed that People's Courts should not refuse to accept indictments on the grounds that the form of the indictment did not meet the requirements, but should accept oral indictments or set up a surrogate office

---

continuously explored. HE XIAORONG (Member of the Party Group and Vice President of the Supreme People's Court), '马锡五审判方式的内在精神及其时代精神' ('The Inner and Contemporary Spirit of Ma Xiwu Way of Trial') (2021) 6, 法律适用 (Journal of Law Application) 3.

11   The Primary People's Court of Guanghan County of Sichuan Province, '我们处理离婚案件是怎样执行'十六字'方针的' ('How We Implement the "Sixteen Words" Policy in Handling Divorce Cases') (1979) 1, 人民司法 (The People's Judicature) 20.

12   HUANG ZONGZHI, '中国法律的实践历史研究' ('A Study of the Practical History of Chinese Law') (2008) 4, 开放时代 (Open Times) 117.

13   See HOU XINYI, '陕甘宁边区司法制度、理念及技术的形成与确立' ('Formation and Establishment of Judicial Systems, Concepts and Techniques in the Shaanxi-Gansu-Ningxia Border Region') (2005) 4, 法学家 (The Jurist) 41–42.

14   See HOU XINYI, '陕甘宁边区高等法院司法制度改革研究' ('A Study of Judicial System Reform Study in the Shaanxi-Gansu-Ningxia Border Region') (2004) 5, 法学研究 (Chinese Journal of Law) 129.

whenever possible, so as to solve the difficulties of illiterate women in litigation concerning marriage issues.[15]

1.5. LEGISLATION FROM JUDICIAL PRACTICE EXPERIENCE

In the face of criticism that 'the provisions of the Marriage Law on divorce are too principled, and there are no conditions for deciding on divorce, thus making it difficult to draw the boundaries of divorce, and thus causing difficulties in the handling of trials', the paper *On the Boundaries of Divorce Policy*, published in 1957, argued that even if the provisions were made, they could not solve the above difficulties:

> Marriage is a complex and diverse social phenomenon reflected by historical, economic and multifaceted ideologies. If fixed conditions are used in deciding on divorce, it will be difficult to fit into the actually changing conflicts and disputes. Therefore, our marriage law does not specify the legal conditions for divorce, which shows the superiority of our marriage law of flexibility and combativeness.[16]

Judicial practice not only complements the application of the law, but also promotes its revision, such as the principles (criteria) for deciding divorce.

When hearing divorce cases, the People's Courts mainly examine whether the grounds for divorce are justified, and whether the relationship between husband and wife is truly unsustainable. Rupture theory and justification theory have been developed in practice.[17] The former advocates that, regardless of whether the grounds for divorce are justified or not, a divorce should be granted when the relationship between husband and wife has completely broken

---

15 '最高人民法院、中央人民政府司法部、内务部关于纠正几个有关婚姻问题的错误的指示' ('Instructions of the Supreme People's Court, the Ministry of Justice of the Central People's Government and the Ministry of Internal Affairs on the Correction of Several Errors Concerning Marriage Issues'), 1951.

16 MA QI, '试论离婚政策界限' ('On the Boundaries of Divorce Policy'), 东北人民大学人文科学学报 (NorthEast People's University Journal of Humanity & Social Science) 173.

17 '中央人民政府法制委员会有关婚姻法施行的若干问题与解答' ('The Central People's Government Legislative Affairs Commission on the Implementation of the Marriage Law and Some Questions and Answers'), June 1950, upheld justification theory. Question 10 therein states that, 'if there are justifiable reasons for not being able to continue the relationship between husband and wife, a judgment of divorce shall be granted; otherwise, a judgment of divorce may also be denied'. '中央人民政府法制委员会关于婚姻问题的解答' ('The Central People's Government Legislative Affairs Commission on the Answer to the Question of Marriage'), 1953, upheld rupture theory. Question 14 therein states that, 'if the mediation is not effective, but it is proven that they [husband and wife] are not to the extent that they cannot continue to live together, the divorce can be denied'.

down, i.e. when it is, in fact, impossible to maintain the relationship; the latter insists that, even if the common life of husband and wife cannot be maintained, a divorce cannot be granted if the grounds are not justified (for example, the bourgeois ideology of liking the new and loathing the old), otherwise it will satisfy the improper demands of those who hold a bourgeois view of marriage.[18] The Supreme People's Court clearly favoured rupture theory, and The Supreme People's Court's Opinions on Several Issues Concerning the Implementation of Civil Policy, in 1963, held that 'whether the relationship is completely broken' was the criterion for deciding whether or not to grant the divorce. In 1979, the Supreme People's Court, at the Second National Conference on Civil Justice, changed the principle of whether the relationship had completely broken down to 'whether the relationship between husband and wife has in fact broken down and whether it can be restored'.[19] This, in turn, formed the Theory of Mutual Feelings Break and the Theory of the Relationship Break, and the Marriage Law of the People's Republic of China 1980 (hereinafter referred to as the Marriage Law 1980) finally adopted the Theory of Mutual Feelings Break.[20] This principle, established in 1980, continues today.

2. DIVORCE LEGAL PRACTICE FROM 1980 TO 2001

2.1. LEGISLATIVE FEATURES AND DIVORCE SYSTEM OF THE MARRIAGE LAW 1980

At the point when China ended the decade of turmoil, and started reform and opening up, the Marriage Law 1980 was promulgated, with 37 Articles. Basing on the Marriage Law 1950, the Marriage Law 1980 was revised according to 30 years of experience in judicial practice, and new situations and problems in marriage and family. It was concise and easy to understand, in line with the legislative style of the Marriage Law 1950. This concept of legislation is similar

---

[18] See You Tong, '对于当前离婚问题的分析和意见' ('Analysis and Opinions on Current Divorce Issues') (1957) 7, 人民日报 (People's Daily),13 April 1957; Liu Yunxiang, '关于正确认识与处理当前的离婚问题 – – 与幽桐同志商榷' ('On the Correct Understanding and Handling of the Current Divorce Issue – Discussion with Comrade You Tong') (1958) 3, 法学 (Law Science) 56–57.

[19] Wu Changzhen and Xia Yinlan, '离婚新探' ('A New Exploration into Divorce') (1989) 2, 中国法学 (China Legal Science) 46.

[20] Art. 25 of the Marriage Law 1980: When one party alone desires a divorce, the organisations concerned may carry out mediation, or the party may appeal directly to a people's court to start divorce proceedings. In dealing with a divorce case, the People's Court should carry out mediation between the parties. Divorce shall be granted if mediation fails because mutual affection no longer exists.

to what was later called the 'coarse rather than fine' view of legislation, but the starting point is different: the former's is to facilitate the people to learn and use the law, while the latter's is to quickly resume the construction of the legal system.[21] The Marriage Law 1980 made few changes to the divorce section, mainly the addition of the legal condition that 'mutual affection no long[er] exists' to the criteria for granting divorce. The legislature believed that, over the years, the courts had been on the strict side when it came to divorce cases, and that adding this condition both upheld the principle of freedom of marriage and gave the courts a certain amount of flexibility.[22] It was also because the new law did not add specific criteria for deciding divorce and the legal consequences of divorce that, by the time the Marriage Law was amended in 2001, the Supreme People's Court had issued several judicial interpretations to deal with the explosive growth of litigation.

2.2. THE IMPACT OF THE REVISION OF THE CIVIL PROCEDURE LAW AND THE REFORM OF THE CIVIL TRIAL METHOD ON THE LEGAL PRACTICE OF DIVORCE

The economic reform that began in 1978 gave birth to China's first Civil Procedure Law (Trial), in 1982. The law was derived from the judicial experience of the past 30 years, and sought to simplify the procedures and norms of civil litigation, emphasising the settlement of disputes by means of mediation rather than trial. However, with the rapid development of the commodity economy, civil disputes have changed dramatically, in terms of quantity and quality. According to a report of the Supreme People's Court, in 1987 the national courts concluded 1,196,494 civil cases, with an increase of 217,504 cases, or 22.2 per cent, over

---

21   Comrade Deng Xiaoping proposed the legislative policy of the 'coarse rather than fine' view of legislation, with the starting point of quickly resuming the construction of the legal system: 'Now the workload of legislation is very large, but in stark contrast is the very-little human resources. Therefore, the legal provisions in the beginning can be a little coarse, and then gradually improve one by one, some places can first try to make some laws and regulations, and then through the summary of the upgrading them to realize the development of the laws and regulations prevailing in all regions of the country, i.e. revising the provision one by one rather than waiting until the "complete set of law system" is established. In short, it's better to have than not to have, and it's better to get it done quickly than slowly.' (DENG XIAOPING, 邓小平文选 (People's Publishing House), vol. 2, Beijing, 1983, p.147.

22   '关于《中华人民共和国婚姻法修改（草案）》和《中华人民共和国国籍法（草案）》的说明' ('Explanation on the Amendment to the Marriage Law of the People's Republic of China (Draft) and Nationality Law of the People's Republic of China (Draft)') made by WU XINYU, Deputy Director of the Legal Affairs Committee of the Standing Committee of the National People's Congress, at the Third Session of the Fifth National People's Congress on 2 September 1980.

1986. Among them, 547,794 marriage and family cases were accepted.[23] In 1991, the courts nationwide concluded 191,013 civil cases, an increase of 59.63 per cent over 1987, and 873,863 divorce cases of first instance, an increase of 59.52 per cent over 1987.[24] The explosive growth of cases put enormous pressure on the work of the People's Courts, and gave birth to the Civil Procedure Law, in 1991. In this law, litigation was changed from mediation-oriented to 'voluntary and lawful mediation', with the principle of mediation considered to be unsuitable for a market economy, the responsibility of collecting and investigating evidence was changed from court-based to party-based, and the civil litigation model was considered to be shifting to an adversarial system.

The reform of the civil trial method within the People's Court system also began in the 1980s, and continues to this day, with the aim of strengthening and improving the courts' own mechanisms, giving full play to their trial functions, and formalising and standardising trial work. The first stage of the reform of the civil trial method is considered to have run from the holding of the 14th National Conference on Court Work, in 1988, to the convening of the 15th Party Congress, in 1997. In the first phase, the responsibility of proof of the parties was strengthened, and the court function was enhanced, the former to resolve 'the contradiction between the lack of trial power and the increasing number of cases faced by the courts at that time, and to free the courts from the heavy work of investigation and evidence collection through the implementation and enforcement of the responsibility of proof of the parties', and the latter to transfer the fact-finding activities previously carried out by the courts before the trial, to the trial itself.[25]

The revision of the rules of civil procedure and the reforms of the civil trial method that have been initiated within the People's Courts have been effective in dealing with the situation of the rapidly growing number of civil disputes. The Ma Xiwu Way of Trial was considered no longer appropriate to the new social environment, and was gradually marginalised, and judges sitting in on cases became the norm. In addition, Civil Procedure Law, in 1992, creatively stipulated a trial limit system, in which ordinary civil case procedures of the first instance need to be concluded within six months, and the situation that existed in the past, in which divorce cases were not decided for a long time, and dragged on for several years, no longer exists.

---

[23]   See Report on the Work of the Supreme People's Court (1988), available at <http://www. gov.cn/test/2008-03/27/content_929873.htm>, last accessed 10.02.2023.

[24]   See Report on the Work of the Supreme People's Court (1992), available at <http://www. gov.cn/test/2008-03/27/content_929905.htm>, last accessed 04.03.2023.

[25]   HUANG SONGYOU, '与时俱进的"两便原则" – – 民事审判改革的指导思想' ('The Up-To-Date Two-Convenience Principle: Guiding Ideas of Civil Trial Reform') (2002) 4, 人民司法 (People's Judicature) 21–22.

2.3. JUDICIAL INTERPRETATION BECOMES AN IMPORTANT SOURCE FOR HANDLING DIVORCE DISPUTES

The principle provisions of the Marriage Law 1980, and the legislative gaps left by it, are filled by the judicial interpretations of the Supreme People's Court, which provide the provisions for handling divorce cases, mainly including the specific conditions for deciding divorce, division of divorce property, and support of minor children after divorce.[26] In 1989, Specific Opinions of the Supreme People's Court on How the People's Court Hearing Divorce Cases Can Determine that the Relationship Between Husband and Wife Has Really Broken Down put forward 14 circumstances to determine the breakdown of a husband and wife's feelings, which are referred to as the 14 Articles. The biggest contribution of the 14 Articles is that they propose a number of specific circumstances under which divorce should be granted, which means that judges have more accurate guidelines for judging cases, and also that they are more efficient, and the biggest breakthrough of the 14 Articles was that divorce could now be granted to a party who is at fault,[27] which means that the principle of granting divorce has completely abandoned the 'Theory of Legitimate Reasons' of the past, and whether divorce is granted or not depends on whether the couple's mutual affection has really broken down. Of course, the promulgation of the 14 Articles may be one of the reasons for the continuous increase in the divorce rate. According to the National Bureau of Statistics, the number of divorcing couples (including registered divorce and litigation divorce) in 1989 was 753,000, and the number of divorcing couples in 2000 was 1,122,900; and the crude divorce rate rose from 0.68 per thousand in 1989, to 0.96 per thousand in 2000.[28]

---

26   The most commonly used include: '最高人民法院关于贯彻执行民事政策法律若干问题的意见' ('Opinions of the Supreme People's Court on Several Issues Concerning the Implementation of Civil Policy and Law'), 30 August 1984; '最高人民法院关于人民法院审理离婚案件如何认定夫妻感情确已破裂的若干具体意见' ('Specific Opinions of the Supreme People's Court on How the People's Court Hearing Divorce Cases Can Determine that the Relationship Between Husband and Wife Has Really Broken Down') in 1989; '最高人民法院关于人民法院审理离婚案件处理子女抚养问题的若干具体意见' ('Specific Opinions of the Supreme People's Court on the Handling of Child Support Issues in People's Courts Hearing Divorce Cases') in 1993; '最高人民法院关于人民法院审理离婚案件处理财产分割问题的若干具体意见' ('Specific Opinions of the Supreme People's Court on the Handling of Property Division Issues in Divorce Cases by the People's Courts') in 1993; etc.

27   Art. 8 of Specific Opinions of the Supreme People's Court on How the People's Court Hearing Divorce Cases Can Determine that the Relationship Between Husband and Wife Has Really Broken Down stipulated one of the circumstances in which divorce should be granted: when a party commits adultery with another person, or illegal cohabitation: if the at-fault party still feels no repentance after education, the no-fault party sues for divorce; or the at-fault party sues for divorce, but the other party does not agree to divorce, after criticism, education or discipline, or after the People's Court ruling not to divorce, and the fault party again sues for divorce with no possibility of reconciliation.

28   Source: National Bureau of Statistics of China, available at <https://data.stats.gov.cn/easyquery.htm?cn=C01>, last accessed 15.07.2023.

3. DIVORCE LEGAL PRACTICE FROM 2001 TO 2020

3.1. LEGISLATIVE FEATURES AND DIVORCE SYSTEM OF AMENDMENT TO THE MARRIAGE LAW 2001

China's economy, with its reform and opening up, has grown at a rapid pace, and the gross domestic product in 2001 had reached 110,86.31 billion yuan, 24.17 times the gross domestic product of 458.76 billion yuan in 1980. With the growth of the economy, and the fast transformation of social life, judicial trial reform was also in full swing, with the legislature amending the Marriage Law in 2001. The Amendment to the Marriage Law 2001 contains 51 Articles, and the main changes in the divorce system were as follows: (1) clarification of the specific circumstances for divorce (elevating some of the specific circumstances in the 14 Articles to law); (2) increasing provisions about rights to visit children (responding to the large number of disputes between spouses over children, after divorce in judicial practice); and (3) improvement of the divorce relief system (the divorce damage compensation system was added to the financial help for divorce, to allow for the punishment for the party at fault in the marriage, the domestic work compensation system was added), etc.

It is worth mentioning that the Marriage Registration Regulations, promulgated and implemented by the State Council in 2003, have made it easier to register divorces. As long as there is proper handling of the child support and property division, the marriage registration authority will neither conduct a substantive examination of the parties' divorce agreement nor be responsible for persuasion and reconciliation, and men and women can receive divorce certificates on the spot. Before that, a person needed a 'letter of introduction' to apply for a divorce, and had to wait for a review period (no more than one month) after filing.[29] The original intention of eliminating the review period was to standardise administrative practices, and to govern the haphazard charging practices of marriage registration authorities (before 2003, there were some marriage registration authorities that charged expedited fees for issuing divorce certificates on the spot). The nature of the administrative review period is different from that of the divorce cooling-off period in the Civil Code 2020. Influenced by the Marriage Registration Regulations, the number of administratively registered divorces soared from 691,000 couples in 2003[30] to 3.736 million couples in 2020,[31] an increase of 535 per cent in 18 years.

---

[29] See Arts. 14 and 16 of the Marriage Registration Regulations 1994.
[30] Source: Statistical Bulletin on the Development of Civil Affairs (2003), available at: <https://www.mca.gov.cn/article/sj/tjgb/200801/200801150093819.shtml>, last accessed 15.07.2023.
[31] Source: Statistical Bulletin on the Development of Civil Affairs (2020), available at: <https://images3.mca.gov.cn/www2017/file/202109/1631265147970.pdf>, last accessed 15.07.2023.

3.2. THE CONTRADICTION BETWEEN DIVORCE CASE TRIAL AND CIVIL LITIGATION REFORM

In 1997, the *Report of the 15th National Congress of the Communist Party of China* put forward the requirement of 'promoting judicial reform', and the Supreme People's Court progressed the reform of the civil trial method to a deeper reform of the civil trial system (including the reform of the court personnel system). Between 1999, when the Supreme People's Court issued the *Five-Year Reform Outline for the People's Courts* as a programmatic document for reform, and 2019, a total of five 'Five-Year Reform Outlines' were issued, and the current one is the *Fifth Five-Year Reform Outline for the People's Courts (2019–2023)*.

However, from the first Five-Year Reform, the reform of the civil trial style has been questioned by many. One aspect of this is the questioning of the direction of reform. For example, Gu Peidong maintained that academics' and practitioners' arguments for potentially making the judicial systems of Western countries the target model for the Chinese judicial system may be untenable, and warned that citing Western judicial systems and their practices in the reform may be counterproductive. He insisted that recognising and upholding the rule of law and the diversity of the judicial system is the basic philosophy of reform, and that 'the actual conditions of Chinese society and the actual requirements of Chinese social governance and social development should be used as the basis for studying and exploring the specific construction of China's judicial system'.[32] Another aspect is the questioning of whether the consequences of reform are in line with the Two-Convenience Principle,[33] considering that judicial reform 'unloaded' the burden on the courts, but gave more burdens to the party, i.e. the convenience has been given to the courts rather than the people.[34] In 2001, the Supreme People's Court promulgated the Certain Provisions on Evidence in Civil Litigation, and the ensuing Mo Zhaojun incident[35] has brought into question the

---

[32] Gu Peidong, '中国司法改革的宏观思考' ('Macro Thinking on China's Judicial Reform') (2000) 3, 法学研究 (Chinese Journal of Law) 15.

[33] The Two-Convenience Principle means that judicial work should facilitate the people's litigation and the courts' exercise of judicial power, with the former taking precedence over the latter. The Two-Convenience Principle is a fine tradition of our judicial work, reflecting the judicial philosophy of justice for the people.

[34] Ren Zhong, '改革开放40年：民事审判程序的变迁' ('40 Years of Reform and Opening Up: Changes in Civil Trial Procedures') (2018) 12, 河北法学 (Hebei Law Science) 13.

[35] In 2001, Judge Mo Zhaogun held a trial on a loan dispute. The plaintiff was in possession of the IOU, and the defendants (a couple) claimed that the plaintiff had used a knife to coerce them to write the IOU. After the trial, Mo Zhaogun ruled that the IOU was valid. The defendant couple committed suicide by taking poison outside the court. Later, the public security investigation found that the plaintiff had indeed used a knife to force the defendants to write the IOU.

strict time limits[36] and burden of proof in these provisions. These questions have led to different implementation of the time limit system by courts around the country, with most courts not fully implementing it, or not implementing it at all. Parties and judges often struggle with the time limits for proof in litigation, and the implementation is in a rather awkward situation.[37] It was not until the amendment of the Civil Procedure Law, in 2012, that the time limit for proof was fundamentally adjusted.[38]

Divorce cases apply the same civil procedure, and are not different because of the special status relationship between the parties or the complete lack of litigation experience of most parties in divorce cases, and so the reforms of the time limit of proof and burden of proof also affect divorce cases. In the general trend of procedural evidence acquisition, courts emphasise the written evidence of the parties, but often the truth is not available using documentary evidence (for example, evidence of abuse and violence in everyday life), which leads to a detachment of the requirements of evidence acquisition from reality.[39] The inability to prove fault further leads to less consideration of fault by the courts, which makes it difficult for the non-fault party to seek justice, and brings a strong sense of denial of justice. In addition, the issue of division of the joint property of the couple, and the issue of recognition and settlement of the joint debts of the couple, are also limited by the evidence system. According to the rule of who claims and who proves, the party who does not govern the common property of the couple at the time of divorce cannot claim the division of the common property, and the presumption rule of the common debt of the couple makes the party who has not raised the debt in the divorce proceeding, unable to prove that he or she has no connection with the debt, when facing the creditor's debit note.[40] The grievances and helplessness of ordinary people, without litigation

---

[36] The People's Court, according to the facts of the individual cases, is to specify the period of proof. In addition, the late submission of evidence is considered a waiver of the right to proof that the People's Court does not recognise in cross-examination. See Arts. 33 and 34 of Certain Provisions on Evidence in Civil Litigation of the Supreme People's Court, 2001.

[37] ZHANG WEIPING, '中国民事诉讼法立法四十年' ('Forty Years of Chinese Civil Procedure Law Legislation') (2018) 7, 法学 (Law Science) 52.

[38] A party can apply for an extension if he or she cannot complete the proof within the time limit of proof; the People's Court could order the party who submits evidence late to give reasons, and even if the reasons are not valid, it does not necessarily lead to a loss of rights. The 2012 amendments actually led to the loss of the importance of the time limit for proof.

[39] See HUANG ZONGZHI and WU RUOZHI, '取证程序的改革：离婚法的合理与不合理实践' ('Reform of Evidence Taking Procedures: Reasonable and Unreasonable Practice of Divorce Law') (2008) 1, 政法论坛 (Tribune of Political Science and Law) 7–8.

[40] Art. 24 of Interpretation of the Supreme People's Court on Several Issues Concerning the Application of the Marriage Law of the People's Republic of China (II)(2003) created the presumption rule of the common debt of the couple: debts incurred by one of the spouses in his or her personal name during the marriage shall be considered as joint debts of the spouses.

experience, in serious court hearings, as well as their disbelief and dissatisfaction with the trial results, have led to a number of extreme cases.[41]

3.3. REINTRODUCING MEDIATION AND INITIATING FAMILY TRIAL REFORM

After the 'mainly relying on mediation' period, from the 1950s to 1970s, the 'emphasising mediation' period, in the 1980s, and the 'voluntary and legal mediation' period, in the 1990s, the civil judicial mediation system has seen a revival at the beginning of this century. In 2004, the Supreme People's Court issued the Regulations on Several Issues Concerning the Civil Mediation Work of the People's Courts, which again emphasised the importance of mediation work. In 2005, the Decision on the Overall Strengthening of the Work of the People's Courts provided that 'the people's courts should conduct mediation throughout the process of hearing the case, so that mediation can be adopted when it is possible and judgment should be made when it is necessary so as to solve cases with such combination of mediation and judgment', which, in Several Opinions on Further Developing the Positive Role of Litigation Mediation in Building a Socialist Harmonious Society, in 2007, was established as a guideline for civil trial work. In 2010, Opinions on Further Implementing the Principle of 'Priority of Mediation and Combination of Mediation and Judgment' were issued, and these established the rule of 'priority of mediation'. In 2014, the Decision of the Central Committee of the Communist Party of China on Several Major Issues in Comprehensively Promoting the Rule of Law put forward the idea that fair justice should 'strive to make the people feel fairness and justice in every judicial case', requiring the improvement of the mechanism for preventing and resolving social conflicts and disputes, the improvement of the diversified dispute resolution mechanism, the strengthening of people's mediation organisations, and the improvement of the linkage system of people's mediation, administrative mediation and judicial mediation.

In 2016, the Supreme People's Court issued the Opinions on the Pilot Reform of Family Judgment Methods and Working Mechanisms. Due to the highly personal, sensitive and complex nature of family cases, family trial reform attempts to distinguish family cases from civil cases, and to explore the trial style and working mechanism suitable for marriage and family relations. The Supreme

---

41 The motives of the suspects for the murders of Judge Ma Caiyun in Beijing, in 2016, and retired Judge Fu Mingsheng in Guangxi, in 2017, both stemmed from family disputes. See Du Wanhua, '论深化家事审判方式和工作机制改革' ('On Deepening the Reform of Family Trial Mode and Working Mechanism') (2018) 2, 中国应用法学 (China Journal of Applied Jurisprudence) 4.

People's Court has selected 100 courts nationwide to carry out a two-year pilot project. Based on the summary of the pilot project, in 2018 the Supreme People's Court issued Opinions on Further Deepening the Reform of Family Trial Methods and Working Mechanisms (Trial) which clearly proposed that the trial of family cases should be different from general civil cases, requiring judges to 'effectively change their working methods, strengthen the judges' authority to explore, discretion and appropriate intervention in the parties' dispositions', and to correctly handle the relationship between protecting freedom of marriage and maintaining family stability. According to the Opinions above, the court can mediate on its own or entrust mediation to invited organisations or persons; establish a cooling-off period for divorce in litigation, with the consent of the parties; require the parties to declare common property in litigation; and investigate common property *ex officio*, etc. The family trial reform has, indeed, played an important role in maintaining the stability of marriage and family, promoting social harmony, and realising social functions.

3.4. EXPLORATION OF LEGISLATIVE JUDICIAL INTERPRETATION

Besides the Marriage Law 2001, the Supreme People's Court has issued several judicial interpretations to guide the work of matrimonial and family trials, among which the interpretation on the treatment of joint debts of husband and wife upon divorce has taken many twists and turns. The Interpretation of the Supreme People's Court of Several Issues on the Application of the Marriage Law (II), in 2003, stipulated that, during the marriage, unless otherwise provided by law, debts incurred by one of the spouses are joint debts. As 'indebted' parties who had no knowledge of the debt continued to press their claims, the Supreme People's Court amended the relevant provisions of the Interpretation above in 2017. However, the amendment does not eliminate the innocent indebtedness, and aggrieved parties still put a lot of pressure on the petition office and the People's Court. In 2018, the Supreme People's Court finally issued a special judicial interpretation for dealing with marital debts, which clarifies that debts raised jointly, debts raised by one of the parties for daily needs, and debts that creditors can prove that one of the spouses raised for the common life and common business of both parties, are joint debts.[42] Because it safeguards both the legitimate rights of creditors and the interests of the people, this judicial interpretation was eventually elevated to a provision of the Civil Code (Article 1064).

---

[42] Interpretation of the Supreme People's Court on Issues Relating to the Application of Law in the Trial of Cases Involving Disputes over Debts of Husband and Wife, 2018.

4. THE CIVIL CODE AND EXPECTATIONS FOR THE FUTURE OF DIVORCE LEGAL PRACTICE

4.1. LEGISLATIVE FEATURES AND DIVORCE SYSTEM OF THE MARRIAGE AND FAMILY PART OF THE CIVIL CODE IN 2020

In 2020, the Marriage Law and the Adoption Law were replaced by the Marriage and Family Part of the Civil Code, with 79 Articles. The Civil Code tightened the rules for administrative registration of divorce, increased the legal conditions for deciding divorce, and expanded the scope of application of the system of compensation for domestic work, etc. The changes are as follows:

1. Considering that administrative registration of divorce is too convenient, and frivolous divorce is difficult to avoid, the Civil Code, which came into force in 2021, adds a divorce cooling-off period system, during which couples are required to wait for one month after filing a divorce application, and if they still decide to divorce, they can obtain a divorce certificate by going to the marriage registration department together again, within one month of the expiration of the cooling-off period. One year after the implementation of the divorce cooling-off period system, 2.411 million divorces were registered by the civil affairs department (3.736 million in 2020), 698,000 divorces were decided and mediated by the court (603,000 in 2020), and the divorce rate was 2 per cent in 2021 (3.1 per cent in 2020).[43] Even excluding the effect of not registering divorces in the first month of the law, the number of registered divorces declined significantly more than the number of litigated divorces.

2. With regard to the maintenance of children after divorce, paragraph 3 of Article 1084 of the Civil Code specifies that 'the people's court shall adjudicate it in compliance with the principle of acting in the best interests of the minor child and in light of the actual situations of both parents', and that the opinions of children over eight years of age are also an important consideration, specifying that the divorce of parents does not affect the parent–child relationship, and that the interests of the minor shall prevail in the event of a conflict of interest between parents and minor children.

3. The scope of application of compensation for domestic work has been broadened by the Civil Code, i.e. by removing the previous requirement of compensation only applying to spouses with separate property.

---

43 Source: Statistical Bulletin on the Development of Civil Affairs (2021), available at <https://images3.mca.gov.cn/www2017/file/202208/2021mzsyfztjgb.pdf>, last accessed 15.07.2023.

4.2. EXPECTATIONS FOR THE FUTURE OF DIVORCE LAW PRACTICE

Firstly, it is necessary to further promote family trial reform. From the reform of the family trial method that has continued from 2016 to date, and the research results of the academic community, it is imperative to formulate an independent family special procedure law to systematically regulate family disputes according to their characteristics. Secondly, judicial civil mediation should have legal protection. The return of mediation is a requirement of the mass line in the judicial field, but also a requirement of the judicial concept of Chinese characteristics; that is, to serve the overall situation, and justice for the people.[44] However, the current rules concerning mediation are of a low rank, and it is recommended that they be stipulated in law, so as to ensure that the reform and improvement of mediation are carried out within a legal framework.

---

[44] Serving the overall situation means giving full play to the political role of justice in national and social governance, accepting the leadership of the Party in judicial work, and serving the overall situation of the Communist Party of China in the governance of the country. Justice for the people means that justice is people-centred, as serving the people wholeheartedly is the purpose of all the work of the Communist Party of China, and we should strive to make the people feel fair and just in every judicial case. See Art. 6 of the Regulations on Political and Legal Work of the Communist Party of China, issued by the Central Committee of the Communist Party of China, in 2019.

FRANCE

SOME REFLECTIONS ON 50 YEARS OF EVOLUTION OF FAMILY LAW THROUGH THE 'DEJUDICIARISATION' OF FRENCH FAMILY LAW

Hugues FULCHIRON*

Résumé

Phénomène marquant du droit français de la famille au cours des trente dernières années, la déjudiciarisation témoigne des évolutions du droit contemporain de la famille. Elle accompagne la reconstruction du règles juridiques régissant la famille sur les droits et libertés de l'individu, une place de plus en plus importante étant donnée à l'autonomie personnelle. Elle traduit également le redéploiement de l'action de l'Etat qui transfère à d'autres acteurs, mais aussi aux intéressés eux-mêmes à travers le contrat, le soin de réguler les relations familiales. Au-delà, elle conduit à s'interroger sur les nouvelles valeurs qui fondent le droit contemporain de la famille.

---

*   This chapter is dedicated to the memory of Marie-Thérèse Meulders-Klein and Jacqueline Rubellin-Devichi, who became friends through the International Society of Family Law, and who, with their own personalities and ideas, were able to analyse, put into perspective and, in some aspects, anticipate the great upheavals in family law at the end of the twentieth century.

1. DEJUDICIARISATION

'Dejudiciarisation' is now one of the main phenomena of French family law. The movement is general, and the policies of dejudiciarisation have been adopted by all the governments that have succeeded in France over the last 30 years. It affects all family law, both property law and non-property law.

'Dejudiciarisation' means, in a very broad sense, the implementation of measures designed to avoid judicial intervention, or to avoid the settlement of disputes by judges themselves, in civil as well as in criminal matters, by favouring the search for a consensual solution, or by entrusting other actors, public or private, to do so. In this sense, dejudiciarisation differs from deregulation, which tends to allow means of regulation other than the law, and in particular State laws. As we will see, it is not because there is dejudiciarisation that there is necessarily deregulation. One might even be tempted to say that the family has never been subject to more legal rules than it is today; the law is everywhere in the family. But it is no longer the judge who will necessarily implement it or ensure its respect.

This is a significant change because, unlike in many countries, in France the judge had a central role in the family. As a representative of society, he ensured the protection of the interests of the most vulnerable people: children, those made vulnerable by age or health, women. He also ensured the protection of a certain social order. Of course, this role was not recognised without some reluctance. Family matters are, above all, private matters. The intervention of the judge, as the representative of society, in the privacy of people, and, more broadly, in the life of the family group, was viewed by many with a certain amount of mistrust. The debates in the nineteenth and early twentieth centuries surrounding judicial control of paternal authority bear witness to this resistance. This is echoed today in the very strict rules governing the intervention of the children's judge[1] – particularly when parents' behaviour puts the child in danger – in domestic law, and in the case law of the European Court of Human Rights. It was also feared that, under the pretext of protection, the judge would be the instrument of control of families by society. The totalitarian regimes of the twentieth century showed that these concerns were not just a fantasy.

But in the event of conflict, or if a person did not fulfil his or her obligations towards the other members of the family, the intervention of the judge seemed to be a necessity: a judge as arbitrator, outside the family (in the collective imagination, the family courts set up by the French Revolution have left a bad memory); a judge to protect the most vulnerable; a judge to guarantee a certain 'family order'.

---

[1] This judge is a special judge in charge of children's issues.

More recently, under the influence of the social and human sciences, the family judge was given another function, that of calming conflicts and treating the ills of the family, particularly the ills of separation: a 'restorative' judge at the service of the family; a tutelary figure who says what is right, and before whom egoism must give way. This new mission, that of a judge coordinating a team of experts and social workers, has only reinforced the judge's role in the family. It should also be noted that, to avoid too much control over families, the legislator, following the advice of Jean Carbonnier, has always refused to entrust all family matters to a single judge. Of course, a judge of family affairs was created, and gradually the judge was entrusted with all separation disputes, for both married and unmarried couples. However, family matters remained divided between several judges: a judge of family affairs, a judge for children in difficulty, a guardianship judge for vulnerable persons, and a collegiate court for matters relating to personal status (marriage and filiation, in particular).

It is these various judicial functions – as guarantor of the social order, arbiter of conflicts, protector of the most vulnerable, and 'healer' of family ills – which reached their peak in the 1960s and 1970s, that are now affected by the phenomenon of dejudiciarisation. Matters that were once at the heart of the judicial role, such as parental authority, maintenance obligations or, even more spectacularly, divorce, are now at least partly lost to the courts. More and more space is left to the individual's will; other actors are invited to take over, either to accompany the parties with a view to reaching agreements (lawyers, notaries, social workers, mediators, etc.), or to take the place of the judge (the public prosecutor's office; the directors of the family allowance funds, in matters of alimony). Moreover, even when the judge retains his or her place, his or her role changes: often, it is less a matter of deciding than of guiding, reconciling and calming, in a permanent search for consensus.

The last 50 years have thus seen the transition from judges who constantly extended their hold on families – to decide, control and assist – to judges who are withdrawing, and whose offices are being modified.

The causes of this shift are multiple, and they are largely separate from the law, which in many ways only records the profound changes in society. Moreover, in these matters, the lawyer must remain cautious, in order not to reduce to simple items what is in reality very complex. However, two main lines can be drawn, which, in fact, largely overlap: individualisation and fundamentalisation, on the one hand (section 2); and privatisation and deregulation on the other (section 3).

2. INDIVIDUALISATION AND FUNDAMENTALISATION

To say that family law has become 'individualised' is to say that it is increasingly built around individuals: their rights and freedoms, their choices and their refusals. Things that are based on status (the major family institutions, such as marriage or inheritance reserves, but also hierarchical relationships within the family) are disappearing, giving instead an increasingly important place to the free choice of the person, and to the instrument which, in law, constitutes the vector of individual autonomy above all: the contract. In a matter that was previously dominated by the mandatory rule and framed by public order, it is in particular through the contract that the individual will now organise the structure of his or her family relationships. This autonomy, which has been won or granted (we shall come back to this) against status, and against the authorities traditionally responsible for ensuring the social control of individuals, in particular the judge, is reflected in an ever-greater freedom in the organisation of the 'constructed' and 'deconstructed' family relationships. At the same time, the judge is disappearing, at least in the 'imperative' sense, i.e. the one that gives the judge the power to say what is right; to order; to impose; and, more generally, to regulate relations within the family.

This can be seen, for example, in the importance given to agreements between spouses in matters of divorce (which led, in 2017, to the consecration of divorce without a judge), but also in matters of parental authority, and even parenthood, with the emergence of the 'parental project' as the basis for parenthood. This is also reflected in the favouring of alternative methods of conflict resolution: mediation, conciliation, participatory procedures and collaborative law are all based on the idea that people are free to make their own choices, and that a solution imposed by the judge should only be used if an agreement cannot be reached.

At the same time, one of the most striking phenomena of contemporary family law, and indeed of law as a whole, is its fundamentalisation. Family relations no longer arise from statutes forged by society: they are now based on the rights and freedoms of individuals, and, if necessary, restructured on this basis. In France, this development takes on a particular dimension because it is part of a twofold European perspective: that of the Council of Europe, with the rights guaranteed by the European Convention on Human Rights; and that of the European Union, with the rights and freedoms granted to European citizens. This fundamentalisation also opens up new fields for the autonomy of individuals, and profoundly modifies the role of the judge: the judge is no longer there to regulate the family, but to ensure the respect of the rights and freedoms of each person.

To put it another way, if the judge continues to play a central role in the family, it is because the judge is invested with a new function: the guardian of individual rights and freedoms. In this sense, the judge is still the guardian of a certain social order, but a renewed social order, at the service of the individual.

3. PRIVATISATION AND DEREGULATION

This phenomenon is closely linked to the previous one in its causes and effects, but it follows its own logic: the need for a reorganisation of State action, as the State withdraws, at least partially, from an area that is increasingly considered to be a matter of individual privacy.

3.1. PRIVATISATION

The time is no longer one for status and coercion, or at least for direct coercion: it is no longer possible to impose, on people, behavioural models whose authority would require a minimum of social consensus. And perhaps there is no longer any need for this: postmodern societies have learned to use other means to manage diversity, in order to ensure, in a new context, the minimum of order required for living in society.

At first, from the end of the nineteenth century to the 1990s, the instrument of this control seemed to be the intervention of the judge: the judge who arbitrates or the judge who decides; the judge who verifies that the interests of each person (and the collective interest) have been respected; the judge who ensures, through an authoritative decision, the legal force of the measures imposed and/or negotiated. But this interventionism of the judge in the private realm, which in its time gave rise to so much controversy, has finally shown its limits: the material limits of a justice system exhausting itself in conflicts that, in a way, feed on themselves; the legal limits of decisions that are difficult to enforce, given the risk of devaluing the justice system's image; and the social limits, because changes in behaviour and the need for autonomy are such that the judge no longer has real control over the situation.

These changes, added to economic constraints and, above all, to a certain social consensus around the 'private' nature of family matters (this old social consensus, which has always made the relationship between family and society a complex issue, and which, from one avatar to the next, is now being rebuilt on an individualistic basis), have led to various forms of disengagement from society and, above all, to the gradual 'exfiltration', if one dares to say so, of its representative: the judge. Nowadays, the judge's intervention tends to focus on emergencies and the protection of the most vulnerable people: women victims of violence, children, and vulnerable elderly people.

However, it would be wrong to speak of a 'withdrawal' of the law. The law remains, but in other forms – less imperative and perhaps less restrictive – and which, in any case, require the participation of the subject: in the absence of the power or desire to impose, we are moving towards a 'collaborative' regulation.

In this perspective, the contract appears, once again, as a particularly relevant instrument. Through the commitments made in and by the contract, through the formalism that surrounds it, through the mandatory rules that govern its formation and effects, and through the sanctions that apply to its non-execution, society has at its disposal a flexible and consensual means of managing the different forms of family life which, beyond the diversity and fragility of the relationships, makes it possible to ensure a minimum of security and predictability, not only for the persons concerned, but also for third parties and, more generally, for the community. More precisely, the law proposes different models and opens up the field of possibilities, while setting out a certain number of common principles. On this basis, it gives individuals the freedom to build their family relationships. But this freedom is doubly constrained: by the rules governing the formation and effects of the contract (if there really is a contract, which is sometimes doubtful, and most often it is an adhesion contract), and by the control exercised in the event of non-execution or incorrect execution.

Both divorce without a judge and registered partnership illustrate this ambivalence towards contractualisation, which is both a vector of autonomy and an instrument of social regulation. It is as if contemporary societies, noting that individuals were claiming more and more freedom, were renouncing the imperative in order to better achieve their minimum objectives of security and predictability, by using the instruments of autonomy to their advantage. In such a context, the judge can only take a back seat.

3.2. DEREGULATION

Privatisation is, in fact, combined with a phenomenon of 'deregulation'. Society no longer intends to control, through the judge, areas of privacy, because the legitimacy of judicial intervention in these areas is contested, and because it is considered no longer socially useful to exercise control in these areas, or at least to exercise this kind of control.

In addition to these sociological considerations, there are also economic reasons: in increasingly complex societies, and societies increasingly regulated by the law, recourse to a judge is becoming more and more common, both in civil and criminal matters. It therefore seems necessary to concentrate the judge's actions in areas where judicial intervention seems essential for living in society. What good is it if the judge is exhausted in managing conflicts that are not conflicts at all, or for which the judicial added value is minor? Consider the example of divorce: today, individuals claim a true 'right to divorce', and society recognises this. What is the sense of maintaining a judicial proceeding that consumes a part of the justice system's resources without any real added value? Of course, the purpose of the judge's intervention is to ensure that the interests of each party are preserved. But, some will say, can one claim a freedom and at the same time ask to be protected against the dangers linked to the exercise of this freedom? To express it even more bluntly, should society cover the cost of the exercise by individuals of their freedom? Would it not be better to concentrate its forces on what seems essential to its functioning today?

Such is the reflection undertaken by the Parliament over the last 20 years. One of the major Dejudiciarisation laws, the law of 18 November 2016 on 'the modernisation of justice in the twenty-first century', had as its leitmotiv the need to 'refocus the judges on their essential missions'. Over the years, this has resulted in the dejudiciarisation of divorce, with the creation of divorce without a judge, even if there are children; the simplification of the judicial divorce proceeding; the increasingly systematic referral to mediation; or the transfer of competence to other public or para-public authorities (the notary, for divorce without a judge, or for the collection of consent in matters of medically assisted procreation or adoption; the directors of the family allowance funds, in matters of maintenance obligations), or even to private actors (lawyers, mediators, and tomorrow perhaps arbitrators, i.e. a form of private justice).

The removal of the judge is, therefore, one of the manifestations of the redeployment of public action with a view to greater efficiency.

Dejudiciarisation of family law is, therefore, a sign of the changes in the family and its law over the last 50 years: a family rebuilt, as has been said, on the basis of individual rights and freedoms; a family largely open to individual choices, since it is true that a family without a judge is also a family that is not 'judged'; a family which, in order to live, calls for greater responsibility on the part of those who build it. If, in fact, individuals – freed from social constraints, freed from the control of the judge – forge their own rules by making their own choices, they are responsible for these choices. As the judge is disappearing, it is on the basis of the combination of freedom and responsibility that the family and its law must be considered today.

JAPAN

HISTORICAL DEVELOPMENT OF JAPANESE FAMILY LAW AND FAMILY POLICY

Ayako Harada*

* This contribution is a revised/updated version of 'Chapter 22: Family', previously published in I. Sato and M. Abe (eds.), *The Standard Textbook of the Sociology of Law (Standard Ho-shakaigaku)*, Kitaohji Shobo, 2022, pp. 213–222. This version is published with permission from Kitaohji Shobo. This work was supported by the Grant-in-Aid for Scientific Research (C) (18K01211) by the Japan Society for the Promotion of Science.

Résumé

Cet article décrit les développements historiques du droit de la famille et des politiques familiales japonais sous l'angle de la sociologie juridique. Après une brève introduction (première partie), la deuxième partie analyse la mise en place de politiques familiales et la reconnaissance par l'État d'un modèle familial ainsi que son intérêt pour la vie des familles. Il explique ensuite comment les modèles familiaux ont été prescrits par les codes civils d'avant-guerre et d'après-guerre au Japon. La troisième partie traite de l'évolution des réalités familiales d'après-guerre au Japon : la multiplication des familles dîtes « nucléaires » a soulevé de nouveaux problèmes qui ont nécessité des changements de politiques familiales, mais ceux-ci ne se sont pas produits assez rapidement. La quatrième partie de l'article plaide en faveur de l'évolution du droit et des politiques familiales japonais qui traitent des questions étroitement liées aux droits et à la dignité des individus dans la vie familiale. Le dernier chapitre conclut l'article par des propositions de recherches supplémentaires sur la vie, les lois et les politiques familiales contemporaines dans une perspective sociojuridique, en tenant compte des pratiques sociétales quotidiennes intéressant la vie des familles.

1. INTRODUCTION

Japanese research in sociology of law takes a keen interest in the family as a key area of research. This is because the family is intimately connected with the workings of the State and society. The family has been constructed on the basis of norms and models regulated and demanded by the State and society. Norms concerning the family emanate from the State and society at the public level – beyond individual human beings and families – and individual families have been formed and managed under the direct and indirect influence of these norms. Meanwhile, the family is also a private domain that allows individuals to enter intimate relationships with others and live their unique individual lives. Furthermore, the family's aspect as a free community can contribute to the formation of civil society. This private aspect of the family is established by the suppression or exclusion of intervention in the family in the public realm. However, in recent years, the boundary between the public and the private aspects of the family has been destabilised by the active intervention of the State and society, in resolving conflicts and protecting victims of violence within the family. Exploring family, which is multifaceted and intricately related to the State and society, should be an important part of sociology of law research. Beyond this is a wider field of research on the intersection of the public and the private in the modern legal order, and the elucidation of conflicts between the two.

2. STATE RECOGNITION OF THE FAMILY MODEL AND FAMILY POLICIES: FROM THE MEIJI TO THE POST-WAR PERIOD

2.1. STATE INTEREST IN FAMILY LIVES

The nature of the family and its activities tend to be easily recognised as natural, and as having endured for a long time. In reality, however, the nature of the family faces strong public and social constraints. The modern State has selected one form of family that is convenient for the State, among the diverse forms of family, creating a legal system and developing policies related to the family, which concern the family, and are based on that family image. The State and society pay attention to the family because the latter functions to create, nurture and educate its members, as well as to mediate the transmission of certain cultural forms, which is the basic condition for the survival of society. The family model set by the State has the policy goal of guiding family relations. Additionally, the State has sought to realise its policy goals by enacting family laws based on that model, and which can be applied in disputes, and while making judgments.[1] The next section gives an overview on the history of Japan's family policy from the perspective of the family model set by the State.

2.2. FAMILY MODEL UNDER THE PRE-WAR CIVIL CODE

The Meiji government created a government-sanctioned family system (called the *ie* system), by making the family order of the former samurai class an ideal family model, and adding to it the element of a family state with the emperor at the top.[2] The newly introduced family register (*koseki*) played a major role in the dissemination of this family system; it was compiled on a nationwide scale in 1872. In this register, a kinship group (household) was described as a unit, and those listed in a unit were catalogued in the order of noble and subordinate genus; lineal and collateral; male and female. These orders were written as relationships with the head of the household.[3] The family register system has been improved since then. It functions not only to help picturise the population, in order to implement measures, such as tax collection, conscription and school

---

[1]   N. Toshitani, *The Family and the State: Laws, Policies, and Ideas that Move the Family (Kazoku To Kokka: Kazoku O Ugokasu Ho, Seisaku, Shiso)*, Chikuma Shobo, 1987, p. 62.

[2]   T. Kawashima, 'Family System as an Ideology *(Ideorogi To Shiteno Kazoku Seido)*' in T. Kawashima, *The Familial Structure of Japanese Society (Nihon Shakai No Kazokuteki Kosei)*, Iwanami Shoten, 2000, pp. 150–238, 150–152 (first published in 1955).

[3]   S. Ninomiya, *Family Register and Human Rights (Koseki To Jinken)*, Kaiho Publishing, 2006, p. 37.

system administration, but also to manage the population: the behaviour of the family is managed by giving authority to the head of the household to report on changes in status, such as the birth and marriage of members. Thus, the family register system creates a family concept by having those listed in the same family register feel cohesion as a family.[4]

After fierce political and legal controversy over the Civil Code (the *Minpoten Ronso*), Japan's first modern Civil Code (Meiji Civil Code) was enacted and effectuated in 1898. The Meiji Civil Code defined a State-recognised family model as the family system already established by the family register system: a household was governed by the head of the household, and maintained permanently by inheritance.[5] The household recognised by the State was to be supported by a respect for the continuity of paternal lineage, subordination of women, a sense of the unity and survival of ancestors and descendants, and the superiority of the family over the individual.[6] This family model, and the sense of family, was convenient for the Meiji government, which sought to form a patriarchal national order led by the emperor. In family moral education, including the Imperial Rescript on Education, the State was likened to a household, so that loyalty to the country (emperor) and filial piety to parents were of the same nature (*chuko ippon*). Such a sense of family system could nurture loyal citizens (subjects) who would serve the family and the State.[7] Authoritarian human relations modelled on patriarchy served as a model for social relations other than the family, including employment relations.[8] It enabled the procurement of cheap and obedient labour, and supported the nation's policy of industrial development. Under the wartime system of national mobilisation, the crackdown on speech and behaviours deemed contrary to family morality was strengthened, and blatant interventions in the family were carried out to foster human resources for the waging of total war.[9] Subsequently, family policy from the Meiji era to the pre-war period defined the family according to the needs of State management, and imposed top-down control over the family and the individual.

2.3. FAMILY MODEL UNDER THE POST-WAR CIVIL CODE

Following Japan's defeat in World War II, the family system was transformed, as part of major reforms concerning the political and legal system. Article 24 of

---

[4]   See ibid., at p. 37. See also TOSHITANI, above n. 1, at pp. 141–148.

[5]   See TOSHITANI, above n. 1, at p. 70.

[6]   See KAWASHIMA, above n. 2, at pp. 155–156.

[7]   Ibid., at pp. 164–170.

[8]   T. KAWASHIMA, 'The Familial Structure of Japanese Society (*Nihon Shakai No Kazokuteki Kosei*)' in T. KAWASHIMA, *The Familial Structure of Japanese Society (Nihon Shakai No Kazokuteki Kosei)*, Iwanami Shoten, 2000, pp. 1–30, 16–23 (first published in 1946).

[9]   See TOSHITANI, above n. 1, at pp. 77–80.

the Japanese Constitution of 1946 stipulates that the laws concerning the family shall be enacted from the standpoint of 'individual dignity and the essential equality of the sexes'. Accordingly, the family system under the Civil Code was abolished, and major revisions were made, such as equal rights for men and women, abolition of patriarchal inheritance, and adoption of a system of equal inheritance (Civil Code amended in 1948). The new family model in post-war family law was the 'modern nuclear family', comprising a married couple and their children.[10] The married couple had to hold the same surname, either the husband's or wife's, under the Civil Code. The principle of family register organisation was changed to the unit of husband and wife and unmarried children with the same surname. However, as a compromise with conservatives in the legislative process, the Civil Code included provisions for clan and ritual succession, and for obligations to support family members, maintaining the system of registering persons with the same surname in family-unit registers, as a remnant of the *ie* system in the new Civil Code.[11] Conservatives continued to resist the family model based on individual freedom and equality, pushing debate on the possible revision of Article 24 of the Constitution. A counterargument was that the democratisation of post-war Japan would not be realised until people overcame the pre-war feudal family system.[12] As described in the next section, as the new family model became more entrenched in Japanese society, arguments for constitutional reform could not gain adequate support, even within the administration. Consequently, the Japanese Constitution, including Article 24, was preserved.[13]

Thus, the Japanese family was transformed under the philosophy of the dignity of the individual and the essential equality of the sexes in the Japanese Constitution, and the 'modern nuclear family' model in the post-war Civil Code, as elucidated in the next section.

3. CHANGING REALITY OF POST-WAR FAMILY LIVES: 'MODERN NUCLEAR FAMILY' MODEL AND REALITY

3.1. EXPANSION OF THE MODERN NUCLEAR FAMILY AND NEW ISSUES

After the war, families rapidly embraced the 'modern nuclear family', not only as an idea, but also in reality. Most people married at a certain age and had a couple of children; the wife managed the home and took care of the family and

---

[10]   See Toshitani, above n. 1, at p. 81.
[11]   See Toshitani, above n. 1, at p. 84.
[12]   See Kawashima, 'The Familial Structure of Japanese Society', above n. 8, at p. 23.
[13]   M. Tsujimura, *The Constitution and the Family (Kenpo To Kazoku)*, Nihon Kajo Publishing, 2016, pp. 325–326.

housework, while the husband worked long corporate hours. More and more nuclear families adapted to this division of labour between men and women – 'men at work, women at home' – leading to the nuclear family's wide popularity in Japan, for the first time in history.[14]

Until around the 1970s, post-war families were handling childcare and the care of older adults through cooperation with three-generation households and relatives; however, with the increase in the number of nuclear families, and the advancement of women in society, it gradually became impossible to carry this burden. Families became weak and faced serious problems, such as marital conflicts and parent–child friction, making it impossible to exercise their family functions without the support of social measures.[15] Nevertheless, the government advocated a 'Japan-type welfare society (*nihongata fukushi shakai*)' theory that differed from those of Western welfare states: it regarded the family as 'an additional welfare asset', and curbed the expansion of social security expenses by continuing to impose care responsibilities on the family.[16] In turn, protecting the position of women as wives, mothers and daughters-in-law who shouldered care responsibilities under the division of labour between men and women emerged as an issue in family law policy. Through the revision of inheritance legislation, in 1980, to protect spouses, which included the increased distribution of inherited assets for bereaved spouses in the statutory inheritance, and the legal restriction of divorce requests from a spouse who was deemed to be responsible for the breakdown of marriage through judicial precedents, the State sought to protect the 'wife's position as a full-time housewife'.[17]

As the period of high economic growth ended in the 1970s, women's entry into the labour market progressed further. In 1985, the Act on Equal Opportunity of Men and Women in Employment was enacted, but the majority of women workers were selected as non-career employees by a course-specific hiring practice. Under such practice, women in career-track positions were required to work on a par with men, including long working hours and transfers, making it difficult for them to balance work with family life. However, instead of pursuing gender equality in labour, the government promoted the tendency of women to assume the role of housewives, and to work only to the extent that it did not harm this role. It did so through various measures, such as tax

---

[14] E. OCHIAI, *Towards the 21st-Century Family: The Postwar Family System and its Transformation (21 Seiki Kazoku E: Kazoku No Sengotaisei No Mikata Koekata)*, Yuhikaku, 4th ed., 2019, pp. 11–28.

[15] S. HARADA, 'The Family Model in "Japan-Type Welfare Society" Theory: In the Context of Family Policy and the Direction of Legislative Development *(Nihongata Fukushi Shakai Ron No Kazokuzo: Kazoku O Meguru Seisaku To Ho No Tenkai Hoko Tono Kanren De)*' in THE UNIVERSITY OF TOKYO INSTITUTE OF SOCIAL SCIENCE (ed.), *The Welfare State at a Turning Point (Tenkanki No Fukushi Kokka)*, Book 2, University of Tokyo Press, 1988, pp. 303–392, p. 310.

[16] Ibid., pp. 378–380.

[17] Ibid., p. 353.

incentives for part-time work, and a national pension system that guaranteed a basic pension for unemployed or low-income persons, namely women, as their spouse's dependents.[18] Subsequently, firms could secure an inexpensive non-regular labour force, comprising women to whom employment adjustments could easily be applied.[19] In this way, a new gender division of labour was established – 'men at work, women at home and at work' – a system maintained by people's, especially women's, consciousness of the importance of family.[20]

Under this new gender division of labour, even if women worked, the main breadwinners were the men; women were employed mainly in part-time roles. In the 1990s, as the deregulation of employment and labour progressed, and non-regular employment spread from women to men, it became difficult for young people to start families. When corporate bankruptcies and layoffs became more common, in the prolonged recession, even the middle class came to see family life as a risk, and the trend toward non-marriage and late marriage progressed. Meanwhile, people diversified their lifestyles: for example, couples now wanted to keep their individual surnames, and did not want to marry legally (or could not, even if they wanted to). The diversification of families progressed to a certain extent. Movement to review discrimination and prejudice against sexual minorities picked up pace. In spite of the many limitations of the legal system, new administrative mechanisms for public recognition of same-sex couples, such as local government partnership certificates, were created.

3.2. DELAYS IN POLICY RESPONSES TO DIVERSIFYING AND INDIVIDUALISING FAMILY REALITIES

The modern nuclear family as the standard family model began to falter, and in the latter half of the 1980s, late marriages, non-marriage and single-person households gradually became more noticeably prevalent. The total fertility rate, referring to the average number of children a woman would give birth to in her lifetime, reached an all-time low of 1.26 in 2005. From the 1980s onwards, the divorce rate rose considerably; in 2003, it reached a post-war high of 2.3 per 1,000 people. The number of couples who remarried after divorce increased, and stepfamily structures were no longer uncommon. Japanese society has transformed into a society in which the majority of people live in other family constellations or alone, rather than in a first-marriage nuclear family, which was once regarded as the standard.

---

[18]   Ibid., p. 383.
[19]   Ibid., p. 351.
[20]   Y. EHARA, 'Changes in Women's Consciousness and Their Impact on the Family: From the Viewpoint of Feminism *(Josei No Ishiki Henka To Kazoku Eno Eikyo: Feminizumu No Kanten Kara)*' (1994) 46 *Journal of Sociology of Law (Hoshakaigaku)* 117, 118–119.

In the 1960s, new trends, such as increases in divorce, cohabitation and children born out of wedlock, along with a decline in the birth rate, and the pervasiveness of dual-income households, became conspicuous in advanced Western countries. In response to the transformation of family realities, legal amendments were made, such as wider availability of no-fault divorce, legal recognition and protection for couples who live together without marriage, and the elimination of discrimination against children born out of wedlock. An increasing number of countries recognised legal effects with regard to same-sex couples or same-sex marriage.[21] Gender equality measures in labour progressed, and to support these, governments reduced the burden of family care by enhancing social welfare and commercial care.[22] Through this series of reforms, various lifestyles once regarded as 'deviations' from standard family life have been normalised and accepted with legal approval. Furthermore, as people moved across borders more frequently, the internationalisation of family relations progressed considerably.[23]

In Japan, in response to changes in families, and growing awareness of human rights, discussions on reviewing family law provisions in the Civil Code intensified from around the latter half of the 1980s. The 1996 Civil Code Amendment Proposal (*Minpo Kaisei Yoko*) was the result of such discussions. Although a major revision of the law in response to changes in the family was proposed, such as the recognition of marriage with different surnames of spouses, the principle of no-fault as the main legal cause of divorce, and an expansion of provisions concerning custody of children after divorce, it was blocked by opposing conservative politicians, and was not submitted as a bill. While Japanese families are diversifying, the government's family policy continues to assume that a family consists of a first-marriage couple and their children. Reforms that approve of diverse families have been inadequate. In terms of values, the 'traditionalisation of modernity', which misunderstands the modern family model as being a Japanese and Asian tradition, although it first became common during the post-war period of high economic growth, has become a drag on reform.[24] While the tax and social security systems provide generous subsidies to 'standard households' of male breadwinners, full-time housewives and children, the redistribution to different types of families such as

---

21   See J. COMMAILLE (translated by S. MARUYAMA and G. TAKAMURA), *The Political Sociology of the Family: Individualization and Society in Europe (Kazoku No Seiji Shakaigaku: Yoroppa No Kojinka To Shakai)*, Ochanomizu Shobo, 2002.

22   See E. ESPIN-ANDERSEN, *The Three Worlds of Welfare Capitalism*, Polity Press, 1990.

23   See U. BECK and E. BECK-GERNSHEIM, *Distant Love*, Polity Press, 2014.

24   E. OCHIAI, 'The 1980s as a Stumbling Block: Human Reproduction of the "Shrinking Postwar System" *(Tumazuki No Ishi To Shiteno 1980 Nendai: "Chizinda Sengotaisei" No Ningen Saiseisan)*' in A. GORDON and K. TAKII (eds.), *Toward an Emerging Japan: Post-'Lost Two Decades' Sketches (Sohatsu Suru Nihon E: Posuto 'Usinawareta 20 Nen' No Dessan)*, Kobundo, 2018, pp. 95–135, 112–113.

single-parent households is weak, with child poverty in these households being neglected or exacerbated.

4. FUTURE PROSPECTS FOR FAMILY AND FAMILY POLICY: SHIFTING PERCEPTIONS ON THE INDIVIDUALS IN THE FAMILY

4.1. NEED FOR AN INDIVIDUAL-BASED FAMILY POLICY

In the future of family law and family policy, the government must consider the nature of the family as a matter of individual choice, and design a fair system wherein individuals are treated equally. Since the 1990s, Japan has increasingly seen a 'constitutionalisation of family law',[25] which proposes a critical examination of family law and family policy from the perspective of constitutional ideals, namely individual human rights and equality.[26] In some cases, judicial decisions have led to legal revisions, such as the Supreme Court ruling the following matters unconstitutional: discrimination concerning children born out of wedlock acquiring nationality,[27] discrimination against children born out of wedlock inheriting,[28] and the period of prohibition on women's remarriage exceeding 100 days after divorce.[29] While these judicial developments can be appreciated as

---

[25] See Tsujimura, above n. 13, at p. 3.

[26] Ibid., at pp. 152–320.

[27] This case concerned a distinction in granting Japanese nationality under Art. 3, para. 1 of the Nationality Act, which provided that a child born out of wedlock to a Japanese father and a non-Japanese mother, and acknowledged by the father after birth, may acquire Japanese nationality only if the child has acquired the status of a child born in wedlock as a result of the marriage of the parents. The Supreme Court declared such legal distinction unconstitutional because it was against Art. 14, para. 1 of the Constitution, which stipulates the people's equality under the law and prohibition of discrimination. See 2008. 06. 04, 2006 (Gyo-Tsu) 135, Minshu vol. 62, no. 6.

[28] This case concerned the constitutionality of the provision of Art. 900 of the Civil Code, which provided that a child born out of wedlock was entitled to inherit only half the value of assets accorded to a legitimate child. The Supreme Court declared such a distinction unconstitutional, due to its violation of Art. 14, para. 1 of the Constitution. See 2013. 09. 04, 2012 (Ku) 984, Minshu vol. 67, no. 6.

[29] This case concerned the constitutionality of the provision of Art. 733, para. 1 of the Civil Code, which prescribed the six-month period of prohibition of remarriage for women. The Supreme Court recognised the necessity of the ban on remarriage to avoid conflicted paternity presumptions, but it also declared that such prohibition exceeding 100 days violated Art. 14, para. 1, which stipulates the people's equality under the law and prohibition of discrimination, as well as Art. 24, para. 2 of the Constitution, which stipulates that laws concerning family shall be enacted from the standpoint of individual dignity and the essential equality of the sexes. See 2015. 12. 16, 2013 (O) 1079, Minshu vol. 69, no. 8. After this Supreme Court decision was made, Art. 733, para. 1 was amended in 2016 to shorten the remarriage prohibition period from 6 months to 100 days. However, discussion continued

pressing for the reform of family law and policy, which would have been difficult to achieve under a conservative administration, the legislature still should be in a position to arouse public debate and engage in reform of the future state of family policy, using those judicial decisions as an opportunity to invigorate its role.

Given that family law and policy need to be reviewed and reformed in terms of individual dignity and human rights guarantees, it is necessary to seriously consider the significance of such individual-based development of family law and policy in a more concrete manner: specifically, three aspects – national sustainability, family violence and conflict, and democratisation of the family – merit consideration.

4.2. NATIONAL SUSTAINABILITY

Population decline owing to a declining birth rate has been threatening the Japanese nation. A major reason for this has been argued to be the familialism that is seen in the familial welfare policy of placing the majority of childcare and nursing care responsibilities on the family.[30] As such, the population recovery of Japan may be achieved by shifting away from conventional familial welfare policy, enhancing social security for the child-rearing generation, and ensuring that support is available to all children and caregivers, regardless of family status. Other Asian countries that experienced a significant decline in birth rate under familial welfare policies have recently seen, at least to some extent, trends suggesting departure from the familialism.[31]

Simultaneously, regarding respect for the individual, situations that encourage interference with, and oppression of, individuals over reproduction must be avoided. In recent years, the development of assisted reproductive technology has given people greater chances to have children. From the viewpoint of population policy, there is a growing debate on improving access to assisted reproductive technology through public subsidies and other means. However, reproductive choices are not always made voluntarily by women, and increased social pressure to use assisted reproductive technologies may threaten individual choice. Moreover, with the development of reproductive technology, it is more likely that adults will have more power to control the fate of children. Children

over the rationality of such prohibition and, eventually, the amendment of the Civil Code in 2022 modified the rule of paternity presumption for children born after maternal remarriage (the modified rule presumes a child born after the mother's remarriage only to be a legitimate child of the husband of the remarriage) and entirely abolished the remarriage prohibition period for women. The amendment will be in force on 1 April 2024.

30   See Espin-Andersen, above n. 22.
31   See Ochiai, 'The 1980s as a Stumbling Block', above n. 24, at p. 123.

must be guaranteed their rights as independent individuals, and the right to know their origins, especially where their conception involves reproductive donors and surrogate mothers. Furthermore, guaranteeing the rights of unborn children should be considered in the construction of systems relating to the use of assisted reproductive technology.

4.3. DEALING WITH FAMILY VIOLENCE AND CONFLICT

When the State or society deals with violence and intra-family conflicts, intervention and support is necessary, focusing on the unique needs of individual family members and their individual relationships with other family members, rather than treating the family as a single unit. In Europe and the United States, civil and family law have played a central role in this regard. In Japan, while the ideological nature of civil law is strong, in that it displays an ideal family model, it has blank provisions that leave dispute resolution to discussions between the parties concerned, with the law functioning weakly in terms of providing clear and specific guidelines for the protection of the vulnerable.[32] In the 2000s, however, Japanese laws were enacted to deal with family violence or abuse, such as child abuse, spousal abuse and elder abuse, and related laws and regulations were established, including the reformed Civil Code provisions on legally restricting the parental authority of abusive parents, and the adult guardianship system to protect older adults against economic abuse.[33] Both the administration and the judiciary played their respective roles in establishing a system for intervention and support provision. This protection for the vulnerable in the family indicates that, even in Japan, the State is changing the public order of the family, from a 'political public order', which defines the nature of the family, to a 'protective public order', for the protection of individuals.[34]

Nevertheless, if the State intervenes directly into the family, even to protect the vulnerable, the risk of the destruction of the private aspect of the family increases. While respecting the individuals subject to intervention as autonomous problem-solving agents, it is necessary to establish a system that supports recovery from violence, and rebuilding safe family relations. In the case of family disputes, such as divorce, a comprehensive support system should be

---

[32] N. MIZUNO, 'The Current Civil Code of Japan as Seen from a Comparative Perspective: Family Law (*Hikakuho Teki Ni Mita Genzai No Nihon Minpo: Kazoku Ho*)' in T. HIRONAKA and E. HOSHINO (eds.), *Centennial of the Civil Code, vol. I., General Discussions (Minpoten No Hyakunen, I. Zentaiteki Kansatsu)*, Yuhikaku, 1998, pp. 651–690.

[33] For the development of child protection law in Japan, see A. HARADA, 'The Japanese Child Protection System: Developments in the Laws and the Issues Left Unsolved' in B. ATKIN (ed.), *International Survey of Family Law: 2010 Edition*, Jordan Publishing, 2010, pp. 217–235.

[34] K. YOSHIDA, 'Reorganization of "Public and Private" in the Family (*Kazoku Ni Okeru "Koshi" No Saihen)*', *Annals of the Philosophy of Law (Ho Tetsugaku Nenpo)*, 2000, pp. 45–61.

constructed, such that the parties receive the necessary services to empower them to actively work for the resolution of their issues.[35] Institutionally, the challenge is twofold: to expand support through the courts for parties in public dispute resolution, and to establish dispute resolution support mechanisms closely linked to everyday family life. From the viewpoint of the organic combination of the two, there is a growing need to re-examine the function of agreement facilitation within the court-annexed family conciliation system, which has functioned as a node intersecting public and private aspects in the process of family dispute resolution.[36]

4.4. DEMOCRATISING THE FAMILY

In a society where the nature of intimate relationships with close family members is left to individual choice, intimate relationships with others (pure relationships, as Giddens describes them), rather than compatibility with existing family systems and behavioural patterns, are valued and pursued.[37] However, pure relationships are fragile, and the more they are pursued, the more unstable they become. Ultimately, problems may arise with stratification, in which the economic power and attractiveness of individuals dominate the creation of intimate relationships.[38] Even in everyday family life, complex and delicate adjustments are required to reconcile the wishes and interests of each family member, and failure can lead to the collapse of the family. However, from another point of view, the modern family is becoming a place where members recognise one another's autonomy, and conduct family life while fully negotiating it with one another. In a free and equal relationship, the path to the democratisation of the family is open, with each person making and negotiating their own decisions.[39]

In political science, research on the possibility of democracy in the family has examined the obstacles to deliberation arising from the nature of the intimate sphere, such as the closed nature of the forum for debate, and inequality

---

[35]   S. Minamikata and T. Tamaki, 'Support and Needs of Parties in Divorce Issues: Based on Field Research *(Rikon Mondai Ni Okeru Tojisha Shien To Nizu: Jittai Chosa O Sozai To Shite)*' (2013) 29 *Socio-legal Studies on Family Law (Kazoku Shakai To Ho)* 79.

[36]   A. Harada, 'Family Reorganization in the Japanese Family Conciliation System: Resolving Divorce Disputes Involving Minor Children' (2019) 33(1) *International Journal of Law, Policy and the Family* 75. See also T. Inada, *Theory of Family Conciliation and Discussion between Parties (Kaji Chotei Kyogi Ron)*, Shinzansha, 2021.

[37]   A. Giddens, *The Transformation of Intimacy: Love, Sexuality, and Eroticism in Modern Societies*, Polity Press, 1992.

[38]   M. Yamada, 'Individualization of the Family *(Kazoku No Kojin Ka)*' (2004) 54(4) *Japanese Sociological Review (Shakaigaku Hyoron)* 341.

[39]   See Giddens, above n. 37. See also Commaille, above n. 21.

among members, and the means to overcome these hurdles.[40] Moreover, from the perspective of the private, such as the personal identity and self-esteem formed in intimate relationships, as well as care and dependency needs, there is an ongoing debate on re-examining the concepts of 'individual', 'autonomy' and 'freedom' in the public, and on reframing human care, which has been trapped in the private sphere, as a public issue.[41] As a social practice, for example, Pacte civil de solidarité (Pacs), a legal partnership system in France, became possible when same-sex couples turned their private problems into political issues, and tied them to social movements.[42] In this way, the possibility of the family as a private sphere that approaches the public one is gaining traction, presenting a new way in which the 'public' can operate.

5. CONCLUSION

The modern family is characterised by the diversification of individual choices regarding the family, under the specific socio-economic conditions and constraints behind individual choices, and by the increasing complexity and instability of human relationships within the family. Multidirectional changes and developments can be observed in the rapidly changing social environment, such as the existence of conflict and violence in the family, and the need to respond to it, along with the internationalisation of family relationships. Amid such complex circumstances, an in-depth consideration of the family is needed, to examine concretely how family-related problems arise, and how people are legally and socially required to deal with them. Instead of presenting a specific 'ideal family' and regulating family relationships based on this ideal, the State needs to develop family law policies that recognise and include diverse family forms, while strengthening the function of individual problem-solving, especially for the protection of vulnerable family members, such as children. This is not so that the 'public' unilaterally regulates the 'private', nor that the 'public' entrusts the family completely to the 'private'; rather, the two spheres should be organically connected, such that the individuals living in any social situations can autonomically create their family lives with others. The relation between the family and the State must be in accordance with contemporary circumstances. The sociology of law, as a field, can expect an even greater need for family research that can contribute to discussions from this perspective.

---

[40] T. TAMURA, *Deliberative Difficulties and Beyond (Jukugi Minshushugi No Konnan: Sono Norikoe Kata No Seiji Rironteki Kosatsu)*, Nakanishiya Publishing, 2017.

[41] See E.F. KITTAY, Y. OKANO and K. MUTA, (eds.), *Theory of Justice from the Ethics of Care: Mutual Equality (Kea No Rinri Kara Hajimeru Seigi Ron: Sasaeau Byodo)*, Hakutakusha, 2011.

[42] See COMMAILLE, above n. 21, pp. 64–65.

Finally, it should be emphasised that the activity of studying, or thinking deeply about, family is not one that researchers should monopolise. Each one of us, as citizens, thinks about our families, based on our own experiences and observations of society. Practicing family life in one's own way directly affects how family works in our society. From this perspective, I would like to ask the following questions to my readers: (1) how should we view the 'diversification' of the family? Are families indeed 'diversifying', when you look at it from the two perspectives of the reality and the ideality of families? (2) If the modern family is, either actually or potentially, a gathering of 'individuals' of different generations and genders (not only sexes, but also sexual orientations and gender identifications), each with their own values and life goals, what are the conditions for such a family to live cooperatively while respecting one another? By facing these simple, familiar, but rather difficult questions about family head-on, we can inspect our views about contemporary family lives and relations.

PORTUGAL

50 YEARS OF PORTUGUESE FAMILY LAW

The Paths We have Followed

Paula Távora Vítor

Résumé

La longévité de la Société Internationale de Droit de la Famille (ISFL) – les 50 dernières années – permet de saisir certains des changements les plus importants du droit de la famille portugais, du processus quasiment tectonique que les exigences d'une démocratie naissante ont provoqué, aux aménagements les plus récents des valeurs qui gouvernent aujourd'hui la vie familiale et le droit de la famille.

En effet, lorsque l'ISFL a été fondée, en 1973, le Portugal vivait encore sous un régime dictatorial et le droit de la famille défini par le code civil de 1966 reflétait cet environnement – en accordant, par exemple, un rôle prépondérant au mari dans le mariage et en discriminant les enfants nés hors mariage. Toutefois, l'année suivante, le changement de régime politique a entraîné l'adoption d'une nouvelle Constitution démocratique qui est rapidement entrée en vigueur (en 1976) et qui a consacré un ensemble de droits et de libertés fondamentaux, sous l'égide du principe d'égalité. La réforme de 1977, qui a adapté le Code civil à la nouvelle Constitution, a profondément remanié le droit de la famille à la lumière de ces nouvelles règles et valeurs.

Depuis lors, non seulement les relations familiales traditionnelles ont été considérablement remodelées, mais de nouvelles relations familiales ont également été reconnues.

Dans cet article, je me propose d'analyser cette évolution au regard de trois différents domaines du droit de la famille afin de comprendre les voies choisies par le législateur portugais.

Tout d'abord, je me concentrerai sur la vie de couple – sur le mariage, qui constituait auparavant le noyau du droit de la famille, et sur l'importance croissante du nouveau mode de vie en couple que constitue l'union de fait. Tant dans le régime du mariage (depuis sa constitution – désormais ouverte aux couples de même sexe – jusqu'à son extinction) que dans le mouvement lent, mais régulier, de consécration juridique de l'union de fait et de la possibilité de vivre en couple dans des conditions différentes, nous parcourrons le chemin de la liberté et de l'égalité.

Ensuite, j'aborderai l'effervescent domaine de la filiation – depuis les profonds changements apportés par la réforme de 1977, qui a consacré le principe de la vérité biologique comme principe supérieur pour l'établissement de la filiation, jusqu'aux nouvelles solutions apportées par la loi en matière de procréation médicalement assistée, qui souligne le rôle du consentement et choisit comme fondement de la filiation la volonté de devenir parent pour les bénéficiaires de ces techniques. Nous parcourrons le chemin de la vérité (définie et redéfinie).

Enfin, j'aborderai les relations entre les enfants et leurs parents (et les personnes qui s'occupent d'eux), *i.e.* l'exercice de l'autorité parentale. Je me concentrerai sur le remodelage de ces relations fondé sur une conception démocratique de la famille, sur la prise en compte de l'intérêt supérieur de l'enfant comme valeur primordiale (ce qui conduit à inclure de nouvelles figures familiales en tant que responsables de la prise en charge de l'enfant et en tant que personne ayant des liens étroits avec l'enfant) et sur l'adoption du principe d'autonomie progressive et de capacité évolutive de l'enfant, qui nous ont permis de parcourir un chemin vers l'autonomie.

1. INTRODUCTION

Fifty years have elapsed since the founding of the International Society of Family Law (ISFL), a time period also corresponding to some of the most significant changes ever made to Portuguese family law, ranging from the tectonic process that the demands of a new-born democracy caused, to the most recent evolutions of values governing both family life and family law.

Indeed, when the ISFL was founded in 1973, Portugal was still under a dictatorial regime, and the family law adopted in the 1966 Civil Code (CC)[1] reflected that political environment. However, in the following year,[2] the change of political regime demanded a new democratic constitution, which soon entered into force.[3] The reform of 1977[4] that adapted the Civil Code to the new 1976 Constitution deeply redesigned Portuguese family law according to these new rules and values, and provided the present structural framework of Portuguese family law. This reform may be encapsulated in two ideas: conformity with the Principles of Family Law and the Principle of Equality enshrined in the Constitution, and respect for the fundamental rights of citizens, even within the most private area of their lives – family life.

The Principle of Equality required the abandonment of hierarchic verticality in the legal regimes of the relations between husband and wife, and between parents and children. And these ideas continued to be strengthened from then on. Since that moment, not only have traditional family relations been subject to a considerable reshaping, but new family relations have also been recognised.

The goal of this chapter is to analyse this evolution, taking into account three different fields that encompass (most of) family law – life as a couple, determination of parenthood, and the relations between children and their parents – and to try to identify the paths chosen by Portuguese family law.

2. THE PATHS OF FAMILY LAW

2.1. LIFE AS A COUPLE: THE PATH TO FREEDOM AND EQUALITY

2.1.1. *Marriage*

It is not surprising that the first field to be explored is 'life as a couple'. When the ISFL was founded, in 1973, the only form of life as a couple that was relevant for family law, under the original version of Portugal's Civil Code, was that which stemmed from marriage. Marriage was defined as a contract between two persons of different sexes who intended to *legitimately* constitute a family

---

[1]   The present Civil Code was approved in 1966 by Decree-Law No. 47344/66, of 25 November, and entered into force the following year.

[2]   On 25 April 1974, a political, social and military movement put an end to the single-party political regime named 'Estado Novo'.

[3]   Decree of 10 April 1976.

[4]   Decree No. 496/77, 25 November.

(emphasis added).[5] This option had implications far beyond the lives of the spouses, and also determined that children born inside or outside of wedlock would be subject to different regimes, thus discriminating against 'illegitimate children'.[6] The reform of 1977 rephrased Article 1577 CC, and referred instead to marriage as a contract between two persons of different sexes who intended to constitute a family according to the provisions of the Civil Code.[7] Therefore, marriage was no longer considered the only way to legitimately constitute family relations.

The subsequent development regarding marriage was driven by the demands of the Religious Freedom Act.[8] Up to the time this Act was enacted, the only other marriage ceremony recognised by the law, besides civil marriage, was that of Catholic marriage. Therefore, as far as religious marriage was concerned, only Catholic marriage had legal effects. It was (as it is today) recognised as an independent institution (even though the Constitution requires that the civil law shall regulate marriage's requisites, regardless of the form of the ceremony).[9] Since the Religious Freedom Act,[10] the Portuguese legal system has also recognised other religious ceremonies as legally valid ways to enter into civil marriage (although not the religious regulation of their content), and named these 'civil marriages under religious form'.[11]

The most relevant change in the concept of marriage was enacted later. In 2010, same-sex marriage ceased to be legally non-existent (the sanction that the system formerly determined). Hence, what was previously considered a matter of public policy – gender diversity of spouses[12] – was overcome by the law, and

---

[5]   See Art. 1577 CC (original version of Decree-Law No. 47344/66, of 25 November); F.M. PEREIRA COELHO and G. DE OLIVEIRA, *Curso de Direito da Família*, vol. I, Imprensa da Universidade de Coimbra, 5th ed., 2016, p. 196. Even after these changes, Antunes Varela wrote against the idea of 'family' outside marriage: A. VARELA, *Direito da Família*, vol. I, Petrony, 5th ed., 1999, p. 177.

[6]   Children born outside wedlock were not only designated differently from a formal point of view (*'filhos ilegítimos'*, *'filhos naturais'*), but they were also discriminated as far as their rights were concerned, namely regarding their inheritance rights (See Arts. 2144, 2150 and 2139, No. 2 and 2140, No. 2 of the original version of the Civil Code – Decree-Law No. 47344/66, of 25 November).

[7]   Art. 1577 CC (version of Decree No. 496/77, 25 November).

[8]   Law No. 16/2001, of 22 June, later regulated by Decree-Law No. 324/2007, of 28 September, which enabled its effectiveness.

[9]   Art. 36, No. 2 of the Constitution of the Portuguese Republic.

[10]   As of 21 November 2022, there were 96 churches or religious communities officially recognised as being 'rooted' in Portugal (http://www.clr.mj.pt/sections/noticias/listagem-dos-atestados2924/downloadFile/file/atestados_de_radicacao__21.11.2022.pdf?nocache=1669046641.72).

[11]   Such ceremonies are the ones performed in the context of a church or religious community officially recognised as being 'rooted' in Portugal, and which obey the formal demands of the Religious Freedom Act (Art. 19 of Law No. 16/2001, of 22 June).

[12]   Decision of the Lisbon Court of Appeal of 15.02.2007 (Proc. No. 6284/2006-8) (http://www.dgsi.pt/jtrl.nsf/33182fc732316039802565fa00497eec/f2c9a606d4e2613180257296004e5975?OpenDocument).

received the seal of approval of the Constitutional Court,[13] which understood that there were 'material grounds' for this legal extension of marriage, and that it was 'reasonable for the legislature to be able to privilege the symbolic effect and optimise the anti-discriminatory social effect ... by extending the protection offered by the unitary framework of marriage to both these unions'.[14]

2.1.2. Divorce

Divorce has been permitted in the Portuguese legal system since 1910.[15] However, in 1973, when the ISFL was founded, most of the Portuguese married population could not dissolve marriage by divorce. As a matter a fact, in 1940 the Portuguese State and the Holy See concluded a concordat that denied Civil courts jurisdiction to decree divorce in Catholic marriages concluded after the entry into force of the concordat (1 August 1940). The fact that the vast majority of marriages were Catholic made divorce almost socially non-existent. In the event of breakdown, Catholic couples retained the option of the separation of persons and assets.[16]

Universal access to divorce[17] was a product of the 1974 change of political regime, and of the new Constitution adopted in 1976. The Constitution (Article 36, No. 2) mandates that all types of marriage may be dissolved by legal

---

[13] Ruling of the Constitutional Court No. 121/2010 (https://www.tribunalconstitucional. pt/tc/acordaos/20100121.html). For an English-language version, see http://www. tribunalconstitucional.pt/tc/en/acordaos/20100121.html.

[14] Such tectonic movement has not only taken place on an internal level – we may witness the adoption of same-sex marriage by other legal systems, and it may be argued that the case law of the European Court of Human Rights has also been following a coherent path regarding same-sex couples, although not as demanding (in *Schalk and Kopf v. Austria*, Application no. 30141/04, ECtHR 24.06.2010 and *Oliari and Others v. Italy*, Application nos. 18766/11 and 36030/11, ECtHR 21.10.2015). This context strengthens the idea that not only did same-sex marriage cease to be contrary to public policy, but that, to the contrary, not recognising it would be. Internally, the revocation, in 2016, of the exceptional rules that prevented same-sex married couples from adopting, or from having access to medically assisted procreation techniques in the same circumstances as different-sex couples, is another element to consider, in order to classify the reception of same-sex marriage as a core option of the system, as a matter of equality.

[15] Decree of 3 November 1910 (the 'Law of Divorce') permitted both litigious divorce and divorce by mutual consent. About the history and the demographics of divorce in Portugal, see N. DE SALTER CID, *O Divórcio em Portugal*, Húmus, 2018.

[16] In the original version of the Civil Code, see Art. 1773 ff. CC. In the present version, see Arts. 1794 ff. The legal separation of persons and assets does not extinguish marriage, but weakens its effects: it eliminates property relations between spouses, and abolishes most personal duties.

[17] Besides the extinction of marriage by death or divorce, both civil and Catholic marriages may be invalidated. The particular regime of invalidation of Catholic marriages – by ecclesiastical courts, grounded on canon law – is a specificity that the Brussels IIb Regulation nowadays (as the Brussels IIa previously did) expressly considers (Art. 99).

divorce (civil and religious marriages, including Catholic). On an international level, an Additional Protocol to the Concordat of 1940, signed in 1975, reframed the position assumed by the Portuguese State regarding Catholic marriage: the duty not to divorce became a religious duty, owed to the Church, that did not bind the State or limit access to legal divorce.[18]

Another important feature of Portuguese divorce law is the fact that non-judicial divorce (for divorce by mutual consent) has long been recognised within the Portuguese legal system.[19] Thus, the current discussion as to the nature of private divorces, and the permissibility of divorce being decreed by an authority other than a Court, took place with the adoption of the 1995 legal changes that permitted the practice of divorce being decreed by an authority other than a Court – by the registrar of the Civil Registry. This became the prevailing way to get a divorce.

In 2008, however, a deeper divorce reform occurred, greatly inspired by the Principles of the Commission on European Family.[20] The 2008 reform maintained the duality between divorce by mutual consent[21] and non-consensual divorce ('divorce without the consent of one of the spouses'), but transformed the Portuguese divorce system into a purely no-fault system, both regarding the grounds for divorce and the consequences of marriage dissolution.[22]

---

[18]   F.M. Pereira Coelho and G. de Oliveira, *Curso de Direito da Família*, vol. I, Imprensa da Universidade de Coimbra, 5th ed., 2016, p. 687; A. Vieira Cura, 'O dever de consciência de os casados catolicamente de não pedir o divórcio nos tribunais civis' in G. de Oliveira, J. Machado and R. Martins (eds.), *Família, consciência, secularismo e religião*, Coimbra Editora, Wolters-Kluwer, 2010, pp. 207–239.

[19]   In 1995, Decree-Law No. 131/95, of 6 June, created the possibility of applying to the Civil Registry Offices for divorce by mutual consent, but only in the absence of minor children, or when parental responsibilities had already been determined. In 2001, Decree-Law No. 272/2001, of 13 October, provided that divorce by mutual consent was to be decreed exclusively by the Civil Registry Office, but demanded several agreements regarding the consequences of divorce.

[20]   See Principles of European Family Law Regarding Divorce and Maintenance Between Former Spouses (http://ceflonline.net/wp-content/uploads/Principles-English.pdf); K. Boele-Woelki, F. Ferrand, C. González Beilfuss, M. Jänterä-Jareborg, N. Lowe, D. Martiny and W. Pintens, *Principles of European Family Law Regarding Divorce and Maintenance Between Former Spouses*, Intersentia, 2004.

[21]   Law No. 61/2008, of 31 October, determined that divorce by mutual consent may be filed either in the Civil Registry Office or in the court (Arts. 1775 and 1778-A CC). Divorce by mutual consent will be filed in the Civil Registry Office where spouses are able to present not only an agreement as to the dissolution of marriage, but also agreements regarding maintenance between former spouses, allocation of the family home, and parental responsibilities, and – since 2017 – allocation of pets (Art. 1775 CC). In the absence of any of these agreements, divorce by mutual consent is still possible to obtain; however, it cannot be decreed by the registrar of the Civil Registry. It must be filed in court, and decreed by the judge. Only the agreement as to the dissolution of marriage is required. Agreements regarding the consequences of divorce will be considered, but not required (Art. 1778-A CC).

[22]   See Art. 1781 CC and Arts. 1790 ff. CC; Arts. 1906 ff., Art. 1676, No. 2 CC.

Current divorce law expressly states that divorce may only be grounded on the irretrievable breakdown of marriage, and the consequences of divorce do not depend on the declaration of the spouses' fault, in the context of this procedure.[23]

2.1.3. De Facto Union

Finally, as far as life as a couple is concerned, the ever-growing importance must be stressed of the new family relation of de facto union, which has benefited from a slow but steady movement to legally strengthen it. The first reference to the concept of a 'de facto union' in the Civil Code was also the result of the 1977 reform – it concerned a minimalistic (but full of symbolic significance) provision that, under certain conditions, granted maintenance, as an obligation of the decedent's estate, to the surviving partner in need.[24] However, only in 1999 (Law No. 135/99, of 28 August) was the first De Facto Union Act created; one that was repealed two years later, in order to include more comprehensive protection for such couples, namely by granting (almost) the same rights to different-sex and same-sex de facto couples (Law No. 7/2001, of 11 May). Since then, the latter Act has been subject to amendments that have widened the effects of this family relation[25] – from social benefits, to the protection of the family home in the event of separation – and have eliminated the last stand of discrimination, in this Act, regarding same-sex couples: the ban on joint adoption by these couples.[26] A similar evolution has taken place within other legal Acts, and many aspects of de facto relationships have received the same

---

[23] These consequences are, among others, the maintenance between former spouses and the compensatory payment, the allocation of the family home, the regulation of parental responsibilities, the distribution of property, the payment of indemnities, and the termination of donations and other benefits. The legislature has, however, in the present author's view, strengthened an idea of responsibility underlying some consequences (maintenance between former spouses, or the newly created compensatory payment) that, unfortunately, has not yet been fully embraced by case law: P. TÁVORA VÍTOR, *Crédito Compensatório e Alimentos pós-divórcio*, Almedina, 2020, pp. 311 ff and 326 ff. R. LOBO XAVIER, *Recentes Alterações ao Regime Jurídico do Divórcio e das Responsabilidades Parentais*, Almedina, 2009, pp. 31 ff.

[24] Art. 2020 CC.

[25] The classification of the de facto union as a 'family relation' has been the subject of an intense debate. Indeed, some authors would classify it as a 'parafamilial relation'; that is, equivalent to a family relation for certain purposes, but not one of the 'family relations' recognised in the Civil Code (Art. 1575 CC). Other authors (especially in the context of constitutional law) have, for a long time, named it a 'family relation'. In the context of this evolution, the positions of GUILHERME DE OLIVEIRA (*Manual de Direito da Família*, Almedina, 2021, pp. 395 ff.) and F.M. DE BRITO PEREIRA COELHO ('Os factos no casamento e o direito na união de facto' in G. OLIVEIRA (coord.), *Textos de Direito da Família para Francisco Pereira Coelho*, Imprensa da Universidade de Coimbra, 2016, pp. 96 ff.) should be stressed, in the way that these authors grant to de facto couples some of the personal effects of marriage, even though the law does not expressly refer to these effects.

[26] Law No. 2/2016, of 29 February.

legal treatment as marriage.[27] In spite of such evolution, the regime of de facto union is not identical to that of marriage. Indeed, regarding property relations, since there is no legal recognition of a 'matrimonial regime' in relation to de facto unions, nor rules regarding debts or administration of assets, the general rules of tort law, contract law and property law will apply, which has generated a rich case law that aims to adapt these rules to the reality of these relations.[28]

2.2. DETERMINATION OF PARENTHOOD: THE PATH TO THE (DEFINED AND REDEFINED) TRUTH

The core of the following analysis is the ebullient field of parenthood, forged by the profound changes brought by the 1977 reform, and challenged by the new issues introduced by the Law of Medically Assisted Procreation (Assisted Reproduction Technologies (ART) Act – Law No. 32/2006, 26 July).[29]

As for the establishment of parenthood, the most fundamental principle – introduced by the 1977 reform (Decree No. 496/77, 25 November) – is the *principle of biological truth.* This public policy principle determines that the system aims to establish the correspondence between parent–child biological and legal bonds, and creates the ways of doing so, by eliminating unnecessary constraints (including those that could derive from the protection of the matrimonial family, or from forms of discrimination against children born out of the wedlock) on this outcome,[30] apparent in the original 1966 version of the Civil Code.

The present system of determination of parenthood may be divided into two fields: a classic one, and a more recent (and still unstable) field that results from the use of ART methods.

Motherhood and fatherhood are the object of the classic system. The criterion to determine motherhood is childbirth (Art. 1796, No. 1 of the CC), hence a biological criterion that allows Article 1796 to be in line with the conclusion

---

[27]   Among many other examples, the regime of exercise of parental responsibilities by married couples applies (Arts. 1911 and 1901 ff CC), and couples married or living in a de facto union have equal access to assisted reproduction technologies (ART) (Art. 6 of Law No. 32/2006, 26 July).

[28]   See, for instance, Decision of the Guimarães Court of Appeal of 19.01.2017 (proc. 1116/14.1TJBNF.G1), and Decisions of the Supreme Court of 24.10.2017 (proc. 3712/15.0T8GDM.P1.S1), and of 14.01.2021 (proc. 1142/11.2TBBCL.1.G1.S1).

[29]   See P. Távora Vítor, 'The Determination of Parenthood in the Portuguese Legal System and the Law of Medically Assisted Procreation: Rolling the Dice Again' in N. Dethloff and K. Kaesling (eds.), *Between Sexuality, Gender and Reproduction: On the Pluralisation of Family Forms*, Intersentia, 2023, pp. 175 ff. and the bibliography quoted.

[30]   G. de Oliveira, 'Critérios Jurídicos da Parentalidade' in G. de Oliveira (coord.), *Textos de Direito da Família para Francisco Pereira Coelho*, Imprensa da Universidade de Coimbra, 2016, p. 273.

mater semper certa est. As for fatherhood, the rule that the father is the man married to the mother at the time of birth or conception (Article 1826 ff. CC – *pater is est quem nuptiae demonstrant*) still applies, although its aim is not to protect marriage: it is, rather, grounded in the presumption that the mother's husband is likely to be the biological father of the child. The same biological criterion also applies to the determination of paternity outside wedlock. *Voluntary acknowledgement* (Articles 1849 ff. PCC) of fatherhood by the father stems from the recognition of a biological (genetic) bond, and in cases where a court has to intervene to *judicially determine fatherhood* (Articles 1869 ff. PCC), the applicable criterion is also the genetic bond between father and child.

Apart from a few exceptions,[31] the principle of biological truth has prevailed in the so-called classic system: the one of the Civil Code. However, and particularly since 2006,[32] the movement toward growing recognition of ART has clearly set aside this principle in several situations.[33] Law No. 32/2006, of 26 July, recognises the fatherhood of the man who did not contribute his gametes;[34,35] the parenthood of the wife or partner of the beneficiary of the assisted reproduction techniques, in a same-sex female couple;[36] and the parenthood of the beneficiaries of gestational surrogacy, based on the surrogacy agreement.[37] These results highlight the role of consent, and signify that the criterion of parenthood is the will to become a parent, at least when it comes to the beneficiaries of these techniques: it is, thus, a volitional criterion.

---

[31] For instance, the rules that determine a deadline either to contest paternity (Art. 1842 CC), or to investigate it (Arts. 1917 and 1873 CC) may be considered contrary to this principle. And the rules that hinder the official inquiry of parenthood in certain situations, such as incest (Arts. 1809 and 1866 CC), also do not pursue the biological truth.

[32] Law No. 32/2006, of 26 July.

[33] In some situations, however, the traditional rules of the Civil Code still apply. For instance, except in the case of surrogacy, the mother is the person who gives birth to the child (Art. 1796, No. 1 CC), regardless of the fact that she may not be the genetic mother (in the event that she benefited from egg donation).

[34] Fatherhood is based on consent: Art. 20, No. 1, Law No. 32/2006, of 26 July. Thus, it is a volitional criterion that prevails.

[35] The possibility of post-mortem insemination has recently been introduced by Law No. 72/2021, of 12 November. According to the new regulations in Articles 22, 22-A, and especially Article 23, of Law No. 32/2006, of 26 July, fatherhood is established with reference to the deceased father, who gave his consent in the context of that parental project.

[36] Co-motherhood is a possibility under Portuguese law. When a same-sex female couple benefits from ART, both the biological criterion regarding the woman who gave birth to the child (Art. 1796, No. 1 CC) and the volitional criterion of the consent given within the parental project by the other woman (Art. 20, No. 1, Law of Medically Assisted Procreation – Assisted Reproduction Technologies (ART) Act – Law No. 32/2006, 26 July (Law of the MAP) will be used to establish the parenthood of each different woman.

[37] Even though the law demands 'recourse to the gametes of at least one of the respective beneficiaries' (Art. 8, No. 4 of Law No. 32/2006, of 26 July), this biological connection is not the relevant criterion: 'The child who is born with recourse to gestational surrogacy shall be deemed to be the son or daughter of the respective beneficiaries.' (Art. 8, No. 9 of Law No. 32/2006, of 26 July).

2.3. PARENTS AND CHILDREN: THE PATH OF CARE AND AUTONOMY

Finally, this chapter will now tackle the relations between children and their parents[38] (and caregivers), namely the exercise of parental responsibilities. In 1973, under the original version of the Civil Code, the expression 'paternal power' reigned, and this reflected the underlying regime: the father exercised 'paternal power', and the mother merely had the 'right to be heard'.[39] This regime would, of course, radically change with the 1977 reform, which introduced not only equal parental rights[40] and equal rights for non-marital children, but also recognition of the evolving capacity of the child.[41] This recognition of greater rights for children – and the corresponding evening-up of the level of parent and child responsibility as the child grows over and obtains more capacity – preceded the ratification of the Convention on the Rights of the Child, by the Portuguese State, in 1990, and has since been increasingly strengthened, with subsequent statutes, for example, giving adolescents legal agency over important issues in their lives.[42]

The regime of parental responsibilities has been subject to different waves (of different dimensions) of reform. Whereas the 1977 reform established the fundamental principles of parental equality and children's rights (even though it retained the phrase 'paternal power'), the 2008 reform, again inspired by the Commission on European Family Law (CEFL) principles,[43] renamed the term 'parental responsibilities', and established the present structure for their exercise. Indeed, it may be argued today that the presumption governing the exercise of parental responsibilities is one of equally shared responsibilities: common exercise by both parents is mandatory, *at least* regarding important matters for

---

[38] This includes, of course, adoptive parents. Indeed, not only is adoption protected by the Constitution itself (Article 36, No. 7: 'Adoption shall be regulated and protected in accordance with the law, which must lay down swift forms for completion of the respective procedural requirements.'), but nowadays only one kind of adoption is available – full adoption – which provides that the legal status of the adopted child is the same as that of a biological child (Art. 1986 CC).

[39] Art. 1882 (original version of Decree-Law No. 47344/66, of 25 November).

[40] The principle of equality between spouses refers also to the maintenance and education of their children (Art. 36, No. 3 of the Constitution). But the Constitution includes, additionally, the principle of attribution to parents of the right and the duty to educate and maintain their children (Art. 36, No. 5), and the principle of inseparability of children from their parents (Art. 36, No. 6).

[41] Art. 1878, No. 2 CC.

[42] For instance, at 16 years old, adolescents may exercise religious self-determination (Art. 1886 CC), and provide informed consent for medical decisions (Art. 38 of the Criminal Code).

[43] Law No. 61/2008, of 31 October. See Principles of European Family Law Regarding Parental Responsibilities, at https://ceflonline.net/wp-content/uploads/Principles-PR-English.pdf.

the life of the child.[44] Contrary to the previous regime,[45] this presumption of shared parental responsibility applies both to married parents and those in de facto unions;[46] parents who live together are presumed,[47] as a matter of law, to have agreed[48] to the common exercise of parental responsibilities. Where such parents disagree on 'matters of particular relevance', however, they may ask a court to resolve their disagreement.[49] The same presumption of shared responsibility applies to parents who live apart,[50] and both parents must agree on 'matters of particular relevance' (Art. 1906, No. 1 CC). Nonetheless, a sole parent caring for a child may decide 'daily living acts',[51] and may act unilaterally in 'urgent situations'.[52] A court may also grant authority to a sole parent when common exercise is *against the best interest* of the child.[53] Thus, the ordinarily principle is one of the common exercise of parental responsibilities, subject to very limited exceptions.

Also, regarding the determination of residence and contact, the trend has been away from the identification of the resident parent as the sole custodial parent, in the event of lack of agreement,[54] and towards the promotion of close relationships with both parents, and shared responsibilities, according to best interests of the child.[55] This does not require the child to alternate between each parent's residence, but does give the court the authority to consider such shared custody arrangements, and the authority to order such arrangements, even where the parents do not agree to such terms.[56]

---

[44]   Residence and custody are no longer identified. About this issue, see M.C. Sottomayor, *Regulação do Exercício das Responsabilidades Parentais nos Casos de Divórcio*, Almedina, 2011, p. 24.

[45]   Prior to 2008, when parents were unmarried, it was presumed that the mother held the child's custody (Art. 1911, No. 2 CC). Whenever non-married parents lived together, the 'paternal power' could be exercised by both parents, if declared in the Civil Registry Office (Art. 1911, No. 3 CC).

[46]   See Arts. 1901–1904 and 1911 CC.

[47]   This agreement is presumed, unless the Law demands express agreement or in cases of 'matters of particular relevance' (Art. 1902, No. 1 CC).

[48]   Art. 1901 CC.

[49]   Arts. 1901, Nos. 2 and 3 CC.

[50]   This applies to parents who are separated, divorced, or whose marriage has been annulled or declared null and void, or to those who have never lived together (Arts. 1904 ff CC).

[51]   The non-resident parent must respect the 'most relevant education guidelines' of the resident parent (Art. 1906, No. 3 CC).

[52]   In such situations, information about the 'urgent situation' should be provided to the other parent as soon as possible (Art. 1906, No. 1 CC).

[53]   An example would be cases of domestic violence (Art. 1906-A, No. 2 CC).

[54]   Art. 1906, No. 2, prior to the 2008 reform.

[55]   The 'availability of each [parent] to promote regular relations of the child with the other' shall be taken into account (Art. 1906, No. 5 CC), as well as the existence of agreements (Art. 1906, No. 8 CC). The child's preferences are another relevant element to be taken into account (Art. 1906, No. 9 CC).

[56]   Art. 1906, No. 6 CC.

Children's relationships with other caregivers, beyond parents, have been subject to growing (although still feeble) recognition. In some cases, step-parents and 'social parents' may exercise parental responsibilities, through the delegation of a parent, regarding daily living matters;[57] but also in a general way, when determined by a court, in cases of the impediment[58] or death of the parents.[59] Finally, courts may recognise a single parent's spouse or cohabiting partner as a de facto second parent, with the full rights and responsibilities of parenthood, even in the absence of adoption (Art. 1904-A CC).

As far as contact rights are concerned, there has not been express legal recognition regarding step-parents and 'social parents', as has, for instance, been given to grandparents and siblings (Art. 1887-A CC).[60] However, Portuguese case law has been quite open to granting contact rights, grounded in the child's best interests, to persons who have a special relationship with the child, such as uncles and religious godparents.[61]

In conclusion, the *democratic view* of the family, the consideration of the child's best interests as the paramount value (leading to the inclusion of new family characters as providers of care, and as significant relations), and the adoption of the principle of the progressive autonomy and evolving capacity of the child, have allowed us to follow a *path of care* that leads towards *autonomy*.

3. CONCLUSION

After centuries of steady balance, Portuguese family law initiated (most notably after the change of political regime of 1974, and the Democratic Constitution of 1976) a movement of reconfiguration that has been increasingly speeding up. And therefore, in several ways, what used to be fundamental no longer is, and what had no relevance has become paramount.

The fundamental values of freedom and equality have reshaped what it means to live as a couple: the ways of entering into intimate relationships, and

---

[57] Art. 1906, No. 4 CC.

[58] Art. 1903 CC.

[59] Art. 1904 CC.

[60] Legal contact rights are also granted to civil godparents (Arts. 16 (e) and 26 of Law No. 103/2009, of 11 September), and to persons of reference when the child is subject to a youth protection measure (Art. 57 (b), Law No. 147/99, of 1 September). R. Martins, and P. Távora Vítor, 'O direito dos avós às relações pessoais com os netos na jurisprudência recente', *Revista 'Julgar'*, no. 10, January–April 2010; and J. Duarte Pinheiro, 'A relação entre avós e netos' in J. Miranda (coord.), *Estudos em Homenagem ao Prof. Doutor Sérvulo Correia*, Faculdade de Direito da Universidade de Lisboa, 2010.

[61] See decisions of the Guimarães Court of Appeal of 10.11.2016 (ECLI:PT:TRG:2016:719.08.8 TBBCL.C.G1.49), of the Oporto Court of Appeal of 07.01.2013, and of the Coimbra Court of Appeal of 20.06.2012 (ECLI:PT:TRC:2012:450.11.7TBTNV.A.C1.07).

of experiencing and abandoning them. The determination of parenthood has become engaged in defining and redefining the relevant concepts of truth for parenthood purposes, and embracing the new principles. And relations between children and their parents and other caregivers have become more democratic, and more focused on the promotion of children's care and autonomy. The abstract verticality of family relations has become obsolete, and 'real relations' between family members have won out as the paramount concern in the legal ordering of family relationships.

SCOTLAND

INCREMENTALISM AND COMPROMISE IN REFORMING CHILD AND FAMILY LAW

Elaine E. Sutherland*

Résumé

Sans surprise – et comme dans beaucoup d'autres États – le droit écossais contemporain de l'enfance et de la famille diffère, parfois assez radicalement, du droit tel qu'il était il y a un demi-siècle. Cet article se concentre sur l'évolution de l'appréhension par le droit des relations intimes entre adultes pour lesquelles la réforme du droit a suivi une trajectoire claire : le système juridique reconnait un plus large éventail de relations et a diversifié les fondements juridiques possibles. Le présent texte examine l'évolution de la loi en s'interrogeant sur les raisons qui ont motivé les différentes réformes et sur la manière dont le processus a fonctionné – un exercice qui peut éclairer ceux qui s'occupent des futures réformes du droit de l'enfance et de la famille.

1. INTRODUCTION

Given the enormous sociopolitical developments of the last 50 years, it would be astonishing – and very disappointing – if the law governing children and

---

*   elaine.sutherland@stir.ac.uk or elaineesutherland@gmail.com.

families had not changed in that time. Thus, it is no surprise to find that, as in many other jurisdictions, contemporary Scots child and family law differs, sometimes quite radically, from the law as it was half a century ago.

That reform of the law has taken place in the context of another major change, with a federal system of government being adopted across the United Kingdom (UK).[1] For Scotland, this means that the Scottish Parliament sits in Edinburgh and legislates on 'devolved matters', while the United Kingdom Parliament continues to sit at Westminster, and retains jurisdiction for Scotland on 'reserved matters'.[2] Most of child and family law is devolved, although some matters that impact on it are reserved to Westminster.[3] In addition, even where an issue is devolved to the Scottish Parliament, it may authorise the UK Parliament to legislate for Scotland,[4] and it has, on occasion, done so.[5]

While Scotland always had its own system of family law, distinct from that operating in other parts of the UK, the creation of a separate Scottish Parliament gave more time for legislation to be passed than had been possible at Westminster. It was also believed that having a legislature within the jurisdiction might enable the law to reflect the will of the Scottish people better than had been the case previously.

Moving beyond the domestic sphere, a range of regional and international treaties have had an impact on Scots law. Of particular significance for child and family law are the European Convention on Human Rights (ECHR)[6] and the United Nations Convention on the Rights of the Child (CRC).[7] The former has been incorporated into the legal systems of the various parts of the UK,[8] and, at the time of writing, efforts continue in Scotland to secure that status for much of the latter.[9]

---

[1]   The National Assembly for Wales was created by the Government of Wales Act 1998. The devolved authority in Northern Ireland is the Northern Ireland Assembly: Northern Ireland Act 1998.

[2]   Scotland Act 1998, ss. 29 and 30 and Sch. 5. Further powers were devolved to the Scottish Parliament by the Scotland Acts 2012 and 2016.

[3]   Reserved matters include immigration, child support (but not aliment) and assisted reproduction.

[4]   This is done by means of a legislative consent motion, formerly known as a 'Sewel Motion': *Scottish Parliament Standing Orders*, The Scottish Government, 6th ed., 6th rev., 1 April 2022, ch. 9B.

[5]   See, e.g. the Gender Recognition Act 2004 and the Civil Partnership Act 2004.

[6]   ETS No. 155, 4 November 1950, entered into force 3 September 1953.

[7]   1577 UNTS 3, 20 November 1989, entered into force 2 September 1990.

[8]   Human Rights Act 1998.

[9]   The Scottish Parliament sought to incorporate into Scots law as much of the CRC as is within its legislative competence, when it passed the United Nations Convention on the Rights of the Child (Incorporation) (Scotland) Bill in 2021. However, the UK Supreme Court found that the bill exceeded that competence in some respects: *Reference by the Attorney General and the Advocate General for Scotland – United Nations Convention on the Rights of the Child (Incorporation) (Scotland) Bill* [2021] UKSC 42. Efforts to produce competence-compliant

Rather than providing an overview of all of the main developments in child and family law over the last 50 years,[10] this chapter focuses on one aspect of it which has changed quite radically over this period: the range of intimate adult relationships recognised by the legal system, and the greater diversity in those to whom they are available. Reviewing how the law has developed, it interrogates what has driven law reform and how the process has worked, an exercise that may inform and assist those seeking further reform of child and family law in the future.

2.   WHERE WE WERE AND THE IMPETUS FOR CHANGE

Our exploration of intimate adult relationships begins in 1973. At that time, there were only two options in Scotland: marriage and 'living in sin'. Marriage was available only to different-sex couples,[11] and monogamy was very much the order of the day, with there being no prospect of entering a polygamous marriage.[12] For those who opted to marry, the relationship brought with it a range of legal consequences both during the relationship and on its termination (whether by divorce or death). Non-marital cohabitation – the 'living in sin' option – was barely recognised by the legal system, save in so far as it involved an infraction of the criminal law.[13] What, then, was the process that brought the legal system to its current, more inclusive and diverse, position?

In Scotland, as in so many other jurisdictions around the world, whether there should be a mechanism by which same-sex relationships could be accorded legal recognition was 'the great debate' in family law in the late twentieth and early twenty-first centuries, with some calling for marriage to be made available to same-sex couples. Lobbying groups on both sides of the debate expended considerable energy in their efforts to shape public opinion and the views of policy-makers, law reform bodies and legislators.

---

legislation continue: *A Stronger and More Resilient Scotland: the Programme for Government 2022 to 2023*, Scottish Government, 2022, p.15 and 'Advancing children's rights', *Scottish Government News*, 27 June 2023, available at <https://www.gov.scot/news/advancing-childrens-rights/> last accessed 04.08.2023.

[10]   For an overview of developments over the previous 30 years, see E.E. SUTHERLAND, 'Scots Child and Family Law: Liberty, Equality and Protection Revisited' (2019) *Juridical Review* 33.

[11]   Marriage (Scotland) Act 1977, s. 5(4)(e) (sub-section now repealed).

[12]   The Matrimonial Proceedings (Polygamous Marriages) Act 1972, s. 2, provides that a Scottish court is 'not … precluded' from granting a decree of divorce, nullity, separation or 'any other decree involving a determination as to the validity of a marriage' and related ancillary orders in respect of a polygamous marriage that was entered into under a law which permits polygamy. The court has the same powers in respect of financial provision in actions of nullity as it has in respect of divorce: Family Law (Scotland) Act 1985, s. 17.

[13]   See, further, below nn. 72–73 and accompanying text.

Domestic law reform does not occur in a vacuum, and, by the end of the twentieth century, a number of jurisdictions in Europe and elsewhere had already made progress on the recognition of same-sex relationships through the mechanisms of civil or registered partnership, when the Netherlands, in 2001, led the way in making marriage available to same-sex couples.[14] The European Court of Human Rights (ECtHR) was showing itself to be increasingly impatient with discrimination based on sexual orientation,[15] albeit it was to be some time before it required recognition of same-sex relationships.

While the Scottish Law Commission had expressly excluded same-sex relationships from its review of adult relationships in 1992, a few respondents urged consideration of their recognition.[16] Reform of the law in Scotland followed the familiar, incremental pattern found elsewhere,[17] with legal recognition of same-sex relationships being preceded by the decriminalisation of homosexuality.[18] By the beginning of the twenty-first century, both same-sex and different-sex couples were being included in legislation on specific issues,[19] and domestic courts were playing their part in the recognition of same-sex relationships.[20]

In all of this, it is worth remembering the human capacity for tenacity – and few are more determined than lovers – since, for a time, some Scottish same-sex couples went abroad and got married in more inclusive jurisdictions. Initially, their marriages were not recognised on their return to Scotland,[21] something

---

[14]   E.E. SUTHERLAND, *Child and Family Law, Vol. II, Intimate Adult Relationships*, W. Green, 3rd ed., 2022, paras. 1-170–1-207.

[15]   See, e.g. *Da Silva Mouta v. Portugal* (2001) 31 EHRR 47, where the Court struck down discrimination on the basis of sexual orientation, in a dispute over a child's residence, as infringing Arts. 8 and 14 of the ECHR.

[16]   Scottish Law Commission, *Report on Family Law*, Scot. Law Com. No.1 35, 1992, para. 8.5.

[17]   W.N. ESKRIDGE, 'Comparative Law and the Same-Sex Marriage Debate: A Step-By-Step Approach Toward State Recognition' (1999–2000) 31 *McGeorge Law Review* 641; K. WAALDIJK, 'Civil Developments: Patterns of Reform in the Legal Position of Same-Sex Partners in Europe' (2000) 17 *Canadian Journal of Family Law* 62.

[18]   Homosexuality was not decriminalised until 1980, when the age of consent was set at 21: Criminal Justice (Scotland) Act 1980, s. 80 (repealed). The age was later reduced to 18, and eventually to 16, bringing it into line with that for heterosexuals: Sexual Offences (Scotland) Act 2009, s. 28.

[19]   See, e.g. the Adults with Incapacity (Scotland) Act 2000; the Protection from Abuse (Scotland) Act 2001; the Housing (Scotland) Act 2001; and the Mental Health (Care and Treatment) (Scotland) Act 2003.

[20]   See, e.g. *Fitzpatrick v. Sterling Housing Association* [2001] 1 AC 27 and *Ghaidan v. Godin-Mendoza* [2004] 2 AC 557.

[21]   There is no reported Scottish case on the point, but, in all likelihood, the courts in Scotland would have responded as they did in England. See *Wilkinson v. Kitzinger* [2006] EWHC 2022 (Fam), where two women who had married in Canada, in 2003, found that their marriage was not recognised when they returned to England. Their challenge, based on Arts. 8, 12 and 14 of the ECHR, was unsuccessful because, by the time the High Court heard their case, their relationship was recognised under the Civil Partnership Act 2004. Ironically, their marriage

---

later resolved by legislation,[22] but the proactivity of these couples served to highlight the need to reform domestic law.

3.   THE 'COMPROMISE': CIVIL PARTNERSHIP

In democratic societies, while some politicians may be driven by noble aspirations, most have an eye to public opinion, not least because their re-election depends on it. Thus, in 2003, in the light of the calls for reform of the law on same-sex relationships – and after a nudge from the Women and Equality Unit at the UK Department of Trade and Industry[23] – the (then) Scottish Executive, as the Scottish Government was known at the time, undertook a public consultation on the introduction of civil partnership in Scotland.[24] Civil partnership was a compromise, designed to create a relationship, exclusively for same-sex couples, that offered most of the legal consequences of marriage, while avoiding the use of the magic word 'marriage', in an effort to appease those opposed to making that institution more inclusive.

The result of that consultation process was clear, with 86 per cent of the 323 responses (222 from individuals and 101 from organisations) supporting civil partnership registration in principle, and 75 per cent supporting the more detailed proposals on registration and dissolution. Forty per cent of respondents believed that civil partnership would undermine marriage, but at least some of them did not see that as a reason to oppose its introduction.[25] The fact that there were only 323 responses should not be read as signalling a lack of concern about the issue, since, traditionally, such consultations have tended to have a low response rate. It does highlight, however, that government consultation is not a referendum. In addition, support for reform was not universal, and particularly strident opposition was voiced by the Roman Catholic Church.[26] While that

---

was eventually recognised in England once the Marriage (Same Sex Couples) Act 2013 came into force, two weeks before same-sex couples were able to marry in England: N. WOOLCOCK, 'Women celebrate as overseas marriage is recognised at last', *The Times*, 10 March 2014.

[22]   Once the Civil Partnership Act 2004, s. 212 came into force, their foreign marriages might have been recognised as an 'overseas relationships': that is to say, as equivalent to a Scottish civil partnership, but not as a marriage. The Marriage and Civil Partnership (Scotland) Act 2014 resulted in foreign same-sex marriages being recognised as marriages in Scotland.

[23]   The Unit published its consultation document in June 2003: Women & Equality Unit, *Civil Partnership: A framework for the legal recognition of same-sex couples*, Women & Equality Unit, 2003.

[24]   *Civil Partnership Registration: A Legal Status for Committed Same-Sex Couples in Scotland*, Scottish Executive, 2003.

[25]   See *The Consultation on Civil Partnership Registration: analysis of the responses*, Scottish Executive Social Research, 2004.

[26]   Y. QURESHI, 'Cardinal calls on Catholics to oppose Government proposals', *Scotland on Sunday*, 14 March 2004.

Church's adherents form a minority of the Scottish population, a significant number of them supported the Labour Party at the time. The Scottish Executive then in power was based on a Labour–Liberal Democrat coalition, and the Labour Party was conscious of the need to tread carefully, in order to avoid alienating a section of its voter base.

It may have been the Executive's desire to distance itself from civil partnership that explains, at least in part, the way law reform was secured.[27] It would have been possible to introduce civil partnership by passing legislation in the Scottish Parliament. However, arguing that any such Scottish legislation would implicate reserved matters, the Executive used the mechanism of the legislative consent motion[28] to hand responsibility over to Westminster, where a statute creating civil partnerships for the whole of the United Kingdom was passed.

Proponents of the legislation argued, inter alia, that Article 8 of the ECHR supported recognition of same-sex relationships, but the impact of the Convention in securing that end was probably fairly minimal. While the Civil Partnership Act was passed in 2004, it was not until 2010 that the ECtHR handed down its decision in *Schalk and Kopf v. Austria*,[29] recognising the right to family life of same-sex couples, and began the evolutive process in its own thinking that led it to conclude that states parties to the ECHR are required to provide a mechanism for the formal recognition of same-sex relationships.[30]

4. SAME-SEX MARRIAGE

If those in government in Scotland hoped that the creation of civil partnership would bring an end to the debate over the legal recognition of same-sex relationships, they were mistaken. The most vocal opponents were not appeased.[31] Recognising that civil partnership is not marriage – otherwise that is what it would be called – supporters of same-sex marriage continued to pursue their quest for full and equal recognition.

---

[27] Another factor may have been that the Executive was still smarting from a recent bruising battle in which it had crossed swords with religious organisations over amending the Local Government (Scotland) Act 1973 to remove the prohibition on discussing homosexuality, described in the Act as a 'pretended family lifestyle', in schools.

[28] On legislative consent motions, see above n. 4.

[29] App. No. 30141/04; (2011) 53 EHRR 20.

[30] *Vallianatos v. Greece*, App. No. 29381/09, (2013) 59 EHRR 12; *Oliari v. Italy*, App. No. 18766/11, (2015) 65 EHRR 26; and *Fedotova v. Russia*, App. Nos. 40792/10, 30538/14 and 43439/14, (2022) 74 EHRR 28.

[31] Roman Catholic Archbishop Mario Conti is reported as commenting, '[t]his new law [the 2004 Act] has created a fiction of marriage by implicitly basing such publicly recognised partnerships on a sexual engagement. This can only diminish the special status of marriage': R. GRAY and A. MACMILLAN, 'Three gay weddings a day in Scotland', *The Scotsman*, 12 February 2006.

In 2011, the Scottish Government consulted on the possibility of extending marriage to same-sex couples.[32] The evolution of public opinion over time is instructive in drilling down into the process at work. When measured by random or structured surveys of the population, it is clear that there was growing support for same-sex marriage. In 2002, 41 per cent of respondents to the *Scottish Social Attitudes Survey* agreed or agreed strongly with the statement, 'Gay or lesbian couples should have the right to marry one another if they want to.' That figure rose to 53 per cent, in 2006, and to 61 per cent, in 2010.[33] An Ipsos MORI poll, in 2012, found that 64 per cent of respondents in Scotland supported a right to marry for same-sex couples.[34] Having reviewed 16 other public opinion surveys that had been conducted for newspapers and organisations in the period 2011 to 2012, the Scottish Parliament Information Centre found 'considerable variations' in the results, concluding that this variation:

> may be explained by differences in the questions that are used to test public opinion on same sex marriage. Polls commissioned by organisations campaigning for and against same sex marriage produced some of the strongest responses both for and against the proposal.[35]

It will be recalled that the 2003 consultation on civil partnership garnered a modest number of responses. The picture was very different with the 2011 consultation on same-sex marriage, which netted 77,508 responses, with 67 per cent of respondents opposing a change in the law to permit same-sex marriage. That dramatic increase reflects concerted efforts by various organisations to rally their supporters. Respondents could reply using the standard form, traditionally employed in consultations, with 10,441 doing so, but some organisations produced abbreviated forms, which were used by 33,634 respondents.[36] Those using prepared forms were split 47 per cent in favour of, and 52 per cent opposed to, extending the right to marry to same-sex couples.[37] Campaigning groups also organised standard letters, postcards and petitions. Postcard responses were 90 per cent against, while the petition signatures were 99 per cent against, the proposed reform. Clearly, those who felt strongly about the issue had become more adept at marshalling their forces.

---

[32]   *The Registration of Civil Partnerships, Same Sex Marriage: A Consultation*, Scottish Government, 2011.

[33]   See *Scottish Social Attitudes Survey 2010: Attitudes to Discrimination and Positive Action*, Scottish Government Social Research, 2011, p. 132 and Table 3.

[34]   Ipsos MORI, *Scottish Public Opinion Monitor – Attitudes towards same-sex marriage*, July 2012.

[35]   *Scottish Parliament Information Centre Briefing on the Marriage and Civil Partnership (Scotland) Bill*, SB 13/51, Scottish Parliament Information Centre, 2013, p. 16.

[36]   *Registration of Civil Partnerships, Same Sex Marriage: Consultation Analysis*, Scottish Government Social Research, 2012, para. 2.8, Table 2.

[37]   Ibid., p. 36, Table 14.

The views of the Scottish population might have been garnered more accurately by having a referendum on the issue rather than relying on those who knew of the government consultation and bothered to respond. Yet whether same-sex couples should be able to marry is not simply a matter of counting votes. If marriage is a fundamental right, then it does not matter what a majority of the population thinks, and it is an essential tenet of democracy that the majority cannot be permitted to oppress a minority. As Sachs J observed in the Constitutional Court of South Africa, in *Minister of Home Affairs v. Fourie*:

> It is precisely those groups that cannot count on popular support and strong representation on the legislature that have a claim to vindicate their fundamental rights through application of the Bill of Rights.[38]

The majority in the US Supreme Court reached much the same conclusion almost a decade later, in *Obergefell v. Hodges*.[39]

While supporters of same-sex marriage founded on the ECHR – and Articles 8, 12 and 14, in particular – in making their case, the ECtHR was of little help, since it had (and, at the time of writing, still has) yet to require states parties to the Convention to extend the right to marry to same-sex couples.[40]

In any event, the Scottish Government introduced the Marriage and Civil Partnership (Scotland) Bill in the Scottish Parliament in June 2013, and it was passed, in a free vote (one not driven by party affiliation), by 105 votes to 18. Most of the legislation came into force on 16 December 2014,[41] and the first same-sex marriages were celebrated in Scotland on Hogmanay (31 December) 2014.[42]

5. DIFFERENT-SEX CIVIL PARTNERSHIP

Once marriage became available to same-sex couples, a number of jurisdictions concluded that civil or registered partnership had outlived its usefulness, and

---

[38] Case CCT/60/04 (2006), at para. 74. At para. 94, he noted further that, 'Majoritarian opinion can often be harsh to minorities that exist outside the mainstream.'

[39] 576 U.S. 644 (2015). At p. 648, Kennedy J. said, 'While the Constitution contemplates that democracy is the appropriate process for change, individuals who are harmed need not await legislative action before asserting a fundamental right.'

[40] That is due, in large part, to the lack of consensus in Europe on same-sex marriage, itself resulting from the hostility to homosexuality in some parts of Eastern Europe: H. FENWICK and D. FENWICK, 'Finding "East"/'West" divisions in Council of Europe states on treatment of sexual minorities' [2019] *European Human Rights Law Review* 247.

[41] Marriage and Civil Partnership (Scotland) Act 2014 (Commencement No. 3, Saving, Transitional Provision and Revocation) Order 2014, SSI 2014/287.

[42] 'First same-sex weddings occur in Scotland', *The Scotsman*, 31 December 2014. At that time, there was a waiting period of 14 days (now 28 days) between lodging the notices of intention to marry and receiving authorisation for the ceremony to proceed.

abolished it, usually prospectively.[43] In others, however, it was retained and marriage and registered partnership co-exist.[44] Thus, it was no surprise when the Scottish Government, like its counterparts elsewhere in the United Kingdom,[45] turned its attention to that issue.

Another, related, matter also required attention. When the Scottish Parliament embraced same-sex marriage, it addressed one form of discrimination, but created another. While same-sex couples could choose between formalising their relationships by means of either civil partnership or marriage, for a time, different-sex couples were limited to marriage. Some different-sex couples who found marriage unattractive, due to its patriarchal, religious or other associations, were keen to formalise their relationships and gain the protections that would afford, and they demanded access to civil partnership.

In 2015, the Scottish Government consulted on both matters – whether civil partnership should be retained, and if so, whether it should be extended to different-sex couples – setting out the following three options:

- No change in the law (civil partnership would remain available to same-sex couples only).
- The prospective abolition of civil partnership (no new civil partnerships, but those already registered would remain valid as such).[46]
- Extending the existing provision for civil partnership to different-sex couples.[47]

It put forward the case for and against each option, making clear that it did not favour the third,[48] and, perhaps remembering the experience of the same-sex marriage consultation, it stressed that this consultation was 'not an opinion poll'.[49]

As if to emphasise that point, the analysis of the 411 responses to the consultation that followed detailed their content, but gave no indication of the number of respondents favouring each option.[50] However, an 'informal

---

43   That was done in the Nordic countries, Ireland and a number of US states.
44   See, e.g. the Netherlands.
45   *Civil Partnership Review (England and Wales) – A Consultation*, Department for Culture Media & Sport, 2014; *Civil Partnership Review (England and Wales) – Report on Conclusions*, Department for Culture Media & Sport, 2014.
46   In a few states in the US, registered partnerships or civil unions were converted into marriages automatically on a specified date. See, e.g. Wash. Rev. Code §26.60.100(4) and 13 Del. Code §218(e). See K.T. Matsumura, 'A Right Not To Marry' (2016) 84 *Fordham Law Review* 1509. That was never the plan in Scotland.
47   *Review of Civil Partnership – A consultation by the Scottish Government*, Scottish Government, 2015.
48   Ibid., p. i.
49   Ibid., p. iii.
50   *Analysis of responses to the consultation on civil partnerships in Scotland*, Scottish Government, 2016.

analysis' of the numbers was provided in the Government's own response to the consultation, revealing that 52 per cent of respondents favoured, and 30 per cent opposed, the extension of civil partnership to different-sex couples, while 9 per cent supported the prospective abolition of civil partnership, and 2 per cent preferred the 'no change' option.[51]

That was not in line with what the Scottish Government wanted to do and, in recent years, it has developed something of a reputation for being determined to the point of intransigence. Rather than appearing to ignore the results of the consultation process, it indicated that it would not legislate immediately, and would gather evidence of the impact of same-sex marriage over the next five years, before reaching a decision on how to proceed.[52] That looked like 'kicking the can down the road', but there was another reason to delay a final decision, since an English case on the matter was due to be heard by the UK Supreme Court.

In England, as in Scotland, civil partnership was available only to same sex-couples, and, in *R (on the application of Steinfeld and Keidan) v. Secretary of State for International Development*,[53] a different-sex couple challenged their exclusion from civil partnership, founding on Articles 8 and 14 of the ECHR.[54] Since it was common ground that access to civil partnership fell within the ambit of Article 8, and that different-sex and same-sex couples were being treated differently in respect of civil partnership, the only way for the Westminster Government to avoid a finding that the law was incompatible with Article 8 was for it to demonstrate that the unequal treatment was justified.[55] Applying the usual four-part test for justification,[56] the Court had no difficulty in concluding

---

51   *Review of Civil Partnership: Scottish Government Response to Consultation*, Scottish Government, 2017, para. 5 (7% of respondents were in an 'other' category). Most of those supporting the 'no change' option were corporate bodies rather than individuals.

52   Ibid., paras. 6–12.

53   [2018] UKSC 32; [2020] AC 1.

54   In *Ratzenböck and Seydl v. Austria*, App. No. 28475/12, [2017] ECHR 947, at para. 42, the ECtHR found no violation of the ECHR in respect of a different-sex couple in Austria who were denied access to civil partnership on the basis that they were not in 'a relevantly similar or comparable situation to same-sex couples', who were denied access to marriage at the time. The case is discussed in R. KELLY and A. PLACE, 'Excluding different-sex couples from registered and civil partnerships: discrimination and proportionality: *Ratzenböck and Seydl v. Austria* and *Steinfeld and Keidan v. Secretary of State for Education*' [2018] *Family Law* 410.

55   [2018] UKSC 32, at para. 19.

56   The test is: (1) that the aim is legitimate, being sufficiently important to justify limiting a fundamental right; (2) that the measures are rationally connected to it; (3) that the measures are proportionate, being no more than is necessary to accomplish the aim; and (4) that they strike a fair balance between the rights of the individual and the interests of the community: [2018] UKSC 32, at para. 41, citing *R (on the application of Aguilar Quila) v. Secretary of State for the Home Department* [2011] UKSC 45; [2012] 1 AC 621, per Lord Wilson at para. 45 and *Bank Mellat v. HM Treasury (No. 2)* [2014] AC 700, per Lord Sumption at para. 20 and Lord Reed at para. 75.

that the Government had failed to make its case,[57] noting, in passing, that it had created the discrimination in the first place.[58] A declaration of incompatibility with the Human Rights Act 1998 was made.[59] That did not resolve the question of what to do about the problem, since the Court, quite properly, left that matter to the legislature.

The Scottish Government consulted again, in 2018.[60] Since the 'no change' option had been ruled out by the Supreme Court, this consultation confined itself to the two remaining courses of action: prospective abolition of civil partnership or its extension to different-sex couples. There was a sense in which the debate was over before it began, because, just two days after the consultation was launched, the (then) prime minister, Theresa May, indicated that civil partnership would be extended to all couples in England and Wales.[61] If Scottish different-sex couples were denied access to civil partnership in Scotland, they could seek to secure that end by travelling over the border to England, albeit there might have been doubt over whether their relationship would be recognised at home.

The 2018 consultation repeated the familiar arguments and sought fresh insights, without actually asking respondents to indicate their preference on how to proceed. Many respondents, like the present author, probably finessed their submissions to make their preference clear. The analysis of the 481 responses received (462 from individuals, and 19 from organisations) confined itself to qualitative analysis and offered no quantitative information,[62] noting that the process 'did not elicit substantial new insight into the arguments'.[63] Hard numbers, albeit for the UK as a whole, were published in the *British Social Attitudes Survey 2019*, which found that 65 per cent of those surveyed supported civil partnership being available to different-sex couples, while only 7 per cent were opposed.[64]

---

[57]   The aim was not legitimate (para. 46); the means used were not proportionate (para. 48); and a fair balance had not been struck (para. 52). Had the aim been legitimate, the Court would have found the requisite rational connection to have been present (para 47).

[58]   In the words of Lord Kerr, at para. 46, '[t]he present case does not involve a form of discrimination that was historically justified but has gradually lost its justification. The exact reverse is the case here. A new form of discrimination was introduced by the coming into force' of the 2013 Act.

[59]   [2018] UKSC 32, at para. 62.

[60]   *The future of civil partnership in Scotland: A consultation by the Scottish Government*, Scottish Government, 2018.

[61]   F. GIBB, 'I will: May promises civil partnerships for all', *The Times*, 3 October 2018.

[62]   *The future of civil partnership in Scotland: Analysis of consultation responses*, Scottish Government, 2019.

[63]   Ibid., para. 11.

[64]   J. CURTICE, E. CLERY, J. PERRY, M. PHILLIPS and N. RAHIM (eds.), *British Social Attitudes: The 36th Report*, The National Centre for Social Research, 2019, at p. 116. Support was even higher amongst those who did not identify with a religion (73%), and those educated to degree level or above (71%).

Given that public opinion was so clear, and with civil partnership becoming available to different-sex couples in the rest of the UK,[65] the Scottish Government had little choice but to change its stance. It introduced the Civil Partnership (Scotland) Bill in the Scottish Parliament in September 2019. Essentially, the bill amended the Civil Partnership Act 2004 to extend civil partnership to different-sex couples in Scotland. It passed by 64 votes in favour, with no votes against or abstentions, in June 2020. Finally, both marriage and civil partnership were available to same- and different-sex couples.

6. MODE OF CELEBRATION OF MARRIAGE AND CIVIL PARTNERSHIP

Historically, in Scotland, celebration of marriage was the province of the Roman Catholic Church. After the Reformation, in the sixteenth century, that function passed to the Church of Scotland. For a time, it had exclusive jurisdiction to perform marriage ceremonies, with that privilege being extended to other religious groups over the following centuries, albeit, religious groups are not treated equally, in terms of being authorised to solemnise marriages.[66] The option of having a civil ceremony was introduced in 1939, when two of the three forms of irregular (common law) marriage were abolished.[67]

When civil partnership was introduced in 2004, legislators were keen to signal that, while it had almost all the same legal consequences as marriage, it was something distinct from marriage. One way that was done was by providing that the relationship could only be formalised by a civil registration process, there being no option of a religious ceremony. That also served to address the concerns of religious groups opposed to recognition of same-sex relationships: that respect for their freedom of religion would be compromised if they were compelled to participate in civil partnership registration.

Not all religious celebrants or groups were opposed to recognition of same-sex relationships, and, indeed, some religious celebrants performed 'commitment ceremonies' which had no legal effect, but which might be important to the couple. As civil partnership became mainstream, and amid plans to permit same-sex couples to marry, the case was made to permit religious celebrants

---

[65]   The Civil Partnerships, Marriages and Deaths (Registration etc.) Act 2019, s. 2 extended civil partnership to different-sex couples in England and Wales, something secured for Northern Ireland as a result of the passing, at Westminster, of the Northern Ireland (Executive Formation etc.) Act 2019.

[66]   For further details, see SUTHERLAND, *Child and Family Law, Vol. II, Intimate Adult Relationships*, above n. 14, at paras. 2-108–2-112.

[67]   Marriage (Scotland) Act 1939. Irregular marriage was a form of civil marriage, since there was usually no religious – and, often, no other – ceremony involved.

who were willing to do so, and whose religious group permitted them to do so, to solemnise both civil partnerships and marriages. That step was taken when the Marriage and Civil Partnership (Scotland) Act 2014 was passed, and it also extended the power to officiate at these ceremonies to authorised 'belief bodies' and celebrants.[68] Once civil partnership became available to different-sex couples, the legislation was amended further, to afford them similar latitude.

Undoubtedly, the statutory scheme has become more complex and efforts to combat both forced and sham marriages and civil partnerships brought further regulation. That may be a small price to pay for respecting inclusion, diversity and protection, but it could be avoided by providing for all marriages and civil partnerships to be solemnised in a civil ceremony, presided over by a registrar,[69] an approach taken in some other jurisdictions.[70] Whether that would be acceptable to the population is, as yet, untested.

One benefit of the current system is the flexibility it offers, in terms of where the ceremony may be performed, and such ceremonies take place in civil registration offices; in buildings associated with particular religious or belief bodies; in hotels; on beaches, lochs and mountainsides; in private gardens and public parks; and in Scottish territorial waters. By and large, location is determined by the couple, the celebrant, and any religious or belief body involved.[71]

7. NON-MARITAL COHABITATION

Even at the beginning of our period of enquiry, in 1973, many couples in Scotland were simply living together without formalising their relationship and, indeed,

---

[68] A religious or belief body is defined as 'an organised group of people – (a) which meets regularly for religious worship; or (b) the principal object (or one of the principal objects) of which is to uphold or promote philosophical beliefs and which meets regularly for that purpose': Marriage (Scotland) Act 1977 Act, s. 26(2) (as amended by the 2014 Act).

[69] E.E SUTHERLAND, 'Giving the state sole jurisdiction over marriage would simplify the law' (2013) 58 (April) *Journal of the Law Society of Scotland*, available at <https://www.lawscot. org.uk/members/journal/issues/vol-58-issue-04/opinion-column-elaine-sutherland/>, last accessed 04.11.2022.

[70] Writing in 2010, Masha Antokolskaia stated the position thus: 'A majority of European jurisdictions provide for a dual system of civil and religious marriage … A minority of European jurisdictions recognise only civil marriage as a legal marriage, however their approach is also not uniform. Some merely do not recognise the legal consequences of religious marriage, without prohibiting its celebration prior to civil registration, while others do prohibit such celebration.' (footnotes omitted): M. ANTOKOLSKAIA, 'Harmonisation of substantive family law in Europe: myths and reality' [2010] *Child and Family Law Quarterly* 397, 402.

[71] Neither civil registration of a civil partnership nor a civil marriage may take place on 'religious premises': Civil Partnership Act 2004, s. 93(1A) and Marriage (Scotland) Act 1977 Act, s. 18, respectively. 'Religious premises' are premises which either are used solely or mainly for religious purposes, or those which have been so used and have not subsequently been used solely or mainly for other purposes.

it was the only option for same-sex couples for many years. In the early days, non-marital cohabitation was largely ignored by the legal system, save in so far as it was criminalised where, for example, the relationship was incestuous,[72] or one of the parties was under the age of consent to sexual activity.[73] There was occasional recognition for specific purposes, like protection from domestic abuse[74] or claiming damages for the death of a partner,[75] but, by and large, parting cohabitants were left to rely on general legal principles, like contract and unjustified enrichment in order to secure a remedy when things went awry in their relationships.

The incidence of non-marital cohabitation increased over the years, and, in 1992, the Scottish Law Commission recommended that the legal system should accord the relationship increased legal recognition during its currency, on breakdown, and on the death of one of the parties. It was quite clear, however, that its goal was not to put non-marital cohabitation on a par with marriage and that any reform should 'neither undermine marriage, nor undermine the freedom of those who have deliberately opted out of marriage'.[76] Legislators endorsed that approach,[77] and the legislation that was eventually passed, the Family Law (Scotland) Act 2006, takes that path.

During the relationship and subject to limited exceptions, Scots law applies a separate property rule to spouses and civil partners, and cohabitants are treated in much the same way.[78] However, unlike spouses and civil partners,[79] cohabitants do not owe each other an obligation of aliment (financial support) during the relationship.

---

[72]   Criminal Law (Consolidation) (Scotland) Act 1995, s. 1, confining the offence to blood relatives and a limited range of parent–child relationships created by adoption or the use of assisted reproductive technology. There is a separate offence of having sexual intercourse with a stepchild: 1995 Act, s. 2.

[73]   Sexual Offences (Scotland) Act 2009, s. 18 (child under the age of 13), and s. 28 (child aged 13 to 15). It is also an offence for a person over the age of 18 to have sexual intercourse with a person under that age where the elder person is in a position of trust in respect of the younger person, something that can arise in respect of people like schoolteachers, but also where the elder person is living with the parent of the younger: 2009 Act, s. 42.

[74]   The Matrimonial Homes (Family Protection) (Scotland) Act 1981, s. 18 provides for different-sex cohabitants to apply to the court in order to benefit from some of the protections under the Act, with the provision being extended to same-sex cohabitants by the Family Law (Scotland) Act 2006, s. 34.

[75]   Damages (Scotland) Act 2011, ss. 4 and 14, replacing the Damages (Scotland) Act 1976, which was in similar terms.

[76]   Scottish Law Commission, *Report on Family Law*, Scot. Law Com. No.135, 1992, at para. 16.1.

[77]   *The Family Law (Scotland) Bill: Policy Memorandum*, Scottish Executive, 2005, para. 65: 'The Scottish Ministers do not intend to create a new legal status for cohabitants. It is not the intention that marriage-equivalent legal rights should accrue to cohabiting couples.'

[78]   There had long been a rebuttable (disputable) presumption that spouses and civil partners owned household goods and savings from housekeeping allowances in equal shares: Family Law (Scotland) Act 1985, ss. 25 and 26. Similar, but not identical, presumptions were created for cohabitants by the Family Law (Scotland) Act 2006, ss. 25 and 26.

[79]   The Family Law (Scotland) Act 1985, s. 1.

Disputes over property arise most often when a relationship ends and Scots law has long had a coherent and sophisticated system in place to assist spouses and civil partners in resolving disputes.[80] The 2006 Act effectively took parts of that system and sought to apply them to parting cohabitants.[81] Even then, the legislation failed to adopt the clear, crisp wording recommended by the Scottish Law Commission in 1992, and the result is a statutory provision that has caused endless problems for parting cohabitants, those advising them, and the courts. Similarly, where a spouse or civil partner dies, there is a system in place to provide for the surviving partner, albeit reform of the law in this area has been debated for the last 30 years.[82] The 2006 Act broke new ground by permitting a surviving cohabitant to seek a discretionary award from the court, and, again, the provision is not without its problems.

In addition to the 2006 Act, the rights of cohabitants to respect for their private and family life, under Article 8 of the ECHR, has sometimes enabled the courts to recognise specific rights for cohabitants. So, for example, the UK Supreme Court, in *Re McLaughlin's Application for Judicial Review*,[83] concluded that a surviving cohabitant was entitled to a widowed parent's allowance, with Lady Hale also finding support for that outcome in the UK's obligations under the CRC.[84]

A number of jurisdictions around the world take a very different approach, treating non-marital cohabitation in much the same way as marriage, with New Zealand being something of a trailblazer in that respect.[85] Given the widespread incidence of non-marital cohabitation in Scotland, that raises the question of whether the case could be made for further reform of the law along similar lines.

In contrast to the issue of recognising same-sex relationships, there has been no grass-roots movement lobbying for radical reform of the law on non-marital cohabitation, with such discussion as there has been being very much the province of academics.[86] The lack of public engagement may be due, in part, to the 'common law marriage myth'; that is, the belief that, by living together, couples establish a common law marriage, giving them the same rights

---

80   Family Law (Scotland) Act 1985, discussed in detail in SUTHERLAND, *Child and Family Law, Vol. II, Intimate Adult Relationships*, above n. 14, at ch. 6.
81   Family Law (Scotland) Act 2006, s. 28.
82   See SUTHERLAND, *Child and Family Law, Vol. II, Intimate Adult Relationships*, above n. 14, at ch. 7, where the position of cohabitants is also discussed.
83   [2018] UKSC 48; [2018] 1 WLR 4250.
84   Ibid., para. 40.
85   Property (Relationships) Amendment Act 2001. That approach was endorsed by the New Zealand Law Commission in *Report on the Review of the Property (Relationships) Act 1976*, New Zealand Law Commission Report No. 143, 2019.
86   F. MCCARTHY, 'Cohabitation: lessons from north of the border?' (2011) 23 *Child and Family Law Quarterly* 277; E.E. SUTHERLAND, 'From "bidie-in" to "cohabitant" in Scotland: the perils of legislative compromise' (2013) 27 *Journal of Law, Policy and the Family* 143.

as spouses. Successive *British Social Attitudes Surveys* demonstrate that this misunderstanding of the law is remarkably widespread throughout the UK,[87] and is more prevalent in Scotland than in the rest of the UK, with some 58 per cent of Scots surveyed believing the myth.[88] While ignorance of the law is a pervasive problem, a contributory factor here may be the fact that, until its substantial and prospective abolition in 2006,[89] Scots law embraced the concept of 'irregular marriage', the Scottish form of common law marriage, which permitted the courts to declare a marriage on the basis of cohabitation, where the couple had lived together in Scotland for an unspecified, but 'substantial' period of time, and were generally regarded by friends and family as married.[90] In any event, this misunderstanding makes public opinion less helpful in driving law reform on non-marital cohabitation than it has been in other areas of family law.

When the Scottish Law Commission returned to the matter of non-marital cohabitation recently, the ambit of its enquiry was narrower than that of its predecessor in 1992. Since the Scottish Government was examining the law of succession (inheritance), the Commission confined itself to reviewing how the law addressed cohabitation during the relationship, and when living cohabitants separate.

It took its customary approach, publishing a Discussion Paper[91] for consultation, and, taking account of the responses it received, making firm recommendations for reform in its final Report. Shortly after the Discussion Paper was published, restrictions were imposed in Scotland as a result of the COVID-19 pandemic, something that may explain why it netted only 46 responses (25 from individuals, and 21 from organisations).[92] However, the Commission secured further input from the specialist Advisory Group it had appointed; through an online survey, to which 243 members of the public responded; and from workshops with the legal profession and an interfaith group.[93]

The Discussion Paper began by asking the fundamental question: whether there should be different regimes for parting spouses and civil partners, on the

---

[87]   In the UK-wide survey for 2018, 47% of respondents believed that couples who have lived together for some time 'definitely do' or 'probably do' have a common law marriage: M. Albakri, S. Hill, N. Kelley and N. Rahim, 'Relationships and gender identity: Public attitudes within the context of legal reform' in J. Curtice, E. Clery, J. Perry, M. Phillips and N. Rahim (eds.), *British Social Attitudes: the 36th Report*, The National Centre for Social Research, 2019.

[88]   Scottish Law Commission, *Report on Cohabitation*, Scot. Law Com. No. 261, 2022, at para. 1.7. The findings for Scotland relied on a small sample of 204 people.

[89]   Family Law (Scotland) Act 2006, s. 3.

[90]   For a discussion of irregular marriage, see Sutherland, *Child and Family Law, Vol. II, Intimate Adult Relationships*, above n. 14, at paras. 2-187–2-201.

[91]   Scottish Law Commission, *Aspects of Family Law: Discussion Paper on Cohabitation*, Discussion Paper No. 170, 2020.

[92]   Scottish Law Commission, *Report on Cohabitation*, Scot. Law Com. No. 261, 2022, at App. D.

[93]   Ibid., at paras. 1.30–1.34.

one hand, and separating cohabitants, on the other. Responses to that question were divided across all groups, and the Commission concluded that:

> in the absence of evidence of clear, unqualified and unequivocal support from a majority of the legal profession, the academic world, equality groups and the general public, it is not possible for us to recommend reform of the law to the extent required to fully align the regimes for financial provision on cessation of cohabitation, divorce and dissolution of civil partnership.[94]

As a result, the Commission's recommendations for reform are largely confined to efforts to modernise and improve the current statutory provisions, by amending or replacing them, while retaining the distinction between cohabitation and the formal relationships. It is too early to assess how the recommendations have been received, and, of course, the Commission's recommendations do not preclude the Scottish Government from taking a different approach, nor the possibility that attitudes will change, leading to calls for more sweeping reform in the future.

8.   LESSONS FOR FUTURE LAW REFORM

There is a tendency, in post-industrial democracies, to equate 'law reform' with 'liberal change', an assumption that is increasingly being called into question.[95] Certainly, over the last 50 years, the Scottish legal system has followed a clear trajectory in recognising an increasingly broad range of intimate adult relationships and in making them more widely available. Both marriage and the newer, equivalent, formal relationship of civil partnership are now available to different and same sex couples. While it has not been placed on a par with these formal relationships, non-marital cohabitation has gained increased legal recognition in so far as it has greater legal consequences than was once the case.

The most significant reforms have occurred in the last 20 years, raising the possibility that a climate has been created that is conducive to further reform. Recently, the minimum age for marriage was raised to 18 in a number of jurisdictions, including England and Wales, the Netherlands and Sweden.[96]

---

[94]   Ibid., at para. 2.38.

[95]   See, e.g. P. ALSTON, 'The Populist Challenge to Human Rights' (2017) 9 *Journal of Human Rights Practice* 1; N. GROSSMAN, 'Populism, International Courts, and Women's Human Rights' (2020) *Maryland Journal of International Law* 104; M.R. MADSEN, J.A. MAYORAL, A. STREZHNEV and E. VOETEN, 'Sovereignty, Substance, and Public Support for European Courts' Human Rights Rulings' (2022) 116 *American Political Science Review* 419; S. MARKS, 'Backlash: the undeclared war against human rights' [2014] *European Human Rights Law Review* 319.

[96]   For a discussion of why the age has been raised, see SUTHERLAND, *Child and Family Law, Vol. II, Intimate Adult Relationships*, above n. 14, at paras. 1-032–1-039.

Discussion is under way in Scotland, where the age is currently 16,[97] over whether to take that step. There is also the possibility, discussed above, of treating non-marital cohabitation in the same way as the formal relationships. A more radical option, at least in Scotland, would be for the legal system to accommodate multi-partner relationships by making provision for polygamy and other consensual non-monogamous relationships.[98] It is doubtful that there would be widespread public support for reform along those lines, but that matter is, as yet, untested.

What lessons might be learned – by both proponents and opponents of reform, and the various state agencies dealing with them – from the developments of the last 50 years? Perhaps the clearest lesson is that securing reform of family law can be frustratingly, if not painfully, slow.

The impetus for reform can come from a wide range of sources. There are the groups lobbying for a particular reform, of course, and they are acutely aware that the strategies they employ may be important in shaping public opinion and the views of policy-makers and legislators. Their activities can do much to get a particular issue on to the Government's agenda, leading to public consultation, and, sometimes, referral to the Scottish Law Commission.

Public opinion itself is important, but precisely how it is measured is challenging. It would be a mistake to place undue reliance on the responses to Government or Scottish Law Commission consultations, since such a small number of individuals and organisations usually respond to them. As the 2011 Scottish Government consultation on same-sex marriage demonstrates, where the response rate is unusually high, that fact alone indicates the need for further enquiry into why that occurred.[99] Opinion polls that seek the views of a cross section of the population may be useful, but care should be taken in noting how questions were framed, and *Social Attitudes Surveys* may provide a more reliable indication. Nor can public opinion be the sole determinant of reform if the result would be the oppression of a minority by the majority.

Domestic courts can play a valuable role in ensuring respect for human rights, and, without wishing to get into the debate surrounding 'judicial activism', they have contributed to law reform in respect of non-marital cohabitation[100] and extending civil partnership to different-sex couples.[101] If campaigners for change are unsuccessful in domestic courts, there is the further option of the ECtHR, albeit it has not proved to be particularly proactive in pushing the boundaries on intimate relationships.

---

[97]   Marriage (Scotland) Act 1977, s. 1.
[98]   See SUTHERLAND, *Child and Family Law, Vol. II, Intimate Adult Relationships*, above n. 14, at paras. 1-053–1-085 (polygamy) and 1-147–1-156 (polyamory).
[99]   See above nn. 36-37 and accompanying text.
[100]   See above nn. 83–84 and accompanying text.
[101]   See above nn. 53–59 and accompanying text.

What of the law reform process itself? Law reform often involves compromise. In this, compromise may be inherently attractive because it carries with it notions of cooperation and reasonableness. More pragmatically, it may be a wise course for the proponents of reform. If they fail to embrace compromise, they may risk ending up with nothing: 'better half a loaf than no bread at all', as the old adage goes. However, as the policy-makers and legislators discovered over civil partnership, compromise should not be viewed as an easy way out. As we have seen, it did not silence those calling for same-sex marriage, nor their opponents, and it set the scene for a fresh battle over making civil partnership available to different-sex couples.

A corollary of compromise is the fact that law reform is often incremental. The most significant driver in broadening the narrow range of relationship options that were available in 1973, and those to whom they are available, was undoubtedly the calls to make marriage available to same-sex couples. That reform was not achieved overnight, being secured a decade after the advent of civil partnership; and it was to be a further five years before that option became available to different-sex partners.

In all of this, perhaps the fundamental message to those seeking a particular reform is not to give up – to be patient, creative and tenacious.

PART III
DEVELOPMENTS IN FAMILY LAW

BRAZIL

THE FAMILY AMONG THE COHABITATION MODALITIES OF THE LAW AND THE DISTINCTION BETWEEN BEING, THINKING, ACTING AND FEELING AS A FAMILY

Antonio Jorge Pereira Júnior*

Résumé

Le présent article expose les perceptions sociologiques, philosophiques, anthropologiques et juridico-constitutionnelles brésiliennes de la famille, afin de permettre la compréhension des observations structurelles qui favorisent l'identification d'une entité comme pouvant être considérée comme une famille par le droit. Il est entendu que l'extension du concept juridique de famille, sans critères objectifs et sans limites, conduit, à proprement parler, à la perte de la compréhension de ses caractéristiques, de ce qui la différencient d'autres groupes et associations de nature « cohabitationnelle ». Ces dernières doivent recevoir un traitement juridique différent, quoique comparable à celui de la famille.

*   Doctor, Master and Bachelor of Law from the University of São Paulo (USP). Professor of the Master's and Doctorate Program in Constitutional Law at the University of Fortaleza (PPGD-UNIFOR). Leader of the Constitutional Law and Private Autonomy Research Group, recognised by the National Council for Scientific and Technological Development (CNPq).

1. INTRODUCTION

The present chapter aims to share sociological, philosophical, anthropological and Brazilian juridical-constitutional views about the family that can help in the reflection on objective observations that enable the legal recognition of an entity such as a family (in relation to being), in the face of the view that the presence of subjective elements such as the imagined family (in relation to thinking), the functional family (in relation to action), or the perceived family (in relation to feeling) are sufficient. It is understood that the extension of the legal concept of family without the consideration of structural or objective considerations, from a social and philosophical perspective, would lead, strictly speaking, to the emptying of the concept itself, covering up attributes that would differentiate it objectively, sociologically and philosophically, from groupings and associations of a similar nature that would justify different legal treatment.

2. A SOCIOLOGICAL PERSPECTIVE OF THE FAMILY

This chapter will maintain that the sociological view of the family provides a foundation for rethinking the legal definitions of what constitutes and what does not constitute a family. Critical to this foundation is a view of society grounded in 'relational realities' that prepare individuals, from birth forward, to function within a web of relationships that connect individuals to each other. This relational concept draws heavily on the work of Pierpaolo Donati, specifically *The family as the root of society*. Donati, a sociologist and professor at the University of Bologna, published this work in Spanish in 2013.[1] The book presents the family as a 'relational reality' that serves as the basis and root for all other social relations, because, in the family, the individual is primarily prepared for sociability.[2]

---

[1] See P. DONATI, *La familia como raíz de la sociedade*, BAC, 2013. Some considerations that follow are taken from Donati's studies, so they will not be deepened or analysed here, as they are separate to the main object, which is the systematisation created by the professor from Bologna. In Donati's book under analysis, the reader will be able to find better references that support his arguments.

[2] Another work of value, for the present study, but which is remarked upon in another article, is *The Family as Educational Environment* (A. BERNAL et al., Madrid: Rialp, 2009). There are several interdisciplinary studies published by the Institute of Sciences for the Family of the University of Navarra. In the first work of the collection, Francisco Altarejos, Full Professor of Philosophy of Education at that University, develops the work *Changes and Expectations in the Family*. He presents, as one of the causes of a crisis in the family, the experience of individualism that generates an experience of the family reality as a society with an associative, mechanical character, where members live for their own satisfaction above all, without entering the context of family education, considering it as a source of growth for everyone who integrates it, with the experience of living as a community; that is, with stronger bonds (pp. 22–23).

Donati considers that society is constituted of the family in a relationship of continuous interdependence. The family should be the primary relational asset. The observations he developed serve for discussions and debates to be carried out by family lawyers, as well as for judicial decisions, especially those of the superior courts. Some of the ideas he developed can help the law to understand the family phenomenon from a sociological perspective.[3]

Donati examines attributes that are permanent in typical family entities through an approach that recognises a certain objectivity of the components of a family structure. At the same time, he presents contemporary situations that make it difficult to identify and perceive those components.

At the beginning of the book, Donati affirms the need to re-evaluate and update the meaning of the family idea. There are different types of cohabitation or coexistence entities in the twenty-first century, but not all of these have a family nature, just as not all contribute equally to the good of society. However, they can still be evaluated or subjectively signified. In this context, in order to distinguish what would be characteristic of a family entity, from a sociological and objective analysis, he traces what he calls the 'genome' of the family, and, as a result, goes through family dynamics, from which he identifies relational effects of the family environment that impact social life and help us to understand why the entity that he considers as a family deserves a different legal treatment.

Although it contains enduring relational attributes, to Donati, the family is not an unchanging structure over time: 'The contemporary family experiences a process of profound social morphogenesis. Morphogenesis, as the term implies, means the production of new social forms that change the previous family structures.'[4] The pluralisation to which the concept is submitted demonstrates its evolutionary perspective. In this sense, Donati recognises a pluralism in which functional and structural changes represent the vitality of the family. At the same time, however, he draws attention to a certain 'pathological pluralism', which, strictly speaking, would culminate in the deinstitutionalisation of the family.[5]

---

[3]   By way of illustration, a summary of the work is set out below, which shows the versatility and verticality of the scientific and philosophical explanation given to the theme, and which serves to inspire the modus operandi of the political, judicial and educational institutions that deal with family: Introduction: Understanding family reasons; Chapter 1: The family as a relational reality; Chapter 2: The family on the horizon of history; Chapter 3: The masculine and feminine identity: distinctions and relations for a family and a society adapted to the human person; Chapter 4: The couple and the family: in search of a 'we' to be ourselves; Chapter 5: The social virtues of the family; Chapter 6: The contemporary family between empirical facts and ethical norms: comparison with Catholic social thought.

[4]   See P. DONATI, *La familia como raíz de la sociedade*, BAC, 2013, p. 56.

[5]   'The family becomes "plural" motivated by two great orders of each epoch or, in any case, of long duration: a) On the one hand, it is modified by the affirmation of a cultural process of "individualization [growing individualist culture] of individuals", that is to say, of the growing importance attached to the subjectivity of persons, in the context of a general increase in the importance of individual citizenship rights (civil, political, social and human);

Therefore, there are limits that suggest conceptualisation, and which are beyond the ordinary subjective readings at the beginning of the twenty-first century.

Donati understands, for example, that the family would not exist completely without sexual difference, because with the composition between man and woman, its truth, beauty and goodness are updated and manifested with greater potential synergy. He develops a rationale about the male and female identity in the family, the role changes, and the different modes of relationship within the family organisation. This is without any kind of discrimination in relation to other cohabitational modalities. He starts from an objective analysis of situations that have passed through the centuries of history without controversy, in regard to the family's nature.

The genome of the relational structure of the family has its own elements of interactive self, reciprocity, generativity and sexuality experienced as conjugal love: 'The familiar form of the interpersonal relationship coincides with a choice of conjugal love that leads to a risk-taking project of common life, seeking its fullness in the means of continuous regenerative living one for the other.'[6] The family is not, therefore, only a place of affections and feelings, much less a residence and a patrimony, but rather, and above all, a social relation that projects itself beyond the home. It can be said that entities of the family profile, as a second nature, go beyond individualities, being a real society or community that, for this reason, are entitled to a differential treatment.

The professor from Bologna University says that the contemporary debate about the pluralism of family forms has been defined by two opposing theses. One thesis understands that pluralism is the product of a determinist evolution, producing, as a result, an increase in the variability and the dismantling of the 'traditional family', which thus becomes marginal. This thesis is, however, contrary to the statistics, which show that the traditional modality of two committed adults (typically a man and a woman, together with the children they produce) continues to form the majority of family relationships, albeit with the adaption of roles. The second thesis, on the other hand, asserts that pluralism would basically result in negative, regressive and socially degrading tendencies, such a view being based on a single-family social representation:

> More than talking about an irreversible crisis, or even the disappearance of the family, one must speak of a process of social differentiation that the family is approaching. This process implies: a) that traditional family structures are being discussed,

---

This process tends to reduce the rights of the family as a supra-personal entity, endowed with its own objectivity external to individuals; b) On the other hand, the family is modified by the prevalence, as a typical principle of modernity, of a systemic process that develops by continually encouraging and reorganizing social bonds. This process entails the continuous deconstruction and reconstruction of family ties based on goals of occasion.' See. ibid., p. 53.

6   Ibid., pp. 17–18.

b) that family expectations and behaviors are subjectivized; and c) that family roles are redefined in an extremely articulated way, that is, the complex of rights and duties, private and public, linked to the status of people as 'relatives' of other people (author's own translation).[7]

It is necessary, therefore, to elaborate new semantics appropriate to plurality, with terms that allow us, at the same time, to differentiate the peculiar identity of the family in contrast to its other analogical and metaphorical forms. In this context, intellectual effort is required for a better understanding of family morphogenesis, in which the co-existent forms are evaluated based on three empirical criteria, being necessary for the consideration of the family: internal vitality (renewal capacity); ability to respond to society's expectations (socialisation, responsibility towards children); and the ability to support oneself when confronted with other family forms (non-Western ethnic groups, for example).

The book also looks at the concept of 'family citizenship'; that is, the family as a civil entity beyond the individual considered in isolation, revealing itself as a real and distinct 'other being'. This idea also transcends the welfare model of the State to act for the family, and it must recognise and fulfil the rights of the family unit, the holder of the rights.

From the group of ideas expressed in *The family as the root of society*, the idea emerges, though the practical legal view, that the family translates into a structural and symbolic relationship capable of generalising its original ethics, while in other diverse situations, it is differentiated by its functions and its respective internal subsystems. This, in itself, leads to the justification of a differentiated normative treatment:

> In short, in the face of the progressive individualism of society, the study claims the family as a social subject and as a humanizing sphere of people and society itself. The family is seen as the paradigm of recognition of the other through the power (especially the power of recognition). Thus, it has a super-functional character, that is, a total social fact that implies all levels of existence (above other primary relationships, such as friendship). And this also explains that the family relationship is the source of specific virtues: unconditional reciprocal belonging, loyalty, availability. In this way, the family is considered an institution that promotes aggregation of social value, since it offers a fiducial model of life that generates primary human and social capital.[8] (author's own translation)

Given the general ideas of a work that deserves attention from scholars of family law, the following is an analysis that is perhaps closer to the Brazilian scenario.

---

[7]   Ibid., p. 54.
[8]   See R. Muñoz, 'Resenha do livro La familia como raíz de la sociedade', *University of Navarra: Scripta Theologica*, vol. 46, n. 03, 2014, 817.

From what has been reported above, attention is drawn to the possibility of reflecting on the diversity of cohabitational situations, with the projection of different effects on to society. Moreover, in contrast to a certain line of thinking from family law educators in Brazil, Donati does not place affection as the main dimension of the family. This is because, in fact, the feelings are not its structuring elements, not even in the current law in the country.

3. A PHILOSOPHICAL PERSPECTIVE OF THE FAMILY

Once we ask the question about the substance of the family entity, it is worth noting that the very notion of 'family-function' – that is, what is done by action – strictly presupposes, logically and ontologically, the family structure, because the functions perceived, even if they want to be reduced to the field of affection or security, arise from a praxis experienced from a sedimented relational structure, since 'action follows being'. That is, the dynamic potentialities of an entity are based on its own structure. In this sense, in the words of John Baptist Villela:

> Marriage is less a creation that is left to be done, to be redone or to be undone for the right of a cultural product sedimented over the millennia. It has certainly evolved over time. It has assumed, from the remotest antiquity, varied forms. But what allows us to say that its *forms* have changed in the time line, without sacrifice of the *content*, is, precisely, the permanence and the immanence of some elements that gave being and identity to the institute. (italics in the original)[9]

Being a phenomenon driven by a social nature and linked to human sustainability, the most common situation of family life observed in history is the experience of the monogamous relationship between man and woman in different civilisations, including those without the influence of the Judeo-Christian ideology. This is intended to go beyond the formal consideration of marriage, to focus on the union formed between a man and a woman with the intention of forming a family unit, especially with the intention of having children. Thus, it is worth noting that the argument for a purely functional family, in fact, incurs the incongruity of naming any kind of cohabitational situation as such. The simple 'living together' of people is not enough to consolidate the idea of family.

The maximum flexibility of the concept of family – for example, in Brazil there are those who believe that the legal concept of family must include a multi-species family, composed of people and animals, or marital relationships between more than two people – means that every imaginary and subjective

---

9   See J.B. VILLELA, *Adoption by Gay Couples: Inadmissibility*, São Paulo: Carta Forense, June 2009, <http://debecaetoga.blogspot.com/2011/06/adocao-por-casais-homossexuais.html>.

situation could be validated by law as a family, having as a source the particular desire or affection of the cohabitants. In this way, the legal concept of family would not be substantial, and the concept itself would lose its meaning, being a mere expression that would translate collective perceptions of subjective perceptions, often fluid and unstable, that would assume, here and there, some of the roles played by the idea of family in social representation. From this same logic, the duties of aid that are linked to the family entity become even more fragile, because they would be hostages to feelings. There would be more insecurity in legal family relations, and thus an unprecedented social instability would be generated.

In this context, it is relevant to go beyond the 'feeling', to look for the remaining ideas of the concept of family that would confirm the family identity as a certain kind of 'coexistence'. Within the concept of the family entity itself, it is also possible and opportune to differentiate modalities or types which manifest the diversity between the modes of family relationships. This perception is implicit in the Brazilian Constitution of 1988, because it is stated there that, '[f]or the protection of the State, the stable union between man and woman as a family entity is recognized, and the law should facilitate their conversion into marriage' (Art. 226, §3). Different modalities are recognised within the category of family, and this happens in the very genesis of the family, and not only in the dynamics of family life. Thus, the constitutional text itself serves as the basis for distinguishing treatment according to the preference of a certain type of coexistence for social life, followed by a stimuli for more complete and stable situations, from the sociolegal structural architecture.[10]

The choice as to how to deal with this legally should be derived from how political society values or hierarchises the co-existing situations in accordance with the common good, so as to prioritise the application of scarce public resources according to a proportional order from the most to the least necessary or convenient, from a social perspective, reflecting principles of distributive justice.[11]

For example, the presence of the terms 'special protection' and 'absolute priority' in Articles 226 and 227 of the Brazilian Federal Constitution of 1988 signify situations that deserve greater attention from the State and civil society, and which should have preferential or differentiated public policies and budget allocations; that is, in Brazil, there is a constitutional basis for legal differentiation of family entities.

---

[10] See A.J. PEREIRA JÚNIOR, 'Hierarquia entre gêneros de convivência na Constituição Federal', *Journal of the Law School, University of São Paulo*, São Paulo, vol. 98, 121–134, 2003.

[11] However, at the same time, it should be remembered that the social recognition of the different ways of human co-existence, as well as the different considerations about the family justice phenomenon, even though they do not impose themselves, logically merit different legal treatment.

Even if a given society decides to prescribe similar or even equal legal effects in relation to diverse cohabitational situations, it would not be correct to deny ontic (in regard to being) and deontic (in regard to ethical obligation) differences between cohabitational situations, connected with the greater or lesser need for one or the other situation for the very sustainability of civil society. This does not depend on, and should not be confused with, the subjective need or aspiration of each person individually considered and involved in their respective situation.

The legal protection of each person, individually considered, is guaranteed by other norms, carried with the greatest coercion, without having to instrumentalise the mechanism of the family for this purpose. In this sense, another provision of Article 226 of the 1988 Constitution states: 'The State shall ensure assistance to the family in the person of each one of its members, creating mechanisms to restrain violence in the context of their relations.' When a practice of intra-family violence threatens a member, the State will take a differentiated action to protect it. But here, again, the emphasis is on the family, in principle a good for everyone, as is clear from the text, which refers to 'assistance to the family in the person of each one'; that is, it does not present an individualistic interpretation, as some authors give to this text, totally displacing the focus of the family. This is different from the legal protection of each person against violence through the Penal Code, which may also co-affect the case, with the immediate intention of defending the person who is the victim of the aggression.

Therefore, the primary function of family norms is, through the logic of Article 226, to address families, in certain social situations, with characteristics that can be seen as necessary in the composition of the social base, without disqualifying other relationships that each person can establish. The prevailing point of view here is that of the 'social order' – the denomination of Title VIII of the Constitution – within which the family theme is regulated. The role of Article 5 of the Constitution, which is part of Title II, devoted to the theme of 'fundamental rights and guarantees', under Chapter 1, specifically designed to deal with 'individual and collective rights and duties', is different.

This is important to assert because the pursuit of legal favouritism for certain co-existing categories has led many to deny the objective distinction between them, even moving away from the banner of diversity, which was the foundation of the LGBT rights movement. João Baptista Villela affirmed, in this sense, that the argumentative line of equalisation between the co-existing entities would reveal incoherence, and weaken the argument of those who defended rights in the name of difference. For this reason, legal institutions or tools that serve diverse situations should be given appropriate names to preserve diversity, even if they prescribe identical legal effects. It would be a better solution to highlight pluralism and respect the consciousness of dissimilarity.

On the other hand, creating the understanding of diverse realities as being equal would, in turn, be inadequate. In this sense, the demand for affirmation of substantial equality between different situations constitutes moral and intellectual coercion. The imposition may cover a strategy of cultural implosion of the notion of family endorsed by a structural perspective, from which it is best understood as the 'basis of society', as expressed in Article 226 of the Federal Constitution.

Another common misconception in this regard is the confusion between individual equality and equality in unequal societies. The dignity of every human person, by the simple fact of being human, is aprioristically equal, because the human condition is not alterable, and the term, dignity, here, has no moral connotation. The assessment of the attitudes practiced by human beings is different. These can be qualified as more or less worthy or more or less unworthy, precisely because the valuation of the conduct and association of human persons varies according to the intent and the action, and their respective effects.

4. THE FAMILY BETWEEN BEING, THINKING, ACTING AND FEELING

The distinction between being, thinking, acting and feeling can serve to guide the reflection on how the law should deal with cohabitational situations that wish to be treated from the family legal perspective. This analysis starts from an anthropological perspective.

In daily life, we can see people who, because they live as a family, and feel like a family, believe that they have the right to receive equal legal recognition to other family modalities. For example, the *Folha de São Paulo* newspaper published a story about a group of three people – two men and one woman – who were said to have been prejudiced by the decision of the National Council of Justice to prohibit the drafting of a public deed[12] of a stable union between three or more people.[13] They felt, subjectively, that they were a family, and believed

---

[12] On the wave of subjectivation of the notary function, in the breaking of the law and the primordial social ends of the activity of the Records, read B. DE AVILA BORGARELLI, 'From Rolandino de Passeggeri to the "deed of polyamory": notarial activity in difficult times', *Boletim Migalhas*, 28 July 2018, online at <http://m.migalhas.com.br/depeso/284568/de-rolandino-de-passeggeri-a-escritura-do-poliamor-a-atividade>.

[13] See 'Com 2 homens e 1 mulher "trisal" deixa o País após decisão do CNJ', <https://www1.folha.uol.com.br/cotidiano/2018/07/com-2-homens-e-uma-mulher-trisal-deixa-o-pais-apos-decisao-do-cnj.shtml>. The Association of Family Law and Succession (ADFAS) filed a Request for Provisions to the National Council of Justice (0001459-08.2016.2.00.0000) on 17 April 2018, in order to prohibit the drafting of public deeds of stable unions between three or more persons. On 18 May 2018, they filed a second Order of Proceedings, in the same sense, in which the reasons for the request were explained. The explanation is also available on the Conjur site: <https://www.conjur.com.br/2018-mai-21/regina-silva-uniao-poliafetiva-efeitos-uniao-estavel-ilegal>. The Requests for Provisions with the CNJ can be accessed through these links: <http://adfas.org.br/wp-content/uploads/2018/06/2-Memoriais-Pedido-de-Providências-0001459-08.2016.2.00.0000.pdf> / <http://adfas.org.br/wp-content/uploads/2018/06/Memoriais-Pedido-de-Providências.pdf>.

that such a perception must lead the State to give them equal treatment with that given to monogamous families.

In other situations, persons who act as father or mother to someone who already has two registered and functional parents would like to be legally incorporated into the legal category of a registered parent, because of 'socio-effectiveness'. It is not that such persons are prevented from doing so – acting, in effect, like another parent – or that they would cease to do so if the State did not attribute such a position to them in the Register. They could even achieve the effects of patrimonial attachment in a similar way to the parental–filial relationship through other mechanisms available in the legal system. But it is more opportune for them, subjectively, to have State recognition, and the desire for juridical-social representativeness would serve them in a more convenient way. Thus, we arrive at the recognition of multiparentality, whereby, from a cohabitational situation, someone claims a corresponding parental legal bond, changing the family identity by registering a third individual where there were already two people in the position of parents.

Finally, there are entities that constitute a family since their origin, according to the law, but whose members, conversely, do not want to assume corresponding duties, and do not even have the slightest affection among themselves. An example would be the case of the refusal of a father to fulfil his duties in the face of an unwanted child. For many in this context, since they are not seen (thought), they do not act (action), and even less want (affections), it would not make sense to be forced to fulfil the demands of a family according to the law.

In the three examples mentioned, there are subjective aspiration to being or not being considered legally as a family, or even as a nuclear family. Would such aspirations be the preponderant factors for civil law? Would the atypical plural of social co-existence – in the way of atypical contracts – serve as a parameter for the legal regulation of the family, which deals mainly with *jus cogen* norms, because of their identification with the constitutive basis of society?

Naturally, the ideal would be for the family structure (plane of being) to be perceived in its essence (plane of thinking), to function as such (plane of action), and to bring full joy to its own members (plane of feeling and desiring). But what is the most important basis for the law to regulate a situation such as a family? To be a family (structure), imagine a family (think, consider), act as a family (dynamic), or to feel as a family (affectivity, desire)?

What is more, is legal regulation a bonus or a burden? What would justify 'special protection'? A reason of social order and a reason of public order.

The social order expresses the importance of the family in the structure of society. It is the basis of society ('the family, the basis of society, will have the special protection of the State' (Article 226 Federal Constitution)). The repercussions of the family for society as a whole makes it a distinct entity. Public order, in turn, will impose limits on the dynamics of the internal and external actions of family members, in connection with public morality and good manners. It is understood, therefore, that the juridical notion of family habitually carries more duties than liberties. Before representing a bonus, the State's interference with the family represents a burden. This is why the liberal movement tends to seek less interference of the State in personal relations.

Do the entities that claim to be treated legally as a family have full awareness of this? Do they know the 'why' of the special protection given by the 1988 Federal Constitution to marriage, to the stable union between man and woman, and to parentage? Should it not be a case of perhaps pleading for their own treatment, possibly similar, because they are not to be confused with the basis of society and, therefore, are not institutions considered simultaneously of social order and public order?

Are they really in need of, or should they be entitled to, equal treatment? Why? Would they not be using family law for another purpose, beyond the scope of the area, such as seeking a sense of social recognition and self-empowerment, through equal legal status? Would that not be using family law for purposes beyond its intended scope? In these cases, how effective would family legislation be in combating prejudice? Could such co-existing realities be exploited in an ideological conflict that escapes them?

'What do I know of what I will be, I who do not know what I am?':[14] this verse is by Álvaro de Campos, from *Tabacaria*. To know the proper way to go through existence, including the juridical, one must first know how to explain what one is. Some people think they *are what they think*, others that they *are what they feel*, and others that they *are what they do*. But they do not know *what they are*. Strictly speaking, first and foremost, each individual is defined by their inherent nature. *What you are* means the structure, essence, nature, the immaterial form of being. Knowing *what you are*, one has a better parameter for knowing how to act. Thus, one seeks to act better, to know one's own being, and one's substantial identity. Equal concern is the co-existence of situations.

'What do I know of what I will be, I who do not know what I am? To be what I think? But I think to be so much! And there are so many who think to be same thing, there cannot be so many!' – this is further verse by Álvaro de Campos in *Tabacaria*.[15] Through thought, we can imagine thousands of things. But, strictly speaking, few of them fit our reality. Should law regulate life in society according to the imagination of people and entities? Is that correct?

I can think of myself as a hero, but that does not make me a hero. Once imagined, I may even feel like one. Moreover, I can read a novel and, from the imagination, experience some of the sensations of the characters. But that does not, in fact, make me any of the characters. It does not change my nature.

---

[14] See F. PESSOA, *Tabacaria* (Álvaro de Campos), online at <http://www.dominiopublico.gov.br/download/texto/pe000010.pdf>.

[15] <https://www.insite.com.br/art/pessoa/ficcoes/acampos/456.php>.

Because neither thinking, acting nor feeling changes the nature of my being. They can, yes, make me evolve or involute within my category of being. From my being, I can align thought, behaviour and feeling to my substantiality; that is, the thought will be better activated from the perception of my objective reality. And so, with self-awareness, with the possession of a better knowledge of oneself, one could better guide one's conduct in harmony with one's being.

The observation of the familial phenomenon throughout history reveals an essential family structure. It is necessary to contemplate this reality and to learn from it, to understand its essential elements. The idea of a father, mother and child make up this nucleus. This is not to belittle other cohabitational situations. It is simply the nucleus from which the general rules of organisation of the family, and of society, have been established over the centuries. There are situations which are analogously similar to it – something similar to something different – without being confused with it. And there are others that are only metaphorically associated with it.

Let us return to the adage 'to act follows being'. Such an affirmation reflects the virtual and imperative order of causality of the ethical 'what should be' mirror of law. It refers to Aristotle's concepts of the 'Actuality' and 'Potentiality': what *should be* (act) according to the *being* (potential) itself. In the previous sentence, expressions derived from the word *be* appear twice: in the first such expression, *be* is a verb, and in the second, *being* is a noun. This *being* at the end of the sentence, the noun, is recognised from the observation of what one is. From *being* follows the *what should be*.

Philosophy, literature and art demonstrate expressions of human excellence, where one perceives the completeness of the human being: the full *being*. At the same time, they also describe the ills, the defects and the atrocities that the human being can commit: the *non-being* which, by derivation, then generates the negative ethical imperative *what should not be*.[16] The call to existence, of course, is an invitation for the consummation of the best, from each individual's situation; an invitation for optimisation, to reach a greater result for private and common good. Hamlet's 'to be or not to be', in Shakespeare, comes from this idea. To *be* (complete), according to the *what should be* of ethical nobility; or non-being (in disagreement with the noblest attitude), to perform revenge.

The term *realisation*, for example, expresses the concrete progress of being as it should be, in the time and circumstances of each individual. The person *realised* from this perspective is the one who has fulfilled in him/herself, through conduct, the high objectives that were potentially in his/her human condition, within the limits of his/her capacity, and according to his/her existential possibilities.

---

16 This chapter does not deal with differentiated psychological situations, which demand treatment and special and particular considerations.

Other maxims of classical ethics translate the ontic presupposition underlying the deontic. The aphorism 'know thyself', which is from the Temple of Delphi, and which Plato expresses as a maxim repeated by Socrates, is a part of this idea. Alongside this, one can place the imperative 'become what you are!', attributed to Pindar. This phrase also expresses the connection between the vocation to excellence and the invitation of the conscience to achieve its realisation in time and space: again, action and power. These are the terms for those who admit that there are essential understandings in the human, which serve as a guide for action.[17] Of course, there is a connection between the two maxims.[18] Without the prospect of an objective reference that inspires and can serve to model thought, there is a tendency to embrace the mirage projected in our imagination by situations and sensations. Sometimes these *sensations* or *imaginations* that predispose to action will be aligned with the very being, from the perspective of the best version of the human. At other times they will not.

In this sense, it should be pointed out that even people who live with references that coincide with an objective basis of being, according to the most complete model, can do so only from the projection of it in their imagination, without reaching the essential understanding of dignity and human categories. That is, they can be situated from a merely subjective perspective, based on sensations and impressions, rather than grounded in the conscious understanding of the human essence.

This could elucidate why existential crises occasionally manifest in seemingly harmonious individuals whose behaviour adheres to the most elevated ethical principles. Suddenly, they start to adopt a lifestyle opposite to their previous one. Perhaps it is simply because they did not possess conscious mastery of the way they lived. They did not grasp reality in its substance. Simply, that way of living coincided with the more common behaviour in the environment in which they were educated, serving as an encouragement or emulation, while they experienced a satisfaction in living in that way. But when they experienced frustration or disgust in that context – incidents that make up the ups and downs of any normal human life – they did not have an adequate understanding of the ethics they practiced, and then they were lost, vulnerable, not knowing how to react.

In this state of anguish, insecurity or circumstantial disappointment – in a word, crisis – they will be drawn to experiencing behaviours that can give them back the sense of comfort they once experienced. Sometimes they will find

---

[17] The very term 'essence' was considered controversial in philosophy, and there are schools that deny its existence, in that it is an agnosticism about the truth.

[18] See L.G. BRAZIL, 'Do "conhece-te a ti mesmo" ao "torna-te o que tu és": Nietzsche contra Sócrates em *Ecce Homo*', *Trágica Magazine*: studies on Nietzsche, 2nd semester of 2012, vol. 5, no. 2, pp. 30–45.

this inspiration exactly in attitudes that are paradoxically opposed to those that they previously practiced, insinuated in the environment. And there they are. Because this orientation, more than objective, had always been more subjective.

Such situations can exactly illustrate the experience by mere reflection of the environment, without the existential incorporation of the reasons that would support the conduct in values organised from a given world view. Educational projects with a rational root in values declined sharply in the twentieth century, with distrust of the possibility of knowing the truth (possible) about things, and the rising tide of moral relativism. This affects the perception of the family and the experience of their reality.

Moving this reasoning to the matter of family, little was known about the structural elements of the family. It was mainly concerned with imagination, action and sensation, rather than with the understanding of being. Imagination and action were dealt with by art and religion, which propitiated the support of maintenance of the structures. But in this scenario, the ethical and cultural change (plane of action) and the massive reduction of religious meaning (plane of feeling), replaced by individualistic and hedonistic bases, made the experience of the family relationship suffer a kind of concussion – a shock in diverse environments – especially influenced by such stimuli.

Thus, an imaginary and fragile construction emerged, a new social representation of the experience of family relationships in a culture that has been massified since the 1960s, competing with the previous perspective, still present, especially in environments less affected by the wave of individualism and hedonism.

In general, however, there is encouragement for the experience of a new way of living, which contrasts with the idea that prevailed until the mid twentieth century. The proposal of the sexual revolution gained ground in the face of the general shallowness of the so-called 'traditional' culture, as well as the actual defects and inequalities that were covered under such a banner. In part, there was intellectual and motivational poverty in the exposition of the potentiality of the traditional family, with respect to their capacity to generate happiness, above all because the image reflected in the mould of religion has decayed with the withdrawal of belief, previously sufficient to sustain the *modus vivendi*. Also, in part, the social representation of the family brought distortions that time would be careful to reveal.

Strictly speaking, the image that succeeded the vision of the traditional family has much less depth. But because of the defects that were often concealed in that social representation, and for the reason that the new modalities have a better dialogue with the sensorial dimension, and have gained space in the collective imagination, especially in the idyllic constructions of a romantic life, the perception of value of the classic model, which was motivational, has fallen. But it did not disappear because of its need for social support.

5. THE FAMILY BETWEEN AFFECTIVITY AND SOLIDARITY

Considering matters of family law, the crisis in the understanding of what the family should be as an existential and social project of transcendent character, allied to a superficial and sensorial environment, enables the attraction and fame of the so-called 'principle of affectivity'. Strictly speaking, what should be solid in the structure of the family relationship is not affectivity, but the very vocation to solidarity that is a reality of sociability. This awareness goes beyond the question of individual feeling, and can provide a foundation for action based on the *being* itself of the family, because it is derived from the human condition, independent of affective instability.[19]

In regard to this, it is worth looking at the work of João Carlos Almeida, Doctor in Education at the University of São Paulo, in his *Anthropology of Solidarity*: 'Solidarity is, today, a space of conceptual consensus. Progressives and conservatives use it without guilt. But what exactly does it mean? The danger of consensus is to mean everything and nothing at the same time.'[20]

Before giving an answer, João Carlos asks a question: 'What reciprocal links of mutual responsibility interfere ontologically in the construction of human identity? Could we call this phenomenon "ontological solidarity?"' In this way, he assumes the challenge of supporting ethical (deontic) inspiration on an ontic basis (the plane of being): 'If we can reasonably answer this question, subsequently we can talk about the "ethical solidarity" that naturally emerges from "ontological solidarity," since action follows being.'

The author explains what 'vertical ontological solidarity' is: 'the bond that exists between the generations from natural bonds, such as those of blood, but also of culture and other forms of memory'. Being essentially historical, that is to say, dependent on time, in the human being this bond would be reciprocal, since 'the father is only a father because he has a son and the son is only [a] son because he has the father'. He then speaks of 'relational reciprocity', constituted of both bonds. Here, he approaches what was said at the beginning of this essay, with

---

[19] The dimension of affections in life should not be overlooked. They are necessary to make life gratifying. One should only understand that they are not the first element when one thinks about the structure of life and the exercise of freedom. In order to better understand the context of affection in personal and family life, and its dynamics in social life, reading the following two texts is suggested: A.J. PEREIRA JÚNIOR, 'Da afetividade à efetividade do amor nas relações de família' in M.B. DIAS, E.F. BASTOS and N.M.M. MORAES, (org.), *Afeto e estruturas familiares*, Del Rey, 2009, pp. 57–77; A.J. PEREIRA JÚNIOR and M.P. NORÕES, 'A abordagem antropológica e jurídica da afetividade no Direito de Família mediante o uso do diálogo socrático em sala de aula', *Argumenta Journal Law*, no. 28, 57–77, Jan/Jun 2018.

[20] <http://www.hottopos.com/notand14/joao.pdf>.

Pierpaolo Donati's approach. However, here the author bases his considerations on the anthropological character of the philosophy of the human being.

This intimate connection between people physically related in a family dimension explains the phenomenon that the death of the parent would also mean the actual death of a part of the child. It is extremely meaningful that the loss of a loved one of such importance as a father, mother or child occupies first place in the causes of stress. It is not reduced to a question of feeling, even though affectivity is the dimension where loss manifests itself immediately, given its connection with sensitivity. Loss affects one's being. It also creates the family bonds in a solid sense; they are beyond affections.

Alongside the category of 'vertical solidarity', is still, according to João Carlos, a 'horizontal ontological solidarity', which only happens 'in the only instant that belongs to us: the present':

> It is at this level that we would like to point out some anthropological presuppositions. It is not a matter of tabulating a philosophical and an ahistorical idealization of the human. It's just the opposite. We want to understand the dynamics of the construction of human identity in the relationships established in this 'eternal present' in which we are immersed. It is necessary to unravel the mystery of existence. For this you will need to consider the person and structures in which you are inserted. Our proposal of didactic elaboration of the concept of horizontal ontological solidarity is to consider the person as a 'knot' of four bonds of reciprocal responsibility, which we will call relations: 1) Relation with materiality; 2) Relation with interiority; 3) Relation with otherness 4) Relation with totality.[21]

Without going further into the study of João Carlos, the selected excerpts serve to contrast the concepts of solidarity and affectivity. It is possible to introduce here the proposal to renew the celebrated 'principle of affectivity' for the 'principle of solidarity'. The first has, as its inner layer, the fluidity of feelings. The second relies on the relational structure and generates duties that last beyond emotional variation. This is also important to have affirmed, because in family law the logic of duty prevails. The minimal social structures, the families, consolidate themselves as nuclei of civil society. Like any co-existing reality, the family relationship is subject to the indulgences of the coming and going of affections and behaviours. But this would not justify the abandonment of duties of solidarity.

Let us consider the marriage between a man and a woman, for example – still one of the social representations of family – for the capacity of generation of civil society itself. This relationship projects and symbolises, apart from the

---

[21]   See J.C. ALMEIDA, 'Antropologia da Solidariedade', *Notandum*, vol. 14, 2007, <http://www.hottopos.com/notand14/joao.pdf>.

desires and contract between the spouses, an institution – consider the theories of marriage as an *institution* – that identifies with the main matrix of civil society itself. That is why it is celebrated socially and supported by the community.

The purpose of the regulation of marriage, in this case, is not to interfere with private life, because even the law does not investigate the intimate feelings and practices of the couple. The requirement of solemnity for their civil constitution, as a social rite, signals that a different, social dimension is being achieved through the actions of the spouses. Therefore, when entering this level of relationship, social obligations impose obligations of solidarity and ties between those directly involved and their families of origin, which will last even beyond the separation of both, as well as kinship of affinity and the impediments to marriage. It is precisely because of the achievement of this generative level of civil society that this union is entitled to special protection, with its burdens and bonuses; that is, social recognition is not based on affectivity, but, rather, is found in the genesis of a relational structure capable of reproducing civil society.

In the past, if this family reality were weakened by a crisis of affection, this was not considered sufficient to give cause for a civil rupture through divorce. Today the situation is different. In Brazil, divorce may be requested on the day after the marriage, unilaterally, without the need for any reason. This ease, regarded by many as an achievement, actually makes it difficult to perceive the differentiated level of the conjugal relationship.[22] It is easier today to dispose of enduring commitments that would affect the whole lives of two people, and eventually even their offspring, than to close a bank account. It is paradoxical to say that such measures are family-friendly. Rather, it seems to denounce an individualist line (family is a society).[23] This contrasts with the legislation of many countries, some of which are even more liberal than Brazil.

It is worth remembering that indissoluble civil marriage lasted in Brazil from 1891 to 1977, based on a cultural conjuncture that believed that such a project was possible and reasonable. Naturally, to live the experience of indissolubility, especially in the hedonistic and predominantly individualistic environment of large urban centres, there should be a public education policy that would prepare people for such an experience. An education which, in the face of crises,

---

[22] A public policy that corresponds with the perception of the social value of civil marriage and effective special protection of the family would be the offer of therapy for the couple in crisis, or of other aid to each separated spouse, in an attempt to help overcome personal or relational difficulties.

[23] Undoubtedly, it is more difficult to resist the crises that erupt during the dismantling of a transcendent family project in the face of the idealisation of an appealing world, with pleasures and satisfactions that are sensorial and accessible for consumption. In this sense, the experience of the burden of the family relationship, in the context of unconsciousness of the peculiarities of a solid family project, would require an education of its own. Without this, it becomes too burdensome for many, because of little apparent bonus.

would help each of the spouses to look beyond themselves and the circumstance itself, in order to glimpse a more attractive perspective that could facilitate the practical updating of the acts, leading to the voluntary maintenance of marriage. It would be a case of having public policies of support, even in times of crisis. If there is a law for helping a company recover, because of the social benefit of its maintenance for society, it would be possible to think of a public policy to assist in the recovery of the conjugal society, before decreeing its bankruptcy.

Today, however, the crisis of the concept of truth, together with hedonistic individualism, enables the maxim of *act following being* to be replaced by *act following feeling*. From this perspective, rather than acting how we should, according to the order of being, we tend to act on the basis of how we feel. Then, as rational beings who hold themselves responsible for the reasons – even if unreasonable – for their own conduct, we tend to make the thought fit the actions, beyond any consideration of the common good.[24] In this way, the objective parameters of consideration for the family as transcending reality, including feelings, are annulled.

Hypersexualisation and a hedonistic culture are expressions of individualism, because sensory pleasure is a tactile and, therefore, epidermal reality, physically limited to the person who feels it. This, naturally, led to the experience of the family project, from a transcendent and permanent perspective, being undermined in contrast to the possibility of experimentation in the market of relationships, variation being seen as a necessary value.

In this way, the situations of living, and the justifications that are made for them, have produced, especially since the 1960s, new ways of understanding the family, and new ways of living: it is for *my* satisfaction. This also occurred, as pointed out above, in the experience of the family living by traditional standards, when the existential and social pillars of this family reality were inadequate, and this denomination was under abuse, and thus internal distortions could not remain. The resilience needed to maintain relationships or tolerate stressful situations has diminished; first, because pretensions to overcome the challenges of life as a couple have been superseded, ceasing to be the goal of overcoming them, once seen as necessary for personal fulfilment; and, secondly, because some of the difficulties pointed out as proper and necessary stages in the life of a couple, were no longer interpreted as such.

In the meantime, in the collective imagination, the idea that situations of family life should be moments of ecstasy was popularised through audiovisual cultural productions. The contrast of this idyllic portrait with reality, and the individualist perspective, enabled the crisis. There was encouragement for new

---

[24]   In this sense, a warning from André Frossard, of the Academy of Letters of France: 'contemporary society, in its incomparable cowardice prefers to legalize its mistakes than combat them'.

experiences and partnerships. At the same time, the supply of consumer goods has increased, making life more enjoyable.

The most intimate human relations of a sexual nature have come to be presented, above all, as situations of pleasure. The idea of family commitment in the face of dissatisfaction has been weakened. In this context, the appeal of affectivity grew along with the 'axis' of family law, on the side of the construction and deconstruction of relationships.

However, strictly speaking, from the perspective of the general theory of law, affectivity could never be a principle,[25] as it is understood by many today, because, as some have defended it, it would be a poison rather than a remedy, given the strictly individualistic understanding of some of the most popular authors in the field of family law.

Thus, in broad strokes – in another article we can more appropriately describe this phenomenon – the transpersonalist family gives way to a hedonistic family, from the civilisation of the liquid love of Zygmunt Bauman.[26] This hedonistic family permeates the imagery of Maria Berenice Dias, when she uses the term 'eudaimonistic', which refers to being from the Aristotelian perspective. However, the term 'eudaimonia', from Aristotle's meaning, translates as happiness derived from virtues, from conduct, which does not coincide with, and need not necessarily be perceived by, the sensorial dimension of affections, but is evidenced by the consciousness of the effective possession of the virtues; that is, the achievement of human excellence by adherence to a set of values, even to the detriment of better feelings or sensations, which is the idea of happiness from Maria Berenice.[27]

6. THE IMAGINARY FAMILY FROM THE 1960S AND THE CONSTITUTIONAL FAMILY IN BRAZIL IN 1988

However, alongside the sexual revolution, and especially since the 1960s, a number of factors have led to variations in the way that members of the family

---

[25] See J.W. DE OLIVEIRA NETO and A.J. PEREIRA JÚNIOR, '(In)viabilidade do princípio da afetividade', *Universitas Jus*, vol. 27, 113–125, 2016.

[26] See Z. BAUMAN, *Amor líquido: Sobre a fragilidade dos laços humanos*, Zahar, 2004.

[27] 'Ethics based on the Aristotelian notion of "eudaimonia" or human happiness ... Although close to the "ethics of virtue", this approach is different to that when the Greek identification between virtuous action and happiness is eliminated. Eudemonism may also vary according to the notions of what happiness, in fact, is. Thus, the Cyrenaic emphasize sensual pleasure; the Stoics emphasize detachment from worldly goods such as wealth and friendship. Thomas Aquinas gives more attention to happiness as an eternal contemplation of God and so on.' (M.B. DIAS, *Manual de Direito das Família*, Editora, Revista dos Tribunais, 4th ed., 2007, p. 52). From the highlighted text, there is an apparent subterfuge in reference to Aristotle.

organise themselves, and thus the structure itself has changed. Such events are also responsible for pluralisation, consistent with the structural view of the family.

Among other changes, there was the progressive separation of the individual's social status from their marital status. Along with this factor, the economic independence of women increased. This made it easier for the family to remain, in the collective imagination, as a personal and microsocial function.[28] Scientific and medical developments allowed for new behaviours that would reconfigure habits. Thus, with contraceptives, it was possible to separate sexuality from reproduction, and the perfection of techniques of assisted human reproduction made it possible to dissociate generation from sexual intercourse. The objectives of marriage – a shared life between spouses, and openness to the procreation and upbringing of children – could be separated. These possibilities influenced life in society and reconfigured relationships.

In the same sense, there was the progressive participation of women in professional activity outside the home, diminishing their economic dependence on their husbands. Family functions were disconnected from the sexual condition of the couple. This advanced the equality of powers and duties between the spouses. In this scenario, the affective-sentimental perspective gained more importance. At the same time, divorce became a more affordable procedure. This does not mean, on its own, that the affective dimension should be imposed as an essential element, simply that it should effectively occupy sufficient space in the family dynamics.

Thus, in the last 40 years of the twentieth century, philosophical and ideological factors affected the vision of human marriage, family and sexuality. Common to the currents of ideas that generated this result was the consideration that marriage and family would cease to be realities viewed from an objective or 'natural' perspective (natural law). On the contrary, they would remain mutable and formable in each epoch by the understanding of each person, without lasting essential attributes.[29]

The Aristotelian notion is connected to the ethics of virtue. Strictly speaking, it would be better, for greater intellectual honesty, not to confuse concepts and ideas. In this sense, it would be better if the author were to withdraw from her explanation the mention of Aristotle and avoid using the term 'eudaimonia', most of which refers to his conception. Otherwise, it gives the impression of false induction or false argument.

[28]   C. Martinez De Aguirre, *Diagnostico sobre el Derecho de Familia*, Rialp, 1996, pp. 17–18. The same author states that, in parallel to these socio-economic factors, it was forgotten that the family performed first-rate training and assistance functions, in relation to which it is practically irreplaceable.

[29]   See A.J. Pereira Júnior, 'A família na Constituição do Brasil – missão, limites e responsabilidades – comentário ao art. 226 da Constituição de 1988' in A.J. Pereira Júnior, D. Gozzo and W.R. Ligiera (org.), *Direito e Dignidade da Família*, Almedina, 2012, vol. 1, pp. 7–34.

Carlos Martinez de Aguirre points out the factors that motivated these changes: *secularisation* and *positivism*, by which the human will and the State were given the power to determine what should be understood, as well as how subjects related to sexuality should be addressed; *liberal individualism*, in the face of which marriage and family would be institutions at the exclusive service of the interests and satisfaction of individuals, without any supra-individual purpose; the increased valuation of the sentimental aspect as the main basis for the emergence and maintenance of marriage, above all other interests; and ideological pluralism and the neutrality of the State in the face of conceptions about marriage, family and sexuality, as well as the different types of citizens organising their affective and sexual relations.[30]

The Brazilian Constitution of 1988 shows signs of the times: next to the matrimonial family, in the sociolegal plan, the family entity formed by a stable union was established, and the family unit of the single-parent form was also established. In addition to the matrimonial family and the family constituted by natural or legal affiliation, the 1988 Constitution recognised the situation of *non-formal legal ties between men and women* as a family entity. Thus, with the consideration of different family units, the base of society was expanded. However, it is worth noting that the situations announced in the 1988 Constitution show the objective potentiality of natural reproduction of society, which is why they are under the special protection of the State. In addition, the matrimonial family was maintained as the most perfect legal and social paradigm. There was still a predominant objectivist perspective.

The Federal Constitution, therefore, listed relations of co-existence that should receive the *special protection* of the State, in spite of other relationship possibilities. On that list, one could note the ontological root of civil society itself, when one thinks of its conservation and perpetuation. Other forms of personal co-existence, which were not considered sufficient and necessary for the preservation of civil society, are entitled to another category of legal protection; that is, in general, something distinctive that might be defined, without involving institutions typical of legal relations.

This means that other categories of co-existence can, from a legal perspective, be conceived and/or protected by law. But the *special protection* of Article 226 would, in principle, be exclusive to situations of *objective interest*, which are necessary for civil society, despite the co-existence of subjective factors that are close to those connected to such relational modalities.

Therefore, legal modalities can be created to serve other interests. One such proposal, for example, is the *vital partnership*, which is based on effective

---

30   See C. MARTINEZ DE AGUIRRE, *Diagnostico sobre el Derecho de Familia*, Rialp, 1996, pp. 23–24. Here, we see observations that would later lead to the decay of the family experience as a reality that transcends the family members, and which would enable the multiplication of different co-existent modalities.

co-existence and cohabitation between people who share the same house, and on solidarity, and could receive a differentiated status before the law that would confer legal benefits, since such an arrangement is effectively meeting mutual needs, in a similar way, albeit not identical, to the family situation that makes up the social base.

The vital partnership has been presented as an idea to be developed, while *lege ferenda*, for situations other than the 'base of society', in the report that accompanied Bill 6.584/13, Family Statute, approved on 26 September 2015 in the Special Commission created for the purpose of examining the aforementioned bill (as of April 2023, it had not yet been voted on in the plenary of the Federal Chamber):

> From the framework and, from an authentic and wide perspective, what to do in the face of situations that are not consubstantiated as a 'base', foundation or condition of existence of civil society, without jus, therefore, for the special protection of art. 226, but which bring some consideration to demand a differentiated protection, beyond the general protection that is already guaranteed to every citizen? Is there any impediment to devising a new category of differentiated protection? For cases that escape the condition of essentiality for civil society, it is possible to envisage, in the current conjuncture, the legal formalization of a 'vital partnership', capable of conferring benefits to the society coming from the deliberate meeting of citizens who share residence and efforts in the maintenance of the common home, with the intention of endurance. The category, of lege ferenda, would be admissible provided it did not affect unavailable rights of third parties. And it could be approved as an initiative of the National Congress in the current legislature.

> Under such a denomination – 'vital partnership' – without a necessary connection to the procreation or creation of the family, the basis of society, one could recognize the bond of solidarity between two persons, who establish a bond of peculiar interdependence among themselves, adjusting the law, between them, for the character of dependency for social security purposes. It would also be appropriate to define the possibility that the partners could also choose to participate as the status of heir of the other, in a position similar to that which would belong to the spouse or companion, if it did not exist, or there is a presumed testamentary heir, in the event of non-existence of such an instrument, to receive 50% of the assets released to be disposed of in a will. This would happen by means of an amendment of the inheritance legislation, to the full reception of the category.

> The unions of brothers, friends and others, regardless of sexual orientation, could be under such denomination. Before this institute, all situations not subject to the categories of art. 226. In the case of inheritance effects could operate when there was no bond of conjugality, since the consort would occupy this position. The foundation of the 'vital partnership' would therefore be the special solidarity between two people, dissociated from conjugality, and united in the maintaining of the common home.

> This would also serve same-sex couples regardless of their sexual orientation, since sexual orientation alone would not justify special rights, at the risk of excluding those

who lived full and effective interdependence, in the simple condition of friends or siblings, without any sexual involvement. Where appropriate, the law would require attributes to confer the status of vital partnership to subsumable situations. It would be limited to a vital partnership per individual, requiring its effective proof at the time of the institution, as well as the manner of its recognition with the competent bodies of the civil registry, with the burden and the bonus of the new situation. A burden that would be expressed in the eventual duty to provide food in case the partner needs, even after the extinction of the bond. Such a procedure would meet the realization of a free, fair and solidary society, an objective of the Federative Republic of Brazil, according to art. 1o, III.

As can be seen, it is possible to design legal institutions that meet the needs of co-existing entities without compromising the nature of institutions typical of familial entities that are assimilable into the basic qualification of society, from an objective perspective.

7.   CONCLUSION

We now reach the conclusion, and those who have had the patience to arrive here have participated in some sociological, philosophical, anthropological and juridical-constitutional readings of the author on the family phenomenon. It is, indeed, believed that it is necessary to establish, through reflection of an interdisciplinary nature, criteria that allow for the identification of the essential attributes of a convivial entity, so that it can be accepted, legally, as a family. At the same time, the author wanted to present a possible explanation about the subjectivation of the concept, as well as to show what contributed to a more individualistic and sentimental perspective of the family. It was considered opportune, still, to point to solidarity as the veritable and main principle of family law, rather than the 'principle of affectivity'. Lastly, it was possible to envisage and conceive different legal institutions that can meet the demand for the security of certain situations of co-existence that are not identified in the basis of society, but are entitled to a different protection.

CHINA

ON THE LEGISLATIVE CONCEPT AND THE NEW RULES OF THE SUCCESSION SYSTEM OF THE CIVIL CODE IN CHINA

CHEN Wei and HE Haiyan

Résumé

Le Code civil de la République populaire de Chine (ci-après dénommé « le Code civil ») est le premier texte portant le nom de « Code » depuis la naissance de la République populaire de Chine, en tant que « Constitution » au sens sociologique du terme. Le Code civil est une garantie importante pour la Chine de réaliser l'objectif des « deux cents ans » et le rêve chinois de parvenir au grand rajeunissement de la nation chinoise. C'est à la fois une création législative et un héritage de l'esprit national de la Chine, de la culture nationale et de l'esprit du temps. Il s'agit d'une loi civile fondamentale aux racines solides, aux objectifs clairs et aux avantages à long terme. La loi relative aux successions est la norme juridique essentielle pour régler les rapports successoraux. Le traitement des successions implique non seulement la protection des intérêts des héritiers, mais aussi la protection des intérêts des créanciers des héritiers et le maintien de la sécurité des transactions. Le Titre VI « Succession » (ci-après dénommé « Succession dans le Code civil ») est une partie importante du Code civil, qui intègre systématiquement la sagesse et les réalisations de la législation sur la transmission des biens tout en tenant compte de la pratique judiciaire depuis la fondation de la République populaire de Chine. Il s'agit d'une loi aux caractéristiques chinoises qui protège les droits et intérêts légitimes des héritiers, des créanciers de la succession et des autres parties prenantes de la succession. Ce texte maintient la sécurité des transactions, développe et consolide le système économique socialiste de marché et améliore le bien-être du peuple.

The Civil Code of the People's Republic of China (hereinafter referred to as 'the Civil Code'), adopted on 28 May 2020 and effective on 1 January 2021, is the first law named after the 'Code' since the founding of the People's Republic of China.[1] The Civil Code is an important step for China in achieving its 'Two Centenary Goals',[2] and realising the Chinese dream of the great rejuvenation of the Chinese nation. The Civil Code is a legislative expression of China's national spirit, national culture and the spirit of the times, and a basic civil law with solid roots, stable expectations and long-term benefits.[3]

Succession law is the basic legal norm for adjusting the inheritance relationship of property, and the handling of inheritance involves not only the protection of the interests of heirs, but also the protection of the interests of the creditors of the heirs, and the maintenance of transaction security. Title VI Succession of the Civil Code (hereinafter referred to as 'Title VI Succession' or 'the Succession Section of the Civil Code' or 'the Succession Section') is an important part of the Civil Code, which systematically integrates the wisdom and achievements of property inheritance legislation and judicial practice since the founding of the People's Republic of China. Title VI Succession is a law with Chinese characteristics that protects the legitimate rights and interests of heirs, safeguards the legitimate rights and interests of estate creditors and other estate stakeholders, maintains the security of transactions, develops and consolidates the socialist market economic system, and enhances the well-being of the people.

1. THE LEGISLATIVE CONCEPT OF THE SUCCESSION SECTION OF THE CIVIL CODE

1.1. REAFFIRMING THE LEGAL PROTECTION OF THE NATURAL PERSON'S RIGHT OF SUCCESSION

The right to private property is the material basis and guarantee of natural persons' rights to subsistence and development. First, Article 13 of our Constitution

---

[1]   SHI JIAYOU, '民法典的"政治性使命"' ('The "political mission" of the Civil Code') (2018) 1山东法官培训学院学报 (*Journal of Shandong Judges Training Institute*) 12.

[2]   'Two centenary goals': the first hundred years is to build a moderately prosperous society in an all-round way by the 100th anniversary of the founding of the Communist Party of China (2021); The second hundred years is to build a prosperous, strong, democratic, civilised and harmonious modern socialist country by the 100th anniversary of the founding of New China (2049).

[3]   XI JINPING, 充分认识颁布实施民法典重大意义 依法更好保障人民合法权益, 2020年5月29 日在十九届中央政治局第二十次集体学习时的讲话 ('Fully understand the great significance of promulgating and implementing the Civil Code and better protect the legitimate rights and interests of the people in accordance with the law', speech at the 20th Collective Study of the 19th Politburo of the 19th Central Committee on 29 May 2020), available at <http://www.xinhuanet.com/politics/leaders/2020-06/15/c_1126116411.htm>.

stipulates that 'the State shall protect the private property rights and inheritance rights of citizens in accordance with the provisions of the law.' The State protection of the inheritance rights of natural persons is an essential requirement for China to protect individual private property, maintain the current distribution system in our country, and consolidate the socialist economic foundation. It is a vital element to fully support the family's function of population reproduction and supporting the elderly and raising children, and to respect the will of the inheritors to freely handle their inheritances. The provisions of the Constitution protecting the inheritance rights of natural persons are the legislative basis for Title VI Succession. Second, paragraph 1 of Article 124 of the General Provisions of the Civil Code stipulates that 'natural persons enjoy the right of inheritance in accordance with law'. This is not only the implementation of the inheritance right of natural persons, protected by the Constitution in the Civil Code, but also the normative source of the independent compilation of inheritance in the Civil Code. Third, the inheritance right is an important way to extend the right to private property, and to obtain property, and the protection of the right to inherit is the starting point and foothold of China's inheritance legislation. Article 1120 of the Civil Code, Title VI Succession, clearly stipulates, '[t]he State protects the inheritance rights of natural persons'. This is a reaffirmation of the Constitution's 'State protection of the inheritance rights of natural persons', and is also the legislative purpose of the Succession Section of the Civil Code. The Succession Section of the Civil Code has four chapters, namely 'General Provisions', 'Statutory Inheritance', 'Testamentary Inheritance and Bequest' and 'Disposition of Inheritance' with a view to 'effectively protecting the inheritance rights of natural persons'.[4]

1.2. PAYING ATTENTION TO PROTECTING HEIRS' FREEDOM TO HANDLE THEIR ESTATES

The principle of autonomy of private law is a fundamental principle of modern civil law, and as a part of civil law, succession law should also follow this principle as an important legislative concept. The principle of autonomy of private law is reflected in the field of succession law, the central tenet of which is that heirs are free to handle their estates.[5] Attention should be paid to the legislative concept of protecting the freedom of heirs to handle their inheritances, which is mainly reflected in the Succession Section of the Civil Code in the following aspects.

---

[4]   CHEN WEI and RAN QIYU, 现代继承法的基本原则研究 ('Research on the Basic Principles of Modern Inheritance Law'); 中国继承法理论与实践研究 ('Research on the Theory and Practice of Inheritance Law in China'), Chinese People's Public Security University Press, 2019, p. 17.

[5]   LI SHAOWEI, 民法法典化与私法价值的实现 ('Codification of Civil Law and the Realization of the Value of Private Law') (2019) 12 河北法学 (*Hebei Jurisprudence*) 28.

1.2.1. Loss of Inheritance and Forgiveness

In the system of loss of inheritance and forgiveness,[6] the first aspect is to examine interference with, or infringement on, the will freedom of the testator, as a statutory cause for the loss of the right to inherit, in order to sanction the illegal interference or infringement of the heir's free disposition of the estate by will. The second aspect is to give the testator the right to forgive the heir who has committed the act of not completely forfeiting the legal cause of the right to inherit.

1.2.2. Intestate Succession

In the intestate succession system,[7] the presumption of the people's willingness to handle the posthumous legacy,[8] the scope and proportion of legal heirs and subrogated heirs, the discretionary claim of inheritance, and the division of estate, are designed to reflect the main will of the majority of the people to handle the estate, and to protect the freedom to handle the estate. If the decedent is unwilling to have their estate handled in accordance with the legal inheritance, they may handle their estate by means of a will.

1.2.3. Testamentary Succession and Bequest

In the system of testamentary succession and bequest,[9] first, the testator has the freedom to determine the content of their will according to their own wishes; that is, the testator has the power to make a testamentary inheritance or bequest with or without obligations, to appoint a will executor, to establish a testamentary trust, to set up a right of residence for others with a will, to appoint a guardian for a child with a will, to donate human organs with a will, and so on. Second, the testator may voluntarily choose the form of will within the scope of the seven statutory forms of will. Third, the testator has the freedom to modify and withdraw the will by means of explicit withdrawal and statutory withdrawal. Fourth, the content of the will should be a true and voluntary expression of the testator's intention. As such, a will made by the testator by means of fraud or coercion is invalid, and the content of a will that has been tampered with is similarly invalid.

---

6   See Art. 1125 of the Civil Code.
7   see Arts. 1127–1131, 1155 of the Civil Code.
8   CHEN WEI, 外国继承法比较与中国民法典继承编制定研究 ('A comparative study of foreign succession laws with the succession of the Chinese Civil Code'), Peking University Press, 2011, p. 417.
9   See Arts. 371, 29, 1152, 1133 (para. 4), 1134–1139, 1142, 1143 of the Civil Code.

1.2.4. Estate Disposal

In the estate disposal system,[10] first, the testator may appoint an executor to ensure that the estate can be handled smoothly. Second, natural persons have the freedom to sign bequest maintenance agreements, in order to respect and maintain the heirs' voluntary arrangements for their lives, deaths, burials, and bequest inheritances.

1.3. PAYING ATTENTION TO THE ROLE OF DEPENDENCY RELATIONSHIPS IN SUCCESSION AND ESTATE HANDLING

In modern society, the succession system is generally based on blood relations and marriage relations, as the basis for obtaining inheritance rights. As the basic unit of societal organisation and population reproduction, the family undertakes the function of supporting the elderly and raising children. In order to provide a foundation for the family system of old-age care and child-rearing, mutual assistance and unity, and harmony and friendship, the Succession Section of the Civil Code adheres to the legislative concept of allocating full weight to the role of the dependency relationship in succession and estate handling.

1.3.1. In-Law Relations under Certain Conditions have the Right to Inheritance

For example, a widowed daughter-in-law or son-in-law who has fulfilled their primary maintenance obligation may, in accordance with the law, be the legal heir in the first order. Stepchildren, stepparents, and step-siblings with a dependency relationship may become legal heirs.[11] Some scholars in China believe that such regulations guide and encourage the support of elders, the raising of children, and the promotion of family unity. However, other scholars have questioned whether it is appropriate to provide inheritance rights for in-laws, who lack a blood tie to the decedent, as not in line with general international legislation,[12] which does not recognise the right of in-law inheritance.[13] Therefore, legislative

---

[10]   See Arts. 1133 and 1158 of the Civil Code.
[11]   See Arts. 1127 and 1129 of the Civil Code.
[12]   The step-parents and stepchildren are originally direct in-laws, and if the step-parents adopt the stepchildren, the two parties are imitation direct blood relatives, and the two parties have the rights and obligations between adoptive parents and children.
[13]   ZHANG PINGHUA and LIU YAODONG, 继承法原理 ('*Principles of Succession Law*'), China Legal Publishing House, 2009, p. 15; GUO MINGRUI, 民法典编纂中继承法的修订原则 ('Principles for The Revision of Succession Law in the Codification of the Civil Code') (2015) 3 比较法研究 (*Comparative Law Research*) 86–92; ZHANG YUMIN, 继承法律制度研究（第二版）('*Research on the Legal System of Succession*'), Huazhong University of Science and Technology Press, 2nd ed., 2016, pp. 131–132.

suggestions have been put forward to make in-laws who have fulfilled their main maintenance obligations discretionary claimants of inheritance.[14] However, China's legislature has not adopted these legislative suggestions. The reason may be that, in the choice of legislative values, compared with the question of whether the in-law relationship (that is, the legal ties that arise from marriage) should or should not give rise to inheritance rights, legislators pay more attention to the role of 'maintenance obligations' in the realisation of the family's old-age support and child-rearing functions. Legislators, accordingly, continue to follow the legislation of the Succession Law 1985 (hereinafter referred to as 'Succession Law'), for in-laws who form maintenance relationships, allowing them to enjoy the right to inherit, which is also in line with the principle of consistency of rights and obligations.

1.3.2. The Performance of the Maintenance Obligations May be Used as a Basis for Distribution of the Estate

For example, heirs who have fulfilled their primary maintenance obligations may receive a greater share of the inheritance, while heirs who have the capacity to meet their maintenance obligations to decedents, but have not done so, may receive a lesser share, or receive none of the inheritance.[15] The legislation regards the existence and extent of the maintenance relationship between the heirs as the basis for more, less, or no inheritance, which reflects not only a concern for the living conditions of the heirs, but also the embodiment of the legislative orientation toward advocating and encouraging respect for the elderly and care of the young, with family members helping each other, and maintaining equal, harmonious and civilised marriage and family relations.

1.3.3. Those Who have a Maintenance Relationship with the Decedent May Share the Inheritance

A maintenance relationship may be used as a basis for the discretionary right to claim an inheritance. For example, a non-heir who depends on the heirs for support, or who gives more life care and material support to the decedent, share a proper portion of the inheritance.[16] Although the above two types of natural persons have no blood or marriage relationship with the decedent, the non-heirs are, based on the simple folk style of advocating respect for the elderly and

---

14   YANG LIXIN and ZHU CHENGYI, 继承法专论 ('*Monograph on Succession Law*'), Higher Education Press, 2006, p. 162; ZHANG YUMIN (ed.), 中国继承法建议稿及立法理由 ('*Draft Proposal on Chinese Succession Law and Legislative Reasons*'), People's Publishing House, 2006, p. 162.
15   See Art. 1130, paras. 2 and 3 of the Civil Code.
16   See Art. 1131 of the Civil Code.

taking care of the young, aiding the poor and helping the weak, given the right to claim inheritance from the decedent's estate. For non-heirs who were supported by the decedent, this is achieved by assigning a proper portion of the estate to them, to play the maintenance function of the estate, and for the non-heirs who gave the decedent more life care and more economic support, by distributing the appropriate part of the estate to them, in the embodiment of the principle of consistency of rights and obligations.

1.3.4. *The Performance of Maintenance Obligations May Constitute a Restriction on Testamentary Freedom and the Settlement of Estate Debts*

For example, a will should retain a share of the estate sufficient to support the 'double-nothing' heirs who are incapacitated and have no means of subsistence. Flesh and blood are close; the way of nature. Retaining the necessary share of the inheritance for heirs who are unable to work, and have no source of livelihood, can give full expression to the role of the inheritance in supporting family members, prevent them from falling into a predicament of survival due to the loss of support from the decedent, and protect the heirs' survival rights.

1.3.5. *Give Priority to Bequest Maintenance Agreements*

The Civil Code stipulates that, when multiple forms of estate disposition exist, the bequest maintenance agreement shall be applied first, followed by testamentary succession, and finally distributed in accordance with intestate inheritance;[17] that is, the legislation gives priority to bequest maintenance agreements, which provide a guarantee for widows, the elderly, and the sick and disabled, to be able to use their inheritance to provide support for the rest of their lives, helping them to secure appropriate living arrangements, and to provide for funeral arrangements and other needs. These principles also reflect the respect for, and maintenance of, the true intentions of the parties, and the fair and reasonable allocation of rights and obligations.

1.4. PAYING ATTENTION TO SAFEGUARDING THE INTERESTS OF ESTATE CREDITORS AND THE SECURITY OF TRANSACTIONS

'The key to governing the country lies in fairness and integrity.'[18] Estate treatment involves not only the protection of the heirs' interests, but also protection of

---

[17] See Art. 1123 of the Civil Code.

[18] (Tang Dynasty) Wu Jing, 贞观政要 ('*Zhenguan Politics*'), Chongwen Book Company, 2017, p. 118.

the interests of the creditors of the estate, and the maintenance of transaction security. Protecting the interests of estate creditors, and maintaining and ensuring the safety of transactions, are embodiments of the principles of good faith and fairness in the inheritance system of civil law, and are also a necessary choice for protecting and promoting social and economic development. The legislative concept of the Succession Section, to safeguard the interests of estate creditors and ensure the security of transactions, is mainly reflected in the aspects described below.

1.4.1. Clarifying the Scope of the Estate[19]

First, it is necessary to determine the scope of the estate and provide for a material basis for the realisation of the interests of the estate's creditors. Second, in order to prevent the improper reduction of the legacy, those who have possession of the inheritance should keep it properly, and no one should embezzle or compete for it. Third, where the joint property of the husband and wife, or the property of others, is involved, the share of such property should be separated first, and the inheritance should be separated accurately. The inheritance should be applied only to the decedent's individual property.

1.4.2. Establishing an Estate Management System[20]

First, the Civil Code stipulates the rules for determining the administrator of the estate, giving him/her the legal status of independently administering the estate. Second, it clarifies the responsibilities of the estate administrator, including clearing the estate and making a list of the estate assets, preventing the destruction and loss of the estate, and dealing with the creditor's rights, and the debts of the estate. Third, clearly defining the liability of the estate administrator for damages is conducive to encouraging the estate administrator to faithfully and prudently exercise their management rights.

1.4.3. Clarifying the Obligation to Pay Off the Debts of the Estate[21]

First, the Civil Code stipulates both the limited and the voluntary unlimited liquidation liability of the heirs for the inheritance debts, and the scope of their respective liabilities for the satisfaction of debts. Second, it stipulates that the claim for inheritance has priority over the right to receive bequests, testamentary inheritance and statutory inheritance rights; that is, the inheritance should first

---

[19]   See Arts. 1122, 1151 and 1153 of the Civil Code.
[20]   See Arts. 1145–1149 of the Civil Code.
[21]   See Arts. 1161–1163 of the Civil Code.

be used to pay off the debts of the estate, and then the bequest or inheritance can be delivered in accordance with the will or law. Third, it stipulates the rules for the distribution of the liability for the repayment of the estate debts between the subject of inheritance rights and the subject of the bequest rights; that is, the inheritance debts shall first be paid off by the legal heirs, and if these debts exceed the actual value of the estate they have obtained, the testamentary heirs and the bequeathed person shall pay off the estate they have obtained in proportion to the proportion of the estate that the heirs received.

1.5. EMPHASISING THE UPGRADING OF EFFECTIVE JUDICIAL INTERPRETATIONS INTO LEGISLATION

In the past, under the legislative guiding principle of 'it should be coarse and not detailed', the Succession Law was brief in its content.[22] Judicial interpretations played an important role in making up for the legislative deficiencies of the Succession Law, and in guiding the judicial trial practice of inheritance. The compilation of the Civil Code elevates effective judicial interpretations to laws, which can overcome the limitations of judicial interpretations issued in the judicial department, and help the broad masses of people to understand and abide by the law. The Succession Section of the Civil Code focuses on the legislative concept of upgrading effective judicial interpretations into legislation, which is reflected mainly in the aspects described below.

First, the presumption rule on the order of time of death, in Article 1121 of the Civil Code, is a simplification and improvement of the presumption rule on the order of time of death in Article 2 of the Opinions on the Succession Law. Second, the provisions of Article 1125, paragraph 2 of the Civil Code, on the relative and absolute loss of inheritance rights, are a modification and improvement of the provisions of Articles 12 and 13 of the Opinions on the Succession Law on the unforgivable and forgivable circumstances in the statutory grounds for loss of inheritance rights. Third, Article 1142, paragraph 2 of the Civil Code stipulates that an act of the testator contrary to the content of the will is regarded as a statutory situation for the withdrawal of the will, which is an absorption and improvement of the provisions of Article 39 of the Opinion on the Succession Law that the specific disposition of the property before the death of the testator is presumed to be the withdrawal of the will. Fourth, the provisions of Article 1152 of the Civil Code, on the transfer of inheritance system before the 'proviso', are an absorption of the provisions on the transfer of inheritance in Article 52 of the Opinions on the Succession Law. Fifth, the provisions of Article 1159 of the

---

[22] On 11 September 1985, the Supreme People's Court promulgated the Opinions of the Supreme People's Court on Several Issues Concerning the Implementation of the Succession Law of the People's Republic of China, hereinafter referred to as the 'Opinions on the Succession Law'.

Civil Code, on the obligations when dividing the estate, are an absorption and perfection of the provisions of Article 61 of the Opinions on the Succession Law that the repayment of the estate debts should be retained for the 'double-no-person' among the heirs.

2. THE NEW INSTITUTIONAL PROVISIONS IN THE 'GENERAL PROVISIONS' CHAPTER OF THE SUCCESSION SECTION OF THE CIVIL CODE AND THEIR LEGISLATIVE RATIONALE

2.1. ADDING THE PRESUMPTION RULE OF CHRONOLOGICAL TIMING OF DEATH

Article 1121 of the Civil Code adds the rule of presumptive time of death. The legislative rationale for this is as follows: first, due to the different rules on the presumption of the time of death, and differences in inheritance methods, and the order of inheritance of several people with mutual inheritance relationships, the actual value of the inheritance obtained by the surviving heirs will be different, and the legislative concepts and values embodied are different as well. Second, from the perspective of extraterritorial legislation, there are two legislative cases concerning the presumption of the death of reciprocal heirs in the same event. One of these is 'presumption of simultaneous death', observed in Italy, Japan and Russia,[23] which simplifies the inheritance relationship, but is not conducive to the downward circulation of the inheritance. The second is the 'presumption of longevity of the strong', as adopted by the British.[24] It is possible to ensure the circulation of inheritance to the younger generations, but it is impossible to avoid the occurrence of no one receiving the inheritance. On the basis of combining China's national conditions and judicial practice, and incorporating the experience of extraterritorial legislation, the Civil Code provides for three types of distinction: (1) the first death of a person without other heirs; (2) the death of an elder first; and (3) the death of a contemporary at the same time. With the first, the Civil Code ensures that those who have other heirs obtain the inheritance of a person without other heirs, so as to avoid the occurrence of no one inheriting the estate. The second is to ensure the circulation of the inheritance of the elders to the blood relatives of the younger generations, through subrogation inheritance, and to function as inheritance support. The

---

[23] See Art. 4 of the Italian Civil Code, Art. 32 of the Japanese Civil Code, and Art. 1114, para. 2 of the Civil Code of the Russian Federation.

[24] A. Iwobi, *The Basis of Succession Law*, Wuhan University Press, 2004, p. 122.

third is to enable the inheritance of the same generation to be inherited by their respective heirs, to simplify the inheritance relationship, and to follow the value of efficiency.

2.2. UPDATING THE DEFINITION OF THE SCOPE OF THE ESTATE

Article 1122 of the Civil Code redefines the scope of inheritance. The legislative rationale for this is as follows: first, the Succession Law, in light of the fact that, at the time of its enactment, most people had relatively little property, and there were relatively few types of property, stipulated the scope of inheritance through 'general provisions', 'positive enumeration' and 'bottom clauses', and through the Opinions on the Succession Law. Types of property such as securities and contracted income were included in the scope of inheritance.[25] However, with the development of China's social economy, and the increase in people's wealth and types of property, and especially the emergence of new types of property, such as game accounts and data, the drawbacks of the enumeration method, which could not cover the full scope of inheritances, became more and more obvious, and it became impossible to meet the new needs of the people for the inheritance of private property.[26] Second, from the perspective of extraterritorial legislation, there are two main types of legislation for defining the scope of inheritance. One is that there is no specific legislation on the scope of inheritance. Examples of this approach are France, Germany and Italy. The second is to define the scope of the estate through 'positive generalisation and negative exclusion'. Examples of this are Japan and Russia.[27] Based on China's legislative tradition and practical needs, and on the basis of drawing on extraterritorial legislation, the Civil Code adopted the method of 'positive generalisation plus negative exclusion' to update the definition of the scope of inheritance. The Civil Code includes inheritable property in the private property of the people within the scope of inheritance to the greatest possible extent, which can save legislative resources, and avoid the problems caused by the lack of enumerative provisions.

---

[25] See Art. 3 of the Succession Law; Arts. 3 and 4 of the Opinions on the Succession Law.
[26] For cases on whether land compensation fees, land requisition and demolition funds, etc. fall within the scope of inheritance, please refer to the Taizhou Intermediate People's Court's（2020）浙10民终430号Second-Instance Civil Judgment, and the Ganzhou Intermediate People's Court's（2019）赣07民终2336号Second-Instance Civil Judgment.
[27] See Arts. 517, 526, 527, 529 and 543 of the French Civil Code; Art. 1992, para. 1 of the German Civil Code; Art. 490, para. 1 of the Italian Civil Code; Art. 896 of the Civil Code of Japan; and Arts. 1110 and 1112 of the Civil Code of the Russian Federation.

2.3. ADDING SUPPLEMENTARY SYSTEM OF ACCEPTANCE AND RENUNCIATION OF INHERITANCE AND BEQUEST

2.3.1. *The Way to Renounce Inheritance Clearly Stipulated*

Paragraph 1 of Article 1124 of the Civil Code specifies the manner in which the right of inheritance is waived. The legislative rationale for this is as follows: first, the Succession Law does not clearly stipulate the way to abandon inheritance. Although Articles 47 and 48 of the Opinions on the Succession Law stipulate that the abandonment of inheritance shall be in writing, if the inheritance is abandoned by oral means, and is recognised or proved by other evidence, this may cause an inheritance dispute, due to the resignation of the head of the inheritance,[28] or an unfounded judgment when a dispute arises. Second, the empirical investigation of the concept of property inheritance, and the inheritance-handling habits of the people in ten provinces and cities in China in recent years, by Chinese scholars (hereinafter referred to as the 'empirical investigation') shows that 50 to 70 per cent of the respondents in these areas were in the habit of abandoning inheritance, meaning that written methods should be used.[29] Third, from the perspective of extraterritorial legislation, France, Germany, Italy, etc. all stipulate that the abandonment of inheritance must be made to the court, or in a credible manner, such as a notarised declaration.[30] Therefore, in order to reduce inheritance disputes, it was necessary to legislate to guide people to adopt the statutory way of abandoning inheritance, and thus the Civil Code clearly stipulates that the abandonment of inheritance must be in writing, on the basis of combining the habits of the people with lessons from extraterritorial legislation.

---

[28] For the relevant cases of inheritance disputes caused by the head of the inheritance indicating that they have renounced inheritance and repented, please refer to the Intermediate People's Court of Hefei City（2020）皖01民终1748号 Second-Instance Civil Judgment; Liaocheng Dongchangfu District People's Court（2017）鲁1502民初8165号; Taihe County People's Court（2016）赣0826民初1647号, and other civil judgments.

[29] The survey data shows that, in the areas where the respondents were located, in the ten provinces and cities of China, the statistics on the habit of abandoning inheritance were as follows: 62.34% in Chongqing Municipality, 67.17% in Jilin Province, 73.00% in Shanghai Municipality, 67.00% in Hebei Province, 51.30% in Hubei Province, 65.03% in Jiangxi Province, 53.19% in Sichuan Province, 64.13% in Guangdong Province, 71.71% in Hainan Province, and 65.65% in Fujian Province: Chen Wei, 当代中国民众财产继承观念与遗产处理习惯实证调查研究 ('*An Empirical Research on People's Concepts of Property Inheritance and Habits of Heritage Disposal in Contemporary China (vols. 1 and 2)*'), Chinese People's Public Security University Press, 2019, pp. 34, 146, 239, 331, 430, 522, 613, 736, 820 and 913.

[30] See Art. 804 of the French Civil Code, Art. 1945 of the German Civil Code, and Art. 519 of the Italian Civil Code.

2.3.2. The Expression of the Time of Renunciation of Bequests Modified

Paragraph 2 of Article 1124 of the Civil Code amends the period for making an expression of intention to accept or renounce a bequest, from 'two months' to 'sixty days', as provided for in Article 25 of the Succession Law. The legislative rationale is that, when the period for accepting or renouncing a bequest is measured in months, it is impossible to avoid the problem that the length of the period for accepting or abandoning a bequest could be either 59, 60, 61 or 62 days, depending on the year or month of death of the heir. Therefore, the modification of the period to 60 days will facilitate the uniformity of the length of the period, and facilitate an easy calculation of the time for the bequeathed person to make an expression of intention.

2.4. ADDING STATUTORY GROUNDS AND CONDITIONS FOR FORGIVENESS FOR THE LOSS OF INHERITANCE RIGHTS

2.4.1. Added Legal Grounds for Loss of Inheritance Rights

Paragraph 1, subparagraphs 4 and 5 of Article 1125 of the Civil Code add a new statutory cause of action for loss of inheritance rights. The legislative rationale for this is as follows: first, there are deficiencies in Article 7 of the Succession Law, on the statutory grounds for the loss of the right to inheritance; that is, heirs who have forged, tampered with or destroyed the will lose the rights to inherit, according to the law, but those who conceal the will, or infringe on the free right to the will of the heir by fraud or coercion, can go unpunished. Second, from the perspective of extraterritorial legislation, Japan, Switzerland and Italy regard the infringement of the testamentary freedom of the heirs by fraudulent or coercive means as a legal reason for the loss of inheritance rights.[31] Therefore, this provision has been added to guarantee the realisation of the heir's free will, and to sanction illegal acts.

2.4.2. Increased Conditions for Relative and Absolute Loss of Inheritance

Paragraph 2 of Article 1125 of the Civil Code adds the conditions for relative and absolute loss of the right of inheritance. The legislative rationale for this is as follows: first, even though Articles 11 to 13 of the Opinion on the Succession

---

[31] See Art. 891 of the Civil Code of Japan, Art. 540 of the Swiss Civil Code, and Art. 463 of the Italian Civil Code.

Law make additional provisions on forgiveness for loss of inheritance rights, the scope of application of the relative loss of inheritance rights is narrow and unreasonable.[32] Second, empirical investigations have shown that 50 to 70 per cent of respondents believed that, if the heirs have lost their right to inherit due to illegal acts of fraud or coercion that infringe on the freedom of the will, they may not lose the right of inheritance after forgiveness of the heirs.[33] Third, from the perspective of extraterritorial legislation, there are two kinds of legislation on the loss of inheritance rights. One type adopts 'relative loss', such as France, Germany, Italy, Russia, etc., all of which stipulate that all situations leading to the loss of inheritance rights can be forgiven by the heirs, which is conducive to promoting the rehabilitation of heirs and maintaining family harmony. The other approach is to adopt 'absolute loss', such as in the United Kingdom and the United States; that is, once the inheritance right is lost, it cannot be restored by the forgiveness of the heir, and the legal deterrent is more than enough, but impersonal.[34] When it was compiled, the Civil Code of China combined the concepts of our people and the experience of extraterritorial legislation. The legislative model combining relative loss of inheritance right with absolute loss of inheritance right can strengthen the protection of the property rights of the heir at fault, safeguard the freedom of the decedent to deal with their own inheritance, advocate good morality, and highlight the gentle feelings of the motherly nature of the civil law.

---

[32] E.g. the act of abusing or abandoning the heir infringes on the personal rights of the heir, and is unfair, but the act of forging, tampering with or destroying the will of the heir is only a violation of the freedom of the heir's will. While the nature of the former act is worse, and its consequences are more serious, the former act cannot lead to the loss of the right to inherit, because of the forgiveness of the heir, whereas the latter act still leads to the deprivation of the right to inherit, even if it is forgiven by the heir, which is unfair, and is not conducive to guiding the people to worship virtue and promote virtue and righteousness.

[33] The survey data shows that, among the respondents in ten provinces and cities in China, specifically those who believed that the heirs had lost their right to inherit due to fraud or coercion that infringed on the free right to the will of the heirs, the statistics on whether the heirs could lose their inheritance rights after forgiveness were: 72.04% in Chongqing City, 75.67% in Jilin Province, 72.20% in Shanghai, 70.04% in Hebei Province, 73.27% in Hubei Province, 64.05% in Jiangxi Province, 78.20% in Sichuan Province, 76.19% in Guangdong Province, 65.63% in Hainan Province, and 50.00% in Fujian Province: CHEN WEI, 当代中国民众财产继承观念与遗产处理习惯实证调查研究 ('An Empirical Research on People's Concepts of Property Inheritance and Habits of Heritage Disposal in Contemporary China (vols. 1 and 2)'), Chinese People's Public Security University Press, 2019, pp. 37, 149, 242, 335, 433, 526, 628, 738, 823 and 914.

[34] See Arts. 726 and 727 of the French Civil Code, Arts. 2336 and 2337 of the German Civil Code, Art. 466 of the Italian Civil Code, and Art. 1117 of the Civil Code of the Russian Federation.

2.4.3. Added Statutory Grounds for Loss of Bequest Rights and Rules for the Handling of Relevant Estates

Paragraph 3 of Article 1125 and paragraph 3 of Article 1154 of the Civil Code add new legal grounds for loss of the right to bequeath, and the treatment of related estates. The legislative rationale for this is as follows: first, the Succession Law does not stipulate the statutory grounds for the loss of the right to bequest, and there is no adjudication basis for adjudicating cases on whether or not the right to bequest is lost, and there has long been a theoretical dispute in China's academic circles over whether the rules on the statutory grounds for the loss of inheritance rights can be applied, in whole or in part, to the loss of the right to bequest.[35] Second, from the perspective of extraterritorial legislation, Japan, Russia and South Korea all stipulate the rules for the admission of the loss of the right to bequeath, or apply the loss of inheritance rights by reference.[36] Therefore, based on the needs of China's social reality, and on learning from extraterritorial legislative experience, the Civil Code stipulates that, if the legatee behaves as stipulated in paragraph 1 of Article 1125 of the Civil Code, that is, if the legatee intentionally kills the decedent, the legatee should bear the consequences of the loss of the bequest right. This makes up for the legislative gap in the rule on the loss of the right to bequest in the Succession Law, so that judicial adjudication has a law to rely on, which is conducive to ensuring the freedom of the heir to handle the inheritance.

3. THE NEW INSTITUTIONAL REGULATIONS IN THE 'STATUTORY SUCCESSION' CHAPTER OF THE SUCCESSION SECTION OF THE CIVIL CODE AND THEIR LEGISLATIVE RATIONALE

3.1. EXPANDING THE SCOPE OF SUBROGATED HEIRS

Article 1128 of the Civil Code expands the scope of subrogated heirs. The legislative rationale for this is as follows: first, the size of the range of subrogated heirs is positively correlated with the probability of subrogation.[37]

---

[35] Liu Chunmao, 中国民法学财产继承 (*'Chinese Civil Law and Property Inheritance'*), People's Court Press, 2008, p. 92; Chen Qiyan, Huang Zongle and Guo Zhengong, 民法继承新论（修订十版）(*'New Theory of Succession of Civil Law'*), Sanmin Bookstore, Revised 10th ed., 2016, p. 353.

[36] See Art. 965 of the Civil Code of Japan, Art. 1117 of the Civil Code of the Russian Federation, and Art. 1075 of the Civil Code of Korea.

[37] Meng Lingzhi, 论我国代位继承制度之完善 (*'On the Improvement of China's Subrogation System'*); 中国继承法修改热点难点问题研究 (*Research on Hot and Difficult Issues in the Revision of China's Succession Law*), Mass Publishing House, 2013, p. 241.

The Succession Law stipulates that the order of legal heirs is small, and the scope is narrow,[38] and that the only subrogated heirs are the direct descendants of the children of the heirs. Therefore, the scope of intestate heirs and subrogated heirs is too narrow to meet the actual needs of some 'families with lost independence', and some unmarried and childless people who have formed new family structures. These changes in family structure have been caused by the implementation of China's family planning policy for more than 30 years, and can easily lead to the inheritance being taken over by no one, and being nationalised, which is inconsistent with the legislative concept of protecting the people's private property.[39] Second, empirical investigations have shown that about 30 to 50 per cent of respondents believe that nieces and nephews should be included within the scope of legal heirs.[40] Third, in extraterritorial legislation, the order and scope of intestate heirs, and the scope of subrogated heirs, are more sequential and broader in Germany, France and Japan than in China, which can better avoid no one inheriting the estate, so as to protect the inheritance rights of natural persons.[41] Therefore, the Succession Section of the Civil Code expands the scope of subrogated heirs, and essentially expands

---

[38] There are only two orders of legal heirs in China, the first-order legal heirs are the spouse, children and parents; the second-order legal heirs are siblings, grandparents and maternal grandparents. Thereinto, the direct inferior blood relatives stop at the children; the direct noble blood relatives stop at the grandparents and maternal grandparents; and the collateral blood relatives stop at the brothers and sisters.

[39] CHEN WEI and DONG SIYUAN, 民法典编纂视野下法定继承制度的反思与重构 ('Reflection and Reconstruction of statutory succession system from the perspective of civil code codification') (2017) 7河北法学 (*Hebei Jurisprudence*) 19.

[40] The survey data shows that, among the respondents in ten provinces and cities in China, the statistics on those who believed that nieces and nephews should be included within the scope of legal heirs were: 24.69% in Chongqing, 26.91% in Shanghai, 32.50% in Hebei Province, 33% in Jilin Province, 31.79% in Hubei Province, 24.87% in Jiangxi Province, 31.71% in Sichuan Province, 50% in Guangdong Province, 26.72% in Hainan Province, and 26.32% in Fujian Province: CHEN WEI, 当代中国民众财产继承观念与遗产处理习惯实证调查研究 (*An Empirical Research on People's Concepts of Property Inheritance and Habits of Heritage Disposal in Contemporary China (vols. 1 and 2)*), Chinese People's Public Security University Press, 2019, pp. 24, 136, 229, 323, 419, 511, 614, 727, 810 and 905.

[41] With regard to the order and scope of intestate heirs, Germany has five or more orders, covering all direct and collateral blood relatives; France has four orders, and direct blood relatives have no restrictions, with collateral blood relatives limited to six kinds; there are three orders in Japan, with no restriction on direct blood relatives – direct blood relatives stop at grandchildren, and collateral blood relatives stop at the children of brothers and sisters. With regard to the scope of subrogated heirs, for example, Japan and France stipulate that the brothers and sisters of heirs can be subrogated, and Germany stipulates that the brothers and sisters of the heirs, and siblings of the parents and cousins, can all be subrogated: see Arts. 1936, 1924–1928 of the German Civil Code, Arts. 734, 735, 739, 740, 744, 745, 752, 754 and 755 of the French Civil Code, and Arts. 887, 889, 891 and 901 of the Japanese Civil Code.

the scope of legal heirs. The Civil Code contributes to the function of the subrogation inheritance system by keeping the estate with blood relations to the decedent, and continuing to circulate it downwards, so as to avoid the loss of inheritance to the family.

3.2.   RELAXING THE CONDITIONS FOR THE DISCRETIONARY CLAIMANT OF THE ESTATE

Article 1131 of the Civil Code relaxes the conditions for the discretionary claimant of the estate. The legislative rationale for this is as follows: first, Article 14 of the Succession Law stipulates that a person dependent on the support of the heir must also 'lack [the] ability to work and lack [a] means of subsistence', in order to enjoy the discretionary claim of inheritance. However, with changes in people's family concepts, the phenomenon of long-term non-marital cohabitation has increased, and although an interdependent dependency relationship often forms between cohabitants, cohabitants are not legal heirs, and cannot participate in the inheritance. Similarly, cohabitants are not, ordinarily, people who lack the ability to work and have no source of livelihood, and so they cannot participate in the discretionary distribution of the inheritance. As a result, the death of one cohabitant may deprive the surviving cohabitant and other dependents of access to the decedent's estate, undermining their economic security.[42] Second, in terms of extraterritorial legislation, both Germany and Switzerland provide for the discretionary division of inheritance among those who depend on the dependent.[43] Therefore, in order to maintain the stability of the maintenance relationship that has been formed during the inherited person's life, the Civil Code, on the basis of learning from extraterritorial legislation, gives non-heirs who relied on the support of the decedent the discretionary right to claim the inheritance. This provision can encourage mutual support within the established maintenance relationships, promote the desirable family style of mutual help and mutual assistance, harmony and friendship, and better allow for the maintenance function of the inheritance.

---

[42]   For dispute cases in which a person who relies on the support of the heir is not a 'double-no-person', and is unable to obtain the discretionary right to claim the inheritance, please refer to the second-instance civil judgment of the Loudi Intermediate People's Court（2020）湘13民终13号Cohabitation Relationship Analysis Dispute; and the first-instance civil judgment of the Youyang Tujia and Miao Autonomous County People's Court（2018）渝0242民初5581号Dispute over the Division of Common Property.

[43]   See Art. 1969 of the German Civil Code and Art. 606 of the Swiss Civil Code.

4. THE NEW INSTITUTIONAL REGULATIONS IN THE 'TESTAMENTARY INHERITANCE AND BEQUEST' CHAPTER OF THE SUCCESSION SECTION OF THE CIVIL CODE AND THEIR LEGISLATIVE RATIONALE

4.1. ADDING A TESTAMENTARY TRUST

Paragraph 4 of Article 1133 of the Civil Code adds a new provision on testamentary trusts. The legislative rationale for this is as follows: first, the increase in private property, and the corresponding increase in the size and complexity of estates, has increased the need to plan inheritances. This increased need for planning includes arrangements for the inheritance of the property after death, especially planning for professional estate management, preserving and appreciating the value of the estate, maintaining specific persons, and avoiding the heirs or bequests squandering their inheritances. As a combination of the testamentary system and the trust system, a testamentary trust can not only meet the above needs of the testator, but also play an important role in protecting the interests of the estate creditors and maintaining the safety of market transactions.[44] Second, from the perspective of extraterritorial legislation, there are two types of legislative examples of testamentary trusts. One is to provide for testamentary trusts in the succession section of the Civil Code, so as to clarify the special rules that distinguish testamentary trusts from general trusts, as seen in Portugal and Chile.[45] The other is for testamentary trusts not to be stipulated in the Civil Code, but only in the trust law, as is the case in Japan.[46] The addition of testamentary trusts is a response from the Succession Section of the Civil Code to the types of testamentary trusts in the Trust Law, which has the significance of filling the legislative gap, and is also a response to the actual needs of the public for wealth inheritance.

4.2. SUPPLEMENTING THE WILL FORM

4.2.1. Added Provisions for Printing Wills

Article 1136 of the Civil Code adds a printed form of will, and clarifies the requirements for its validity. The legislative rationale is that the wide application

---

[44] CHU XUEFEI and XU TENGFEI, 试论我国遗嘱信托制度之构建 ('On the Construction of Testamentary Trust System in China') (2015) 8河北法学 (*Hebei Jurisprudence*), 171–178.

[45] See Arts. 2286 to 2296 of the Portuguese Civil Code, and Arts. 1311 to 1316 of the Chilean Civil Code.

[46] N. MASATOSHI, 信托法判例研究 ('*Research on The Jurisprudence of Trust Law*'), translated by Zhang Junjian, China Founder Publishing House, 2006, p. 313.

of computers and printing equipment has greatly changed the way people record, write and communicate. What is the nature of the will produced by printing? There are four theories: 'self-written wills', 'proxy wills', 'compromise theories' and 'new forms of wills'.[47] In judicial practice, there are also problems of inconsistent adjudication standards on the nature and validity of printed wills.[48] In order to provide testators with more options and freedom in relation to the form of wills, the Civil Code adopts the 'new type of testamentary form theory', which also stipulates more stringent effective elements than proxy wills, to ensure the authenticity of the expression in the will.

4.2.2. Added Provisions for Video Wills

Article 1137 of the Civil Code adds a new video will, improving the requirements for the validity of audio and video wills. The legislative rationale is that, previously, video wills have been used as auxiliary tools, or as evidence to verify the authenticity of holographed testament and allograph testament, but have not been regarded as an independent form of wills. In judicial practice, the court can usually apply the rules of audio or oral wills by analogy, to determine the nature and validity of a video will, but it is easy to cause the will to be invalid due to the lack of formal requirements,[49] which is not conducive to guaranteeing the true expression of the testator's intention. Therefore, recognising video wills as a new form of wills is a legislative response to practical needs, and also provides a legal basis for judicial practice to judge the nature and validity of video wills.

---

[47] ZHAO CHUN, 民法典编纂视野下的遗嘱形式及其形式要件完善 ('The form of wills and their formal requirements under the perspective of the codification of the Civil Code') （2019）4北方法学 (*Northern Jurisprudence*), 77.

[48] E.g. the Fuzhou Intermediate People's Court believes that printing a will is a self-written will. For details of the case, please refer to the Fuzhou Intermediate People's Court's（2020）闽01民终2014号 Second-Instance Civil Judgment; The Xingcheng People's Court believes that the printing of the will is an allograph testament. For details of the case, please refer to the first-instance civil judgment of the Xingcheng People's Court（2018）辽1481民初1762号.

[49] E.g. the Yancheng Intermediate People's Court believes that a video will is not a form of will stipulated in China's law, but that it is most similar to the audio will, and can be reviewed according to the relevant provisions on the audio will. For details of the case, see the Civil Ruling of the Yancheng Intermediate People's Court（2019）苏09民申302号; for another example, the Duyun Municipal People's Court held that, although China's Inheritance Law does not explicitly cover a video will, its nature is similar to that of an oral will, so it can be reviewed with reference to the effective elements of an oral will. The details of the case can be found in the First Instance Civil Judgment of the Duyun Municipal People's Court（2017）黔2701民初2893号.

4.3. EXPANDING THE SCOPE OF WITNESSES TO A MISSING WILL

Paragraph 1 of Article 1140 of the Civil Code expands the scope of witnesses to a missing will. That is, the following persons cannot be witnesses to the will: (1) persons without capacity for civil conduct, persons with limited capacity for civil conduct, and other persons who do not have the capacity to witness; (2) heirs and legatees; (3) persons who have an interest in the heirs or legatees. The legislative rationale is that the ability of the testamentary witness is the key to ensuring the authenticity and validity of the will. Witnesses to a missing will can be divided into two categories, according to the different reasons for their lack of qualification: first, those who have an interest in the will; second, those who do not have the ability to witness, which refers to those who are, in fact, unqualified. In extraterritorial legislation, in addition to persons who do not have full capacity for civil conduct, Russia also stipulates that illiterate citizens, citizens with physical defects, and who are unable to fully understand the nature of what is happening, and persons who are not sufficiently fluent in the language used in the will, are not able to serve as witnesses. Chile stipulates that all persons who are losing their senses, blind, deaf or mute cannot be witnesses to a will.[50] In order to ensure the authenticity of wills, the Civil Code adds 'other persons who do not have the ability to witness' as the final provision on persons who do not have the ability to witness wills, which excludes those who cannot read and write, who are not sufficiently familiar with the language used in the will (such as a minority language, a certain foreign language, Braille, sign language, etc.), or who cannot know or understand what is happening due to physical defects (such as deaf, blind or mute people, or other disabled people who do not have audiovisual capacity), thereby improving the provisions on China's testamentary witnesses.

4.4. IMPROVING THE SYSTEM FOR WITHDRAWING A WILL

4.4.1. 'Revocation of Will' Amended to 'Withdrawal of Will'

Article 1142 of the Civil Code amends 'revocation of wills' to 'withdrawal of wills'. The legislative rationale for this is as follows: a will withdrawal is a unilateral civil juristic act, in which the testator withdraws a will that has not yet taken effect, so that it does not take legal effect. The revocation of a will is the legal act of revoking the effective will from the People's Court after the testator's

---

50 See Art. 388 of the Civil Code of the Russian Federation, and Art. 1012 of the Civil Code of Chile.

death. The nature of these two acts is different. Article 20 of the Succession Law stipulates that the testator may 'revoke' the will he or she has made, which means that the testator withdraws his/her will that has not yet taken effect before his/her death, and the essence is the withdrawal of the will. The Civil Code amends this to make the legislative expression more rigorous and scientific.

4.4.2. *Added Provisions on Will Withdrawal*

Paragraph 2 of Article 1142 of the Civil Code adds statutory circumstances for the withdrawal of a will. The legislative rationale for this is as follows: in jurisprudence, 'there are two types of withdrawal of wills. One is explicit withdrawal, the other is statutory withdrawal'.[51] The latter is when the testator does not express the withdrawal of the will, but if the subsequent will contradicts the previous will, or the will and the testator's behaviour conflict, and it can be presumed that they intend to withdraw the will, and so are legally regarded as having done so. In extraterritorial legislation, many countries provide for the statutory withdrawal of wills. For example, Japan stipulates that there can be statutory withdrawal of a will for three reasons, namely conflict between the former will and the latter will, the situation where the act of disposing of property after the establishment of a will and other legal acts contradict the will, and the testator's intentional destruction of the will or the subject matter of the bequest.[52] Incorporating lessons from the experiences of extraterritorial legislation, the Civil Code expands the applicability of statutory withdrawal of wills, avoids unnecessary disputes, and more comprehensively guarantees the freedom of the public to withdraw wills.

4.5. AMENDING THE NOTARISED WILL VALIDITY RANK

Article 1142 of the Civil Code deletes the provision, in paragraph 3 of Article 20 of the Succession Law, which stated that 'notarised wills shall not be revoked or modified by self-written, written by proxy, audio recordings and oral wills', which negates the priority application rule of notarised wills and establishes the rules of priority application of final wills. The legislative rationale for this is as follows: first, the testator has the right to change or withdraw their will at any time before the will takes effect. However, the establishment, modification or withdrawal of notarised wills must be carried out under the complicated procedures stipulated in the Notary Law and the Rules for Notarisation of Wills,

---

[51] SHI SHANGKUAN, 继承法论 (*'Succession Law'*), China University of Political Science and Law Press, 2000, p. 472.

[52] See Arts. 1023 and 1024 of the Civil Code of Japan.

and certain notarisation fees must be paid. This not only limits the testator's freedom to change or withdraw their will, but also increases the economic cost and difficulty of making a notarised will, compared with other forms of will.[53] Second, empirical investigations have shown that about 50 to 75 per cent of respondents believe that the validity of the last established will should take precedence over a notarised will established earlier.[54] Third, from the perspective of extraterritorial legislation, there is currently no legislative precedent that gives priority to notarised wills. Therefore, the establishment of the rule of priority application of the last will guarantees the testator's freedom to establish, modify or withdraw the will, and helps realise the testator's final expression of his/her true intention.[55] In addition, the legislative reform should reduce the economic costs and procedural difficulties faced by members of the public when making, changing or withdrawing wills, which is in line with the orientation of efficiency value of the law.

4.6. IMPROVING THE SYSTEM OF ATTACHING OBLIGATIONS AND WILLS

Article 1144 of the Civil Code improves the system of compulsory wills. The legislative rationale for this is as follows: Article 21 of the Succession Law[56] has the following four deficiencies: first, 'unit', as a product of the planned economy era, is not a legal term; its connotations and extent are not clearly defined, and it cannot accurately express or cover the relevant legal subjects that may be involved. Second, the term 'individual' does not specifically describe the

---

[53]　CHEN FA, 论我国公证遗嘱适用的效力位阶— – 以法律的价值理论与民众继承习惯的现实为视角 ('Legal Effects of Notarial Will in China: A Perspective of Legal Value and Inheritance Practice') (2012) 5现代法学 (*Modern Jurisprudence*) 64.

[54]　The survey data shows that, among the respondents in ten provinces and cities in China, the statistics on those that believed that the validity of the last established will should take precedence over the notarized wills established earlier were: 70.82% in Chongqing City, 47% in Jilin Province, 64.58% in Shanghai, 65.30% in Hebei Province, 72.67% in Hubei Province, 71.06% in Jiangxi Province, 71.80% in Sichuan Province, 65.08% in Guangdong Province, 75.78% in Hainan Province, and 75.94% in Fujian Province: CHEN WEI, 当代中国民众财产继承观念与遗产处理习惯实证调查研究 ('*An Empirical Research on People's Concepts of Property Inheritance and Habits of Heritage Disposal in Contemporary China (vols. 1 and 2)*'), Chinese People's Public Security University Press, 2019, pp. 30, 143, 235, 329, 426, 574, 621, 734, 816 and 911.

[55]　LIN XIUXIONG, 继承法讲义（第八版）('*Lecture Notes on Succession Law*'), Taipei Yuanzhao Publishing House, 8th ed., 2019, p. 257.

[56]　Art. 21 of the Succession Law stipulates that, if an obligation is attached to testamentary inheritance or bequest the successor or legatee shall perform the obligations. If this person fails to perform their obligations without justifiable reasons, the People's Court may cancel their right to accept the estate, at the request of the concerned unit or individual concerned.

characteristics of the subject enjoying the right, which is too broad without appropriate restrictions. Third, there is no restriction on the scope of 'one's acceptance of inheritance'. It is a question as to whether the estate is the whole inheritance accepted, or only for the obligatory part. Fourth, 'one' can cover only natural persons, and cannot include other civil entities, such as legal persons or unincorporated organisations, as legatees, and the expression is not thorough enough. Therefore, two improvements drawing from Article 21 of the Succession Law have been made in the Civil Code: one is to amend 'units and individuals' to 'interested parties or relevant organisations', limiting the subject of claims to those who have an interest in the relevant will, which can cover a variety of civil subjects arising from the rapid development of the social economy, so that the legislative expression can be more accurate. The other is to amend 'one's right to accept the estate' to 'one's right to accept part of the inheritance with obligations', expanding the scope of bequeathed persons from natural persons to civil entities, such as legal persons or unincorporated organisations, and narrowing the scope of liability for not performing the obligations attached to acceptance of the will, so as to make the legislative expression more comprehensive and rigorous, and also in line with the principle of consistency of rights and obligations.

5. THE NEW INSTITUTIONAL REGULATIONS IN THE 'HANDLING INHERITANCE' CHAPTER OF THE SUCCESSION SECTION OF THE CIVIL CODE AND THEIR LEGISLATIVE RATIONALE

5.1. ADDING A SYSTEM OF ESTATE ADMINISTRATORS

Articles 1145 to 1149 of the Civil Code add a system of estate administrators, the four main aspects of which are described below.

5.1.1. Added Rules for Determining the Administrator of the Estate

Articles 1145 and 1146 of the Civil Code establish rules for determining the administrator of an estate. The legislative rationale for this is as follows: first, due to the lack of an estate management system in China, disputes over inheritance have occurred frequently, due to improper estate management, transfers of estate by heirs, and infringements of the legitimate rights and interests of estate creditors.[57] Second, empirical investigations have shown that 65 to 95 per cent

---

[57]   CHEN WEI and SHI TING, 我国设立遗产管理制度的社会基础及其制度构建 ('The social basis for the establishment of the heritage management system in China and its institutional construction') (2013) 7 河北法学 (*Hebei Jurisprudence*) 19.

of respondents believe that heirs should act as estate administrators, and 15 to 30 per cent believe that the deceased's unit or village (residence) committee should act as estate administrators.[58] Third, from the perspective of extraterritorial legislation, there are three main types of inheritance administrators, such as those in France, Germany and Japan, who are mainly designated by the will, elected or appointed by heirs, and designated by the court in special circumstances.[59] Therefore, the Civil Code stipulates the way to determine the estate administrator on the basis of respecting the habits of the people, and learning from extraterritorial legislation, which is conducive to the realisation of the testator's wishes, respecting the independent choice of the heirs, and the fairness and efficiency of the estate management.

5.1.2. *Added Provisions on the Duties of Estate Administrators*

Article 1147 of the Civil Code specifies the duties of the estate administrator. The legislative rationale for this is as follows: first, the Inheritance Law fails to designate the responsibilities of the estate administrator, which is not conducive to guiding them in legally performing their management duties. Second, empirical investigations show that, in relation to six particular duties, including making and producing the estate inventory, and preserving the heritage properly, about 45 to 95 per cent of respondents believe that the estate administrator has such duties, depending on the particular duty in question.[60] Third, from the

---

[58] The survey data shows that, among the respondents in ten provinces and cities in China, the statistics on those who believed that the heirs should serve as the estate administrator, or that the unit or village (residence) committee where the deceased was located should do so, were as follows: 99.86% and 25.39%, respectively, in Chongqing; 85.5% and 26% in Jilin Province; 90% and 17.1% in Shanghai; 90.47% and 31.44% in Hebei Province; 88.46% and 31.87% in Hubei Province; 63.54% and 15.16% in Jiangxi Province; 89.72% and 28.57% in Sichuan Province; 69.59% and 13.78% in Guangdong Province; 88.84% and 25.65% in Hainan Province; 85.71% and 25.56% in Fujian Province: CHEN WEI, 当代中国民众财产继承观念与遗产处理习惯实证调查研究 ('*An Empirical Research on People's Concepts of Property Inheritance and Habits of Heritage Disposal in Contemporary China (vols. 1 and 2)*'), Chinese People's Public Security University Press, 2019, pp. 21, 133, 224, 319, 414, 507, 609, 724, 806 and 902.

[59] See Arts. 790, 800, 809-1, 813–815 of the French Civil Code; Arts. 1959–1961, 1981, 2032 and 2038 of the German Civil Code; and Arts. 918, 926, 936, 952, 1006 and 1012 of the Japanese Civil Code.

[60] The survey data shows that, among the respondents in the ten provinces and cities in China, the numbers who believed that the responsibilities of the estate administrator are: (1) inventory of the heritage and the preparation of the heritage list; (2) proper custody of the estate; (3) identifying the claims and debts of the inherited person, before actively recovering the creditor's rights or paying off the debts; (4) finding out whether the heir has a will, and determining whether the will is true and legal; (5) participating in any litigation arising from the inheritance, as plaintiff or defendant; (6) the statistics on the regular production of estate management reports and the reporting of estate management to heirs,

perspective of extraterritorial legislation, France, Japan, Vietnam, and other countries, have stipulated the responsibilities of making an inheritance list, managing the estate, disposing of the creditors' rights and the debts of the estate, and distributing the remaining inheritance.[61] In summary, clearly stipulating the scope of responsibilities of the estate administrator, and attaching a catch-all clause, is conducive to confirming the scope of the estate, ensuring the accuracy of the estate list, the safety and value of the estate, the settlement of the estate debts, and the orderly division of the estate, safeguarding the interests and transaction security of the interested parties to the estate, and avoiding the deficiency of the enumerative provisions.[62]

5.1.3. Added Provisions on Liability for Fault of Estate Administrators

Article 1148 of the Civil Code clearly establishes the fault liability of the administrator of the estate. The legislative rationale for this is as follows: first, the Inheritance Law does not stipulate the fault liability of the estate administrator. Moreover, in the inheritance activities, if the administrator of the estate does not properly manage the estate, and causes damage, there is no legal basis for holding them liable. Second, empirical investigations have shown that between 45 and 70 per cent of respondents believe that the administrator of an estate is liable for compensation in the event of intention or gross negligence.[63] Third, from

---

were: 88.96%, 91.20%, 71.84%, 56.48%, 80.16%, and 58.56%, respectively, in Chongqing; 91.33%, 91.67%, 72.17%, 56.83%, 71.83% and 61.17%, respectively, in Jilin Province; 92.30%, 94.00%, 69.10%, 59.40%, 65.40% and 48.50%, respectively, in Shanghai; 92.18%, 93.88%, 71.41%, 48.08%, 65.01% and 56.61%, respectively, in Hebei Province; 91.81%, 94.08%, 73.29%, 53.57%, 65.10% and 59.18%, respectively, in Hubei Province; 90.97%, 91.82%, 71.55%, 47.36%, 54.00% and 43.10%, respectively, in Jiangxi Province; 93.21%, 96.34%, 75.09%, 61.32%, 70.91% and 57.67%, respectively, in Sichuan Province; 92.64%, 91.92%, 65.80%, 65.32%, 57.48% and 41.80%, respectively, in Guangdong Province; 90.50%, 92.64%, 60.33%, 42.28%, 62.23% and 58.43%, respectively, in Hainan Province; 94.73%, 93.98%, 78.20%, 80.45%, 58.65% and 62.41%, respectively, in Fujian Province: CHEN WEI, 当代中国民众财产继承观念与遗产处理习惯实证调查研究 ('An Empirical Research on People's Concepts of Property Inheritance and Habits of Heritage Disposal in Contemporary China (vols. 1 and 2)'), Chinese People's Public Security University Press, 2019, pp. 22, 134, 225, 320, 416, 508, 611, 725, 807 and 902–903.

61   See Arts. 789–792, 796–810 and 811-1 of the French Civil Code; Arts. 920 and 934 of the Civil Code of Japan; and Arts. 617 and 618 of the Civil Code of Vietnam.

62   CHEN WEI and LIU YUJIAO, 中国民法典继承编之遗产清单制度系统化构建研究 ('A Study on the Systematic Construction of Inheritance List System in the Succession Code of the Chinese Civil Code') (2019) 5 现代法学(Modern Jurisprudence) 62.

63   According to the survey data, among the ten provinces and cities in China, the statistics on those who believed that the administrator of the estate only bears the liability for compensation in the event of intent or gross negligence were: 56.62% in Chongqing Municipality, 69.66% in Jilin Province, 62.90% in Shanghai Municipality, 52.63% in Hebei Province, 55.67% in Hubei Province, 50.43% in Jiangxi Province, 55.57% in Sichuan Province, 52.25% in

the perspective of extraterritorial legislation, such as that in Japan and Vietnam, the administrator of the estate should be liable for damage caused by breach of his/her obligations or gross negligence.[64] Therefore, clarifying the liability for damages due to the fault of the estate administrator helps to encourage the estate administrator to perform his/her duties faithfully and prudently.

5.1.4. Increased Rights for Estate Administrators to Claim Remuneration

Article 1149 of the Civil Code clarifies the right of the administrator to claim remuneration. The legislative justification for Article 1149 of the Civil Code is: first, the estate administrator receives remuneration in accordance with the law, in accordance with the will or agreement, or the affirmation of the value of the estate administrator's labour, or the autonomy of the testator's intention, or the freedom agreed upon by both the heirs and the estate administrator, and also conforms to the principle of consistency of rights and obligations, and the legislation should be recognised and protected. Second, empirical investigations have shown that, in the ten provinces and cities of China, in the area where the respondents live, about 30 to 60 per cent of the respondents have the habit that the administrator elected by the heirs who did not have the status of heir and the court-appointed administrator had the right to request remuneration.[65] Third, from the perspective of extraterritorial legislation, Germany, Japan and Vietnam all stipulate that the administrator of the estate may reach a remuneration agreement with the heirs, or the court shall determine the remuneration for the management.[66] Therefore, giving the estate administrator the right to receive remuneration in accordance with the law, or by agreement, can encourage the estate administrator to perform his/her management duties with the attention of a good administrator.

Guangdong Province, 46.32% in Hainan Province, and 46.62% in Fujian Province: CHEN WEI, 当代中国民众财产继承观念与遗产处理习惯实证调查研究 ('An Empirical Research on People's Concepts of Property Inheritance and Habits of Heritage Disposal in Contemporary China (vols. 1 and 2)'), Chinese People's Public Security University Press, 2019, pp. 23, 135, 227, 321, 418, 510, 613, 726, 809 and 903.

[64]   See Art. 934 of the Civil Code of Japan and Art. 617 of the Civil Code of Vietnam.

[65]   The statistics are: 56.62% and 67.19% in Chongqing, 44.67% and 66.00% in Jilin Province, 33.70% and 52.00% in Shanghai, 34.85% and 56.05% in Hebei Province, 35.81% and 54.02% in Hubei Province, 32.54% and 49.57% in Jiangxi Province, 40.77% and 63.94% in Sichuan Province, 29.69% and 65.08% in Guangdong Province, 38.24% and 52.49% in Hainan Province, 27.07% and 45.86% in Fujian Province: CHEN WEI, 当代中国民众财产继承观念与遗产处理习惯实证调查研究 ('An Empirical Research on People's Concepts of Property Inheritance and Habits of Heritage Disposal in Contemporary China (vols. 1 and 2)'), Chinese People's Public Security University Press, 2019, p. 22, 134, 226, 321, 418, 509, 611–612, 726, 808 and 903.

[66]   See Art. 2221 of the German Civil Code, Arts. 29 and 1018 of the Civil Code of Japan, and Art. 618 of the Civil Code of Vietnam.

5.2. ADDING A SYSTEM OF INHERITANCE TRANSFER

A new system of succession has been added to Article 1152 of the Civil Code. The legislative rationale for this is as follows: first, there are applicable needs for the succession system in the inheritance activities of Chinese people, and in judicial practice. There are particular folk customs of inheritance division in some parts of China;[67] that is, some children wait for both parents to die before dividing the estate. This delay results in a longer period from the beginning of inheritance to the division of the estate, during which the number of heirs who die may be larger, or the probability of this increases, resulting in a large number of inheritance cases involving many people and complex circumstances, and in many inheritance cases that require the application of the succession system.[68] Second, although Article 52 of the Opinions on the Succession Law provides for the transfer of inheritance,[69] it is a judicial interpretation with a low level of validity, and the general public is often unaware of this judicial adjudication rule. Third, from the perspective of extraterritorial legislation, France, Switzerland and Russia all provide for a system of succession.[70] Therefore, the Civil Code elevates the system of succession to legislative status, and clarifies that succession applies to both statutory and testamentary succession. However, if the will contains other arrangements, testamentary succession shall apply, rather than the transfer of a deceased heir's interest to his successors. This not only respects the deceased's free intention to dispose of the inheritance, but also helps to reduce inheritance disputes.

---

[67] The survey data on the inheritance habits of the people in the ten provinces and cities of our country show that, in the areas where the respondents in the ten provinces and cities of China are located, after the death of the heirs, the heirs of their children will not submit a request for the division of the inheritance to the surviving spouse of the heirs. The data on the use of folk customs in inheritance division are: 78.55% in Chongqing City, 80.70% in Jilin Province, 58.66% in Shanghai, 77.38% in Hebei Province, 75.19% in Hubei Province, 70.53% in Jiangxi Province; 74.74% in Sichuan Province, 76.01% in Guangdong Province, 66.27% in Hainan Province, and 84.85% in Fujian Province: CHEN WEI, 当代中国民众财产继承观念与遗产处理习惯实证调查研究 ('*An Empirical Research on People's Concepts of Property Inheritance and Habits of Heritage Disposal in Contemporary China (vols. 1 and 2)*'), Chinese People's Public Security University Press, 2019, pp. 48, 158, 253, 343, 441, 538, 639, 747, 833 and 924.

[68] The authors' searches produced 4,577 judgment documents, from 1 January 2005 to 31 December 2019, using 'transfer inheritance' as a keyword, in the 'China Judgment Documents Network', which shows that the inheritance activities and judicial practices of the Chinese people have applicable needs for the inheritance transfer system.

[69] This means that, if a father dies, leaving his estate to his three children and his wife, and the children wait for the mother to die before distributing the father's estate, one of the children might die before then. In that case, that child's share of the estate would be transferred to their heirs.

[70] See Art. 775 of the French Civil Code, Art. 542 of the Swiss Civil Code, and Art. 1156 of the Civil Code of the Russian Federation.

5.3. EXPANDING THE SCOPE OF SUBJECTS OBLIGATED BY BEQUEST MAINTENANCE AGREEMENTS

Article 1158 of the Civil Code expands the scope of subjects of obligations under bequest maintenance agreements. The legislative rationale for this is as follows: Article 31 of the Succession Law stipulates that the scope of the subjects of obligations in bequest maintenance agreements is narrow, and limited to those other than the heirs and collective ownership organisations, excluding other organisations with old-age functions. It cannot meet the actual needs of elderly people who have lost their only child, social and economic development, and the increase in the number of migrant workers during the implementation of the family planning policy. The Civil Code expands the scope of obligatory subjects of bequest maintenance agreements, including to organisations and individuals other than heirs, which is conducive to giving full play to the supplementary functions of bequest maintenance agreements for family pensions and social security pensions.

5.4. CLARIFYING THE USE OF THE NATIONALISED UNINTENDED HERITAGE

Article 1160 of the Civil Code clearly states that inheritances that no one inherits and no one is bequeathed shall belong to the State, and shall be used for public welfare. The legislative rationale for this is as follows: empirical surveys show that about 60 to 80 per cent of respondents believe that, where the decedent does not write a will, and has no heirs, then, pursuant to the intestate succession law, their estate should belong to the State, the national treasury, the social welfare agencies of the civil affairs departments, etc.[71] Therefore, the Civil Code stipulates that the use of State-owned unintended heritage for public welfare undertakings can promote the development of social welfare undertakings, reflect the State's people-oriented concept, help enhance the governments' ability to ensure people's basic livelihoods and social governance, and also implement the policy of 'taxes come from the people and are used for the people', thus maximising the social utility of 'the heritage that no one inherits'.

---

[71] The survey data shows that, among the respondents in ten provinces and cities in China, the statistics on those that believe that the unintended heritage should belong to social welfare institutions, such as the State, the national treasury, and the civil affairs departments, are: 67.98% in Chongqing City, 80.09% in Jilin Province, 62.50% in Shanghai, 70.18% in Hebei Province, 70.64% in Hubei Province, 61.65% in Jiangxi Province, 72.39% in Sichuan Province, 82.55% in Guangdong Province, 66.68% in Hainan Province, and 59.13% in Fujian Province: CHEN WEI, 当代中国民众财产继承观念与遗产处理习惯实证调查研究 ('*An Empirical Research on People's Concepts of Property Inheritance and Habits of Heritage Disposal in Contemporary China (vols. 1 and 2)*'), Chinese People's Public Security University Press, 2019, pp. 23, 135, 227, 321, 418, 510, 613, 726, 809 and 903.

5.5. ADDING RULES ON LIABILITY FOR THE SETTLEMENT OF ESTATE DEBTS

Article 1163 of the Civil Code adds rules for the allocation of responsibilities between the subjects of inheritance rights and the subjects of bequest rights, when settling inheritance debts. First, the Succession Law does not stipulate the distribution of responsibility for the repayment of inheritance debts between such subjects. Although Article 62 of the Opinions on the Succession Law stipulates that the division of an estate should only occur when the unpaid estate debts have been paid, and suggests that will beneficiaries may be liable if the debts are not paid before the distribution of the estate, these rulings can neither guide the public to pay off the estate debts first and divide the estate later, nor avoid the division of the estate first, and the repayment of the debts later, which leads to new disputes.[72] Second, from the perspective of extraterritorial legislation, German law stipulates the principle that the debts of the estate should be paid before dividing the estate, which is conducive to the protection of the legitimate rights and interests of the estate's creditors.[73] Therefore, the Civil Code extends the distribution of the liability for the repayment of estate debts to the subjects of inheritance rights and bequest rights. This changes the situation from one where 'the estate has been divided and the unpaid debts are paid' to the whole process of the division of the estate, which can prevent the heirs from maliciously evading the settlement of the inheritance debts and infringing on the interests of the estate creditors after dividing the estate. The new provisions are conducive to the building of a good order of inheritance distribution, reducing disputes over inheritance debts, and ensuring the legitimate rights and interests of the estate creditors, together with the safety of market transactions.

6. OTHER NEW REGULATIONS RELATING TO THE WILL SYSTEM UNDER THE CIVIL CODE AND THEIR LEGISLATIVE RATIONALE

6.1. ADDING A TESTAMENTARY GUARDIANSHIP SYSTEM

Article 29 of the Civil Code introduces a system of testamentary guardianship. The legislative rationale for this is as follows: first, before the promulgation of

---

[72] Regarding the relevant cases of disputes caused by the division of the estate infringing on the interests of the estate creditors, see the Second-Instance Civil Judgment of the Intermediate People's Court of Xiangxi Tujia and Miao Autonomous Prefecture（2018）湘31民终871号, and the Second-Instance Civil Judgment of the Intermediate People's Court of Bayingolin Mongolian Autonomous Prefecture of Xinjiang Uygur Autonomous Region（2020）新28民终373号.

[73] See Arts. 1975, 1980 and 1986 of the German Civil Code.

the General Provisions of the Civil Law 2017, in China, parents' ability to name testamentary guardians for their children was difficult to ensure, due to the lack of a legal basis in judicial practice, which tended to cause disputes.[74] Second, from the perspective of extraterritorial legislation, Germany, South Korea and Chile have all provided for a system of testamentary guardianship.[75] Therefore, the establishment of the testamentary guardianship system is the embodiment of the principle of autonomy of private law, the principle of freedom of will, and the principle of maximising the interests of children. It also provides a legal basis for guiding testators to establish testamentary designated guardianship, and guiding judicial practice to confirm the effectiveness of testamentary guardianship.[76]

6.2. ADDING A WILL TO ESTABLISH THE RIGHT OF RESIDENCE

Article 371 of the Civil Code adds a new provision for the establishment of the right of residence by means of a will. The legislative rationale for this is as follows: in real life, a second order of intestate heirs living with the heirs, or non-heirs (such as long-term non-marital cohabitants, elderly nannies, de facto dependent children, widows and the elderly, etc.) may have no place to live after the death of the heir, because the heirs who inherited the ownership of the house in the inheritance used the house themselves or sold it. Moreover, the publicity of testamentary inheritance, bequest or obligation-bearing wills is weak, and it is often difficult to avoid the unstable factors caused by the settlement of the residence problems of the above-mentioned special groups through borrowing and leasing, and disputes are likely to arise.[77] Therefore, the establishment of the right of residence through the will can meet and protect the residence needs of the above-mentioned types of people, which is conducive to social stability and harmony.

---

[74] For details of disputes arising from the appointment of a guardian via a will, please refer to the Civil Judgment of the People's Court of Tiexi District of Anshan City（2017）辽0303民初44号, and the Civil Judgment of Youjiang District People's Court of Baise City（2015）右民特字第16号.

[75] See Art. 1777 of the German Civil Code, Art. 930 of the Korean Civil Code, and Art. 354 of the Civil Code of Chile.

[76] MENG QINGUO, TANG RUI, 论遗嘱指定监护的完善 – – 以民法典《婚姻家庭编》的编纂为重点 ('On the Perfection of Guardianship Designated by Wills: Focusing on the Compilation of the Marriage and Family Code of the Civil Code') (2019) 5 河北法学 (*Hebei Jurisprudence*) 23.

[77] For dispute cases over claims of permanent residence and long-term residence, for the property subject of inheritance, see the Zhongshan Intermediate People's Court（2016）粤20民终2106号, Second-Instance Civil Judgment; Shanghai Jiading District People's Court（2016）沪0114民初2949号, Civil Judgment.

6.3. ADDING PROVISIONS ON THE DONATION OF HUMAN ORGANS THROUGH A WILL

Article 1006 of the Civil Code adds a provision for the donation of human organs through a will. The legislative rationale is that Article 8 of China's Human Organ Transplant Action Regulations stipulates that, for persons with full civil capacity, donations of human organs before death should be in writing, but the effectiveness of donating human organs through a will is not clear. The Civil Code adds a will method of donating human cells, tissues, organs and remains, without compensation, which respects the testator's intention to voluntarily donate organs, provides a response to the actual needs of human organ transplantation, and helps to make up for the current large imbalance between supply and demand, in organ transplantation and donation in China.[78] The Civil Code provisions are conducive to the promotion of public interest, and the enhancement of social welfare.

6.4. DELETING THE PROVISION ON THE VALIDITY OF PROPERTY RIGHTS UNDER BEQUEATHED RIGHTS

Article 230 of the Civil Code deletes the provisions of Article 29 of the Property Law 2017 in China, on the validity of property rights under bequeathed rights. The legislative rationale for this is as follows: first, China takes whether a person is a legal heir as the criterion for distinguishing between testamentary succession and bequest. If the bequeathed person is not a legal heir, and if they cannot be the testamentary heir, they will not enjoy the right to inherit what is stated in the will, so the bequest designated by the will only has effect in relation to creditor's rights. Moreover, the fact that the inherent jurisprudence of the inheritance claim, embodied in Article 34 of the Succession Law, is superior to the right to receive the bequest, also shows that the bequest does not have the effect of property rights. However, Article 29 of China's Property Law 2017 used to stipulate that both the right of inheritance and the right to receive bequests have the effect of property rights, which makes the nature of the validity of the right of bequest controversial in theory, and difficult to operate in practice. Second, from the perspective of extraterritorial legislation, in countries that do not recognise a general or partial general bequest, like Germany and Switzerland, the validity of

---

[78] According to statistics, as of 15 July 2020, there were 2,187,738 people registered for valid voluntary donation; as of 30 June 2020, 29,650 people had donated a total of 86,086 organs. Although China's human organ donation work has developed rapidly, it is still one of the countries with the lowest rate of organ donation in the world: see The Red Cross Society of China Chinese Organ Donation Management Center, available at <https://www.codac.org.cn>.

the bequest is a creditor's right.[79] Therefore, the Civil Code deletes the provisions on the validity of property rights under bequeathed rights, which is conducive to the coordination and unification of the connection and application of the inheritance section and the property rights section.

In summary, the new rules of the relevant system in the Succession Section of the Civil Code have made great progress. Meanwhile, 'the tree of life is evergreen', and people's new demands of the law are also growing. In view of the limitations of statutory law, the promulgation and implementation of the Succession Section of the Civil Code does not mean the cessation of theoretical research on inheritance law and legislative reform, and some of its systems should and can be further supplemented and improved. In the future, on the basis of studying the inheritance habits of the Chinese people, summing up judicial practice experience, and learning from the experience of extraterritorial legislation, suggestions should continuously be put forward for the refinement, supplementation and improvement of the Succession Section of the Civil Code, and to contribute to the realisation of the benign interaction between law and social reality.

---

[79] See Arts. 2174 and 2176 of the German Civil Code; Arts. 562 and 563 of the Swiss Civil Code.

ISRAEL

ISLAMIC LAW IN THE JEWISH STATE

The Formation of an Israeli Shari'a

Karin Carmit Yefet* and Ido Shahar**

Résumé

Cet article présente les développements récents et passionnants du droit musulman de la famille dans l'État juif. Plus précisément, il explore les processus peu étudiés d' « israélisation du droit musulman », *i.e.* la convergence de facteurs légaux « externes » qui ont eu un impact sur l'évolution du droit musulman. L'analyse se concentre plus particulièrement sur deux formes « d'israélisation » : l'une concerne l'interprétation « civile » de la loi musulmane par les juges aux affaires familiales, l'autre est relative aux conséquences d'une réforme législative, introduite en 2001, qui a mis en place une compétence concurrente entre les tribunaux civils de la famille et les tribunaux de la *charia* pour la plupart des questions relatives au statut personnel des musulmans en Israël. L'étude est fondée sur la jurisprudence en matière de pension alimentaire pour l'épouse musulmane. Elle identifie la dynamique de deux processus parallèles, voire paradoxaux : d'une part, les tribunaux de la sharia ont eu tendance à introduire des réformes internes

---

* Senior Lecturer, Faculty of Law, University of Haifa; member of the Global Young Academy.
** Senior Lecturer, Middle Eastern and Islamic Studies, University of Haifa.
   This research was supported by the Israel Science Foundation (grant no. 607/17).

en faveur des femmes et à adopter des interprétations du droit musulman de la famille relativement libérales et favorables aux femmes au cours des deux dernières décennies ; d'autre part, les tribunaux civils de la famille ont développé une jurisprudence conservatrice et patriarcale qui est systématiquement défavorable aux femmes musulmanes et à leur famille. Cette étude se termine par un aperçu de la manière dont le droit musulman pourrait évoluer au sein de l'État juif.

1. INTRODUCTION

Israeli family law is unique among the law of Western countries: it is patterned after the Ottoman *millet* system, which imbued communal-religious courts with jurisdiction in the personal status matters of their respective community members.[1] The Israeli pluri-legal family law regime accords official recognition to 14 religious communities, including Jews, Muslims, Druze, Baha'i, and 10 different Christian denominations. Each recognised religious community possesses its own State-sanctioned tribunals and a separate set of legally binding religious codes. This State-administered religious court system co-exists alongside a parallel system of civil family courts, which have been vested with concurrent jurisdiction over the ancillary matrimonial matters of property distribution, wife maintenance, and child support and custody.[2] Family law in the Jewish state is, thus, a hybrid of civil and religious legal elements, where the interplay between the sacred and the secular unfolds in many manifestations.

---

[1]   Y. SEZGIN, 'A Political Account for Legal Confrontation between State and Society: The Case of Israeli Legal Pluralism' (2004) 32 *Studies in Law, Politics, and Society* 197; M. ABOU RAMADAN, 'The Shari'a In Israel: Islamization, Israelization and the Invented Islamic Law' (2006) 5 *UCLA Journal of Islamic and Near Eastern Law* 81; M. ABOU RAMADAN, 'Notes on the Anomaly of the Shari'a Field in Israel' (2008) 15 *Islamic Law and Society* 84; K.C. YEFET, 'Unchaining the Agunot: Enlisting the Israeli Constitution in the Service of Women's Marital Freedom' (2009) 20 *Yale Journal of Law & Feminism* 101; K.C. YEFET, 'Israeli Family Law as a Civil-Religious Hybrid: A Cautionary Tale of Fatal Attraction' (2016) *University of Illinois Law Review* 1505; D. HACKER, 'Religious Tribunals in Democratic States: Lessons from the Israeli Rabbinical Courts' (2011) 27 *Journal of Law and Religion* 59. It should be noted that the Ottoman *millet* system underwent far-reaching transformations during the British Mandate in Palestine: G. AMIR, 'The Institution of the "Religious Community" in Israeli Jurisprudence as a Mechanism for Ethnic Sorting and Control' (2014) 23 *Politika* 46 (in Hebrew); I. AGMON, 'There are Judges in Jerusalem and there were legislators in Istanbul: On the History of the Law Called (mistakenly) "The Ottoman Law of Family Rights"' (2017) 8 *Family in Law* 125 (in Hebrew).

[2]   F. RADAY, 'Israel – The Incorporation of Religious Patriarchy in a Modern State' (1992) 4 *International Review of Comparative Public Policy* 209; R. HALPERIN-KADDARI, *Women in Israel: A State of Their Own*, University of Pennsylvania Press, 2004; Y. SEZGIN, 'The Israeli Millet System: Examining Legal Pluralism through the Lenses of Nation-Building and Human Rights' (2010) 43 *Israel Law Review* 631; D. HACKER, 'Religious Tribunals in Democratic States: Lesson from the Israeli Rabbinical Courts' (2012) 27(1) *Journal of Law and Religion* 59.

For example, religious courts enjoy exclusive jurisdiction over matters of marriage and divorce, which they adjudicate according to religious law. However, religious and civil courts share concurrent jurisdiction over specified family law matters, and both must either apply religious law, as in matters of spousal and child support, or secular civil law, as in matters of child custody and property distribution.[3] Put differently, Israel maintains a pluri-legal system of personal status law which combines normative pluralism in the civil family courts (i.e. the application of different norms to different segments of the population) with institutional pluralism (i.e. there are designated communal-religious tribunals with exclusive jurisdiction in matters pertaining to their community members).[4]

While a wealth of literature has lavished attention on the Jewish family and the law that regulates its intimate affairs, the personal status law applicable to Israel's religious minorities has been understudied in legal scholarship. This chapter contributes to the narration of the intriguing story of Islamic law in the Jewish state. Conceptually speaking, the regulation of the Muslim-Palestinian family has given rise to two remarkable and dialectical phenomena: the Islamisation of Israeli law, and the Israelisation of Islamic law.[5] Islamisation takes place when 'Israeli legal norms are repackaged as norms that already exist in Islamic law, and are applied in the Shari'a Courts as pure, authentic Islamic law'.[6] The case of child custody, which the shari'a court is obliged to adjudicate according to the civil law principle of the child's best interests, is a paradigmatic example of such a process. This principle has no mention in Islamic doctrine, and yet Israel's shari'a courts have read it into classical sources, and have thus bestowed Islamic legitimacy upon a civil principle. By 'Islamising' Israeli law, the shari'a courts have suggested that child welfare is every bit as Islamic a term as it is Israeli.[7]

The other side of the coin, so to speak, is the Israelisation of Islamic law, i.e. the application of Islamic law within the framework of a civil 'Westernised' legal system, and within the complex context of the interrelations between a non-Muslim hegemonic majority and a Muslim minority. Broadly speaking, this process includes the confluence of 'external' legal forces and apparatuses that have impacted, overtly or covertly, on the development of Islamic doctrine. The repertoire of such secular/Israeli influences may be vast and varied, and encompass situations in which civil law criminalises Islamic practices; subjects

---

3 YEFET, 'Israeli Family Law as a Civil-Religious Hybrid', above n. 1.

4 For further discussion on institutional and normative pluralism, see Y. SEZGIN, *Human Rights under State-Enforced Religious Family Laws in Israel, Egypt, and India*, Cambridge University Press, 2013, pp. 5–8.

5 To the best of the authors' knowledge, these concepts were first introduced by Mousa Abou Ramadan. See ABOU RAMADAN, 'The Shari'a In Israel', above n. 1.

6 Ibid., at 81.

7 M. ABOU RAMADAN, 'The Transition from Tradition to Reform: The Shari'a Appeals Court Rulings on Child Custody (1992–2001)' (2002) 26 *Fordham International Law Journal* 595.

shari'a courts to the normative hierarchy of the Israeli Constitution, or to the ultimate authority of Israel's Supreme Court; introduces forum competition by administering concurrent jurisdiction of the civil and religious tribunals; or empowers civil judges to experiment with the interpretation and implementation of Islamic norms.

While Islamisation of Israeli civil law has received considerable academic attention – primarily by Abou Ramadan[8] – Israelisation of Islamic law has, thus far, remained grossly understudied. This chapter thus seeks to shed light on this underexplored process. The formation of an 'Israeli shari'a' gives rise to a series of pivotal queries which remain largely unanswered to date: does the constitutional character of Israel as a Muslim-minority democracy that is an avowed *Jewish* nation state have any bearing on its particular development of Islamic law? What sociolegal and structural forces work to shape the design and application of Islamic law in a Jewish state? Has Islamic law been 'feminised' and harmonised with Israel's liberal constitutional scheme? Or does it hold tightly to the traditional patriarchal regime that classically defined it? In short, what characterises Israeli-Islamic law?

In addressing some of these questions, this chapter focuses on developments that have extended Israel's civil-religious family law hybrid to Muslims. Specifically, the chapter will examine the effects of a 22-year-old momentous legislative reform which granted Israel's civil family court system concurrent jurisdiction – alongside the shari'a courts – over personal status matters, other than the marriage and divorce, of Muslim litigants. From roughly 2002 onwards, civil courts have been tasked with the application of Islamic family law and with the expounding of its various doctrines. This statutory reform thus allows us a rare glimpse into the operation of two components of 'Israelisation': one relates to the 'civil' interpretation of Islamic law by family judges, while the other relates to the effects of competition arising from the concurrent jurisdiction accorded to the civil courts on the evolution of judicial Islamic doctrine in the shari'a courts.

An examination of these two features of 'Israelisation' requires both an intra-tribunal comparison of the sharia courts' pre- and post-reform jurisprudence, and an inter-tribunal comparison between the case law of the shari'a court and family court systems. Our case study under investigation is Muslim wife maintenance suits – a classic subject matter over which both the civil and shari'a courts enjoy concurrent jurisdiction, and which treads into an uncharted territory of Islamic interpretation. Methodologically speaking, the proposed comparative analysis is based on a textual analysis of: (1) a case law corpus made up of hundreds of wife maintenance decisions passed by the shari'a courts before, and especially after, the jurisdictional reform, and which were published

---

[8]   Ibid.

on the Shari'a Courts Administration website; and (2) several dozen family court decisions passed between 2002 and 2020 which were published in computerised judicial databases, or which were never published, but kindly shared with us by judges, attorneys and litigants.[9]

As this chapter will show, the seemingly procedural, progressive and feminist-driven reform led to substantive and, at least in part, regressive results: on one hand, the shari'a courts introduced internal reforms into Islamic law, in an attempt to thwart the anticipated reform, and, after its passage, to contain and constrain its impact. On the other hand, the civil family courts paradoxically developed a conservative and patriarchal Islamic jurisprudence that systematically operates to the detriment of Muslim women.

Structurally, the rest of the chapter proceeds as follows: the second section provides a brief introductory background, in order to understand the particularities and peculiarities of the shari'a field in Israel. The third section introduces the 2001 jurisdictional reform and the impetus behind its initiative. The fourth and fifth sections analyse the aftermath of the reform in the shari'a and civil family court systems, respectively, by focusing on wife maintenance jurisprudence. The sixth section concludes the chapter and outlines insights that may be distilled from the case study about the evolution of Islamic law in the Jewish state.

2. THE FORMATION OF AN ISRAELI SHARI'A: AN OVERVIEW

An investigation of the evolution of Israeli-Islamic law must be conducted against the backdrop of the unusual framework governing the regulation of shari'a courts in Israel. Under the Mandate, these courts enjoyed not only the broadest jurisdiction of all the recognised religious tribunals, but also the broadest institutional autonomy.[10] The State of Israel, established in 1948, adopted the

---

[9]   Locating family court decisions is a considerable challenge. The Israeli Courts Administration does not publish family court decisions on any official website, and proprietary computerised databases only publish them partially, sparingly, and at the family court judges' discretion. This practice prevents scholars from accessing a representative sample of these court decisions, and makes it difficult to identify and corroborate wide-ranging arguments and generalised trends. The following findings should, therefore, be read with this caveat on the inherent limitations of studying Israeli family court decisions in mind.

[10]   While the shari'a courts held exclusive jurisdiction in *all* matters of personal status of Muslims, the other religious tribunals have had exclusive jurisdiction only in *some* matters of personal status of their respective community members. In addition, whereas the shari'a courts were fully funded by the Mandate government, the other courts were funded by their respective communities. See I. SHAHAR, 'Islamic Law as Indigenous Law: The Shari'a Courts in Israel from a Postcolonial Perspective' (2015) 5 *Journal of Levantine Studies* 83.

quasi-*millet* system introduced by the British,[11] yet while the broad jurisdiction of the shariʿa courts was retained (at least until 2001), they were stripped of any vestige of institutional autonomy. Undeniably, the shariʿa court system is the most regulated and subordinated legal system among the 14 recognised religious communities in Israeli law,[12] and this relatively tight civil oversight manifests in various ways.

For one thing, while Israel has avoided institutional and normative unification, the shariʿa court system is integrated into the Jewish state, with its judges appointed by a secular and non-Muslim civil body, and subject to oversight by the Israeli Supreme Court in its capacity as a High Court of Justice (HCJ).[13] The HCJ may intervene in shariʿa court decisions if they exceed their jurisdiction, if they violate the principles of natural justice, or if they disregard legal provisions that are specifically applicable to the religious tribunals.[14] A notable example is the HCJ decision which forced the nomination of female arbitrators to family councils – the quasi-judicial bodies that execute the dissolution process – in order to make divorce more woman-sensitive and promote gender mainstreaming.[15]

For another thing, while shariʿa courts enjoy formal exclusive jurisdiction over matters of marriage and divorce, Islamic law is subject to key civil legislation that imposed certain liberal norms on the shariʿa courts. These include, for example, the Israeli Constitution,[16] the Women's Equal Rights Act, and secular criminal law severely restricting polygamous and underage marriages,[17] and

---

11 The Law and Administration Ordinance, the first act of legislation to be enacted by the Knesset, determined that the laws and regulations in force prior to 15 May 1948 would continue to apply.

12 ABOU RAMADAN, 'Notes on the Anomaly', above n. 1.

13 Ibid.; Y. SEZGIN, 'Human Rights under State-Enforced Religious Family Laws', above n. 4; A. NATOUR, 'The Role of the Shariʿa Court of Appeals in Promoting the Status of Women in Islamic Law in a Non-Muslim State (Israel)' (JSD dissertation, American University Washington College of Law, 2009).

14 M. ABOU RAMADAN, 'La loi applicable à la minorité roum orthodoxe de l'état d'Israël' [The law applicable to the Rum Orthodox Minority in the State of Israel] (2000) 50 *Proche-Orient chrétien* 105, 109.

15 HCJ 3856/11 *Doe v. Supreme Sharia Court of Appeals* (published on Nevo, 27 June 2013) (Isr.); M. PINTO, 'The Absence of the Right to Culture of Minorities Within Minorities in Israel: A Tale of a Cultural Dissent Case' (2015) 4 *Laws* 579; M. ABOU RAMADAN, 'Islamic Legal Hybridity and Patriarchal Liberalism in the Shariʿa Courts in Israel' (2015) 4 *Journal of Levantine Studies* 39; I. SHAHAR, 'Standing at the Barricades of Patriarchy: The Israeli Shariʿa Courts and the Appointment of Women Arbitrators' (2017) 8 *The Family in Law* 81; YEFET, 'Israeli Family Law as a Civil-Religious Hybrid', above n. 1.

16 By 'Constitution' we mainly refer to Basic Law: Human Dignity and Liberty 1992, s. 11 (Isr.).

17 A. LAYISH, 'Muslim Women's Status in the Shariʿa Court in Israel' in C. SHALEV and M. LIBAN-KOBI (eds.), *Women's Status In Law and Society*, Schocken Publishing, 1995 (in Hebrew); NATOUR, above n. 13; K.C. YEFET, 'Feminism and Hyper-Masculinity: A Case Study in Deconstructing Legal Fatherhood' (2015) 27 *Yale Journal of Law and Feminism* 49; YEFET, 'Israeli Family Law as a Civil-Religious Hybrid', above n. 1.

outlawing Muslim men's right to a unilateral *talaq* (repudiation), while making repudiation without wifely consent actionable in tort.[18]

Yet, as argued by Shahar, despite the shariʿa courts' formal lack of autonomy, these tribunals have evolved, over the years, into an arena for autonomous Muslim (and Palestinian) agency: a distinct politico-legal field, circumscribed by Israel's outer political framework yet retaining its own inner logic, values and normative system.[19] The qadis (Muslim judges) presiding in Israeli shariʿa courts have thus demonstrated their ability to initiate internal reforms, and to promote innovations in Islamic law by way of court rulings, or by issuing special 'judicial circulars' (*marasim qada'iya*).[20]

The qadis have, presently, largely remained the sole source of Islamic legal reform, in light of both Israel's restrictive policy concerning Islamic colleges and *Iftā*ʿ institutions, and the persistent reluctance of Palestinian-Israeli Muslims to accept reform from a non-Muslim Israeli legislative body.[21] Accordingly, the Ottoman Family Law of 1917 – the first State codification of family law in the Islamic world – has remained binding and unreformed in Israel until this day.[22] Yet, while the Israeli legislature did not introduce substantive reforms into

---

[18] See. e.g. Arts. 176 and 181 of Penal Law, 5737-1977 (Isr.); s. 8(b) of the Women's Equal Rights Law 5711-1951 (Isr.); CA 245/81 *Sultan v. Sultan* 38(3) PD 169 (1984) (Isr.) (recognising unilateral divorce as vesting women with a civil cause of action against their husbands). It is noteworthy, however, that some of the protective civil and criminal norms are underenforced: see, e.g. A. RUBIN PELED, 'Shariʿa' under Challenge: The Political History of Islamic Legal Institutions in Israel' (2009) 63(2) *Middle East Journal* 241, 259; I. SABAN, 'The Minority Rights of the Palestinian-Arabs In Israel: What Is, What Isn't and What Is Taboo' 26 *Iyunei Mishpat* (2002) 241, 274 (in Hebrew); R. ABURABIA, *Within the Law, Outside of Justice: Polygamy, Gendered Citizenship and Colonialism in the Israeli Law*, Hakibbutz Hameuchad – Sifriat Poalim, 2022 (in Hebrew).

[19] I. SHAHAR, 'State, Society and the Relations Between Them: Implications for the Study of Legal Pluralism' (2008) 9(2) *Theoretical Inquiries in Law* 417; I. SHAHAR, 'A Tale of Two Courts: How Organizational Ethnography Can Shed New Light on Legal Pluralism' (2013) 36 *PoLAR: Political and Legal Anthropology Review* 118; SHAHAR, 'Islamic Law as Indigenous Law, above n. 10; I. SHAHAR, *Legal Pluralism in the Holy City: Competing Courts, Forum Shopping, and Institutional Dynamics in Jerusalem*, Routledge, 2015.

[20] About the judicial circulars, see I. SHAHAR, 'Legal Reform, Interpretive Communities and the Quest for Legitimacy: A Contextual Analysis of a Legal Circular' in R. SHAHAM (ed.), *Law, Custom, and Statute in the Muslim World: Studies in Honor of Aharon Layish*, Brill Publishing, 2007. Notably, a recent HCJ decision has questioned the validity of these circulars, but they are still widely used: see HCJ 3910/13 *Plonit v. The Sharia Court System Administration* (published on Nevo, 9 March 2015) (Isr.).

[21] ABOU RAMADAN, 'Notes on the Anomaly', above n. 1. This reluctance was revealed once again in 2015, when Muslim Knesset members led the objection to a new draft of Muslim family law, prepared by women's organisations. See <http://bokra.net/Article-1318780>, last accessed 22.05.2023.

[22] About the application of the Ottoman family law in Israel, see I. SHAHAR, 'A law one hundred years young: The interpretive viability of the Ottoman Family Law in Palestine/Israel, 1917–2017' (2022) 65 *Journal of the Economic and Social History of the Orient* 890.

Islamic family law, it did intervene by reducing the jurisdictional scope of the shari'a courts' judicial authority. This issue will be addressed in what follows.[23]

3. SUBSTANTIVE REFORM IN PROCEDURAL GARB: INTRODUCING CONCURRENT CIVIL-RELIGIOUS JURISDICTION

As mentioned above, until November 2001 the shari'a courts had the broadest jurisdiction of any religious courts in Israel, holding exclusive authority over all matters pertaining to the personal status of Israel's Palestinian-Muslims.[24] Thus, while Jewish and Druze women who sought wife maintenance had the option to choose the forum in which to file their suits – their respective religious tribunals or the civil family court – Muslim women's only recourse was to approach their communal religious tribunal and to present their claims before an all-male panel of qadis.[25]

As a whole, Muslim women fared badly in pre-reform era shari'a courts. Most notably, the shari'a courts were taken to task for awarding women meagre and unrealistic maintenance payments that ignored their lived realities.[26] Consequently, in the mid 1990s, several human and women's rights organisations sought to better the position of Palestinian-Arab Muslim and Christian women within the legal sphere of family law. They joined forces as the 'Action Committee for Equality in Personal Status Issues', and set out 'to act in order to advance equality between the genders in family law, as well as to advance the rights of Arab litigants in religious courts and in civil family courts through the utilization of both legal and social tools'.[27] In 1995, shortly after the Knesset (Israeli Parliament) approved the Family Courts Law, the Committee initiated a draft amendment to the new law, with a view to furnishing Muslim and Christian women with the statutory option of turning to civil courts in all matters of personal status other than marriage and divorce.

---

[23]   The empirical examples discussed hereinafter have been extensively presented and analysed elsewhere: see W. Hleihel, I. Shahar and K.C. Yefet, 'Transforming Transformative Accommodation: Muslim Women Maintenance Suits in Israel as a Case Study', *Law and Social Inquiry* (forthcoming). See also W. Hleihel, K.C. Yefet and I. Shahar, 'The Muslim Wife Between the Israeli Shari'a Court and the Family Affairs Court: A Conservative Revolution in Liberal Clothing' (2022) 52 *Mishpatim* 319 (in Hebrew).

[24]   Yefet, 'Israeli Family Law as a Civil-Religious Hybrid', above n. 1.

[25]   Israel's first female qadi was only appointed in 2017. See S. Jacobs, 'Opposition to Israel's first Qadiya' (2020) 47(2) *British Journal of Middle Eastern Studies* 206; T. Zion-Waldoks, R. Irshai and B. Shoughry, 'The First Female Qadi in Israel's Shari'a (Muslim) Courts: Nomos and Narrative' (2020) 38(2) *Shofar: An Interdisciplinary Journal of Jewish Studies* 229.

[26]   A. Kaplan, *Invisible Work: Work Time and Gender Information and Policy Principles*, the Van Leer Institute, 2012.

[27]   Quoted from a draft prepared by the Action Committee. No author nor date mentioned.

The rationale undergirding the proposed jurisdictional reform was the Committee's working hypothesis that the shari'a courts were androcentric institutions which placed women in an inherently inferior position in relation to men, and that 'substantive and full equality between men and women can only be attained in civil courts and not in patriarchal Sharī'a Courts'.[28] More specifically, it was posited that, 'when a woman files a maintenance suit in the civil court, even if her case is handled according to religious law, she will be compensated differently, she will be treated differently, [and] consequently, what she will receive will be different'.[29]

The reform initiative quite expectedly encountered resounding resistance from officiating qadis and their political allies. In the months and years that followed, a stormy controversy developed over the issue of concurrent jurisdiction: one which not only reached academic and professional circles, but also the pages of Israel's Arabic-language press. The parties facing each other on either side of the ring were clear cut: on one side, feminist and liberal speakers, who sought to break down the shari'a courts' monopoly, and, on the other, conservative and Islamic speakers, who joined forces with the qadis in calling for the preservation of the shari'a courts' exclusive authority over the Muslim community.[30] In their efforts to thwart the reform initiative, the qadis introduced a series of internal women-friendly reforms – which will be discussed in the next section – designed to persuade their feminist audience that demonopolisation was unnecessary and unwarranted.[31]

The ideological battles continued unabated in the parliamentary debates. While the reform's supporters insisted that concurrent jurisdiction was a key mechanism in ensuring women's rights, the opponents decried the 'contamination' of shari'a law's purity and authenticity by civil intervention. MK 'Abd al-Malek Dahamsheh of the United Arab Party, for example, exclaimed passionately:

> I think that it is not every day, not even every month, nor even every week or two that this house is called to deliberate laws that so directly touch the thing most precious to a group of people that live in this state … this draft amendment to the law that is before you purports to do justice with Arab women, whether Muslim or Christian. It purports to achieve equality … Who determined that the most appropriate forum, the best and most fitting court, for a Muslim woman in order to be accorded maintenance and in order to sue for the paternity of a child or to litigate in any personal matter is

---

28 Ibid.
29 Y. Dayan, MK, Minute No. 208, The Constitution, Justice and Law Committee (1998), p. 12 (Isr.), available at <https://fs.knesset.gov.il/14/Committees/14_ptv_485638.PDF>, last accessed 22.05.2023.
30 Hleihel, Yefet and Shahar, 'The Muslim Wife Between the Israeli Shari'a Court and the Family Affairs Court', above n. 23.
31 See Shahar, Legal Pluralism in the Holy City, above n. 19, at pp. 116–118.

not the shari'a court ... presided upon by experienced and skilled judges and qadis? [Who determined] that we should bring her to a family court – a court that knows nothing about shari'a laws, that doesn't know them ... For they [civil judges] will have to rule according to these laws. So we will throw upon them women, men and families, when they are not skilled, not trained, not capable, have not studied, and are not eligible to rule on Islamic family laws. What are we doing?!?[32]

Taleb al-Sanaa of the Mada-Ra'am party echoed this last point, professing that the ultimate victims of putting the shari'a in the incapable hands of civil courts would, paradoxically, be women:

My colleagues say that we care about the wellbeing of women ... but we aren't changing the material law according to which these cases are adjudicated, because if it's in a shari'a court, the judge will rule on the basis of [Muslim] personal law, and if it's in a family court, he will rule on the basis of [Muslim] personal law. So what, in essence, have we changed? We have only changed the judge, because the law is the same law. Only the judge has changed – there, there's a Muslim judge, and here there is a Jewish judge. In essence, by passing this law we are saying that we don't trust Muslim judges. We trust Jewish judges ... I understand the motivations, I understand that you want the best, but sometimes you want to do good and it turns out that you have actually caused damage.[33]

These passionate parliamentary polemics culminated in the passage of Amendment No. 5 to the Family Courts Law, in November 2001. Thus, after a fierce and multi-year struggle, Muslim (and Christian) women were finally granted a forum-selection privilege – already enjoyed by Jewish women for half a century – between their communal religious tribunals and the civil family courts.

Interestingly enough, however, there has been a perplexing lack of research into the aftermath of this landmark legislative amendment: did the statutory reform achieve its stated feminist goals and live up to the hopes and expectations of its initiators? How do civil judges administer Islamic law, and to what extent have they succeeded in introducing gender-equalising and women-sensitive doctrines into their rulings? These questions have only marginally been discussed to date, let alone critically examined.

As will be demonstrated below, it appears that both the opponents and the proponents of the statutory reform were right in their estimations: whereas the shari'a courts responded to the competition by adopting a gender-sensitive approach towards their female constituency, the family courts seem to have

---

32   Ibid., at p. 58.
33   Knesset Plenum Minute no. 234, DK (1998) 1, p. 336, available at <https://main.knesset.gov.il/Activity/plenum/Pages/SessionItem.aspx?itemID=437573>, last accessed 22.05.2023.

fallen prey to an inherent cultural bias that imagines the shari'a as intrinsically patriarchal, static and monolithic. In line with this view, the civil family courts tend to rule in accordance with patriarchal values perceived as mandatory Islamic norms.

4. ISRAELISATION OF ISLAMIC LAW IN THE SHARI'A COURTS

The normative basis for Islamic maintenance rules rests on several key Qur'anic verses, which construct the Muslim marriage not as a relationship between equals, but rather as hierarchical relations reflecting the husband's supremacy and his wife's subordination. It is based on these patriarchal relations that the shari'a constructs a well-defined division of labour between the spouses: the wife is to obey her husband and to accept his authority as the head of the family, while the husband, in return, commits himself to supporting his wife and providing for her needs.[34]

These basic principles of classical Islamic law have been refined into modern shari'a codes that guide the rulings of Israel's shari'a courts.[35] The major prerequisite for a wife to be entitled to maintenance, apart from a valid marriage contract, is the fulfilment of her duty to be confined (muhtabasa) in the marital house. According to this condition, the wife is obligated to reside in her husband's lodgings as long as he requires it, and she will be exempted from this duty if there are legal impediments (mawani' shar'iyya), or if the dwelling that he provided her does not meet the legal requirements (maskan ghayr shar'i).[36]

During the pre-reform era, female litigants often found themselves ineligible for maintenance and, moreover, even when they were considered eligible, the level and scope of maintenance was insufficient and awarded parsimoniously.[37] For example, the shari'a courts made it ever more difficult for women to receive maintenance, by broadly construing the female duty of confinement such that

---

[34] HLEIHEL, YEFET and SHAHAR, 'The Muslim Wife Between the Israeli Shari'a Court and the Family Affairs Court', above n. 23.

[35] The main normative source in this regard is the Ottoman Family Law of 1917, and in cases of legislative lacunas, the qadis turn to the legal literature of the Hanafi school of law, which is perceived as the 'default' source of law, and especially to the private codification of Hanafi family law compiled by the Egyptian jurist Qadri Pasha (1875).

[36] Arts. 70-2, the Ottoman Family Law.

[37] SHAHAR, Legal Pluralism in the Holy City, above n. 19, at pp. 116–118. See also HLEIHEL, YEFET and SHAHAR, 'The Muslim Wife Between the Israeli Shari'a Court and the Family Affairs Court', above n. 23; A. LAYISH, Women and Islamic Law in a Non-Muslim State: A Study Based on Decisions of the Shari'a Courts in Israel, Routledge, 1975; See the analysis of the case law in Y. MERON, Islamic Law in Comparative Perspective, Magnes Press, 2001 (in Hebrew).

a wife who 'misbehaves in the household', performs her duties sloppily, or otherwise disobeys her husband, forfeits her monetary entitlement.

However, in the period of struggle against the reform, and even more so in the post-reform era, the shariʿa courts enriched their wife maintenance jurisprudence with an expansive range of women-friendly developments that have become an organic part of Israeli-Islamic law. For example, consistent case law has construed a man's duty of support as absolute, and as one which may only be revoked if the wife has left the marital house unjustifiably.[38] Even in such cases, a husband's refusal to allow his wife back into the marital home, or a woman's declaration of willingness to return to the marital home, reactivates her eligibility for maintenance. The shariʿa courts' reformist efforts also extend to approving situations in which a wife departed from the marital home for work purposes or academic studies which commenced prior to marriage as being in perfect harmony with her duty of confinement.[39] Moreover, the shariʿa courts have strictly confined the duty of confinement, and have unwaveringly dismissed any grievances concerning a wife's misbehaviour, disobedience or alleged violations of her sexual duties.[40] In its reconstructed wife maintenance jurisprudence, the one and only foundation on which the duty of confinement is predicated is residing in the marital home and not leaving it without a justified shariʿa cause.

Simultaneously, the shariʿa courts introduced innovations into the construction of the 'shariʿa justification' that allows women to leave their husbands yet still remain entitled to their support. For example, the shariʿa courts adopted an exacting and onerous definition of the 'legal abode' *(maskan shar'i)* a husband is required to provide for his wife.[41] Thus, if a household fails to live up to the ideals of a serene, secure and private dwelling, as well as one which provides a healthy and peaceful environment for married life alongside congenial neighbours, then this constitutes a valid shariʿa justification for a wife to not live with her husband.[42]

---

38   Case 124/2006 (published on the Shariʿa Courts Administration website, 8 October 2006) (Isr.); Case 400/2017 (published on the Shariʿa Courts Administration website, 14 March 2018); Case 201/2018 (published on the Shariʿa Courts Administration website, 3 October 2018) (Isr.).

39   For more on this, see Appeal 262/2003 (unpublished, 24 February 2004) (Isr.); Appeal 252/2011 (published on the Shariʿa Courts Administration website, 11 December 2011) (Isr.).

40   Appeal 10/1997 (published in Al-Kashaf, 1997, vol. 1, p. 78); Appeal 37/2006 (unpublished, 28 February 2006); Case 124/2006, above n. 38; Case 358/2017 (published on the Shariʿa Courts Administration website, 15 March 2018); Appeal 315/2013 (published on the Shariʿa Courts Administration website, 27 November 2013); Appeal 201/2018, above n. 38; Case 904/2016 (unpublished, 5 June 2016) (Isr.).

41   See I. SHAHAR, 'A New Look at the Agency of Qāḍīs: Israeli Shariʿa Courts as a Case Study' (2019) 59(1) *Die Welt des Islams* 70.

42   Appeal 173/2005 (published on the Shariʿa Courts Administration website, 30 May 2005) (Isr.); Case 106/2020 (published on the Shariʿa Courts Administration website, 10 May 2020) (Isr.);

The post-reform era also saw the shari'a courts breaking sharply from their traditional invidious treatment of wife-battering. Earlier rulings sought to distinguish between different forms of violence, and to apply varying normative significance according to the severity, frequency and form of violence. Thus, for example, light and sporadic violence, especially if the husband expressed remorse for it, was not held to be a legitimate shari'a justification for leaving the matrimonial home.[43] Post-reform jurisprudence, however, has witnessed a remarkably pro-woman interpretive trend that construes domestic violence as impairing a house's capacity to constitute a 'legal abode'.[44] More specifically, the shari'a courts introduced a doctrinal shift that no longer places the analytical centre of gravity on the 'level of violence' by the husband, but rather on the level of security experienced by the wife in the marital home. Put differently, if the wife does not feel safe in her own home, and supports this feeling with evidence, then she has a right, and even an obligation, to leave the nuptial home. Operating as it did from within this gender-sensitive interpretive framework, recent case law, in particular, embodies a decidedly pronounced intolerance towards any form of violence: the duty of confinement is voided even if the severity and frequency of violence is objectively negligible, even if it is verbal or financial abuse, and even if it is a mere threat rather than a concrete act of violence.[45]

Case 453/2012 (published on the Shari'a Courts Administration website, 30 January 2013) (Isr.); Case 190/2005 (unpublished, 21 March 2006) (Isr.); Case 312/2005 (unpublished, 28 December 2005) (Isr.); Appeal 277/2007 (published on the Shari'a Courts Administration website, 2 March 2008) (Isr.); Case 150/2005 (published on the Shari'a Courts Administration website, 2 March 2008) (Isr.); Case 150/2005 (published on the Shari'a Courts Administration website, 18 July 2005) (Isr.). See also Appeal 106/2020 (unpublished, 20 May 2020) (Isr.); Appeal 115/2005 (published on the Shari'a Courts Administration website, 30 June 2005) (Isr.); Case 281/2004 (unpublished, 20 December 2004) (Isr.). See also Shari'a Appeal 165/1996, and its translation in FC (Krayot) 14737-10-09 A. v. A. (published on Nevo, 22 March 2010) (Isr.).

[43] See Appeal 25/2007 (published on the Shari'a Courts Administration website, 9 May 2007) (Isr.); Appeal 238/2017 (published on the Shari'a Courts Administration website, 7 March 2018) (Isr.); See also Shari'a Case 3106/18 (published on the Shari'a Courts Administration website, 5 March 2019) (Isr.).

[44] Appeal 51/2009 (unpublished, 20 December 2009) (Isr.); Case 24/1996 (published on the Shari'a Courts Administration website, 1 April 1996) (Isr.); Case 39/1996 (published on the Shari'a Courts Administration website, 3 April 1996) (Isr.). It should, however, be noted that earlier Shari'a Court case law tended to distinguish between different types of violence, and to imbue its levels of severity and frequency with normative significance. Thus, for example, minor and 'one-time' violence, especially if it was regretted by the husband and if the husband promised it would not occur again, was not perceived as a justified Shari'a ground for leaving the marital residence. See LAYISH, 'Muslim Women's Status in the Shari'a Court in Israel', above n. 17, at p. 108.

[45] Appeal 290/14 (published on the Shari'a Courts Administration website, 15 July 2014) (Isr.); Appeal 281/2008 (published on the Shari'a Courts Administration website, 18 December 2008) (Isr.); Case 59/2012 (published on the Shari'a Courts Administration website, 7 May 2002) (Isr.); Appeal 419/2016 (published on the Shari'a Courts Administration website, 26 February 2017) (Isr.); Case 285/2019 (published on the Shari'a Courts Administration website, 28 November 2019) (Isr.); Case 80/2020 (published on the Shari'a Courts Administration website, 30 June 2020) (Isr.).

A final example relates to a procedural reform that was introduced by the shariʿa courts in the wake of the struggle against the above-mentioned legislative reform, in order to placate feminist circles that threatened their jurisdictional monopoly. The shariʿa courts sought to establish a judicial policy that would consider their female litigants' real social needs. The present authors discuss this procedural innovation – its logic, form and effects – in detail elsewhere.[46] For present purposes, it suffices to focus on its cumulative impact: it allowed the qadis to increase the amount of wife maintenance by almost 50 per cent – well beyond the average rate awarded by either the civil family courts or any other religious tribunal in Israel.[47] Moreover, the shariʿa courts held, in a long line of cases, that a woman's economic status or independent income, whether from work or any other source, has no bearing on the level and scope of maintenance she is due.

In sum, the qadis in the shariʿa courts have demonstrated an impressively creative interpretive agency in inducing changes from within the Islamic traditions. By so doing, they were literally aiming to appease not only their women constituents, but also to reduce the tension between Islamic law and the liberalised and feminist legal discourse, which had become hegemonic in the Israeli civil legal system.[48] In that sense, the Israelisation of Islamic family law meant a remarkable liberalisation and feminisation of the latter.

5. THE ISRAELISATION OF ISLAMIC LAW IN THE CIVIL FAMILY COURTS

While the story told thus far appears quite optimistic – from a feminist perspective, of course – the tables turn dramatically when we shift our gaze to the civil family courts. The Israelisation of Islamic family law in these courts appears to be proceeding in a very different direction: instead of liberalising Islamic family law, the Israelisation processes taking place in the civil courts are bringing about a stark patriarchalisation of this law. The reasons for this unexpected – and, one would add, gloomy – phenomenon will be discussed below, but first we will provide some empirical examples to illustrate this trend.

---

[46] HLEIHEL, YEFET and SHAHAR, 'The Muslim Wife Between the Israeli Shariʿa Court and the Family Affairs Court', above n. 23; See also SHAHAR, *Legal Pluralism in the Holy City*, above n. 19, at pp. 116–118.

[47] See N. BARKALI, *Periodical Survey No. 315: Women Receiving Maintenance Payments from the National Insurance Institute 2018*, Table 15, 2020 (in Hebrew), available at <https://www.btl. gov.il/Publications/survey/Documents/seker_315.pdf>, last accessed 22.05.2023.
See SHAHAR, *Legal Pluralism in the Holy City*, above n. 19, at p. 116.

[48] See SHAHAR, 'Legal Reform, Interpretive Communities and the Quest for Legitimacy', above n. 20.

Consider, for example, maintenance's constitutive condition: the duty of the wife's confinement to the marital home. The family courts have demonstrated a tendency to construe this duty ever more broadly, demanding that a wife must not only reside in the nuptial home, but must also perform all manner of wifely duties. Thus, in sharp contradistinction to the shari'a courts, the family courts do not settle for the narrow and restricted concept of residing in the nuptial home alone, but keep on raising the bar required for the satisfaction of the female duty of confinement. At the same time, the family courts have also substantially narrowed the ambit of the justified shari'a causes that may allow wives to relieve themselves from their wifely duties without losing their eligibility for maintenance. Thus, a series of additional variables have been introduced by the civil family courts into the gendered equation, such as a woman's behaviour and her fulfilment of her intimate marital duties, as a precondition for wife maintenance. In one such case, the family court deemed a wife's 'expression of sincere desire' to 'maintain a harmonious joint life'[49] insufficient, and thus required actual adherence to the 'sum total' of her 'duties and obligations' – including sexual duties.[50]

The family courts also went so far as to impose the onerous burdens the *Halakha* (Jewish law) prescribed for Jewish women, on Muslim women. For example, the courts equated the position of a rebellious wife in Jewish law with that of a rebellious wife in Islamic law, and thus wrongfully denied Muslim women maintenance if they had failed to provide sexual services to their husbands.[51] The 'Judaisation' of Islamic law has become even more pronounced in recent years, as the family courts subjected Muslim wives to three *halakhic* grounds that would cost a Jewish wife her maintenance. To wit, these are adultery, an 'act of ugliness' (a sexual act with another man for which there is only circumstantial evidence), and *overet 'al dat*, i.e. 'a wife who violates religious precepts, a wife who does not respect her husband and goes out with other men on a non-sexual basis'.[52]

What makes this injurious judicial trend even more indefensible is the fact that, whereas the civil courts defied Jewish law in releasing Jewish women from a strict code of sexual conduct,[53] the same courts defied shari'a law in subjecting Muslim women to a strict code of sexual conduct which does not apply to them.

---

[49] FC (Tiberias) 59344-02-15, *S.N. v. S.N.* (published on Nevo, 23 March 2016) (Isr.), paras. 44 and 47.

[50] FC (Tiberias) 30980-02-13, *Plonit v. Ploni* (unpublished, 7 June 2015) (Isr.), para. 32.

[51] See *S.N. v. S.N.*, above n. 49. It should be noted that this decision severely contradicts the decision passed by the Shari'a Appeals Court which states that 'a wife that prevents her husband from enjoying her', as the latter court phrases it, is not considered a rebellious wife. See Appeal 37/2006 (unpublished, 28 February 2006) (Isr.); Case 124/06 (published on the Shari'a Courts Administration website, 8 October 2006) (Isr.).

[52] See *S.N. v. S.N.*, above n. 49, at para. 71.

[53] In a series of illuminating articles, Ruth Halperin-Kaddari provides an excellent demonstration of the ways in which the Israeli Supreme Court devalues the meaning ascribed to a wife's deviation from the code of proper sexual conduct. It does this, for example, by increasing the

The civil court jurisprudence thus not only Judaises and patriarchalises Islamic law, but also unduly discriminates between Muslim and Jewish women.

Another example of the differential judicial interpretation of the duty of confinement between the civil and religious courts relates to the circumstances in which a woman expresses her willingness to return to the marital home. In sharp contradistinction to established shariʿa court precedent, the family court has been reluctant to award women maintenance in such circumstances. The family court also boldly suggested that an abused wife's claim of willingness to return to the marital home is necessarily unreliable.[54]

The civil courts further resorted to a woman-unfriendly application of Islamic law by deviating yet again from shariʿa court precedent which construed husbandly consent to the issuance of protective or restraining orders against him as a waiver of the duty of confinement.[55] For the civil courts, the very pursuit of such orders is a sheer testament to a wife's disobedience, which, in turn, disentitles her to maintenance.[56] In one case involving a Muslim wife with five minor children, who had never left the marital household, the court held that the husband should 'not be obliged to pay for his wife's maintenance even though Islamic law establishes such an obligation'.[57] In rationalising this perplexing decision, the civil court reasoned that 'their [marital] path had reached its endpoint in light of the continuing dispute between them as is reflected by the motions for a court protective order filed by one party against the other and by the interventions made by the Israel Police Force and the local Welfare Services office'.[58] The court thus effectively penalises women who seek State protection with the loss of their maintenance.

---

weight of evidence which is required for proving such a deviation, by devaluing the meaning ascribed to such a deviation, and by introducing a reciprocity metric. See R. HALPERIN-KADDARI, 'Marriage and Divorce Law and Gender Construction' in *To Be A Jewish Woman: Proceedings of the First International Conference in Israel: Woman and Her Judaism*, 2001, pp. 155, 161–62 (in Hebrew); R. HALPERIN-KADDARI, 'Wife Support: From Perception of Difference to Perception of [In]Equality' (2005) 7 *Mishpat u'Mimshal* 767 (in Hebrew); R. HALPERIN-KADDARI, 'Moral Considerations in Family Law and a Feminist Reading of Family Cases in Israel' in D. BARAK-EREZ et al. (eds.), *Readings in Law, Gender and Feminism*, Nevo publishers, 2007 (in Hebrew); See also, e.g. CA 277/81, *Grinhaus v. Grinhaus* PD 36(3) 197 (1982) (Isr.), with respect to the introduction of a dimension of gender equality, and for the blunting of the discrimination against women caused by the existence of a double standard in personal status law with respect to the duty of sexual faithfulness between married partners.

54 FC (Nazareth) 14135-09-14, *M.M. (A Minor) v. Y.M.* (published on Nevo, 26 April 2015) (Isr.).

55 Appeal 30/2012 (published on the Shariʿa Courts Administration website, 28 May 2012) (Isr.); Case 213/2013 (published on the Shariʿa Courts Administration website, 4 September 2013) (Isr.); Case 104/2014 (published on the Shariʿa Courts Administration website, 10 June 2014) (Isr.); Case 372/2018 (published on the Shariʿa Courts Administration website, 16 January 2019) (Isr.).

56 See *S.N. v. S.N.*, above n. 49, para. 47. See also para. 45.

57 FC (Tiberias) 30980-02-13, *Plonit v. Ploni*, above n. 50, para. 32.

58 Ibid.

The 'civil' version of Islamic law also differs substantially from shari'a court doctrine in its radically stingy interpretation of a legitimate 'shari'a justification' for violating the duty of confinement. The following example – of a maintenance suit that reached both the civil and religious instances – is particularly striking. In *Plonit*, the family court rejected Plonit's maintenance suit, finding her a 'rebellious wife' (*nashiz*) for preventing her husband from entering the marital household.[59] By so ruling, the family court deviated from a previous shari'a court ruling – adjudicating Plonit's divorce – that acknowledged her right to do so since her husband had married other women surreptitiously while wasting all their money on his new wives. According to the civil tribunal, however,

> shari'a law is an archaic and patriarchal legal system which authorizes a husband to marry up to 4 wives at once. Might the wedding of additional wives justify the wife's refusal to permit her husband to enter the marital household? I believe the answer to this question is negative.[60]

A few months after the civil decision was rendered, the shari'a court awarded Plonit interim maintenance (*nafaqat 'iddah*), a special type of short-term support paid for a period of three months after a divorce has been finalised. The shari'a court found that the family court had fundamentally erred in conceptualising the wife as rebellious, and in unlawfully stripping her of her Islamic entitlement to maintenance. The shari'a court also called its civil counterpart to task for its Orientalist labelling of Islamic law as an 'archaic and patriarchal legal system', counselling it to become conversant in classical shari'a law sources that protect women's status and celebrate their rights.[61] This decision, which provides a rare glimpse into divergent rulings by the family court and the shari'a court in the very same case, reveals the extent to which the civil instance is impeded by Orientalist constructions which limit the range of its interpretive creativity, and empty Islamic law of its ameliorative and emancipatory potential.[62]

Another paradigmatic example of the women-unfriendly interpretation of Islamic law that differs sharply from the qadi-made Islamic law is the family court ruling that wife-battering is the only valid justification for departing from the marital household.[63] Even this limited exception was construed so narrowly as to flip the religious paradigm entirely on its head and render the wife's duty of confinement, rather than the husband's duty of support, as an absolute mandate.

---

[59] FC 34133-09-13, *Plonit v. Ploni* (unpublished, 15 May 2014) (Isr.).

[60] Ibid., para. 23.

[61] Case 1682/2014 (unpublished, 15 November 2014) (Isr.).

[62] Another example of this judicial worldview can be found in FC (Nazareth) 54724-02-13, *M.A.N. v. A.A.N.* (published on Nevo, 23 December 2013) (Isr.).

[63] FC (Nazareth) 24824-04-12, *N.H.H. v. S.H.* (published on Nevo, 21 May 2013) (Isr.), paras. 24 and 11.

Thus, several family court decisions have ruled that 'ongoing violence' cannot constitute a justified legal ground for leaving the marital household: a wife in such circumstances must return, and once again be confined to her husband, if she wishes to get paid.[64] The family courts also held that 'moderate violence'[65] or verbal or financial abuse constitute part of a husband's prerogative to discipline his wife and, as such, do not amount to a 'shari'a justification' for departing the marital household.[66] By so ruling, the civil family courts thus (ab)use Islamic law so as to 'civilise' and trivialise various forms of violence against Muslim women, and to entrench hegemonic Orientalist stereotypes that depict Palestinian-Muslim society as inherently savage.

Adding insult to injury, civil court jurisprudence also imposes a heavy evidentiary burden on Muslim women in order to prove domestic abuse.[67] For example, the family courts – in square contradiction to the shari'a courts[68] – refused to consider court protective orders obtained by wives with their husband's consent as evidence of domestic abuse. The civil courts have also ascribed negative evidentiary value to a delay in filing a police complaint, and to the fact that no indictment resulting in a conviction had been filed.[69] In one case, the court held that a claim of marital violence should be doubted, since 'the wife, who is both educationally and behaviorally savvy, did not file a motion for a court protective order or a police complaint alleging violence, and this suffices to show that we are concerned with claims that are difficult to accept'.[70] The court

---

64   *M.M. (A Minor) v. Y.M.*, above n. 54; FC (Nazareth) 47674-06-14, *H.Y.S. v. M.Y.A.* (published on Nevo, 12 May 2015) (Isr.).

65   FC (Tel Aviv) 12810/06, *A.A.A.R. (A Minor) v. A.A.A.R.* (published on Nevo, 1 March 2009) (Isr.).

66   Ibid.; FC (Jerusalem) 10711/09, *A.T. v. S.T.* (published on Nevo, 11 January 2012) (Isr.). See also *M.A.N. v. A.A.N.*, above n. 62.

67   An example of such discrimination can be found in a case where a wife's departure from the marital household was caused by the mutual fault of both husband and wife, a state of affairs known in Jewish *halachic* law as a 'his and her preclusion'. In such cases, the family courts ruled – contrary to Jewish law, as well as Rabbinical Court case law – that a Jewish wife is nonetheless entitled to the award of maintenance payments. On the other hand, the same family courts ruled – contrary to shari'a court case law – that a Muslim wife is not entitled to the award of maintenance. To the family court, a Muslim wife is only entitled to maintenance when the preclusion of joint residence is a 'his' preclusion; that is to say, is caused by the husband alone rather than being shared by both partners: FC (Krayot) 7161/05, *Plonit v. Almoni* (published on Nevo, 1 November 2016) (Isr.); FC (Nazareth) 2881/03, *Plonit v. Ploni* (published on Nevo, 29 May 2006) (Isr.). See also FC (Tiberias) 30980-02-13, *Plonit v. Ploni*, above n. 50, para. 20. But see also FC (Nazareth) 48375-12-11, *A.A. v. A.D.* (published on Nevo, 10 June 2012) (Isr.).

68   Appeal 30/2012, above n. 55; Case 213/2013, above n. 55; Case 104/2014, above n. 55; Case 372/2018, above n. 55; Case 56/2020 (published on the Shari'a Courts Administration website, 14 May 2020) (Isr.).

69   See, e.g. *S.N. v. S.N*, above n. 49; *A.A.A.R. (A Minor) v. A.A.A.R.*, above n. 65, as well as the decisions mentioned below.

70   *N.H.H. v. S.H.*, above n. 63, para. 37.

reiterated its disbelief in claims of domestic violence in another decision, since the wife's 'testimony repeatedly noted her desire for matrimonial reconciliation, something which does not accord with her claims of violence and abuse ... It is thus unclear how the wife expects this court to believe her.'[71]

The same is true with regard to a wife who claimed to have been physically and verbally abused during 14 years of marriage. The very claim of protracted violence was, in and of itself, a valid reason to suspect the woman's credibility: 'This court wonders and enquires how a battered and humiliated wife, [who] was also a rape victim, lived with a so-called violent and dangerous husband yet withstood [his conduct] for 14 years?'.[72] This judicial trend, which is oblivious to the severe under-reporting that is a hallmark of Arab-Palestinian women victims of domestic violence,[73] fails to make allowances for the cultural, social and economic impediments which lock many of them in abusive relationships, or hinder their approaching external State agents.[74]

A final illustration of judge-made Islamic law that is diametrically opposed to qadi-made Islamic law concerns the level and amount of maintenance. The family courts have released husbands from their support obligation where their wives worked for a living, and at times even in cases where the wives worked in the *un*paid labour market, and after offsetting their potential earning capacity against their maintenance.[75] In straying from established shari'a court jurisprudence on the matter, the family courts relied on *halakhic* principles of Jewish law, and on liberal values of formal equality.[76] For the civil courts, wife maintenance belongs in 'the distant past', where a gendered division of labour reigned supreme in the family and society, and has no place 'today', since 'life has changed, and most women have joined the labor force and earn a respectable wage'.[77] In other words, the family courts adopted a false premise of imagined gender parity

---

[71]   *M.M. (A Minor) v. Y.M.*, above n. 54, para. 36.6.

[72]   See *S.N. v. S.N.*, above n. 49, para. 66.

[73]   S. Salim, 'Economic violence between spouses in the Arab Muslim sector in the State of Israel as reflected in the ruling of the Sharia court' (MA Thesis, University of Haifa, Faculty of Law, 2019), pp. 25, 28.

[74]   As Abu-Rabia-Queder and Weiner-Levy put it, '[an] Appeal to an external body is perceived as involving not only an alien cultural factor but also an entity in conflict with the nation, thus rendering such an appeal tantamount to treason.': see S. Abu-Rabia-Queder and N. Weiner-Levy, 'Between local and foreign structures: Exploring the agency of Palestinian women in Israel' (2013) 20(1) *Social Politics* 88, 97; A. Sa'ar, 'Contradictory location: assessing the position of Palestinian women citizens of Israel' (2007) 3(3) *Journal of Middle East Women's Studies* 45, 64.

[75]   See, e.g. FC (Tiberias) 30980-02-13, *Plonit v. Ploni*, above n. 50; FC 30459-03-16, *Plonit v. Ploni* (unpublished, 2 April 2020) (Isr.); FC 7161/05, *Plonit v. Almoni*, above n. 67; FC (Nazareth) 37345-12-15, *R.A. v. S.H.H.* (published on Nevo, 25 September 2018) (Isr.); see *S.N. v. S.N.*, above n. 49.

[76]   FC (Krayot) 7161/05, *Plonit v. Almoni*, above n. 67, para. 51.

[77]   See *S.N. v. S.N.*, above n. 49, para. 50 (emphasis ours). See also *R.A. v. S.H.H.*, above n. 75. See also FC 30459-03-16, *Plonit v. Ploni*, above n. 75.

which applies the rhetoric of equality to an avowedly unequal reality, and makes glib analogies between Muslim women, Muslim men and Jewish women. This judicial approach is oblivious to both inter-gender and intra-gender differences, and to the multiple marginalities of Muslim women along the axes of gender, class, religion and ethnonational status. Indeed, Muslim women are the most discriminated-against population in the Israeli labour force: they suffer from the highest unemployment rates, and from the lowest wages.[78]

The 'Israelisation' of the shari'a, as mediated by the civil family courts, thus contributes to the patriarchalisation of Islamic law, to the feminisation of poverty, and to a gross gender injustice.

6. CONCLUSION

This chapter sought to shed light on 'Israeli shari'a' – that is, on the impact of Israelisation processes on Islamic family law – taking place in two institutional venues: the shari'a courts and the civil family courts. By investigating the aftermath of a momentous legislative reform that affected both these courts, the chapter strived to depict the paradoxical effect of these Israelisation processes. As illustrated above, the reactions of the two tribunals to the reform were diametrically opposed: whereas the qadis presiding in shari'a courts invested concerted efforts in internal reforms designed to address the distinct vulnerability of Muslim women in a patriarchal Muslim-Palestinian society, the judges presiding in the civil family courts tended to apply Islamic substantive law in a conservative and patriarchal manner that, paradoxically, did not correspond either with the shari'a or with liberal norms of gender justice.

The civil family courts appear always to opt for bad solutions: they apply conservative and traditional values in situations where a liberal and gender-sensitive interpretation would have been advisable, and they apply liberal values of formal equality in situations that call for a multicultural and intersectional feminist prism. The result is a judicial policy that is oblivious to the multiple marginalisations and intersectional vulnerability of Muslim women, located at the bottom of Israel's stratified social hierarchy.

---

[78] See the 2019 data from Israel's Central Bureau of Statistics, 'The Muslim Population in Israel – Data on the Occasion of Eid al-Adha (The Feast of the Sacrifice)', 28 July 2020 (in Hebrew), available at <https://www.cbs.gov.il/he/mediarelease/DocLib/2020/230/11_20_230b.pdf>, last accessed 22.05.2023. See also generally V. Kraus and Y.P. Yonay, *Facing Barriers: Palestinian Women in a Jewish-Dominated Labor Market*, Cambridge University Press, 2018. Indeed, beyond the commonplace wage gaps Palestinian women suffer by virtue of being women, they also suffer from an inbuilt inferiority caused by their ethnonational status, an inferiority which is reflected in their dismal pay data: their mean monthly pay is 45% lower, compared with their Jewish sisters: Knesset Research and Information Center, *Employment among Arab Women*, 2016 (in Hebrew).

How may we explain this paradoxical and Janus-faced appearance of the Israeli shari'a? In the present authors' opinion, the answer resides, at least in part, in the domains of Orientalisation, expertise and motivation. The qāḍīs are – naturally – all Muslims with an excellent command of Islamic legal sources, so they obviously felt secure enough to introduce liberalising reforms in their rulings.[79] The civil judges, however, who are almost invariably non-Muslims with almost no knowledge whatsoever of Islamic law[80] – obviously did not feel authorised or capable to introduce innovation, and resorted, instead, to uninformed and prejudiced Orientalist stereotypes that prompted them to patriarchalise Islamic law. Moreover, the qāḍīs appear to be genuinely troubled about the possibility of Muslim litigants abandoning their communal tribunal, which is perceived as the final arbiter of the shari'a, in favour of a non-Muslim tribunal. In order to prevent this danger from materialising, and considering that about 70 per cent of the cases adjudicated in the Israeli shari'a courts are initiated by women,[81] the qāḍīs were prepared to go to great lengths in their introduction of pro-women reforms. In contrast, the civil judges lack any incentive to attract Muslim litigants, and assume upon themselves the unwieldy task of mastering and applying Islamic law. From their perspective, losing litigants to the shari'a court would only mean a welcome relief in their workload.[82]

It remains to be seen whether these two modes of Israelisation will converge or remain bifurcated. If they converge, it would be intriguing to see the form a unified Israeli shari'a might assume. Would it be modelled along the liberalised and feminised jurisprudence developed by the qadis in the shari'a courts, or would it resemble the patriarchal and conservative shari'a applied by the civil family courts? Only time will tell.

---

[79]   Y. REITER, 'Judge Reform: Facilitating Divorce by Shari'a Courts in Israel' (2009) 11(1) *Journal of Islamic Law and Culture* 13, 30.

[80]   Y. SEZGIN, 'Reforming Muslim family laws in non-Muslim democracies' in J. CESARI and J. CASANOVA (eds.), *Islam, Gender and Democracy in Comparative Perspective*, Oxford University Press, 2017, pp. 160, 166.

[81]   SHAHAR, *Legal Pluralism in the Holy City*, above n. 19, p. 79.

[82]   For a detailed discussion of the reasons behind the civil court jurisprudence, see HLEIHEL, SHAHAR and YEFET, 'Transforming Transformative Accommodation', above n. 23.

KENYA

PRESUMPTION OF MARRIAGE BY REPUTE (COHABITATION) IN KENYA

Jamil Ddamulira Mujuzi*

Résumé

En 1976, la Cour d'appel d'Afrique de l'Est a invoqué la présomption de mariage prévue par la common law anglaise pour reconnaître un mariage coutumier au Kenya. Dans la même décision, la Cour a également estimé qu'un mariage peut bénéficier d'une présomption d'existence fondée sur une longue cohabitation. Telle fut sa décision, alors que la question du mariage « par réputation » ne lui était pas posée. Depuis lors, les tribunaux ont été confrontés à la question de savoir si cette décision est uniquement applicable lorsque les parties ont respecté les principaux éléments d'un mariage coutumier ou si elle s'applique également au mariage « par

---

*   Professor of Law, Faculty of Law, University of the Western Cape. Email: djmujuzi@gmail.com.

réputation ». Cette problématique est, en outre, accentuée par le fait que le Kenya ne dispose d'aucune législation prévoyant ou interdisant le mariage « par réputation ». Les tentatives d'inclure le mariage « par réputation » dans la loi sur le mariage et dans d'autres textes ont jusqu'à présent échoué. Dans cet article, je m'appuie sur plus de 100 décisions de la Cour d'appel et de la Haute Cour rendues entre 1976 et novembre 2022 pour illustrer les problèmes auxquels les tribunaux se sont heurtés lorsqu'ils ont été confrontés à la question du mariage « par réputation ». Je traite de la manière dont les tribunaux ont abordé : l'établissement de la présomption; le type de présomption applicable au mariage « par réputation » ; la charge et les moyens de preuve ; les éléments à prendre en compte pour déterminer l'existence d'un mariage par réputation ; les droits des parties dans un mariage par réputation ; et la dissolution d'un mariage par réputation.

1. INTRODUCTION

In 1976, the Court of Appeal for East Africa recognised the principle of presumption of marriage in Kenya. Since then, Kenyan courts have developed rich and sometimes controversial or inconsistent jurisprudence on issues such as the meaning of this presumption, its legality, and its scope. In June 2021, the High Court held that '[p]resumption of marriage is part of the law in this country'.[1] The High Court held that '[a]side from the form of marriages envisioned under the [M]arriage [A]ct, parties can be presumed to be married based on their actions'.[2] The presumption has become so entrenched that the High Court has decried the prevalence of some people attempting to invoke the presumption of marriage for the purpose of enriching themselves.[3] For a better understanding of the issue of presumption of marriage in Kenya, it is important to point out, at the outset, that whenever one talks about the concept of presumption of marriage, it is vital to distinguish between two different situations: firstly, where a marriage ceremony took place, or where the essential ingredients of a marriage were satisfied; and, secondly, where no marriage ceremony took place, or where the essential elements of a marriage were not satisfied. In a case where a marriage ceremony took place, or the essential elements of a marriage were met, the presumption is that the marriage complied with the necessary legal requirements, and it is thus presumed to be valid. In a case where no effort was made to comply with any essential requirements of a marriage, the fact that people have lived together as husband and wife for a long period means that they are presumed to be married

---

1   *PWN v. JHOM* [2021] eKLR, para. 38.
2   *MNN v. GMN; SNN (Interested Party)* [2022] eKLR, para. 40.
3   *Raphael Ratemo & another v. Emily Nakhanu Musinai* [2017] eKLR, para. 48.

(marriage by repute/cohabitation).[4] This distinction was blurred by the Kenyan Court of Appeal in *MNM v. DNMK & 13 others*,[5] when it held that:

> The presumption of marriage is not dependent on the parties who seek to be presumed husband and wife having first performed marriage rites and ceremonies, otherwise there would be no need for the presumption because performance of rites and ceremonies would possibly result in a customary, Mohammedan or statutory marriage.[6]

There are also instances where the Kenyan High Court has blurred the distinction between marriage by repute, and presumption of marriage where the marriage ceremony took place. For example, in *MWM v. WEL*,[7] the applicant asked the Court to presume the existence of a customary marriage between her and the respondent. The Court held that, '[t]his court does hereby presume the applicant and the respondent as married under the Turkana custom and by virtue of their long co-habitation, ten years, and coupled with the birth of two children'.[8] Likewise, in *In re Estate of Peter Simel Muse Lengakah (Deceased)*,[9] the Court held that the marriage between the applicant and the deceased was valid on the basis of the presumption of marriage under customary law, and long cohabitation. The Court held that it also had to rely on the presumption of marriage by repute as a safety measure, in case its conclusion on the validity of the customary marriage was incorrect.[10] Practice from some African countries demonstrates how the above two situations work in different countries. In Uganda, for example, courts have held that the presumption of marriage is only applicable where a marriage ceremony is alleged to have taken place, or where it is alleged that the essential elements of a marriage were complied with. Legislative attempts to provide for presumption of marriage by repute have, so far, been unsuccessful.[11] However, in Malawi and Tanzania, legislation recognises marriage by repute.[12]

Before 1976, neither Kenyan legislation nor case law provided for a presumption of marriage. However, everything changed on 6 August 1976,

---

4   R. PROBERT, 'The presumptions in favour of marriage' (2018) 77(2) *CLJ* 375–398.

5   *M N M v. D N M K & 13 others* [2017] eKLR.

6   Ibid., p. 25.

7   *M W M v. W E L* [2017] eKLR.

8   Ibid., para. 9.

9   *In re Estate of Peter Simel Muse Lengakah (Deceased)* [2019] eKLR.

10   See also *In re Estate of Tom Otieno Ngoe (Deceased)* [2020] eKLR.

11   See, generally, J.D. MUJUZI, 'Presumption of Marriage in Uganda' (2020) 34(3) *International Journal of Law, Policy and The Family* 247–271.

12   S. 22(5) of the Constitution of Malawi (1994) recognises 'marriages by repute or by permanent cohabitation'. See also s. 74 of the Marriage, Divorce and Family Relations, Act. No. 4 of 2015 (Malawi); s. 160 of the Marriage Act (Tanzania).

when the then Court of Appeal for East Africa, in the case of *Hortensiah Wanjiku Yawe v. Public Trustees*,[13] held unanimously that the presumption of marriage was applicable to all marriages. Since then, this case has been relied on by subsequent courts to hold that Kenyan law recognised the concept of presumption of marriage, whether or not a marriage ceremony took place. Subsequent courts have done so despite the fact that the court in *Hortensiah Wanjiku Yawe v. Public Trustees* acknowledged the marriage ceremony that had taken place in that case as a factor in its decision. Several attempts have been made by some legislators to include a provision in Kenyan law recognising marriage by repute. However, all these attempts have, so far, failed.[14] Although the 2014 Marriage Act defines 'cohabitation', it is silent on whether cohabitation is recognised as a form of marriage. The drafting history of the 2014 Marriage Act shows that attempts to provide for cohabitation as a form of marriage failed. Despite this, some Members of Parliament and courts argue that the fact that 'cohabitation' is defined in the Marriage Act means that it is a type of marriage under Kenyan law.[15] In this chapter, the author analyses over 100 cases decided between 1976 and January 2023, to illustrate how courts have dealt with the issue of presumption of marriage. Since the presumption of marriage is a creature of Kenyan courts, the author will start with the facts, arguments and holding in the leading case of *Hortensiah Wanjiku Yawe v. Public Trustees*,[16] not only to show what the issues before the Court of Appeal were, but also to demonstrate how and why subsequent courts have expanded the ambit of this decision.

2. THE FACTS AND HOLDING IN *HORTENSIAH WANJIKU YAWE v. PUBLIC TRUSTEES*

The decision in *Hortensiah Wanjiku Yawe v. Public Trustees* introduced the concept of presumption of marriage in Kenyan law. The applicant's partner was a Ugandan citizen resident in Nairobi, when he died intestate in a car accident in May 1972.[17] In July 1972, the 'Public Trustee of Kenya was granted letters of Administration to his estate in Kenya'.[18] It was the applicant who reported the deceased's death to the Public Trustee of Kenya, and she 'claimed that she was the deceased's widow and that she had four children by him'.[19] When the

---

13   *Hortensiah Wanjiku Yawe v. Public Trustees* (EACA C.A. No. 13 of 1976) (Unreported).
14   J.D. Mujuzi, 'The Contentious Legal Status of Marriage by Presumption/Repute in Kenya' in J.M. Scherpe and S. Gilmore (eds.), *Family Matters – Essays in Honour of John Eekelaar*, Intersentia, 2022, pp. 419–431.
15   Ibid.
16   *Hortensiah Wanjiku Yawe v. Public Trustees* (EACA C.A. NO. 13 OF 1976) (Unreported).
17   Ibid., p. 1.
18   Ibid.
19   Ibid.

Public Trustee of Kenya contacted the Administrator General of Uganda, he was informed that there were Ugandan claimants to the estate. The Ugandan claimants, through their advocate, 'alleged that the appellant was not married to the deceased'.[20] Because of this uncertainty, the Public Trustee of Kenya approached the High Court for 'directions' on a number of questions, one of them being whether the deceased was 'properly married to the appellant'.[21] On this issue, the High Court held that 'the appellant was not the deceased's wife'.[22] Its reasoning was based on the fact that, although evidence showed that the parties and their respective families had consented to the marriage, the existence of a marriage either by 'Kikuyu custom or at all' was not proved, on a balance of probabilities.[23] The applicant appealed to the Court of Appeal against the High Court's ruling that she was not the deceased's wife.[24] She argued that the High Court had erred in concluding that there was no marriage between the deceased and the appellant, because it 'had failed to consider the presumption of marriage in favour of the appellant arising from long cohabitation'.[25] The appellant argued that:

> [S]he met the deceased in 1962, that they decided to marry, and in March, 1963 she went through a Kikuyu customary marriage with him, and had since lived with him as husband and wife until his death, and during that period bore him 4 children. They had a matrimonial home in Nairobi West. That she had lived for over 9 years with the deceased and bore him children was not challenged.[26]

The witnesses for the appellant testified before the High Court that 'the deceased used to call the appellant his wife and that the appellant was regarded as the deceased's wife for all purposes'.[27] The deceased's mother also testified that the deceased had introduced the appellant to her as his wife.[28] She also testified that she had visited the appellant's parents in the company of the deceased and one of his daughters.[29] The Court of Appeal observed that the 'uncontradicted' evidence by the witnesses 'indicated that the appellant and the deceased were living together as man and wife in a matrimonial home with the children of their union ... for a period of over 9 years'.[30] The trial judge did not accept the

---

20   Ibid.
21   Ibid.
22   Ibid., p. 2.
23   Ibid., p. 3.
24   Ibid., p. 2.
25   Ibid., p. 3.
26   Ibid., p. 3.
27   Ibid.
28   Ibid.
29   Ibid.
30   Ibid., p. 4.

evidence of witnesses who testified that the appellant and the deceased had performed the ceremonies related to the Kikuyu marriage.[31] The evidence also showed that, in his job application, the deceased had mentioned the appellant as his wife.[32] Against that background, the Court of Appeal held that:

> By general repute and in fact the parties had cohabited as man and wife in a matrimonial home for over 9 years before the deceased died ... and during that period the appellant bore him four children. Evidence was led on behalf of the appellant that a Kikuyu customary marriage between her and the deceased took place and that various ceremonies and rituals were duly performed. The deceased's mother appeared to deny that any such ceremonies took place in her presence as alleged by the appellant and her witnesses ... But in assessing the evidence on this issue, the trial judge omitted to take into consideration a very important factor. Long cohabitation as man and wife gives rise to a presumption of marriage in favour of the appellant. Only cogent evidence to the contrary can rebut such a presumption, see re *Taplin- Watson v. Tate* (1937) 3 ALLER 105. The trial judge did not consider this factor. The trial judge was not satisfied that the appellant had established, on a balance of probabilities, that the Kikuyu customary marriage was performed in accordance with all the necessary ceremonial rituals. It is not clear whether he found that the marriage was not valid because all the rituals were not performed, or that no marriage of any kind had taken place at all. However in considering whether there was a marriage the trial judge ought to have taken account of the presumption of marriage in the appellant's favour. Such a presumption carries considerable weight in the assessment of evidence. Once that factor is put into the balance in the appellant's favour, the scale must tilt in her direction.[33]

Against that background, the Court observed that there was evidence that the deceased's mother had visited the appellant's parents, and that English case law showed that, '[e]ven if the proper ceremonial rituals were not carried out, that would not invalidate the marriage'.[34] The lawyers for the Ugandan claimants and the lawyers for the Public Trustee 'appeared to doubt whether a presumption arising from long cohabitation based on English Common Law was an element in Kikuyu customary marriage'.[35] They also argued that, 'perhaps the presumption in English Common Law arose because of the public concern regarding illegitimate issue and inheritance; in the Uganda Law of Succession, illegitimacy is no bar to inheritance'.[36] They added that, in the High Court, the appellant did not 'rely on cohabitation as a factor in her favour', and they doubted if this matter

---

31 Ibid.
32 Ibid.
33 Ibid., pp. 4–5.
34 Ibid., p. 6. The Court relied on the English cases of *Sastry Aronegary v. Sembecutty Vaigalil* (1880–1) 6 Appeal Cases 364 and *Re Shephard, George v. Thyer* (1904) 1 Ch. 456.
35 Ibid.
36 Ibid.

could be raised before the Court of Appeal.[37] In response to these submissions, the Court of Appeal held that:

> [A]ll marriages in whatever form they take, civil or customary or religious, are basically similar, with the usual attributes and incidents attaching to them. I do not see why the concept of presumption of marriage in favour of the appellant in this case should not apply just because she was married according to Kikuyu customary law. It is a concept which is beneficial to the institution of marriage, to the status of the parties involved and to issue of their union, and … is applicable to all marriages howsoever celebrated.[38]

The Court held that, had the High Court relied on the evidence before it, and the concept of presumption of marriage, it 'would probably have held that the appellant was married to the deceased and was his wife'.[39] Against that background, the Court held that 'the appellant was the deceased's wife', and was entitled to a share of the inheritance as the deceased's widow.[40] By that holding, the Court of Appeal introduced the concept of marriage by reputation in Kenyan law. It is important to take a close look at this judgment before discussing how courts have relied on it to deal with many other issues relevant to the presumption of marriage.

3. UNDERSTANDING *HORTENSIAH WANJIKU YAWE* v. *PUBLIC TRUSTEES*

This case raises a very important issue in Kenyan family law, and ever since it was handed down, many courts have followed it. However, before discussing the jurisprudence of Kenyan courts since this decision was handed down, it is important to know what was being presumed by the Court of Appeal. As mentioned above, when dealing with the concept of presumption marriage, one should distinguish between two situations. The first situation is where the court deals with the question of whether a marriage ceremony took place, or whether the essential elements of the marriage in question were complied with. In this case, what is being presumed is the validity of the marriage ceremony or the compliance with the rites of a given marriage, and if that presumption is not rebutted, then the marriage is presumed to be valid (because the ceremony was valid or the requirements were complied with). The second situation is where a marriage ceremony did not take place at all, or where the parties did not

---

[37] Ibid.
[38] Ibid., pp. 6–7.
[39] Ibid., p. 7.
[40] Ibid.

comply with the essential requirements of any of the marriages provided for in legislation. In this case, a marriage is presumed based on long cohabitation – marriage by repute.[41] The facts of the case in *Hortensiah Wanjiku Yawe v. Public Trustees* show that the Court of Appeal was dealing with the question of whether a marriage ceremony took place. In other words, it was dealing with the first scenario above. The English cases it referred to also dealt with the presumption of marriage on the basis that a marriage ceremony had taken place. However, in the process of resolving the issue before it, the Court of Appeal also held that 'long cohabitation as man and wife gives rise to a presumption of marriage'. As will be illustrated below, subsequent case law shows that courts are still divided on the correct interpretation of the Court of Appeal's judgment. Nonetheless, this judgment has been relied on by many judges to find that the Court of Appeal recognised the presumption of marriage by repute. In the author's opinion, this approach broadens the ambit of the Court of Appeal's holding, since the facts of the case show that the Court of Appeal was dealing with presumption of marriage where the appellant had submitted that her marriage had complied with the necessary requirements of a customary marriage. This understanding also explains why the Court held that the presumption of marriage was applicable to all marriages, and reasoned that 'all marriages in whatever form they take, civil or customary or religious, are basically similar'. Case law from Kenyan courts shows that courts have adopted two different interpretations of the Court of Appeal's decision: the strict interpretation and the broad interpretation. The strict interpretation is to the effect that the Court of Appeal's decision means that the presumption of marriage is only applicable to cases where a marriage ceremony is alleged to have taken place. The broad interpretation is that long cohabitation can be relied on to presume a marriage, even in the absence of a ceremony or a claim that a ceremony occurred.[42] Against that background, it is important to consider the issues that Kenyan courts have considered in relation to marriages by repute.

4. REOPENING THE DEBATE AND CASTING DOUBT ON *HORTENSIAH WANJIKU YAWE v. PUBLIC TRUSTEES*

The Court of Appeal, in some of the cases decided after *Hortensiah Wanjiku Yawe v. Public Trustees*, has cast doubt on the issue of presumption of marriage

---

41   R. PROBERT, 'The presumptions in favour of marriage' (2018) 77(2) *CLJ* 375–398.
42   In *MNK v. POM; Initiative for Strategic Litigation In Africa (ISLA) (Amicus Curiae)* [2023] KESC 2 (KLR), para. 36, the Court held that: 'Presumption of marriage is a well-settled common law principle that long cohabitation of a man and woman with a general reputation as husband and wife raises a presumption that the parties have contracted marriage. However, a presumption of marriage is a rebuttable presumption and can disappear in the face of proof that no marriage existed.'

by repute. For example, in *Mary Njoki v. John Kinyanjui Mutheru*,[43] the Court of Appeal, by majority, held that the concept of 'common law wife' was not known in Kenya, and that a presumption of marriage was only applicable where the parties had complied with most of the requirements of one of the types of marriages recognised in Kenyan legislation.[44] In other decisions, the same Court has also held that Kenyan law did not recognise marriage by repute. For example, in *Machani v. Vernoor*,[45] the Court of Appeal held that, '[w]here there is no marriage but parties are living together in an association that could be seen as that of a husband and wife they are living so in a state of concubinage'.[46]

However, the Court reconsidered its position in subsequent cases. For example, in *MWG v. EWK*,[47] the Court held that the ruling in *Machani* was *obiter*. In this case (*MWG v. EWK*), the appellant was married to the deceased under Kikuyu customary law in 1968. However, the respondent lived with the deceased as 'husband' and 'wife' from 1986 until his death in 2002, 'a continuous period of approximately fifteen years during which period three children were born of the relationship'.[48] The appellant recognised the respondent's three children as heirs to the estate of the deceased, but did not recognise the respondent as one of the heirs of the deceased. However, the respondent, on the basis of section 3(5) of the Law of Succession Act, had applied for the letters of administration, 'as a wife so as to take part in the administration of the deceased estate and partake her share of the estate'.[49] The High Court held that there was a presumption of marriage between the deceased and the respondent, and declared her as a widow accordingly. The issue before the Court of Appeal was whether the respondent was one of the deceased's heirs. The majority held that there was a presumption of marriage between the deceased and the respondent, because they had cohabited together for 15 years, had children together, the deceased paid the rent, the deceased's family had accepted the respondent as his wife, and the appellant knew that the deceased lived with the respondent.[50]

The majority held that there was also a customary marriage between the deceased and the appellant because:

> The deceased according to Kikuyu Customary Law is the one who was obliged to pay dowry for the petitioner. As at the date of his death he had not done so. Cohabitation

---

43 *Mary Njoki v. John Kinyanjui Mutheru* [1985] eKLR.
44 Ibid. (especially the decision of Justice Kneller).
45 *Machani v. Vernoor* [1985] eKLR.
46 Ibid., p. 9. See also *In Kituu v. Nzambi* [1984] KLR 411.
47 *M.W.G v. E.W.K* [2010] eKLR.
48 Ibid., p. 7.
49 Ibid.
50 Ibid., p. 4.

is one of the essentials of a Kikuyu marriage. Likewise providing residence and maintenance for a wife are among the other essentials of a Kikuyu marriage. The main component lacking here is dowry. There is no fixed time for paying dowry.[51]

Against that background, the Court presumed the existence of a Kikuyu customary marriage between the appellant and the deceased. The Court also held that the facts in the case of *Machani v. Vernoor* were distinguishable from those in the case before the court. This is so because, in the *Machani* case, the man rejected both the children and their mother; in other words, he 'neither accepted the respondent as wife nor did he accept the children as his'.[52] The Court also added that the *Machani* decision and similar decisions 'were based on the old thinking', and that, in 1981, section 3(5) was included in the Law of Succession Act because 'Parliament realized that some women who genuinely had been taken as wives were discriminated against merely because ... dowry had not been paid, or that there had not been any ceremony to solemnize the union'.[53] However, the decision in *MWG v. EWK*[54] was not unanimous. In his dissenting (minority) decision, Justice Nyamu held that the Court should have been guided by section 6 of the Judicature Act, which provides that:

> The High Court, the Court of Appeal and all subordinate courts shall be guided by African customary law in civil cases in which one or more of the parties is subject to it or affected by it, so far as it is applicable and is not repugnant to justice and morality or inconsistent with any written law, and shall decide all such cases according to substantial justice without undue regard to technicalities of procedure and without undue delay.

He held that:

> The court's findings concerning the existence of a Kikuyu customary law marriage was not based on any evidence at all and was with respect a finding plucked from the air and an unfortunate imposition of a presumption of marriage to the well documented requirements of a Kikuyu customary marriage.[55]

He referred to case law to the effect that African customary law was part of Kenyan law and had to be recognised, and that courts should take judicial notice of such customary law. Against that background, he held that:

> [A]lthough the payment of rent and cohabitation might appear attractive attribute of marriages pursuant to the English common law or any other Kenyan communities,

---

51 Ibid.
52 Ibid., p. 5.
53 Ibid.
54 *M.W.G v. E.W.K* [2010] eKLR.
55 Ibid., p. 10.

they do not constitute acceptable ingredients of a marriage under the Kikuyu customary law and this finding constitutes a serious misdirection both in fact ... [and] in law.[56]

He referred to the case of *Hortensiah Wanjiku Yawe v. Public Trustee* and held that:

Even going by the wording of the above observation it cannot be said that in a relationship such as that of [the appellant] and the deceased, where there was no proof of the well-known major ingredients of the Kikuyu customary law marriage ... the evidence of cohabitation and repute perse would constitute a valid marriage under the Kikuyu customary law. It becomes a customary marriage recognized by virtue of section 3(2) of the Judicature Act because of the presence of the specified customary ingredients. It is a massacre of such a custom for anyone to suggest that a presumption of marriage per se can constitute a marriage under any system of law whether customary or common law unless it is accompanied by the other essential ingredients pertaining to a particular system of marriage. A presumption based on cohabitation remains a presumption but it cannot constitute a customary law marriage without the essential ingredients. The presumption cannot itself form the super structure of a Kikuyu customary law marriage or any other, it can only be part of the issue whether factually there is a marriage. The contention that there can be a Kikuyu customary law marriage by virtue of a presumption imposed by a court is fallacious and hollow even on the basis of *YAWE* case.[57]

What is common between the majority and dissenting judgments is that, for a presumption of marriage to be applicable to a customary marriage, there has to be evidence to show that the parties intended to enter into a customary marriage, and that the major ingredients of such a customary marriage were complied with. This is the same approach that the Court followed in the *Hortensiah Wanjiku Yawe v. Public Trustees* decision. However, the majority and minority judgments differed on the essential ingredients of the customary marriage in question. It is, therefore, important that, before a customary marriage is presumed, the essential elements of such a marriage have to be in place. This is an approach that the Court of Appeal[58] and the High Court[59] have followed in other cases. The same applies to other types of marriages. For example, the High Court has

---

[56]   Ibid.
[57]   Ibid., p. 11.
[58]   See, e.g. *William Situma & another v. Mathew* Mabusi [2016] eKLR. However, some judges have held that marriage by repute is not recognised in Kenyan law, and that people who are living together as husband and wife without being marriage 'are living so in a state of concubinage': see *M v. R M* [1985] eKLR, p. 9 (Court of Appeal).
[59]   *Mary Wanjiku Gitau v. Mary Wanjiku Gitau & Stephen Kimwaki* [2021] eKLR; *CNG v. DMN* [2018] eKLR; *Rosa Adisa Magala v. Boniface Amwayi* [2012] eKLR (court presumed the existence of a customary marriage).

held that the common law principle of presumption of marriage by repute is not applicable to Muslim marriages.[60] This is because, '[a]ny cohabitation outside marriage is … condemned as illicit and the woman involved in it, is punishable for Zina (fornication)'.[61] However, a presumption of marriage, where the requirements of a Muslim marriage were met, is applicable.[62] It is important to emphasise that a marriage by repute (cohabitation) is just that – marriage by repute. It not one of the marriages mentioned in the Marriage Act.

Should the essential elements of the marriage in question be missing, then a court will have to decide whether the facts call for reliance on the presumption of marriage by repute.[63] This means that such a marriage is one by repute; it is not a customary, civil or religious marriage. That is why both the Court of Appeal and the High Court have referred to it as common law marriage,[64] or marriage by conduct.[65] A marriage by repute cannot be presumed if it is contrary to the law. For example, cohabitation between people of the same sex cannot result in a marriage by repute. This is because Article 45(2) of the Constitution prohibits same-sex marriages. A marriage by repute will be presumed even if it is not recognised by the Church or the customs of the parties.[66] As the High Court

---

60   *SR v. RR* [2019] eKLR.

61   *In re Estate of CCBH (Deceased)* [2017] eKLR, para. 27. See also *In re Estate of Salim Juma Hakeem Kitendo (Deceased)* [2022] eKLR, para. 81.

62   *Chengo Karisa Nyuchi v. Mwanamkuu Harun Ndole & 3 others* [2020] eKLR; *In re Estate of Ramadhan Hassan (Deceased)* [2014] eKLR (Kadhi's Court). In *H. W. v G. D. B.* [2016] eKLR, the High Court was willing to presume the existence of a marriage between Muslims, but there was no evidence that the parties had indeed met the requirements for such a presumption. However, the Court of Appeal has not found it necessary to decide whether the concept of presumption of marriage is applicable to Muslim marriages: see *CKC & another (Suing through their mother and next friend JWN) v ANC* [2019] eKLR.

63   *M N M v. D N M K & 13 others* [2017] eKLR, p. 25; *Nderitu Ndirangu v. Patrick Mwago Wanjau* [2011] eKLR; *K O & another v. J O* [2018] eKLR; *ASA v. NA & another* [2020] eKLR; *Vincent Aliero Ayumba v. Livingstone Eshikuri Liakayi & 2 others* [2017] eKLR; *Eva Naima Kaaka & another v. Tabitha Waithera Mararo* [2018] eKLR (Court of Appeal); *Anastasia Mumbi Kibunja & 4 others v. Njihia Mucina* [2013] eKLR (Court of Appeal); *Lucy Wambui Maina v. Dickson Muhia Mutty & 2 Others* [2007] eKLR; *In re Estate of Morris Kilonzo Musyimi (Deceased)* [2018] eKLR; *In Re Estate of Wakaba (Deceased)* [2004] eKLR.

64   *R.M.M v. B.A.M* [2015] eKLR, para. 8 (Court of Appeal); *Mary Njoki Kamau v. Jane Wanjiru Kiarie* [2017] eKLR, para. 28; *In re Estate of the late Nelson Ndara Koibita (Deceased)* [2018] eKLR, para. 15. However, in *CWN v. DK* [2021] eKLR, p. 6, the High Court held that marriage by repute 'is ordinarily referred to as "common law marriage" though this characterization is misnomer. It is a misnomer because in English law it is not a term that connotes marriage as known in law but it is used to refer to unmarried, cohabiting heterosexual couples. It is a term that does not confer on cohabiting parties any of the rights or obligations enjoyed by spouses or civil partners.'

65   *ERK v. JCC* [2020] eKLR, para. 12.

66   *Christopher Nderi Gathambo & Samuel Muthui Munene v. Samuel Muthui Munene* [2003] eKLR (not recognised by Church and custom); *B C C v. J M G* [2018] eKLR (not recognised by custom).

held in *Raymond Kamwanza Ndolo & another v. Christopher Kiamba Maingi,*[67] 'it is possible for parties to be presumed married in instances where no single customary rite has been performed or they do not meet the threshold of a customary marriage rite'.[68] The consent of the woman's family to the relationship between her and the man is not necessary for the validity of a marriage by repute.[69] If, after cohabiting for a long period of time, the parties enter into one of the marriages provided for under the Marriage Act, the subsequent marriage takes precedence over the common law marriage.[70] It is, therefore, important that, when a court concludes that the presumption of marriage is applicable, it clarifies which of the two presumptions – presumption where a marriage ceremony took place, or presumption of marriage by repute – is applicable. In some cases, it is not clear which presumption was relied on.[71] This raises the question of whether a court, in the event that there is no evidence to prove that a marriage ceremony took place, or that the main requirements of the marriage in question were met, for it to presume the existence of such a marriage, can, of its volition, conclude that there was marriage by repute. It is to this issue that we turn.

5. ESTABLISHING THE APPLICABLE PRESUMPTION

Kenyan law provides for presumptions of fact and presumptions of law.[72] The Court of Appeal has held that, for it to presume the existence of a marriage by repute, the party alleging the existence of such a marriage must plead that issue specifically.[73] In some cases, the presumption of marriage has been

---

[67] *Raymond Kamwanza Ndolo & another v. Christopher Kiamba Maingi* [2018] eKLR.

[68] Ibid., para. 98.

[69] *Christopher Nderi Gathambo & Samuel Muthui Munene v. Samuel Muthui Munene* [2003] eKLR; *B C C v. J M G* [2018] eKLR; *Lucy Wambui Maina v. Dickson Muhia Mutty & 2 Others* [2007] eKLR, p. 11.

[70] *R.M.M v. B.A.M* [2015] eKLR, para. 8 (Court of Appeal) (the parties had cohabited for 23 years before entering into an Islamic marriage); *M W K v. A M W* [2017] eKLR, para. 40 (the parties had cohabited before entering into a short-lived official wedding).

[71] See, e.g. *Hellen Omwoyo v. David Ouma Gor* [2017] eKLR (the High Court found that most of the elements of a customary marriage had been met, but did not clarify which presumption was applicable).

[72] See, e.g. *In re an Application for Presumption of Death of Danson Machaga Muturi* [2017] eKLR; *In Re Estate of George Okello Noballa (Deceased)* [2008] eKLR (presumption of death is one of law).

[73] *William Situma & another v. Mathew Mabusi* [2016] eKLR (the applicant failed to convince the court that he had entered into a customary marriage with the deceased, for him to be allowed to bury her body). See also *Raymond Kamwanza Ndolo & another v. Christopher Kiamba Maingi* [2018] eKLR, para. 102; *Samuel Kiarie Kirimire (deceased)* 1999 eKLR.

pleaded specifically.[74] However, there are cases in which the facts are silent on whether one of the parties pleaded the issue of marriage by repute, before the High Court held whether or not a marriage by repute could be presumed.[75] In some cases, the High Court makes it clear that the applicant or petitioner did not plead presumption of marriage by repute, but nonetheless goes ahead and makes a finding on that issue.[76] However, courts should also be aware of the fact that some cultural practices change over time, and that what were considered to be essential elements of a customary marriage in the past may no longer be necessary today.[77] This raises the question of whether the presumption of marriage by repute is a presumption of law or of fact. It is to this issue that we now turn.

6. THE TYPE OF THE PRESUMPTION OF MARRIAGE BY REPUTE, AND THE BURDEN AND STANDARD OF PROOF

The Court of Appeal has held that the presumption of marriage is based on section 119 of the Evidence Act.[78] This section provides that '[t]he court may

---

74   *Vincent Aliero Ayumba v. Livingstone Eshikuri Liakayi & 2 others* [2017] eKLR (High Court); *Beth Nyambura Kimani v. Joyce Nyakinywa Kimani & 2 others* [2006] eKLR (Court of Appeal); *Anastasia Mumbi Kibunja & 4 others v. Njihia Mucina* [2013] eKLR (Court of Appeal); *PWN v. JHOM* [2021] eKLR, para. 37; *In re Estate of Shem Marcaad Nyamai alias Shem alias Shem M O Nyamai (Deceased)* [2021] eKLR, paras. 20–21; *In re Estate of Margaret Wanjiru Karenju (Deceased)* [2016] eKLR.

75   See, e.g. *ASA v. NA & another* [2020] eKLR; *CKK v. PM* [2019] eKLR, para. 12 (court held that there was a marriage by repute); *Fatiah Wamuyu Abdalla v. Consolata Njagi Njiru* [2016] eKLR (court found that the facts did not show marriage by repute); *In re Estate of Jecinter Njoki Okoth (Deceased)* [2020] eKLR (court found that the facts disclosed marriage by repute); *In The Matter Of The Estate Of Francis Kambo Ndirangu – Deceased* [2012] eKLR (court found that the facts disclosed marriage by repute); *In re Estate of Morris Kilonzo Musyimi (Deceased)* [2018] eKLR; *In re Estate of Mungiiria Silas Muriithi (Deceased)* [2021] eKLR (court found that the facts disclosed a presumption of marriage); *In re Estate of Tom Otieno Ngoe (Deceased)* [2020] eKLR, para. 120 (the court found that it was duty-bound to consider the question of presumption of marriage, and held that the facts showed that there was indeed such a presumption); *In re Estate of Karia Getao Gicheru (Deceased)* [2021] eKLR (in this case, the applicant failed to adduce the evidence of a marriage ceremony, and the fact that she had lived with the deceased for over 30 years, as she had alleged); *ERK v. JCC* [2020] eKLR.

76   See, e.g. *In re Estate of James Njenga Kinuthia (Deceased)* [2018] eKLR, paras. 26–28; *Phylis Wangari Kiragu v. Henry Githinji, Samuel M. Nyingi, Benjamin Ireri James* [2002] eKLR; *Raphael Ratemo & another v. Emily Nakhanu Musinai* [2017] eKLR, para. 42 (the court found that, on the facts before it, there was no evidence to presume a marriage by repute); *John Wachanga Kiama v. Beatrice Njambi Ndirangu* [2010] eKLR (the court held that there was evidence to presume a marriage by repute).

77   *Mary Wanjiku Gitau v. Mary Wanjiku Gitau & Stephen Kimwaki* [2021] eKLR, para. 15.

78   Cap. 80, Laws of Kenya.

presume the existence of any fact which it thinks likely to have happened, regard being had to the common course of natural events, human conduct and public and private business, in their relation to the facts of the particular case'.

In *MWG v. EWK*,[79] the Court of Appeal referred to section 119 of the Evidence Act and held that:

> The existence or otherwise of a marriage is a question of fact. Likewise, whether a marriage can be presumed is a question of fact. It is not dependent on any system of law except where by reason of a written law it is excluded. For instance a marriage cannot be presumed in favour of any party in a relationship in which one of them is married under statute. However, in circumstances where parties do not lack capacity to marry, a marriage may be presumed if the facts and circumstances show the parties by a long cohabitation or other circumstances evinced an intention of living together as husband and wife.[80]

The Supreme Court also held that a marriage by repute is a presumption of fact under section 119 of the Evidence Act.[81] Other courts came to the same conclusion in earlier cases.[82] Some judges have gone to the extent of holding that section 119 of the Evidence Act recognises 'the concept of presumption of marriage'.[83] The presumption of marriage is applicable where there is no evidence of marriage. In other words, 'presumption is not itself evidence' but, rather, 'a rule of law applied in the absence of evidence'.[84] Therefore, this 'presumption is not dependent upon the existence of a marriage'.[85] The purpose of the presumption is to 'rescue' a marriage which 'does not comply with the relevant formalities provide[d] under the marriage Act or under customary law'.[86] In light of the above discussion, the High Court's view that the presumption of marriage is a presumption of law[87] is not the dominant one.

Courts have been inconsistent on which party has the burden to prove whether there was a marriage by repute. In some cases, courts have held that, if

---

[79] *M.W.G v. E.W.K* [2010] eKLR.
[80] Ibid., p. 3.
[81] *MNK v. POM; Initiative for Strategic Litigation in Africa (ISLA) (Amicus Curiae)* [2023] KESC 2 (KLR), paras. 39–40.
[82] See, e.g. *EMP v. FNM* [2020] eKLR, para. 20; *A M D N v. S M L* [2017] eKLR, p. 4; *Raphael Ratemo & another v. Emily Nakhanu Musinai* [2017] eKLR, p. 7; *In re Estate of Peter Simel Muse Lengakah (Deceased)* [2019] eKLR, pp. 5–6; *In re Estate of Daniel Olal Nyawawa (Deceased)* [2019] eKLR, p. 7.
[83] *In re Estate of Morris Kilonzo Musyimi (Deceased)* [2018] eKLR, para. 46; *In re Estate of D N M (Deceased)* [2018] eKLR, para. 18. See also *In re Estate of Mungiiria Silas Muriithi (Deceased)* [2021] eKLR, para. 20, where the Court held that, '[t]he doctrine of presumption of marriage has its genesis in Section 119 of the Evidence Act.'
[84] *In re Estate of Daniel Olal Nyawawa (Deceased)* [2019] eKLR, p. 7.
[85] *In re Estate of Morris Kilonzo Musyimi (Deceased)* [2018] eKLR, para. 48.
[86] *In re Estate of Joseph Abongo Odipo (Deceased)* [2019] eKLR, para. 25.
[87] *CWN v. DK* [2021] eKLR.

one of the parties alleges that there is a marriage by repute, the burden is on the person who disputes the existence of that marriage to disprove the presumption.[88] However, there are also cases where courts have held that, whichever party alleges the existence of marriage by repute, he/she has the burden to prove that such a marriage exists.[89] The best approach, which has also been followed by the Supreme Court,[90] would be to require the person who alleges the existence of marriage to adduce evidence to that effect, and the party disputing that claim to rebut it.[91] If the defendant does not contest the validity of a marriage, a court will presume its validity.[92] It is, thus, important to know the factors that a court has to consider in determining whether or not to presume the existence of a marriage by conduct.

7. FACTORS TO CONSIDER IN DETERMINING THE EXISTENCE OR OTHERWISE OF A MARRIAGE BY REPUTE

Before the 27 January 2023 Supreme Court decision in *MNK v. POM; Initiative for Strategic Litigation in Africa (ISLA) (Amicus Curiae)*,[93] case law showed that, for a court to find that there was marriage by repute, it had to consider three factors: 'the length of the period the parties were together, their general conduct and reputation and how they held themselves out and were perceived'.[94] These three factors were categorised into two broad elements: the qualitative and the quantitative elements. The quantitative element related to 'the length of time the two people have cohabited with each other',[95] and the qualitative element related to 'acts showing general repute that the two parties held themselves out as husband and wife'.[96] As the Court of Appeal held in *Eva Naima Kaaka & another v. Tabitha Waithera Mararo*,[97] the facts must 'establish a prolonged period of cohabitation',[98] and that '[a]cts of general repute, are synonymous

---

[88]   *N L S v. B R P* [2016] eKLR, p. 12.
[89]   See, e.g. *M W K v. A M W* [2017] eKLR, para. 26; *Mwangi v. Maina* [2022] KEHC 14303 (KLR), para. 36; *Karuku & another v. Njogu* [2022] KEHC 665 (KLR), para. 11.
[90]   *MNK v. POM; Initiative for Strategic Litigation in Africa (ISLA) (Amicus Curiae)* [2023] KESC 2 (KLR), para. 61.
[91]   *CNG v. DMN* [2018] eKLR, para. 26.
[92]   *Christine Cherubet & another v Romana Jepkoechkebenei* [2019] eKLR.
[93]   *MNK v. POM; Initiative for Strategic Litigation in Africa (ISLA) (Amicus Curiae)* [2023] KESC 2 (KLR).
[94]   *PWN v. JHOM* [2021] eKLR, para. 42.
[95]   *P M K v. G N & 5 others* [2018] eKLR, para. 47(a).
[96]   Ibid., para. 47(b). See also *M W K v. A M W* [2017] eKLR, p. 8.
[97]   *Eva Naima Kaaka & another v. Tabitha Waithera Mararo* [2018] eKLR.
[98]   Ibid., p. 6.

with the impression, or assessment of the couple as perceived by the general public, including relatives and friends. By their nature they are a determinant of whether a presumption of marriage can be found to exist.[99] In other words, the relationship should not be clandestine.[100] In *MNK v. POM; Initiative for Strategic Litigation in Africa (ISLA) (Amicus Curiae)*,[101] the Supreme Court outlined the following as the factors which must be considered in determining whether or not a presumption of marriage was applicable:

> [1]. The parties must have lived together for a long period of time. [2]. The parties must have the legal right or capacity to marry. [3]. The parties must have intended to marry. [4]. There must be consent by both parties. [5]. The parties must have held themselves out to the outside world as being a married couple. [6]. The onus of proving the presumption is on the party who alleges it. [7]. The evidence to rebut the presumption has to be strong, distinct, satisfactory and conclusive. [8]. The standard of proof is on a balance of probabilities.[102]

The Court added that, although it had laid down the above 'strict parameters within which a presumption of marriage can be made',[103] it should be remembered 'that the doctrine of presumption of marriage is on its deathbed of which reasoning is reinforced by the changes to the matrimonial laws in Kenya. As such, this presumption should only be used sparingly where there is cogent evidence to buttress it.'[104] As the discussion below will show, all the above factors that the Supreme Court outlined have always been considered by courts in determining whether or not the presumption of marriage is applicable. The evidence needed to prove the three major factors (cohabitation, the conduct of the parties, and how the parties were/are perceived by others) is discussed next.

The first factor relates to the duration of the cohabitation. The Supreme Court held that 'the parties must have lived together for a long period of time.'[105] However, it did not stipulate the minimum duration of the cohabitation. The Court of Appeal held that 'long cohabitation is not mere friendship [and] … the woman is not a mere concubine but … the long cohabitation has crystallized into a marriage and it is safe to presume the existence of a marriage.'[106] A court

---

99   Ibid., p. 9. See also *Joseph Gitau Githongo v. Victoria Mwihaki Munya* [2014] eKLR (High Court), p. 5.
100   *In re Estate of EAK (Deceased)* [2022] eKLR, para. 50.
101   *MNK v. POM; Initiative for Strategic Litigation in Africa (ISLA) (Amicus Curiae)* [2023] KESC 2 (KLR).
102   Ibid., para. 64.
103   Ibid.
104   Ibid., para. 65.
105   Ibid., para. 64.
106   *Phylis Njoki Karanja & 2 others v. Rosemary Mueni Karanja & another* [2009] eKLR, p. 6. See also *Ndunda v. Mutunge* (Civil Appeal 47 of 2018) [2022] KECA 1308 (KLR) (2 December 2022), para. 23.

will not find a marriage by repute if there is no evidence of cohabitation, even if '[t]here is material ... establishing that the parties had an intimate relationship'.[107] If the parties have been in a relationship, but have not lived under the same roof all the time, the court will only consider the time they have 'effectively' lived together, in deciding whether there is a presumption of marriage.[108] This is because, in cases of presumption of marriage by repute, 'the issue of cohabitation takes a central stage'.[109] Therefore, there has to be 'actual cohabitation',[110] as opposed to 'intermittent' visits,[111] casual sexual encounters,[112] or a mere sexual relationship.[113] The High Court held that, '[c]ohabitation ... entails the long-term continuous living together of a couple holding themselves out as a husband and wife but in the absence of any formal marriage'.[114] The Court also added that, '[o]n the nature and length of the cohabitation, there is no doubt that the period of cohabitation should be long enough, continuous and not a sojourn, a habit of visiting or waiting for a time'.[115] Cohabitation can be proved by rental agreement, oral evidence (witnesses) or other evidence.[116] Case law shows that courts have recognised marriages by repute where parties have cohabited for 5 years,[117] 6 years,[118] 9 years,[119] 10 years,[120] 12 years,[121] 13 years,[122] 14 years,[123]

---

107   *S.W.G v. H.M.K* [2015] eKLR, para. 20. See also *Vincent Aliero Ayumba v. Livingstone Eshikuri Liakayi & 2 others* [2017] eKLR; *In re Estate of Makokha Idris Musindalo* [2022] KEHC 13765 (KLR), para. 48.

108   *Christopher Nderi Gathambo & Samuel Muthui Munene v. Samuel Muthui Munene* [2003] eKLR, p. 4. See also *In re Estate of George Kamwanga (Deceased)* [2023] KEHC 19418 (KLR) para. 28.

109   *K O & another v. J O* [2018] eKLR, para. 32.

110   *ASA v. NA & another* [2020] eKLR, p. 7. See also *Anastasia Mumbi Kibunja & 4 others v. Njihia Mucina* [2013] eKLR, p. 7 (Court of Appeal).

111   *N L S v. B R P* [2016] eKLR, p. 14. See also *In re Estate of Kisinga Kinothya (Deceased)* [2020] eKLR, para. 19, where the Court did not find evidence of cohabitation.

112   *In re Estate of Stephen Ngigi Karwigi (Deceased)* [2020] eKLR, para. 34.

113   *In re Estate of the Late Alex Okungulo Mukongi* [2022] KEHC 14551 (KLR), para. 67.

114   *K O & another v. J O* [2018] eKLR, para. 35.

115   Ibid., para. 36.

116   *M W K v. A M W* [2017] eKLR, p. 8; *In re Estate of Joseph Mwaura Nderi (Deceased)* [2022] KEHC 598 (KLR) (Family), para. 57 (oral evidence).

117   *In re Estate of Njeru Njagi (Deceased)* [2019] eKLR.

118   *BCC v. JMG* [2018] eKLR; *In re Estate of George Owino Onyango (Deceased)* [2017] eKLR.

119   *Christopher Nderi Gathambo & Samuel Muthui Munene v. Samuel Muthui Munene* [2003] eKLR; *In re Estate of Tom Otieno Ngoe (Deceased)* [2020] eKLR.

120   *Geoffrey Waruru Kinyua v. Susan Wambui Waruru* [2010] eKLR, p. 6; *Grace Wanjiku Kimani & 2 others v. Peter Kimanga Kimani & another* [2017] eKLR.

121   *RM & 3 others v. EAO* [2022] KEHC 12074 (KLR) (Family).

122   *Mary Njoki Kamau v. Jane Wanjiru Kiarie* [2017] eKLR, para. 28.

123   *In re Estate Robert Ngundo Nyiva (Deceased)* [2021] eKLR.

15 years,[124] 17 years,[125] 18 years,[126] 20 years,[127] 23 years,[128] 24 years[129] and 34 years.[130] The above duration could be spent either in Kenya or abroad.[131] Based on the above case law, it can be argued that the minimum period of cohabitation should be five years.

The second factor relates to the conduct of the parties, in addition to cohabitation. This could be evidenced by having a child or children (biological or adopted) together, and informing their friends and/or relatives that they are husband and wife;[132] staying together, and one of them paying rent;[133] acquiring property or loans together;[134] the deceased asking the applicant to bury him;[135] the deceased introducing the petitioner to his employers[136] or church[137] as his wife; the children adopting the deceased's surname,[138] or the deceased sharing confidential information with the applicant.[139]

---

124   *V R M v. M R M & another* [2006] eKLR; *R N N v. P S* [2016] eKLR; *Mwangi v Maina (Probate & Administration Appeal 4 of 2020)* [2022] KEHC 14303 (KLR) (26 October 2022).

125   *Nderitu Ndirangu v. Patrick Mwago Wanjau* [2011] eKLR.

126   *Beth Nyambura Kimani v. Joyce Nyakinywa Kimani & 2 others* [2006] eKLR.

127   *In re Estate of Margaret Wanjiru Karenju (Deceased)* [2016] eKLR.

128   *EMP v. FNM* [2020] eKLR, para. 24.

129   *In re Estate of Peter Simel Muse Lengakah (Deceased)* [2019] eKLR.

130   *Jedidah Mathembo Ndunda v. Rael Mutunge* [2015] eKLR, para. 29.

131   *R N N v. P S* [2016] eKLR (the 15 years were spent in Kenya and the Netherlands).

132   *Christopher Nderi Gathambo & Samuel Muthui Munene v. Samuel Muthui Munene* [2003] eKLR; *B C C v. J M G* [2018] eKLR; *M.W.G v. E.W.K* [2010] eKLR; *M N M v. D N M K & 13 others* [2017] eKLR; *Nderitu Ndirangu v. Patrick Mwago Wanjau* [2011] eKLR; *V R M v. M R M & another* [2006] eKLR (Court of Appeal); *In re Estate of Njeru Njagi (Deceased)* [2019] eKLR, para. 59 (child by adoption). However, having children together is not, per se, a sufficient ground to presume the existence of marriage. There has to be long cohabitation: see *Ann Wanjiru Njonge v. Newton Gikaru Gathiomi & 2 Others* [2007] eKLR; *In re Estate of the Late Alex Okungulo Mukongi* [2022] KEHC 14551 (KLR); *James Odhiambo Nyawade v. Philip Otieno & another* [2017] eKLR. Likewise, the High Court held, in *A W M v. R M* [2005] eKLR, p. 5, that the inability of the woman to have children does not prevent it from presuming the existence of a marriage by repute, especially when the couple 'tried to conceive but failed and this aggravated her position and was the cause of the breakdown of the relationship'. In *Raphael Ratemo & another v. Emily Nakhanu Musinai* [2017] eKLR, para. 43, the Court held that, 'if the deceased considered himself married to the applicant and carried himself out as such, then he would have not only introduced the applicant as his wife to his relatives and work colleagues, but would have also nominated her as his next of kin or at his place of work'.

133   *M.W.G v E.W.K* [2010] eKLR.

134   *Mary Njoki v. John Kinyanjui Mutheru* [1985] eKLR, p. 15; *V R M v. M R M & another* [2006] eKLR (Court of Appeal).

135   *P M K v. G N & 5 others* [2018] eKLR, para. 55.

136   *In re Estate of Charles Anyanda Luyudi (Deceased)* [2020] eKLR.

137   *RM & 3 others v. EAO* [2022] KEHC 12074 (KLR) (Family).

138   *Ndunda v. Mutunge (Civil Appeal 47 of 2018)* [2022] KECA 1308 (KLR) (2 December 2022), para. 29.

139   *In re Estate of D N M (Deceased)* [2018] eKLR, para. 24 (his M-Pesa password).

The third factor relates to how the parties were/are perceived by others. This is proved by evidence such as church members, neighbours or family members testifying that they considered the parties to be married;[140] the inclusion of each other's name,[141] or the name of the applicant,[142] on official documents;[143] the appointment of the surviving party as one of the managers of the deceased's property;[144] or the applicant's active participation in the deceased's burial arrangements.[145] The bottom line is that the parties behaved as married people, and intended to be treated as such: as the High Court held, that '[t]here is obviously a legitimate expectation by either party that having stayed together for such a long period of time, invested together and gotten children, they are for all purposes and intents husband and wife hence the relevance of the presumption of marriage'.[146] If there is insufficient evidence for a court to find whether there is a marriage by repute, it will not make a finding.[147]

The presence of the above three factors does not mean that a marriage by repute will always be presumed. For such a marriage to be presumed, both parties must also have the capacity to marry, and must consent to the marriage.[148] For example, where one of the parties has already entered into a statutory monogamous marriage, the court cannot invoke a presumption of marriage where he/she cohabits with another person.[149] Likewise, if the woman was in a customary or civil marriage at the time she allegedly entered into a marriage by

---

140   *Christopher Nderi Gathambo & Samuel Muthui Munene v. Samuel Muthui Munene* [2003] eKLR (church, family members of the husband, and neighbours); *P M K v. G N & 5 others* [2018] eKLR, para. 53 (church members); *PWN v. JHOM* [2021] eKLR, para. 41 (neighbours and family members); *John Wachanga Kiama v. Beatrice Njambi Ndirangu* [2010] eKLR (the church, neighbours, the community, the district administration and family members). In re *Estate of Justus M'murithi M'bagiri (Deceased)* [2019] eKLR, para. 30, the Court held that '[t]he evidence by the petitioner and her witnesses did not show that the petitioner and the deceased lived together as husband and wife or that they were regarded as such by the community.'

141   *B C C v. J M G* [2018] eKLR; *EMP v. FNM* [2020] eKLR, para. 24.

142   *M N M v. D N M K & 13 others* [2017] eKLR.

143   However, in *Vincent Aliero Ayumba v. Livingstone Eshikuri Liakayi & 2 others* [2017] eKLR, the High Court held that the mere fact that the deceased had included the appellant on her medical aid was not enough to prove the existence of marriage by presumption.

144   *M N M v. D N M K & 13 others* [2017] eKLR.

145   In re *Estate of Margaret Wanjiru Karenju (Deceased)* [2016] eKLR.

146   *Mary Njoki Kamau v. Jane Wanjiru Kiarie* [2017] eKLR, para. 34.

147   *Ruth Njeri v. Charles Lilechi Lugano* [2007] eKLR.

148   *Phylis Njoki Karanja & 2 others v. Rosemary Mueni Karanja & another* [2009] eKLR, p. 6 (Court of Appeal); *E.N. W v. G.N. K & another* [2010] eKLR.

149   *O K N v. M P N* [2017] eKLR, p. 9 (Court of Appeal); *MNK v. POM* [2020] eKLR 5 (Court of Appeal); *POC v. JB & another* [2021] eKLR, para. 70; *EMP v. FNM* [2020] eKLR, para. 24; In re *Estate of Jackson Nduva Kathula (Deceased)* [2018] eKLR, paras. 15–16; In re *Estate of the late Nelson Ndara Koibita (Deceased)* [2018] eKLR, para. 19; In re *Estate of Salim Juma Hakeem Kitendo (Deceased)* [2022] eKLR, paras. 90–92.

repute, the court will hold that the marriage by repute was invalid.[150] If it is alleged that a person did not have the capacity to enter into a marriage by cohabitation, because of his/her previous marriage, the alleged previous marriage must be proved.[151] The Supreme Court held that a presumption of marriage does not exist unless 'cogent evidence' shows, inter alia, that 'the parties must have intended to marry'.[152] In other words, such intention must be proved. This implies that it is not sufficient to infer such intention from long cohabitation and conduct. Both parties must have intended to enter into a marriage by repute.[153] Both parties must also have consented to the marriage by reputation. It is important, at this point, to take a look at the rights of people who are in a common law marriage.

8. THE RIGHTS OF PARTIES IN A MARRIAGE BY REPUTE

Kenyan courts have been inconsistent on the issue of the rights of parties in a marriage by repute. In some cases, courts have held that, where a marriage by repute is presumed to exist, parties in such a marriage have all the rights that spouses have in other marriages.[154] These have included the rights: to bury their deceased partners;[155] to an equitable share of the jointly acquired matrimonial property;[156] to administer the estate of the deceased spouse,[157] and to inherit the

---

[150] *Raphael Ratemo & another v. Emily Nakhanu Musinai* [2017] eKLR, p. 6 (customary marriage); *TMG & another v. AP* [2022] KECA 612 (KLR) (civil marriage); *MNK v. POM; Initiative for Strategic Litigation in Africa (ISLA) (Amicus Curiae)* [2023] KESC 2 (KLR) (civil marriage).

[151] *MWN v. TIM* [2022] KEHC 13771 (KLR) (23 September 2022), para. 18.

[152] *MNK v. POM; Initiative for Strategic Litigation in Africa (ISLA) (Amicus Curiae)* [2023] KESC 2 (KLR), para. 64.

[153] Ibid., paras. 66–68.

[154] *Christopher Nderi Gathambo & Samuel Muthui Munene v. Samuel Muthui Munene* [2003] eKLR, p. 10.

[155] Ibid.; *B C C v. J M G* [2018] eKLR, para. 16; *Nderitu Ndirangu v. Patrick Mwago Wanjau* [2011] eKLR (the right of the husband to bury the deceased wife); *Rosa Adisa Magala v. Boniface Amwayi* [2012] eKLR (the right of a husband to bury a customary law wife). However, where customary law does not allow the wife to bury a husband, the court will order that he should be buried by his relatives, and not by his common law wife: see *Lucy Wambui Maina v. Dickson Muhia Mutty & 2 Others* [2007] eKLR, p. 11.

[156] *ERK v. JCC* [2020] eKLR; *S.W.G v. H.M.K* [2015] eKLR; *P M K v. G N & 5 others* [2018] eKLR, para. 1; *CKK v. PM* [2019] eKLR; *PWN v. JHOM* [2021] eKLR, para. 61; *EMP v. FNM* [2020] eKLR (property declared matrimonial property and distributed); *N L S v. B R P* [2016] eKLR, p. 14 (the Court did not uphold the presumption of marriage by repute, and found that the issue of matrimonial property fell away).

[157] *Beth Nyambura Kimani v. Joyce Nyakinywa Kimani & 2 others* [2006] eKLR (Court of Appeal); *Esther Wanjiru Kiarie v. Mary Wanjiru Githatu* [2016] eKLR, para. 9; *In re Estate of Fred Barasa Waswa (Deceased)* [2020] eKLR, p. 4; *In re Estate of Daniel Olal Nyawawa (Deceased)* [2019] eKLR.

estate or part of it (as a beneficiary/dependant);[158] and to getting an injunction to prevent the common law spouse from contracting a statutory marriage.[159] Additionally, the wife is entitled to maintenance from the husband after the dissolution of the marriage,[160] and the children are considered to have been born in wedlock.[161]

One of the contentious issues relates to the distribution of property at the dissolution of a marriage by cohabitation. In *MNK v. POM; Initiative for Strategic Litigation in Africa (ISLA) (Amicus Curiae)*,[162] the Supreme Court held that:

> Kenya, just like many other countries, does not have laws to protect parties to cohabitation in case of a dispute relating to property acquired during the subsistence of such cohabitation. However, the issue of cohabiting couples' property has increasingly become a social problem due to the high number of people resorting to cohabitation and in the process of acquiring properties, upon separation there is no legislation governing the division of property.[163]

The Court added that:

> While we acknowledge the difficulties of resolving such disputes, a *laissez fair[e]* approach can result in injustice for parties to a relationship who might be more vulnerable or who contribute less in financial terms than their partners. Conversely, we do note that the interventionist approach risks creating uncertainty, and attaching a monetary value to the party's actions within this type of relationship is often highly complex as is in the present case.[164]

Against that background, the court held that the distribution of property acquired during cohabitation should be governed by the principles of constructive trusts.[165] This is meant to prevent one of the parties from unjustly enrichment

---

158   *Phylis Njoki Karanja & 2 others v. Rosemary Mueni Karanja & another* [2009] eKLR (Court of Appeal); *In re Estate of Peter Simel Muse Lengakah (Deceased)* [2019] eKLR; *In The Matter Of The Estate Of Francis Kambo Ndirangu – Deceased* [2012] eKLR; *In re Estate of Morris Kilonzo Musyimi (Deceased)* [2018] eKLR; *John Wachanga Kiama v. Beatrice Njambi Ndirangu* [2010] eKLR; *Jedidah Mathembo Ndunda v. Rael Mutunge* [2015] eKLR; *In re Estate of Mungiiria Silas Muriithi (Deceased)* [2021] eKLR; *In re Estate of Charles Anyanda Luyudi (Deceased)* [2020] eKLR; *In re Estate of George Owino Onyango (Deceased)* [2017] eKLR.

159   *E.N. W v. G.N. K & another* [2010] eKLR.

160   *A W M v. R M* [2005] eKLR, p. 6; *R N N v. P S* [2016] eKLR.

161   *Nderitu Ndirangu v. Patrick Mwago Wanjau* [2011] eKLR; *Geoffrey Waruru Kinyua v. Susan Wambui Waruru* [2010] eKLR, p. 6.

162   *MNK v. POM; Initiative for Strategic Litigation in Africa (ISLA) (Amicus Curiae)* [2023] KESC 2 (KLR).

163   Ibid., para. 82.

164   Ibid., para. 83.

165   Ibid., paras. 84–89.

him or herself with the property meant to benefit both of them.[166] This is based on the common intention for the parties to have beneficial interests in the jointly acquired property.[167] This common intention can be 'inferred' from the parties' 'conduct during the subsistence of their relationship'.[168]

In other cases, courts have held that parties in a marriage by repute have one right: to inherit from the estate of the deceased. This reasoning has been based on section 3(5) of the Succession Act, which provides that:

> Notwithstanding the provisions of any other written law, a woman married under a system of law which permits polygamy is, where her husband has contracted a previous or subsequent monogamous marriage to another woman, nevertheless a wife for the purposes of this Act, and in particular sections 29 and 40 thereof, and her children are accordingly children within the meaning of this Act.

Strictly interpreted, section 3(5) is only applicable in cases where the 'questionable' marriage is recognised under Kenyan law.[169] However, courts have extended this provision to marriages by repute, although such recognition is limited to succession purposes.[170] In other words, '[s]ection 3(5) recognizes such marriage for purposes of succession only'.[171] The applicability of section 3(5) to marriages by repute means, inter alia, that these marriages are not monogamous. Thus, a man who is married under customary law can enter into a valid common law marriage.[172] The High Court held that a common law wife is a competent and compellable witness against her husband, because case law shows that the presumption of marriage by repute is resorted to when a party 'is seeking relief to obtain inheritance or in matrimonial property action'.[173] In effect, the Court did not recognise the wife as such, within the meaning of the Marriage Act and the Evidence Act, for the purposes of marital/spousal privilege.[174] In the author's view, if a marriage by repute is presumed to exist, there is no reason why the parties should not enjoy all the rights that parties in other marriages enjoy. Otherwise it would not amount to a marriage. It could also be argued that treating people in marriages by repute differently from those in other marriages

---

[166] Ibid., para. 91.
[167] Ibid., para. 90.
[168] Ibid., para. 91.
[169] *Irene Njeri Macharia v. Margaret Wairimu Njomo & another* [1996] eKLR.
[170] *In re Estate of Jackson Nduva Kathula (Deceased)* [2018] eKLR, paras. 16–17.
[171] *In re Estate Robert Ngundo Nyiva (Deceased)* [2021] eKLR, para. 51. See also *Mary Njoki Kamau v. Jane Wanjiru Kiarie* [2017] eKLR; *Grace Wanjiku Kimani & 2 others v. Peter Kimanga Kimani & another* [2017] eKLR, p. 7.
[172] *A K M & another v. A K A* [2015] eKLR, para. 40.
[173] *Republic v. George Mwangi Kabira & 2 others* [2017] eKLR, para. 12.
[174] For a detailed discussion of this privilege, see *Republic v. Maxwell Kipruto & 2 others* [2019] eKLR.

amounts to discrimination within the meaning of Article 27 of the Constitution, which prohibits discrimination on many grounds, including marital status.

9. TERMINATING A MARRIAGE BY REPUTE

Although, in most of the cases, courts have presumed the existence of a marriage by repute after the death of one of the parties, and, as a result, such marriages have been dissolved by death,[175] there are also cases where such marriages have been presumed when both parties are still alive. In such cases, and where necessary, courts have dissolved such marriages.[176] As is the case with a statutory marriage, parties that would like to have their marriage by repute dissolved have to 'file their Petition for Divorce in the normal procedure'.[177] In other words, the termination of a marriage by repute requires 'a formal divorce'.[178] Case law shows that a court will dissolve a marriage by repute when there is evidence that it has irretrievably broken down. This could be because of reasons such as cruelty,[179] adultery[180] or hostility.[181] However, if one of the parties to a marriage by repute permanently deserts the other and enters into a marriage with another person, the Court will understand the marriage to 'have ended by presumption of divorce, notwithstanding that no formal petition was filed in a Court of Law to be decreed as such in accordance to the Law'.[182] A marriage by presumption can either be monogamous or polygamous.[183]

---

[175] In *N L S v. B R P* [2016] eKLR, p. 13, the High Court observed that '[m]ost of the decided cases involving presumption of marriage involved issues dealing with succession'. See also *Raphael Ratemo & another v. Emily Nakhanu Musinai* [2017] eKLR, para. 41.

[176] *ERK v. JCC* [2020] eKLR. In *E.N. W v. G.N. K & another* [2010] eKLR, the Court indicated that it needed more evidence before it could resolve a common law marriage.

[177] *A M D N v. S M L* [2017] eKLR, p. 5.

[178] *In the Matter of The Estate of the Late G K G* [2006] eKLR, p. 3.

[179] *Geoffrey Waruru Kinyua v. Susan Wambui Waruru* [2010] eKLR. In this case, the High Court dissolved a marriage by repute on the following grounds: 'cruelty attributed to the defendant ... namely neglect of children of the marriage, disappearances from home to unknown places, obtaining money by false pretences from the plaintiff's friends thereby humiliating and embarrassing the plaintiff, refusing to contribute to domestic household expenses, removing the children of the marriage from the home without the plaintiff's knowledge, neglecting her house hold and maternal duties to the children, by being a habitual drunkard, using children as a weapon to fight the plaintiff and using the plaintiff's ATM card without his consent' (see p. 2).

[180] *EMP v. FNM* [2020] eKLR, para. 30.

[181] *A W M v. R M* [2005] eKLR, p. 5: the High Court dissolved the marriage 'due to the cruelty, hostility and total breakdown of the relationship'.

[182] *In re Estate of Jecinter Njoki Okoth (Deceased)* [2020] eKLR, p. 6. However, see *In re Estate of Mungiiria Silas Muriithi (Deceased)* [2021] eKLR, where the deceased had 'abandoned' his common law wife in Kenya and travelled to America, where he died, but the Court held that she was still his common law wife, and was entitled to a share of his estate.

[183] *In re Estate of Eliud Kiarie Mutembei (Deceased)* [2022] eKLR, para. 65 (it was polygamous).

10. CONCLUSION

This chapter has discussed the history of the presumption of marriage in Kenya, and the issues surrounding this presumption. The issues discussed have been: facts and holding in *Hortensiah Wanjiku Yawe v. Public Trustees*; understanding *Hortensiah Wanjiku Yawe v. Public Trustees*; reopening the debate and casting doubt on *Hortensiah Wanjiku Yawe v. Public Trustees*; establishing the applicable presumption; the type of the presumption of marriage by repute, and the burden and standard of proof; factors to consider in determining the existence or otherwise of a marriage by repute; the rights of parties in a marriage by repute; and terminating a marriage by repute. I have argued, inter alia, that if a marriage by repute is presumed to exist, the parties to such a marriage should have the same rights as those married in terms of the Marriage Act.

PACIFIC ISLAND COUNTRIES

LEGAL REGULATION OF SAME-SEX RELATIONSHIPS IN PACIFIC ISLAND COUNTRIES

A Conflict of Values

Jennifer CORRIN

Résumé

Dans les petites îles indépendantes du Pacifique Sud, les couples de même sexe sont placés dans une situation juridique difficile. Dans beaucoup de ces pays, ils ne sont pas autorisés à se marier ou à conclure une union civile. Dans certains de ces États, les actes sexuels entre partenaires de même sexe sont d'ailleurs toujours criminalisés. Le présent article examine les dispositions légales qui régissent les relations entre personnes de même sexe dans une sélection de pays insulaires du Pacifique. Il étudie également les garanties constitutionnelles d'égalité et de non-discrimination et la manière dont elles s'appliquent aux couples de même sexe. Il analyse ensuite la manière dont les tribunaux réagissent face aux contradictions entre le droit pénal et les dispositions relatives aux droits de l'homme lorsqu'il s'agit de relations entre personnes de même sexe. Enfin, il aborde les perspectives de réforme.

1. INTRODUCTION

In small island countries of the South Pacific, same-sex couples are placed in a difficult legal position. In many of these countries, they are not entitled to marry or form a civil union that is recognised by State laws. In some countries, sexual acts by same-sex partners are still criminalised. This chapter examines the legal provisions that govern same-sex relationships in a selection of Pacific Island countries.[1] It also explores the constitutional guarantees of equality and freedom from discrimination, and the limits that have been placed on those rights, which may impact on same-sex couples. The chapter then goes on to consider the courts' approach to the tensions between criminal laws and human rights provisions, in the context of same-sex relationships. Finally, the chapter considers prospects for reform.

2. MATRIMONIAL LAWS

In some Pacific Islands countries, such as Nauru[2] and Fiji,[3] marriage is expressed to be the union of a man and a woman. In Fiji, for example, the Marriage Act provides: 'Marriage in Fiji shall be the voluntary union of one man to one woman to the exclusion of all others'.[4] Consequently, same-sex marriages cannot be celebrated under the Act. While the Marriage Act prescribes the only legally recognised way of formalising a marriage in Fiji, in practice parties do go through other ceremonies of marriage in accordance with their customs or religion. However, these processes are not available to same-sex partners, and, in any event, they are not recognised under State law.[5] Consequently, in order to have their marriages recognised by the State, parties usually follow a customary or religious marriage with a civil ceremony, referred to by Indo-Fijians as a 'court marriage'.[6] A similar practice is followed in many Pacific Island countries.[7]

In many parts of the region, however, the relevant legislation does not expressly limit marriage to a man and a woman. Examples can be found in

---

[1] While Papua New Guinea is not a small island country, it shares a colonial history and cultural considerations with many of its neighbours, and so it has been included in the discussion in this chapter.

[2] Births Deaths and Marriages Registration Act 2017 (Nauru), s. 3.

[3] 1968, s. 13.

[4] Ibid.

[5] See, e.g. *Haseena v. Saajid* [2021] FJHCFD 6 para. 05, where a Nikah ceremony, recognised by Islamic law, was held not to be legally binding.

[6] Many religious leaders are also certified marriage officers, which allows them to conduct civil and religious marriage ceremonies: P.I. JALAL, *Law for Pacific Women*, Fiji Women's Rights Movement, 1998, p. 203.

[7] See, e.g. *Marriage in Papua New Guinea*, Monograph 4 [1986] PNG Law Reform Commission, 1 January 1986, p. 5.

Samoa,[8] Solomon Islands,[9] Tonga,[10] Tuvalu[11] and Vanuatu.[12] The question then arises whether the common law definition of marriage, as expressed in *Hyde v. Hyde*,[13] applies in those countries. As there was a general application or adoption of the principles of common law throughout the region during the colonial era,[14] the answer would appear to be in the affirmative. The English common law position has been endorsed by the courts in a number of regional countries. For example, in Solomon Islands, the Chief Justice held, in *Hepworth v. Sikela*,[15] that: 'marriage is essentially a voluntary union for life of one man and one woman to the exclusion of all others. That union can be entered into between an indigenous and a non-indigenous Solomon Islanders or between two indigenous Solomon Islanders'.

More recently, *Hyde v. Hyde* was endorsed by the National Court of Papua New Guinea, in *Loni v. Loni*.[16] Accordingly, in the absence of a statutory provision to the contrary, a marriage must be between 'one man and one woman'. Certainly, it seems to be widely accepted in the region that marriage is only permitted between parties of the opposite sex.[17]

The provisions governing nullity in the region do not expressly stipulate that a marriage will be void if the parties are of the same sex.[18] However, this would seem to be the result of a marriage ceremony performed in a country where only heterosexual marriage is recognised by the State.

In some countries of the region, for example Solomon Islands[19] and Vanuatu,[20] customary marriages are recognised by the State. However, as in Fiji, customary marriage is not open to same-sex partners, as such unions are not recognised by customary laws. In one area of Solomon Islands, customary marriage is defined

---

[8] Marriage Ordinance 1961 (Samoa).

[9] Islanders' Marriage Act, Cap. 171 (Solomon Islands).

[10] Births, Deaths and Marriages Registration Act, Cap. 6.01 (Tonga); Solemnization of Marriage Regulations (Tonga).

[11] Marriage Act, Cap. 17.25.

[12] Marriage Act, Cap. 60 (Vanuatu).

[13] (1886) LR 1 P&D 130.

[14] See, e.g. Supreme Court Ordinance 1875 (Fiji), s. 35; Pacific Order in Council 1893 (UK), s. 20, applying in British Solomon Islands Protectorate, Gilbert and Ellice Islands Colony, New Hebrides, and Tonga. See, further, J. CORRIN and V. NAROKOBI, *Introduction to South Pacific Law*, Intersentia, 5th ed., 2022. In Vanuatu, the civil law also applies; see, further, J. CORRIN, 'Comment Ca Va? The Status of French Law in Vanuatu', *American Journal of Comparative Law* (in press).

[15] [1994] SBHC 2. See also *Ashika v. Vinay* [2017] FJHCFD 5 para. 12; *LK and JVR* [2009] FJHC 60 para. 4.28.

[16] [2020] PGNC 57 para. 14.

[17] Vanuatu Law Commission, *A Review of the Marriage Act*, Issues Paper No. 2, 2014, p. 13.

[18] See, e.g. Marriage Ordinance 1961 (Samoa), Part 2, and Divorce and Matrimonial Causes Ordinance 1961 (Samoa), s. 9; Islanders' Divorce Act, Cap. 170 (Solomon Islands), s. 12.

[19] Islanders' Marriage Act, Cap. 171 (Solomon Islands), s. 4.

[20] Marriage Act, Cap. 60 (Vanuatu), s. 10.

in provincial legislation as, 'the union of a man and woman under customary law or practice'.[21] This has also been emphasised in Vanuatu, where the Vanuatu Law Commission's 2014 Issues Paper reviewing the Marriage Act noted that, while Vanuatu's Constitution guarantees freedom from discrimination:[22] '[i]n church and tradition[al] beliefs of the people of Vanuatu, it is widely accepted that marriage is a union between the opposite sexes although this is not explicitly stated in the legislations'.[23]

The only country which permits marriage by same-sex couples is Pitcairn Island.[24] Of course, Pitcairn is in a different position to the other countries under discussion, as it is a United Kingdom Overseas Territory, and the legislation in question was made by the Governor of the Islands of Pitcairn, Henderson, Ducie and Oeno, rather than a local institution. There is no provision for civil unions between same-sex partners in any small Pacific Island country. However, in Pitcairn Island, such unions, when validly entered into overseas, are recognised as marriages.[25]

3. FAMILY PROTECTION FROM VIOLENCE

In many Pacific Island countries, recent reforms have extended family protection provisions to de facto partners. However, in most countries, these reforms do not extend to same-sex couples. For example, in Vanuatu, a spouse is defined to mean:[26]

> an individual of the opposite sex to the person who:
>
> (a) is or has been married to the person; or
> (b) although not married to the person, is living with the person in a marriage-like relationship or has lived with the person in such a relationship; or
> (c) is a biological parent of a child with the person (whether or not they are or have been married or are living or have lived together).

It has been suggested that, as the Act extends protection to a 'family member', and that term is broadly defined,[27] the legislation could extend to same-sex relationships. However, it seems doubtful whether the courts would interpret it in this way, given the prevailing norms. These norms were well illustrated

---

21 Moli Ward Customary Law Ordinance 2010 (Solomon Islands), s. 33(1).
22 Vanuatu Law Commission, above n. 17.
23 See also *Re MM Adoption Application by SAT* (Unreported, Supreme Court, Vanuatu, Harrop J, 3 July 2014), available via www.paclii.org at [2014] VUSC 78.
24 Same Sex Marriage and Civil Partnerships Ordinance 2015, Part II, s. 7(a).
25 Ibid., s. 7(b).
26 Family Protection Act 2008, (Vanuatu), s. 5.
27 Ibid., s. 3.

in the case of *In Re MM Adoption Application by SAT*,[28] where the Supreme Court sought the opinion of the Malvatumauri (National Council of Chiefs) on whether a single man might adopt a female child under customary law. The response of the Council focused on the fact that the single man in question was in a same-sex relationship, and held that this was not acceptable in custom. The court therefore rejected the adoption application.[29]

In Solomon Islands, protection from domestic violence has been extended to a 'spouse or de facto spouse'.[30] There is no definition of spouse, so it would appear that the Act may be interpreted as extending to same-sex couples. However, interpretation may be influenced by the criminalisation of sexual activity between such couples, which is discussed in the next section of this chapter.

In Fiji, on the other hand, in the Domestic Violence Act 2009, which introduces measures to protect victims of domestic violence, the term 'spouse' is defined as including 'a person who is or has been in a de facto relationship with the other person',[31] thus extending all protections in the Act to same-sex partners in a de facto relationship. In Tuvalu, protection is extended in gender-neutral terms to a complainant who 'lives or works temporarily or permanently with the defendant, or where the act of domestic violence occurred or is occurring', or, in the event that the complainant is unable to apply personally, to 'a family member, guardian or friend' or a person from a comprehensive list of responsible officials.[32]

4. CRIMINALISATION OF SAME-SEX RELATIONSHIPS

In a number of Pacific Island countries, same-sex sexual activity is still criminalised. These include Cook Islands,[33] Kiribati,[34] Papua New Guinea,[35] Samoa,[36] Solomon Islands,[37] Tonga[38] and Tuvalu.[39] In all these countries, this includes sexual activity in private between consenting adults. In Solomon Islands, the High Court confirmed this in the case of *Director of Public Prosecutions v. Bowie*,[40]

---

[28]   Above n. 23.
[29]   See, further, J. CORRIN and S. FARRAN, 'The Law of Adoption in Vanuatu' in J. CORRIN and S. FARRAN (eds.), *The Plural Practice of Adoption in Pacific Island States*, Springer, 2019, p. 147.
[30]   Family Protection Act 2014 (Solomon Islands), s. 6(2)(a).
[31]   S. 2.
[32]   Family Protection Act and Domestic Violence Act 2014 (Tuvalu), s. 8.
[33]   Crimes Act 1969, ss. 154 and 155.
[34]   Penal Code, Cap. 67 (Kiribati), ss. 153–155.
[35]   Criminal Code, Cap. 262 (Papua New Guinea), ss. 210 and 212.
[36]   Crimes Act 2013 (Samoa), ss. 67 and 68.
[37]   Penal Code, Cap. 62 (Solomon Islands), ss. 161 and 162.
[38]   Criminal Offences Act, Cap. 4.04 (Tonga), ss. 136 and 137.
[39]   Penal Code Cap 10.20 (Tuvalu), ss. 153–155.
[40]   [1988–1989] SILR 113.

which is discussed later in this chapter. Samoa has an additional criminal offence of keeping a place of resort for the purpose of 'indecent acts' between males.[41]

The penalties for such offences are severe. In Kiribati, Papua New Guinea, Solomon Islands and Tuvalu, for example, 'buggery' with a person of either sex, whether in private or in public, is punishable by imprisonment for up to 14 years.[42] Even more severe is the penalty in Tonga, where the Court may, in lieu of, or in addition to, a sentence of imprisonment of up to ten years, order the convicted person to be whipped.[43]

In Fiji, same-sex relationships were criminalised until 2009,[44] when the Crimes Decree repealed the Penal Code.[45] Sexual offences are now limited to rape, sexual assaults, indecent assault, abduction of a minor with the intent to have carnal knowledge, defilement of children or intellectually impaired persons, unnatural offences with animals, incest, and various associated offences, such as attempts and procurement.[46]

Another exception is Vanuatu, where same-sex sexual activity is only illegal if either party is under 18.[47] This age of consent is higher than the 15 years required for girls engaging in heterosexual sexual activity. The penalty for the former offence is imprisonment for up to two years.[48]

5. CONSTITUTIONAL PROMOTION OF CHRISTIAN VALUES, CULTURAL NORMS AND HUMAN RIGHTS

The strong Christian values prevailing in the region are emphasised in many regional constitutions.[49] Most contain at least one reference to God in the preamble. For example, the Constitution of Tuvalu states:

> WHEREAS the people of Tuvalu, acknowledging God as the Almighty and Everlasting Lord and giver of all good things, humbly place themselves under His good providence and seek His blessing upon themselves and their lives.[50]

---

41 Crimes Act 2013 (Samoa), s. 71.
42 Penal Code, Cap. 67, s. 153 (Kiribati); Criminal Code 1974 (Papua New Guinea), s. 210; Penal Code, Cap. 26 (Solomon Islands), ss. 160–162; Penal Code, Cap. 10.20 (Tuvalu), s. 153.
43 Criminal Offences Act, Cap. 4.04 (Tonga), s. 142.
44 Penal Code, Cap. 17 (Fiji), ss. 175–177.
45 Crimes Act 2009 (Fiji), s. 391.
46 Crimes Act 2009 (Fiji), ch. 3, Part 12B.
47 Penal Code, Cap. 135 (Vanuatu), s. 99.
48 Ibid.
49 See Constitution (Amendment) Act 1997 (Fiji), Preamble, s. 5; Constitution of the Independent State of Papua New Guinea, Preamble; Constitution of the Independent State of Samoa 1961 (Samoa), Preamble; Constitution of 1978 (Solomon Islands), Preamble; Constitution of Tonga, Cap. 1.01, s. 1; Constitution of the Republic of Vanuatu 1980, Preamble.
50 Constitution of Tuvalu, Cap 1.02, Preamble.

In Samoa, the Constitutional preamble states:

IN THE HOLY NAME OF GOD, THE ALMIGHTY, THE EVER LOVING WHEREAS sovereignty over the Universe belongs to the Omnipresent God alone, and the authority to be exercised by the people of Samoa within the limits prescribed by God's commandments is a sacred heritage.

In 2017, this was taken further, by adding to the body of the Constitution, 'Samoa is a Christian nation founded on God the Father, the Son and the Holy Spirit.'[51]

In Pacific Islands, Christian values are generally conservative and homophobic. Indeed, they formed the basis of the 'one-man, one-woman' approach enshrined in the common law and many marriage Acts.[52] Thus, the Vanuatu Law Commission's Issue Paper stated:

Vanuatu's Constitution is established on Christian values as ... dictated in the preamble. Christian values [state] that provision of same sex marriage is unacceptable and is improper. In a place where the custom and Christian beliefs and practice of the people dominates their lives, recognizing same sex marriage may be an issue.[53]

In addition to the endorsement of Christian values, many regional constitutions promote local culture and custom. For example, the Constitution of Tuvalu contains Principles, which provide that:[54]

While believing that Tuvalu must take its rightful place amongst the community of nations in search of peace and the general welfare, nevertheless the people of Tuvalu recognize and affirm, with gratitude to God, that the stability of Tuvaluan society and the happiness and welfare of the people of Tuvalu, both present and future, depend very largely on the maintenance of Tuvaluan values, culture and tradition, including the vitality and the sense of identity of island communities and attitudes of co-operation, self-help and unity within and amongst those communities.

Amongst the values that the people of Tuvalu seek to maintain are their traditional forms of communities, the strength and support of the family and family discipline.

Alongside these Christian and traditional values, most regional constitutions[55] also contain a Bill of Rights, including the right to protection from discrimination on the grounds of gender. For example, in Samoa, it is provided that, 'no law

---

51   Constitution of Samoa 1960, Art. 1(3), inserted by the Constitution Amendment Act 2017 (Samoa).
52   *Anskar v. Yansuan* [1985] PNG Law Reports 1.
53   Vanuatu Law Commission, above n. 17, p. 13.
54   Constitution of Tuvalu, Cap. 1.02, Constitutional Principles, paras. 3 and 4.
55   The exception is Niue.

and no executive or administrative action of the State shall, either expressly or in its practical application, subject any person or persons to any disability or restriction or confer on any person or persons any privilege or advantage on grounds including sex and family status'.[56]

Fiji has the strongest provision in this regard, with specific constitutional protection from discrimination on the grounds of 'gender, sexual orientation, gender identity and expression'.[57] Interestingly, the precursor of the current Bill of Rights contained exceptions to the right to equality, in favour of a law which declared 'marriage to be the voluntary union of one man to one woman to the exclusion of all others' and provided 'for the prosecution of unnatural offences or indecent practices'.[58] These provisions do not appear to have been expressly repealed, but the relevant Decree does not appear in the 2016 Revised Edition of the Laws of Fiji, and in any event, they are void to the extent that they are inconsistent with the Constitution.[59]

The inclusion in constitutions of both anti-discrimination provisions and promotion of the conservative norms that accompany culture and custom gives rise to a conflict of values in relation to sexual preference. In Tuvalu, the tension is resolved in favour of custom, with the Constitution providing that the rights and freedoms enshrined in the Constitution may be exercised only 'in acceptance of Tuvaluan values and culture, and with respect for them'.[60] Further, the national interest, in accordance with which constitutional rights and freedoms must be exercised,[61] is defined as including 'the protection and development of Tuvaluan values and culture'. Similarly, in Solomon Islands, customary law, and implicitly its underlying norms, are shielded from the right to freedom from discrimination.[62] The latest draft of a new, federal constitution for Solomon Islands contains a Bill of Rights that prohibits the government from discriminating directly or indirectly against anyone on a broad range of grounds. 'Sex' is included, but with the proviso that this must 'not be interpreted as including sexual orientation'.[63]

In addition to the constitutionally protected rights, Papua New Guinea[64] and Samoa[65] are parties to the International Covenant on Civil and Political Rights (ICCPR). This binds them to respect, and to protect, the rights recognised in

---

[56] Constitution of Samoa 1960, Art. 15(2).
[57] Constitution of the Republic of Fiji 2013, s. 26(3).
[58] Fundamental Rights and Freedoms Decree 2000, s. 19 (7)(F) and (G).
[59] The Constitution is the supreme law: Constitution of the Republic of Fiji 2013, s. 2.
[60] Constitution of Tuvalu, Cap. 1.02, s. 11(2)(b).
[61] Ibid., s 11(2)(a).
[62] Constitution of Solomon Islands 1978, s. 15(5)(d). The Constitution is contained in the schedule to the Solomon Islands Independence Order 1978 (UK).
[63] Draft Federal Constitution of Solomon Islands 2014 No. 2, cl. 19(3).
[64] 21 July 2008.
[65] 15 February 2008.

that document, without distinction of any kind,[66] for all individuals within their jurisdiction, including those of non-heterosexual orientation. However, neither country has ratified the Optional Protocol to the ICCPR, which would have subjected them to the jurisdiction of the UN Human Rights Committee.

6. JUDICIAL CONSIDERATION OF CONFLICTING VALUES

The issue of sexual activity between same-sex partners was examined by the Fijian High Court in two cases dealt with together: *Nadan v. The State*[67] and *McCoskar v. The State*.[68] The cases involved appeals by a Melbourne tourist, Mr McCoskar, and his male Fijian partner Mr Nadan, both of whom had been sentenced to two years' imprisonment for engaging in consensual homosexual sex. At the time of the offence, section 175 of the Penal Code[69] criminalised 'carnal knowledge against the order of nature'. Section 177 criminalised acts of 'gross indecency' between males.[70] Consent was not a defence to either of these provisions. The 1997 Fijian Constitution, however, contained a Bill of Rights that guaranteed rights to privacy[71] and equality before the law on grounds of gender.[72] The court, therefore, held that sections 175 and 177 had to be construed 'with such modifications and qualifications as are necessary to bring them into conformity with the Constitution'. The court considered that there must 'exist particularly serious reasons before the State or community can interfere', and that any limitations on the right to privacy must be 'prescribed by law and be reasonable and justifiable in a free and democratic society'. On this basis, it was held that section 175 was an unjustifiable interference of the State into the private lives of consenting men and women. Moreover, section 177 amounted to a breach of the right to equality before the law regardless of sex, as it concerned only the sexual activities of men. Ultimately, the court stated that both sanctions were invalid to the extent that they were inconsistent with the rights to privacy and equality guaranteed by the Constitution.

As mentioned above, since these cases were decided, the Penal Code has been repealed by the Crimes Act 2009,[73] which does not criminalise consensual sexual activity between same-sex partners.

---

[66]   International Covenant on Civil and Political Rights, opened for signature 19 December 1966, 999 UNTS 171 (entered into force 23 March 1976), Art. 2(1).
[67]   [2005] FJHC 252.
[68]   [2005] FJFC 500.
[69]   Cap. 17 (Fiji).
[70]   Penal Code, Cap. 17 (Fiji), s. 177.
[71]   Constitution (Amendment) Act 1997 (Fiji), s. 37.
[72]   Ibid., s. 38.
[73]   Crimes Act 2009, s. 391.

In Solomon Islands, a different aspect of discrimination has been examined. As in many of the countries under discussion, the Penal Code of Solomon Islands, as originally enacted, was framed in terms of acts committed by males. It provided that:

> Any male person who, whether in public or private, commits any act of gross indecency with another male person, or procures another male person to commit any act of gross indecency with him, or attempts to procure the commission of any such act by any male person with himself or with another male person, whether in public or private shall be guilty of a felony, and shall be liable to imprisonment for five years.[74]

This wording formed the basis of a defence argued in the Solomon Islands case of *Director of Public Prosecutions v. Bowie*.[75] In that case, the defendant had been prosecuted under this section for gross indecency. It was submitted that this section of the Code discriminated against men, and was therefore unconstitutional, as it contravened the right to freedom from discrimination enshrined in section 15 of the Constitution. The Magistrates Court accepted this argument, and acquitted the accused on the basis that the section was void.[76] This decision was overturned on appeal. Ward CJ held that the word 'male' should be severed from the section, thus making the offence applicable to both men and women.

Following this case, in 1989, the Penal Code was amended to make the offence gender-neutral, by deleting the word 'male' from the section. The amending Act did not alter the wording of section 160, which is, in part, still not gender-neutral, providing:

> Any person who-
>
> (a)   commits buggery with another person or with an animal; or
> (b)   permits a male person to commit buggery with him or her,
>
> shall be guilty of a felony, and shall be liable to imprisonment for fourteen years.

Discriminatory wording is still on the statute books in some countries. For example, in Kiribati it is provided that:[77]

> Any male person who, whether in public or private, commits any act of gross indecency with another male person, or procures another male person to commit any act of gross indecency with him, or attempts to procure the commission of any such

---

[74]   Penal Code, Cap. 26 (Solomon Islands), s. 160.
[75]   [1988–89] SILR 113.
[76]   The Magistrates' Court's decision is unreported, but the author was counsel for the defendant in this case.
[77]   Penal Code, Cap. 67 (Kiribati), s. 155.

act by any male person with himself or with another male person, whether in public or private, shall be guilty of a felony, and shall be liable to imprisonment for 5 years.

As in Solomon Islands, the Constitution of Kiribati guarantees the right to freedom from discrimination.[78] However, the definition of 'discriminatory' does not include different treatment on the grounds of gender,[79] which would appear to rule out a challenge to any allegation of gross indecency on that basis.

7. CULTURAL PRACTICES

In Samoa and Tonga, there is a particular cultural practice to be considered. In Samoa, *fa'afafine*, and in Tonga, *fakaleiti*, are 'biological males who express feminine gender identities in a range of way[s]'.[80] Typically, *fa'afafine* live, work and dress as women throughout most of their lives.[81] In this role, they contribute to the family, and there does not appear to be a particular focus on sexuality.[82]

Legal questions arise in relation to marriage and *fa'afafine* and *fakaleiti*. *Fa'afafine* and *fakaleiti* have received significant anthropological and sociological attention, but there has been little legal analysis. As mentioned above, the legislation governing marriage in both Samoa and Tonga does not state that parties to a marriage must be of the opposite sex.[83] Neither is it stipulated that a marriage will be void if the parties are of the same sex.[84] However, as noted above, both Samoa and Tonga have inherited the common law, and with it the definition of marriage as the union of one man and one woman. The practice in both countries accords with the common law, and, to date, it appears that the only option for *fa'afafine* and *fakaleiti* who wish to marry is to marry a woman.[85]

Recent Australian and New Zealand case law has highlighted that, while a marriage must be between a man and a woman, the concepts of men and women

---

[78] Constitution of Kiribati 1979, s. 15. The Constitution is contained in the schedule to the Kiribati Independence Order 1979 (UK).

[79] Constitution of Kiribati 1979, s. 15(3).

[80] J. SCHMIDT, 'Redefining Fa'afafine: Western Discourses and the Construction of Transgenderism in Samoa' (August 2001) 6, *Intersections: Gender, History and Culture in the Asian Context*, accessed via intersections.anu.edu.au/issue6/schmidt.html, last accessed 23.07.2023.

[81] Ibid., 40.

[82] K. POASA, 'The Samoan Fa'afafine' (1992) 5(3) *Journal of Psychology & Human Sexuality* 15: the words *fa'afafine* and *fakaleiti* literally mean 'the way of a woman' (39).

[83] Marriage Ordinance 1961 (Samoa); Births, Deaths and Marriages Registration Act, Cap. 6.01 (Tonga); Solemnization of Marriage Regulations (Tonga).

[84] Divorce and Matrimonial Causes Ordinance 1961 (Samoa). Tongan legislation makes no mention of void or voidable marriages: Divorce Act, Cap. 6.09 (Tonga). See, further, S. FARRAN, 'Transsexuals, *Fa'afafine, Fakaleiti* and Marriage Law in the Pacific: Considerations for the future' (2004) 113(2) *Journal of the Polynesian Society* 119, 124.

[85] S. FARRAN, 'Transsexuals, *Fa'afafine, Fakaleiti* and Marriage Law in the Pacific', above n. 84, 138.

'are both social and policy issues and need not be immutable'.[86] The courts of Samoa and Tonga have yet to consider whether and how this transsexual jurisprudence can be translated into the cultural position of *fa'afafine* and *fakaleiti*. While there may be room for reinterpretation of what it means to be a 'man' and a 'woman', in light of prevailing culture, in practice it has been suggested that courts will be 'reluctant to set off on a path that is bound to attract social and moral condemnation, especially from church groups'.[87] It has also been suggested that judges may find it difficult to distance themselves from their own moral and religious beliefs.[88]

A further issue arises from the fact that, as noted above, homosexual acts are illegal in both Tonga[89] and Samoa.[90] It is unclear whether these offences apply to sexual activities between a *fa'afafine* or *fakaleiti* and a man, or whether such behaviour is legitimated by the cultural context, on the basis that *fa'afafine* and *fakaleiti* cannot be categorised as either women or homosexual men. Culture appears to bestow on them a 'distinct androgynous gender category'.[91] They do not 'neatly fit into Western categories of male, female, heterosexual, homosexual or transsexual, but would appear to be unique to the Pacific region'.[92] Again, this question has yet to come before a Samoan or Tongan court.

8. THE FUTURE

Cultural norms and the influence of churches weigh heavily against reform of the law to permit marriage or civil unions between same-sex couples. In this environment, the prospect for legalising sexual activity between same-sex partners, even in the case of consenting adults in private, appears slim. In Solomon Islands, the Law Reform Commission's Second Interim Report on Sexual Offences[93] mentions the offence of 'buggery', but makes no recommendation in this regard. In 2016, the Penal Code (Amendment) (Sexual Offences) Act was passed, to amend the Penal Code in relation to sexual offences. However, the sections prohibiting 'buggery', and the indecent practices between persons of the same

---

[86]   Ibid., 132. See *Re Kevin* (2001) 165 FLR 404; *Attorney General for the Commonwealth v. Kevin and Jennifer* (2003) 172 FLR 300; *Attorney General v. Otahuhu Family Court* [1995] 1 NZLR 603. See, further, ibid., 133.

[87]   S. FARRAN, 'Transsexuals, Fa'afafine, Fakaleiti and Marriage Law in the Pacific', above n. 84, 139.

[88]   Ibid.

[89]   Criminal Offences Act, Cap. 18, s. 136.

[90]   Crimes Act 2013, s. 67.

[91]   K. POASA, above n. 82, 50.

[92]   S. FARRAN, 'Transsexuals, Fa'afafine, Fakaleiti and Marriage Law in the Pacific', above n. 84, 137.

[93]   Solomon Islands Law Reform Commission, *Review of Penal Code and Criminal Procedure Code: Sexual Offences*, 2013, Second Interim Report.

sex offences, were left unchanged. In 2017, the Commission published an Issues Paper on the Penal Code. It considered the law relating to homosexual conduct as encapsulated in the Penal Code, and posed the question, '[s]hould homosexual activity which is consensual and done in private be prohibited?'.[94] Unfortunately, the responses to this question do not appear to be publicly available.

In Fiji, extensive reforms to family laws, in 2012, recognised de facto relationships, but only between a man and a woman. However, this was hardly surprising, given the opposition to same-sex relationships reflected in the Fiji Law Reform Commission's Report and its final recommendations.[95]

In other countries, it has been suggested that, while 'legal reform might eventually encompass unmarried heterosexual couples', law reform is 'unlikely to encompass same-sex couples in the foreseeable future.'[96] This has been attributed largely to the influence of Christian church groups.[97] In Samoa, the 2017 endorsement of Christianity in the body of the Constitution, referred to above, could arguably be relied on to legitimise a moral stance that inhibits the reform of the law relating to same-sex partners.

In countries where the constitutional Bill of Rights enshrines the right to equality and freedom from discrimination, the current position is arguably unconstitutional. That would certainly seem to be the case regarding marriage in Fiji, where the Constitution guarantees non-discrimination on the grounds of sexual orientation.[98]

However, there is evidence of some advocacy for reform. In Vanuatu, for example, the Law Reform Commission's Issues Paper, quoted from above, goes on to state:

> Everyone is a part of a family and a citizen of a country. Those who have feelings for the same sex may try to repress their natural feelings and unhappily try to live according to the standard expected from their families. The Law would not benefit all people of the country if it simply ignores these individuals.[99]

This notwithstanding, given the resistance to granting formal legal status to same-sex relationships, it seems unlikely that such reform will occur within the near future.

---

[94] Solomon Islands Law Reform Commission, *Review of Penal Code and Criminal Procedure Code*, 2017 Issues Paper 1, p. 92.

[95] Fiji Law Reform Commission, *Family Law Report 1999: Making a Difference to Families*, 1999, pp. 42–43.

[96] S. FARRAN, 'Living in Sin in Paradise: Cohabitation in the South Pacific' in A. BAINHAM and B. RWEZAURA (eds.), *The International Survey of Family Law*, Jordan Publishing, 2006, pp. 407, 408–409.

[97] S. FARRAN, 'Transsexuals, *fa'afafine, fakaleiti* and marriage law in the Pacific', above n. 84, 135.

[98] Constitution (Amendment) Act 1997, s. 38. See, now, Constitution of the Republic of Fiji 2013, s. 26(3).

[99] Vanuatu Law Commission, above n. 17, p. 13.

POLAND

POLISH SOLUTIONS IN THE PROTECTION OF ELDERLY RIGHTS

Małgorzata Balwicka-Szczyrba and Anna Sylwestrzak*

Résumé

Selon les dernières recherches, la Pologne devrait, d'ici 2100, occuper la première place en termes de proportion de personnes âgées par rapport au reste de la population, et être ainsi le pays le plus âgé d'Europe. Il est donc important d'évaluer le système actuel du droit de la famille, du droit des successions et du droit civil en Pologne, afin de sauvegarder de manière adéquate les intérêts des personnes âgées dans les actes de la vie civile. Il faut partir du principe que les personnes âgées devraient pouvoir contracter aussi longtemps que possible, grâce à un soutien adéquat. En outre, le recours à l'incapacité légale, qui est fréquemment utilisé à l'encontre des personnes âgées en Pologne, ne contribue pas à la protection de leurs droits fondamentaux, mais est au contraire discriminatoire dans de nombreux cas.

L'objectif scientifique de cet article est d'identifier les tendances et d'analyser les solutions existantes dans le droit civil polonais pour la protection des intérêts des personnes âgées, y compris dans le droit de la famille et le droit

---

* This publication has been prepared as part of the NCN OPUS 22 project entitled 'Zdolność do uczestnictwa w obrocie cywilnoprawnym osób starszych. Instytucje wsparcia – perspektywa prawna' (*The elderly ability to engage in civil-law transactions. Support institutions – a legal perspective*), funded by the National Science Centre, Poland, contract no: UMO-2021/43/B/HS5/00916. Małgorzata Balwicka-Szczyrba ORCID: 0000-0002-7981-5602. Anna Sylwestrzak ORCID: 0000-0001-8346-1926.

des successions. La possibilité pour ces personnes de participer à des actes civils est particulièrement préoccupante. L'article propose de définir un cadre optimal pour la protection des intérêts des personnes âgées en Pologne. Celui-ci impliquera la détermination de principes généraux et de lignes directrices pour la protection des personnes âgées, tout en essayant de construire de nouvelles solutions statutaires pour répondre au problème de plus en plus visible du vieillissement de la population en Pologne.

La législation polonaise comporte certaines dispositions utiles pour la protection des droits des personnes âgées. Il s'agit, par exemple, de mécanismes du droit des successions tels que la succession par les grands-parents du testateur et le droit des grands-parents à une quasi-créance alimentaire. Toutefois, de nouvelles dispositions restent attendues. Il semble nécessaire de supprimer l'incapacité légale et de la remplacer par des institutions basées sur la prise de décision assistée, comme le mandat de protection future donné à un mandataire ou encore un modèle plus flexible d'intervention judiciaire ou administrative adapté aux besoins des personnes âgées. L'objectif d'une telle législation devrait être de fournir un soutien aux personnes âgées, tant matériel qu'immatériel, afin qu'elles puissent participer activement le plus longtemps possible aux actes de la vie civile et à la vie sociale.

1. INTRODUCTION

The latest research shows that, by 2100, Poland will become Europe's leading country in terms of the ratio of the elderly to the overall population, and therefore the oldest country on the continent. Indeed, the senior population has recently experienced a rapid rise, with a simultaneous decline in other age groups. This translates into a considerable surge in the old-age dependency ratio, understood as the number of persons aged 65 and over per 100 people within the 15–64 age bracket. The figure stood at 28.9 in 2021.[1] Another emerging demographic trend relates to the oldest-old (aged 80 and over): in 2000, their number amounted to 774,000, accounting for 2 per cent of the total population, while in 2021 it exceeded 1.6 million, representing a good 4.3 per cent.[2]

With Polish society ageing, and a fast-growing number of the oldest-old, it is important to examine whether the current legal system in Poland provides adequate measures to safeguard elderly interests in civil law transactions. Senior citizens may prove to be particularly vulnerable to the adverse consequences of

---

[1]   Polish Central Statistical Office, *Sytuacja osób starszych w Polsce w 2021 r* (*The situation of elderly in Poland in 2021*), Warsaw, 2022, p. 15.

[2]   Polish Central Statistical Office, *Ludność. Stan i struktura oraz ruch naturalny w przekroju terytorialnym w 2021 r.* (*Population. Numbers, structure and natural shifts according to territory in 2021*), Warsaw, 2022, p. 18.

legal transactions, due to old-age dementia.[3] However, it is the present authors' position that elderly persons should be able to engage in legal transactions for as long as possible, given appropriate support and protection of their interests. Active participation of the elderly in the social sphere should extend to include family law.

The objective of this chapter is to analyse the existing legal arrangements designed to protect the lawful interests of the elderly under Polish civil law, including family law. The focus will be on measures for the protection of the elderly, both of a general and a specific nature, as well as desirable directions of change that would serve to further strengthen the position of senior citizens in Polish law.

2. MEASURES FOR THE PROTECTION OF THE ELDERLY AS PARTIES TO A CIVIL LAW RELATIONSHIP: GENERAL CONSIDERATIONS

Capacity for legal acts in Polish law extends to natural persons and legal entities, with its scope subject to age-based restrictions for the former group. Under Article 10 of the Polish Civil Code, full capacity for legal acts is granted to natural persons who have attained the age of majority (18 years) or, exceptionally, through marriage. There is no upper age that would deprive the person who has attained it of their legal capacity, so elderly people can, as a rule, engage in legal transactions unless they become fully legally incapacitated. Full legal incapacitation results in what is known as 'civil death', depriving the person of their capacity for legal acts.[4]

The civil law system envisions general measures to be applied for the protection of the rights and interests of the elderly, as inherently weaker parties to a legal transaction. Therefore, it appears that the institution of legal incapacitation should not be applied to the elderly as unduly interfering in their legal activity.[5] The corrective and protective function is more appropriately fulfilled by the institutions of defects in a declaration of intent, and of exploitation, as well as

---

[3]   Dementia is a natural consequence of human ageing. See P. Błędowski, T. Grodzicki, M. Mossakowska and T. Zdrojewski (eds.), *Badanie poszczególnych obszarów stanu zdrowia osób starszych, w tym jakości życia związanej ze starzeniem*, Gdański Uniwersytet Medyczny, 2021, p. 297.

[4]   See M. Balwicka-Szczyrba and A. Sylwestrzak, 'Legal effects of Incapacitation in Polish Family Law' in R. Fretwell Wilson and J. Carbone (eds.), *International Survey of Family Law*, Intersentia, 2022, p. 277.

[5]   See M. Balwicka-Szczyrba and A. Sylwestrzak, *Instytucja ubezwłasnowolnienia w świetle unormowań konstytucji RP oraz konwencji o prawach osób niepełnosprawnych*, GSP, 2018, vol. XL, p. 167.

nullity of a legal act performed in violation of the principles of community life, as discussed below.

The institution of defects in a declaration of intent is covered under Article 82 *et seq.* of the Polish Civil Code. The legal regulation of defects in declarations of intent ensures the security of civil law transactions, including by providing a 'level playing field' for all parties involved.[6] A central component to safeguarding elderly interests is the defect of lack of consciousness or freedom, as defined in Article 82 of the Polish Civil Code. The sanction of nullity attaches to a declaration of intent made by a person who, for any reason, is in a state which precludes the conscious or free making of a decision and the declaration of intent. This includes, in particular, mental illness, mental impairment, or other, even temporary, mental disorders. These kinds of disorders should be regarded as resulting from deteriorating old-age dementia that precludes consciousness. Consequently, this ever-growing, at-risk social group will potentially be the most frequent beneficiary of the protections granted under Article 82 of the Polish Civil Code.

The construal of the premise of lack of consciousness or freedom seems to be commensurate with the potential risks associated with old age. It will be seen that an individual's state of consciousness is not a separate process from external events, and that a disruption or impairment of mental functions in the cognitive and communicative spheres, or in decision-making, may be so aggravated by external events as to meet the prerequisites of Article 82 of the Polish Civil Code.[7] For example, manipulative actions of others, and pressure from third parties, may preclude decision-making freedom.[8] Furthermore, the state of lack of consciousness or freedom does not have to be total and complete; it suffices that it is so significant that specific factual circumstances can be shown to have led to a defect in the declaration of intent. On the other hand, the reasons for the lack of consciousness or freedom are secondary, since only effect truly matters under the law.[9]

On the other hand, the institution under discussion does not take effect automatically, and its applicability is verified on a case-by-case basis. Case law[10] points out that even persons with mental disorders may, at times, act with discernment, a condition described as a 'lucid interval'. It should be stressed that not every Alzheimer's disease-induced impairment of cognitive function necessarily meets the prerequisites under Article 82 of the Polish Civil Code. A defect in the declaration of intent, as contemplated in Article 82 of the Polish

---

[6]   K. Południak-Gierz, *Wady oświadczenia woli w umowach zawieranych na internetowym rynku konsumenckim*, C.H. Beck, 2020, p. 7 ff.

[7]   Polish Supreme Court Order of 21.12.2021, II CSK 459/21, LEX No. 3322184.

[8]   A. Wilk, *Wady oświadczenia woli – wybrane problemy praktyczne*, C.H. Beck, 2018, p. 10.

[9]   Appellate Court Judgment, Gdańsk, 14.12.2020, V ACa 356/20, LEX No. 3189590.

[10]   See Appellate Court Judgment, Białystok, 15.10.2015, I ACa 491/15, LEX No 1842188.

Civil Code, exists only when the condition of the affected person is such that they cannot reasonably be assumed to act with awareness of external circumstances, or the nature of the action (its circumstances, meaning or effects) is so complex or confusing that they would be incapable of giving it any proper consideration. The mere diagnosis of an illness, however, is not a ground for such a claim.[11] Consequently, the existence of a state precluding consciousness cannot be assumed a priori, even in mentally ill or mentally impaired individuals, or even when they are fully or partially legally incapacitated. This applies even more so to elderly persons, whose declarations of intent may need to be verified for validity by a court-appointed expert witness.

Another protective measure is the institution of exploitation, under Article 388 of the Polish Civil Code. This protective device has recently been modified to provide parties to civil law transactions, including the elderly, with a wider scope of protection. Under this regulation, a person who lacked sufficient knowledge of the subject-matter of the contract, or was infirm or inexperienced, may demand that their performance be reduced or the performance due to them be increased, or even that the contract should be declared invalid. Following a recent amendment to the Polish Civil Code, these rights expire after the lapse of six years, where the contracting party is a consumer.

The prerequisites for the application of the protective measures under Article 388 of the Polish Civil Code seem to adequately counteract potential risks associated with the elderly engaging in legal transactions. Indeed, the core feature of 'exploitation' is that it plays a grossly disproportionate role in the parties' performances. Another premise refers to the infirmity or inexperience of, or exertion of force against, a party, or their ignorance of the subject-matter of the contract, envisioning a grossly disproportionate performance. The third condition, which is subjective in its nature, for the application of Article 388§1 of the Polish Civil Code, is taking advantage of the situation. It is irrelevant who executed the contract and who incorporated the inequitable provisions into the contract. For this particular prerequisite to be effective, it is necessary to demonstrate that the exploiting party took advantage of the situation in their interests, i.e. 'acted opportunistically' to secure a special advantage by exploiting the vulnerable situation of the other party.[12] There is no doubt that the indicated prerequisites may arise from old-age infirmity; consequently, one of the claims available under Article 388 of the Polish Civil Code will be available to senior citizens.

Legal acts involving elderly persons may be assessed through the lens of the principles of community life set out in Article 58§2 of the Polish Civil Code. According to the wording of this Article, a legal act contrary to the principles

---

[11]   Appellate Court Judgment, Szczecin, 28.03.2019, I ACa 612/18, LEX No. 2668049.
[12]   See Appellate Court Judgment, Szczecin, 20.06.2019, I ACa 703/18, LEX No. 3123412.

of community life shall be declared invalid. It appears that the invalidity of a legal act could be invoked where an elderly person with dementia is a party, and especially when the declaration of intent itself is not found to be defective, and the prerequisites of exploitation are not met. The principles of community life constitute a general clause that embodies a set of moral practices accepted in society, changeable over time, and variable depending on the particular facts of the case.[13] Consequently, Article 58§2 of the Polish Civil Code prevents a legally unacceptable contradiction between the substance of a norm arising from a legal act and the substance of the moral norms accepted by society. This provision will be applicable where such a contradiction involves an elderly person.

The general legal measures discussed above serve corrective, protective and verificatory purposes. The possibility of their application in the case of legal transactions involving elderly persons, subject to conformity with statutory provisions, is beyond doubt. In fact, it should be emphasised that the disadvantages related to age constitute an additional argument for the possibility of applying these measures, whose purposes are to ensure the regularity of civil law transactions, and to protect their vulnerable actors. Therefore, it should be pointed out that the current legal system envisions protective mechanisms to defend against defective legal acts and prevent the violation of the principles of community life. Consequently, full legal incapacitation of an elderly person does not appear to be necessary, in order to protect their rights and interests.

Under certain circumstances, the effective utilisation of these legal instruments may be problematic, especially where lasting old-age dementia makes impossible the unaided discernment of defective legal acts. The disadvantages of old age, and its associated lack of assertiveness in the pursuit of rights and claims, make a case for implementing legal remedies to support elderly persons in their legal transactions.[14] This role could be filled by an attorney-in-fact, appointed for an elderly person. The attorney would ensure that legal acts performed by the elderly person were legally valid, and intervene if necessary, including through the courts, to protect the interests of the elderly person.[15]

3. MEASURES FOR ELDER PROTECTION IN FAMILY LAW

The provisions of the Polish Family and Guardianship Code (PFGC) concerning the institution of marriage do not introduce special solutions to take account

---

[13] More in A. DOLIWA, *Funkcje zasad współżycia społecznego*, C.H. Beck, 2021, p. 47.
[14] See M. BALWICKA-SZCZYRBA and A. SYLWESTRZAK, above n. 5, p. 166.
[15] See ibid. See also M. BALWICKA-SZCZYRBA, *Ubezwłasnowolnienie całkowite osoby starszej* (in press).

of advanced age. However, the disabilities of the elderly, both in the physical and psychological senses, trigger a number of general protective instruments designed to prevent the defective celebration of marriage; counteract its defective functioning; and prevent the dissolution of marriage, where this would harm the spouse's legally protected personal interests.

First of all, it should be pointed out that full legal incapacitation and mental illness are impediments to marriage (Articles 11 and 12 of the PFGC). Due to the lack of a universal register of incapacitated persons, as well as the ease of concealing mental disorders from the registrar of marriages, these circumstances are difficult to verify during the marriage ceremony, and may potentially lead to a celebration of a defective marriage. In the case of elderly persons suffering from old-age dementia who are not fully legally incapacitated, the application of Article 12 of the PFGC is problematic, since it is unclear whether dementia, which is an age-related decline in mental ability, meets the prerequisites of mental illness to preclude marriage. Indeed, dementia is a symptom that can be caused by a number of diseases, such as Alzheimer's disease, or vascular and other diseases,[16] but is not in itself an illness.[17] Accordingly, there is a body of scholarship in support of the view that, since the premise of Article 12 of the PFGC should be narrowly construed,[18] dementia should not be considered to fulfil the premise.[19] The doubts related to the determination of the scope of impediments to marriage under Article 12 of the PFGC arise mainly from the term 'mental illness', which from the medical point of view is outdated, and which scholars advocate should be replaced by the modern concept of 'mental disorder'.[20] It has even been postulated that Article 12 of the PFGC should be repealed as discriminating against mentally disabled persons, since the verification of legal validity of marriage should be based on the examination of the occurrence of defects in the declaration of intent at the celebration of marriage, rather than on the rigid criterion of mental illness.[21]

A defective celebration of marriage by an elderly person suffering from dementia may also arise from the occurrence of one of the defects in the declaration of intent, as listed in Article 15[1] of the PFGC, in particular the

---

[16] J. ANDREWS, *Demencja. Kompleksowy przewodnik po chorobie*, Harmonia Universalis Publishing House, 2017, pp. 28–33.

[17] T. GABRYELEWICZ, 'Czym jest otępienie?' in T. GABRYELEWICZ, A. BARCZAK and M. BARCIKOWSKA (eds.), *Otępienie w praktyce*, Termedia Wydawnictwa Medyczne, 2017, p. 11.

[18] A. ZIELONACKI, in H. DOLECKI and T. SOKOŁOWSKI (eds.), *Kodeks rodzinny i opiekuńczy. Commentary*, a Wolters Kluwer business, 2010, p. 55.

[19] M. BALWICKA-SZCZYRBA, 'Sytuacja osób starszych w prawie rodzinnym i opiekuńczym' in J. ŁUKASIEWICZ and M. ZAŁUCKI (eds.), *Prawo rodzinne i spadkowe wobec współczesnych zjawisk technologicznych i społecznych*, Adam Marszałek Publishing House, 2018, p. 212.

[20] M. BALWICKA-SZCZYRBA and A. SYLWESTRZAK, above n. 5, no. 40, pp. 151–167.

[21] A. SYLWESTRZAK, *Konwencja o prawach osób niepełnosprawnych a unormowania Kodeksu rodzinnego i opiekuńczego*, Acta Iuris Stetinensis, 2014, no. 6, pp. 611–623.

existence of a state precluding conscious declaration of intent, or error as to the other party's identity. Marriage by persons suffering from dementia may lead to a number of undesirable outcomes, for example where the mental disorder of a prospective spouse involves difficulty identifying other people (for example, they might mistake a nursing home room-mate for a loved one). Also, an elderly person's mental disorder can be deliberately exploited by another person who induces the senior citizen into marriage in the hope of an inheritance. While a spouse can petition for dissolution of marriage, based on PFGC provisions on divorce, only spouses can do so, making it difficult, if not impossible, for spouses suffering from mental illness to do so. In order to protect the elderly effectively, therefore, it would be advantageous to classify the above scenarios as grounds for the annulment of marriage, since public prosecutors are empowered to motion the court for annulment.

Dementia also adversely affects the ability to manage one's own assets, such as paying bills or accepting payments from third parties. Article 29 of the PFGC introduces the institution of statutory spousal representation,[22] whereby a spouse affected by a temporary impediment may have the other spouse appointed to act on their behalf in day-to-day affairs, as long as the spouses live together, and unless the affected spouse opposes the appointment. This arrangement helps the affected spouse manage their personal property in order to preserve the continuity of management and prevent damage. However, its application in the event of one of the spouses being afflicted with old-age dementia raises doubts, as it is premised on the temporary (and therefore reversible, though not necessarily short-lived) nature of the impediment.[23] It should be noted that, in the initial period of dementia, the affected person's mental condition is variable, with periods of distress interspersed with episodes of full mental capacity, making it possible to argue that the premise under Article 29 of the PFGC has been fulfilled. The non-affected spouse may then act as a legal representative to assist the other spouse in difficult times. However, as dementia deteriorates, the disordered state becomes progressively worse, such that the impediment suffered by the elderly person becomes permanent rather than temporary. At this stage, a problem may arise as to the legal validity of the other spouse's assumption of management activities, if they have not obtained a power of attorney, and it cannot now be obtained due to the potential principal's mental disorder. In such a situation, it would be permissible to apply for full legal incapacitation; however,

---

[22] S. Szer, *Prawo rodzinne*, Państwowe Wydawnictwo Naukowe, 1966, p. 93. This concept was subsequently adopted by other authors.

[23] M. Jadczak-Żebrowska, *Prawa i obowiązki małżonków*, Wolters Kluwer, 2017, p. 160. Illness of the spouse is given as an example of such an impediment: Supreme Court resolution of 24.05.2012, II CSK 466/11, LEX No. 1211145. See also P. Bodył-Szymala and M. Wojcieszak, *Ustawowy ustrój majątkowy po nowelizacji k.r.o. z perspektywy stosunków prawnych z udziałem banków*, Prawo Bankowe, 2005, no. 10, p. 39.

this is not standard practice in Polish society, as often the affected spouse remains under the de facto custody of the unaffected spouse, who continues to exercise management responsibility even after the affected spouse's condition has eliminated the original legal basis for doing so. The non-affected spouse can, therefore, continue to have access to the affected spouse's bank account for household expenses, as well as contracting household repairs or improvements on their behalf. This continued activity by the non-affected spouse is necessary to secure the existence, treatment and recovery of the affected spouse. However, the legal validity of this spousal activity usually goes unchallenged, due to the absence of interested parties, so the effects of these defective acts persist. On a positive note, this situation prevents legal incapacitation, which could be perceived by a spouse suffering from dementia as an infringement of their independence and dignity, reducing them to what they see as a helpless object. As a result, it should be considered desirable to allow the non-affected spouse to continue the ordinary management of the personal property of the spouse suffering from dementia, despite the fact that their mental disorder has deteriorated. It would, therefore, be appropriate to reform the regulation of the statutory representation of spouses, by extending it to cover cases in which the impediment suffered by one spouse has become permanent. After all, a permanent impediment often implies the spouse's continuing need for assistance in asset management. It should also be borne in mind that a spouse who receives such assistance will not, as a rule, be in a position to properly control the actions of their spouse, and it would therefore be necessary to ensure adequate external supervision. It would, therefore, appear that, in view of the risk of damage to the interests of the spouse suffering from a permanent impediment, the empowerment of the other spouse should not arise by operation of the law, as is the case for a temporary impediment, but should instead be court-ordered. The guardianship court would make a comprehensive assessment of the situation of the person with dementia, as well as the needs of the family, enabling the other spouse to represent the person with dementia either to the existing extent, or to the extent individually specified in the order. The granting of such a power of attorney would, under Article 12 of the UN Convention on the Rights of Persons with Disabilities, require it to be subject to periodic judicial review, while the duties of the empowered spouse could be given a form similar to the reporting duties of a guardian, which primarily include the submission of periodic reports, including an account of the management. It should be possible for the court to grant the mandate either for an indefinite period of time or for a fixed period of time; in the latter case, the possibility of a further extension would arise after the end date. It would be advisable to shape this institution as flexibly as possible, to match the circumstances of the specific case.

Slightly less problematic are the consequences of spousal dementia with regard to management of joint spousal property, since, as a rule, each spouse is entitled to perform acts of management with respect to the property (Article 36§2 of the PFGC), and this competence is independent of the analogous competence of the spouse.[24] Therefore, if one spouse ceases to manage the property, the other spouse can take over the entire management without the need for additional authorisation. A spouse suffering from dementia is often incapable of active participation in the management and running of the household, resulting in a de facto extension of the freedom of the other spouse, henceforth unhindered by the risk of objection to their intended activities (Article 36[1] of the PFGC). The limits of this freedom are then designated by a set of actions requiring mandatory spousal consent, as listed in Article 37 of the PFGC. If, due to dementia, the spouse cannot give informed consent, their declaration must be replaced by a court order under Article 39 of the PFGC.[25] The regulations on the management of joint property, under which the non-affected spouse may take over the majority of management activities without additional authorisation, enable matrimonial property regimes (statutory and contractual property regimes) to better protect the interests of the affected spouse than property separation regimes. In the latter, there is no statutory authority for a spouse to manage personal property in the event of the permanent exclusion from management activities of the other spouse; the spouses should, therefore, in anticipation of future complications, give each other authority to perform legal acts in the event that one of them is afflicted with a mental disorder.

Also notable is the issue of elderly divorce.[26] Advanced age, as such, is not recognised in case law as an impediment to divorce.[27] However, in specific circumstances, and especially when, in the case of a significant age difference between the spouses, the younger spouse applies for divorce from the older spouse, and the main motive for doing so is the desire to avoid the hardship of providing assistance to the ageing partner, a divorce may prove to be inadmissible on the grounds of conflict with the principles of community life (Article 56§2 of the PFGC).[28] Indeed, age, health, and especially an incurable illness of the spouse, make up the totality of the circumstances considered by the court when assessing the admissibility of divorce from an ethical point of view.

The material needs of an elderly person are primarily secured, under family law, by the maintenance obligation, which is primarily incumbent on the spouse,

---

[24] More extensively, in K. GOŁĘBIOWSKI, *Zarząd majątkiem wspólnym majątków małżonków*, a Wolters Kluwer business, 2012, pp. 308–311; and A. SYLWESTRZAK, in M. BALWICKA-SZCZYRBA (ed.), *Zarząd majątkiem wspólnym. Komentarz*, Warsaw, 2016, p. 290.

[25] The present case fulfils the prerequisite for judicial interference in the management of joint property, which Art. 39 of the PFGC defines as 'insurmountable obstacles to communication with the spouse'.

[26] In 2021, the number of divorces between spouses over 60 years of age was 3,661, representing 7.1% of the total number of divorces in Poland: *Demographic Yearbook of Poland*, Główny Urząd Statystyczny, 2021, p. 240.

[27] Appellate Court Judgment, Poznań, 5.10.2004, I ACa 683/04, LEX No. 163577.

[28] M. BALWICKA-SZCZYRBA, above n. 19, pp. 214–216.

even after divorce (Article 60 of the PFGC),[29] as well as after separation. The maintenance obligation of separated spouses is always indefinite, whereas after divorce, it expires five years after the divorce is pronounced, except when one spouse has been found to be at fault for the breakdown of the marital relationship, in which case it continues indefinitely. This time-frame may, however, be extended by the court at the request of the entitled person, but only on account of exceptional circumstances. Exceptional circumstances do not include events that normally occur in a person's life, such as the ageing process,[30] so the process of worsening dementia does not warrant an extension of the maintenance obligation beyond the statutory five-year term. Failing that, the next step for the elderly person should be to claim maintenance from descendants, ascendants, siblings, and possibly stepchildren. Due to the lengthening of the human lifespan, a phenomenon has emerged whereby both living parents and their children are elderly, and if both of these generational groups become destitute, they may turn to their descendants for maintenance, which can put a significant strain on the grandchildren and great-grandchildren, especially given the reduced number of offspring in modern families.[31] In addition to the maintenance obligation, parents and children are obliged to respect and support each other (Article 87 of the PFGC), so elderly parents can expect assistance not only in the form of means of subsistence, but also in the form of support and assistance, for example in the use of electronic devices, the internet, entering into contracts, etc. A single, destitute elderly person with no spouse or relatives may, therefore, find themselves in a difficult situation, without being able to benefit from a maintenance claim or a claim for personal support.

In addition to statutory inheritance in the fourth group (in the first group are descendants and spouses; in the second, parents; and in the third group siblings and descendants of siblings), the law of succession provides grandparents with recourse to a maintenance claim, as set out in Article 938 of the Polish Civil Code, known as a quasi-maintenance claim,[32] that operates against the heirs of a deceased grandchild, as long as the grandparents are destitute and cannot obtain maintenance from persons on whom such an obligation rests.[33] The obligation

---

[29] The amount of the maintenance award on divorce depends on which one of the spouses has been pronounced to be at fault in the divorce decree; the obligation continues until the beneficiary remarries. More extensively, see A. Sylwestrzak, *Obowiązek alimentacyjny rozwiedzionego małżonka ponoszącego wyłączną winę rozkładu pożycia*, Gdańskie Studia Prawnicze, 2005 r., vol. XIV, pp. 851–865.

[30] Supreme Court Judgment of 29.07.2020, I UK 10/19, OSNP, 2021, no. 4, item 45.

[31] M. Balwicka-Szczyrba, above n. 19, p. 219; M. Łączkowska, *Prawo alimentacyjne jako przykład regulacji prawnej solidarności międzypokoleniowej*, RPEiS, 2012, no. 3, pp. 165–173.

[32] See J. Kremis and E. Gniewek, in E. Gniewek (ed.), *Kodeks cywilny. Komentarz*, C.H.Beck, 2011, p. 1550.

[33] For a broader discussion of the grandparents' entitlement and its relation to their statutory inheritance, see A. Sylwestrzak, *Sytuacja prawna dziadków w świetle norm prawa spadkowego*, Gdańskie Studia Prawnicze, 2011, vol. XXVI, pp. 426–430; see also J. Haberko,

passes to the heir of the grandchild; this could be, for example, the grandchild's spouse. The obligor is obliged to provide the grandparent with maintenance in the form of periodic cash or in-kind payments.[34] This provision supplements the maintenance protection system by extending the circle of persons obliged to support an elderly person. However, we are not dealing here with a maintenance claim in the strict sense of the term, due to the specific nature of the obligation, i.e. the obligation originates not so much from the family relationship with the beneficiary, but from succession from a grandchild; the responsibility is distributed among the inheritors in proportion to their share in the inheritance, and the debtor may discharge the obligation by making a single payment of an amount corresponding to the value of one-quarter of the debtor's inheritance share. This protection cannot be barred by a legal act, including by the testator's will,[35] nor does it become time-barred, as the claim can materialise even long after the opening of the inheritance.[36] Humanitarian considerations designed to protect the elderly from destitution have led to postulates for an extended construal of Article 938 of the Polish Civil Code, by awarding an extended scope of protection to great-grandparents as well;[37] moreover, an amendment is postulated which would grant analogous rights to the parents of the testator.[38]

4. SUMMARY

In view of the visible process of ageing of the Polish population, it is necessary to revise the existing legal regulations in order to provide this social group with the broadest possible protection. As they are an inherently weaker social group, supporting them will help to mitigate the risk of their discrimination, while also having a positive impact on the certainty of legal transactions involving senior citizens.

The analysis of the regulations of the Polish Civil Code and the PFGC leads to the conclusion that Polish law contains favourable regulations, both general

---

Dziadkowie-wnuki. Osobista więź prawnorodzinna i relacja prawnospadkowa, RPEiS, 2012, no. 3, pp. 149–152.

34   The admissibility of non-monetary benefits is supported by A. KALLAUS, *W kwestii uprawienia dziadków spadkobiercy przewidzianego w art. 938 i 966 k.c.*, Rzeszowskie Zeszyty Naukowe, 1993, no. 3, pp. 141 and 143.

35   See ibid., p. 144; J. STRZEBIŃCZYK, *Roszczenia dziadków spadkobiercy według art. 938 i 966 k.c.*, Nowe Prawo, 1980, no. 1, p. 80.

36   On the other hand, awarded claims that have already fallen due are time-barred after six years (Art. 125), and contractually agreed claims are time-barred under Art. 118 after three years, as claims for periodic benefits.

37   K. OSAJDA, in K. OSAJDA (ed.), *Kodeks cywilny. Komentarz*, vol. 3, C.H.Beck 2013, p. 475.

38   P. KSIĘŻAK, *Zachowek w polskim prawie spadkowym*, LexisNexis, 2012, p. 72; A. SYLWESTRZAK, above n. 33, p. 429.

and specific, concerning protection of the lawful interests of weaker parties, including senior citizens. The legal instruments discussed in the present study seem to adequately counteract the potential negative effects resulting from progressive medical conditions, such as infirmity or dementia, in the areas of both civil and family law.

It is also possible to identify areas that require new solutions for the elderly. In particular, it was noted that problems may arise with effective use of the institutions envisioned in the law, especially where ongoing old-age dementia prevents independent discernment of irregular legal transactions. The disadvantages of old age, and its associated lack of assertiveness in the pursuit of rights and claims, make a case for implementing legal remedies to support elderly persons in their legal transactions, in particular the institution of an attorney for the elderly.

In conclusion, it should be emphasised that the present authors believe there is a definite need to abandon the institution of incapacitation for the elderly, as an institution which excessively interferes with the legal situation of senior citizens, and to replace it with institutions based on assisted decision-making, such as an attorney for the elderly. There is no doubt that the aim of modern legislation should be to support senior citizens so that they can actively participate in civil law transactions and social life for as long as possible.

UNITED STATES AND ISRAEL

THE RIGHT TO PRIVACY

A Comparative Legal Analysis Marking the End to US Legal Exceptionalism

Pamela Laufer-Ukeles[*]

Résumé

Dans cet article, l'auteur soutient que si l'affaire *Dobbs v. Jackson Women's Health* concerne le droit à l'avortement, sa portée est exponentiellement plus large. Elle marque la fin de l'exception juridique américaine, telle que personnifiée dans la sanctification du droit au respect de la vie privée. Contrairement à ceux qui soutiennent que le droit à l'avortement aurait dû être fondé sur le droit à l'intégrité corporelle, à l'égalité ou à l'autonomie, l'auteur affirme que le juge Blackmun a eu tout à fait raison dans la décision *Griswold v. Connecticut* : seul le droit au respect de la vie privée peut protéger l'individu des interrogatoires et de l'humiliation et conférer ainsi aux citoyens le droit d'être « laissés en paix » en tenant l'État à distance. L'invocation du droit au respect de la vie privée est particulièrement pertinent en matière familiale, cette dernière constituant le principal domaine dans lequel ce droit est protégé. L'affaiblissement du droit au respect de la vie privée aura très certainement des répercussions dans les nombreuses situations dans lesquelles il

---

* Professor of Law and Public Health, Academic College of Law and Science, Hod Hasharon, Israel.

est mis en balance avec une vie potentielle, y compris en-dehors de l'avortement : contrôle des naissances, droits des femmes en matière de soins et de santé pendant la grossesse, poursuites pénales contre les femmes enceintes, hypothèses de vie et de naissance illicites, gestation pour autrui et PMA, pour n'en citer que quelques-uns. Un tel affaiblissement aura également, en toute logique, des répercussions sur les cas dans lesquels le droit au respect de la vie privée n'est pas seulement mis en balance avec une vie potentielle, mais avec la vie réelle des enfants. En effet, en matière d'éducation, de soins, de santé et d'autres décisions ayant des conséquences sur les enfants, l'affaire *Dobbs* provoque également, aux États-Unis, un affaiblissement des prérogatives liées au droit au respect de la vie privée des parents. Bien que cela puisse être bénéfique à certains égards, notamment en ce que cela permet à l'État de protéger les droits des enfants, il en résulte également un paternalisme lourd, un État qui contrôle tout et impose une vision unique de l'intérêt supérieur des enfants.

Pour parfaire cette analyse, l'auteur oppose le système juridique américain sur l'avortement et les droits parentaux, au système juridique beaucoup plus interventionniste et paternaliste d'Israël, dans lequel les décisions en matière d'avortement sont prises par un comité devant lequel les femmes doivent comparaître. Quant aux décisions relatives aux enfants en matière de soins et de santé, lorsque les parents ne sont pas d'accord avec les médecins, elles sont régulièrement prises par l'État après avis des tribunaux sur l'intérêt supérieur de l'enfant dans l'affaire en cause. Cette comparaison permet de clarifier l'ampleur des pertes résultant de l'affaire *Dobbs* et de démontrer le potentiel changement radical de la notion de vie privée aux États-Unis ainsi que ses répercussions mondiales. En effet, en Israël, dans l'ombre de l'arrêt *Dobbs*, le corps législatif a adopté de nouvelles réglementations visant à accroître la protection de la vie privée des femmes dans le processus d'avortement, démontrant ainsi l'impact potentiel de la jurisprudence américaine sur la procédure régulière substantielle, autrefois phare de la protection de la vie privée familiale, et sur la façon dont le droit au respect de la vie privée est perçu et défendu dans le monde entier.

1. US LEGAL EXCEPTIONALISM AND THE RIGHT TO PRIVACY

This chapter will argue that beyond (just) curtailing access to abortion, *Dobbs v. Jackson Women's Whole Health* is especially significant for its impact on the constitutional right to privacy.[1] In *Dobbs*, the Court held that the right to have an abortion is not constitutionally protected by the right to privacy because

---

[1]   *Dobbs v. Jackson Whole Health*, No. 19-1392, 597 US ___(2022).

abortion involves potential life.[2] Prior to the *Dobbs* holding, the right to privacy had been crafted and protected in US jurisprudence in a manner that made the US legal system exceptional in providing a heightened protection for the privacy of personal judgement, and of individual world views. By harming this protected right, *Dobbs* changed something fundamental in the US legal tradition.

This introductory section 1 sets out the thesis that the right to privacy was precisely the right basis upon which to grant the right to abortion, and that its curtailment diminishes US legal exceptionality. Section 2 will sharpen the importance of the right to privacy, by comparing the US protection of privacy in the context of abortion, overturned by *Dobbs*, to the abortion process in Israel. Section 3 will discuss the impact of the curtailment of privacy in *Dobbs* in other contexts where potential life is relevant, and where the State's interest in the actual life of children is present. In section 4, I will conclude where I started, by explaining why *Dobbs* signals the end of US legal exceptionalism. I will use a comparative frame, by highlighting the way privacy has been exceptionally pronounced and characteristic of the US legal system, and contrasting it with the mitigated privacy and paternalism in the Israeli legal system.

The right to privacy was established in the seminal case of *Griswold v. Connecticut*.[3] Prosecuted for distributing birth control to married couples, Griswold argued that the state law prohibiting such distribution, and the use of birth control by married couples, was unconstitutional. The Supreme Court agreed with Griswold that the statute was unconstitutional, but the grandeur of the case lies in the basis of this decision. Justice Douglas argued that the law violated the 'right to privacy' – but the right to privacy is not written anywhere in the US constitution. Instead, he explained that, 'the foregoing cases suggest specific guarantees in the Bill of Rights have penumbras formed by emanations from those guarantees that help give them life and substance'.[4] Essentially, the right to privacy can be understood from the Bill of Rights more generally – it is an essential part of the US constitutional system, and does not even need to be explicitly mentioned. On the one hand, this perhaps weakens the right, as it is left unrooted to any specific amendment, although it was later held to be derived from the Fourteenth Amendment Due Process Clause, as part of substantive due process.[5] Indeed, scholars have argued that penumbras are a 'flimsy' basis for a grounding of any right.[6]

---

2 Ibid., at 32.

3 *Griswold v. Connecticut*, 381 US 479 (1965).

4 Ibid., at 484.

5 *Poe v. Ullman*, 367 US 497, 523 (1961) (Harlan, J., dissenting) (noting that Connecticut's anti-birth control laws 'violate[d] the Fourteenth Amendment, in that they deprive[d] appellants of life, liberty, or property without due process'); *Griswold*, 381 US, at 500 (Harlan, J., concurring).

6 'Penumbras and emanations are a flimsy foundation for fundamental rights, which is why they never again have been mentioned by the Court. We believe it would have been far better

On the other hand, there is something prescient about recognising that the right to privacy is so fundamental to the US constitutional framework that it does not need mentioning. Indeed, the reason that there were no enumerated rights in the original US Constitution was because to enumerate those rights would be to limit them; whatever rights were not granted to the government were to be retained by the people. In his concurrence in *Griswold*, Justice Goldberg emphasised this point in addressing the intent of James Madison in drafting the Ninth Amendment: 'It was proffered to quiet expressed fears that a bill of specifically enumerated rights could not be sufficiently broad to cover all essential rights and that the specific mention of certain rights would be interpreted as a denial that others were protected.'[7] This basic premise of the US Constitution reinforces the sense that the essence of privacy – the right to be left alone, free of State interference – is so essential to the constitutional framework that to mention it only weakens its primacy to the constitutional framework. A right as fundamental as decision-making on intimate subjects like what occurs in the bedroom between married persons remains firmly in the realm of privacy, protected from state law regardless of the precise words of the Constitution.

Thereafter, this right to privacy was developed through a series of US cases over the 50 years following *Griswold*. The right to privacy was expanded in *Eisenstadt v. Baird*, where the right to use birth control was extended to non-married individuals.[8] The Court held, 'if the right to privacy means anything, it is the right of the individual, married or single, to be free from unwarranted governmental intrusion into matters so fundamentally affecting a person as the decision whether to bear or beget a child'.[9] Essentially, the right to privacy encapsulates the driving constitutional force in the US: that government should be limited, and has no place in the bedrooms of its citizens, in weighing in on questions of marriage and family, in telling a citizen how best to live, or in questioning a citizen's judgement. It is a right grounded in anti-paternalism and anti-government control, at its very core.

This right to privacy was extended to include the right to abortion in *Roe v. Wade*.[10] In *Roe*, the Court held that, at least until the third trimester of a pregnancy, at which time a foetus becomes viable outside the womb of the

---

for the Court to explain why reproductive autonomy is safeguarded under the liberty right of the Due Process Clause, as Justice Harlan urged.': E. CHEMERINSKY and M. GOODWIN, 'Abortion: A Woman's Private Choice' (2017) 95 *Texas L. Rev.* 1189, 1202.

7   301 US, at 492.

8   *Eisenstadt v. Baird*, 405 US 438 (1972); *Cassey v. Planned Parenthood*, 505 US 833 (1992), at 851 (freedom to make 'intimate and personal choices' that are 'central to personal dignity and autonomy').

9   405 US, at 453.

10   *Roe v. Wade*, 410 US 113 (1973).

woman, a woman's right to privacy protects her right to abort, and overwhelms any interest of the State in the unborn foetus. Justice Blackmun, writing for the majority, explained,

> [t]his right of privacy, whether it be founded in the Fourteenth Amendment's concept of personal liberty and restrictions upon state action, as we feel it is, or ... in the Ninth Amendment's reservation of rights to the people, is broad enough to encompass a woman's decision whether or not to terminate her pregnancy.[11]

Justice Blackmun further explained that banning or limiting abortion for the sake of the foetus, prior to the third trimester, unconstitutionally violates the woman's right to privacy by imposing on a woman's decision-making in a manner that burdens her physical and emotional state.

The right to privacy's reach in protecting abortion was limited but also reinforced in *Cassey v. Planned Parenthood*,[12] which held that State interests in protecting foetal life were valid beginning at the time of conception. Therefore, based on balancing the valid State interests in foetal life against a woman's right to privacy, regulations put into place to restrict abortion – such as informed consent statutes, waiting periods, and procedural and administrative requirements that limit access and create burdens on women – are constitutionally valid. However, the ultimate choice (the privacy) of the pregnant woman remains intact prior to the point of viability and, thus, regardless of procedural hurdles, women must retain the choice to abort until viability, at which point abortion can be banned.

The right to privacy is elicited in particularly self-defining and self-actualising choices. As the Court in *Cassey* explained, '[a]t the heart of liberty is the right to define one's own concept of existence, of meaning, of the universe, and of the mystery of human life.'[13] The right to privacy has been held to be fundamental, especially in the context of marital, sexual and reproductive matters.[14] In sum, the right to privacy involves a constitutional right to personal, self-defining choices, which has been held to include the right to birth control, abortion, marriage, reproduction and child-raising.

Still, there are those that argue that privacy is too amorphous, and was the wrong hook on which to hang the right to abortion. Abortion is not private in the same manner as the intimate privacy of the bedroom, referred to in *Griswold*. It is much more public, and requires surgical intervention by a doctor. Accordingly, scholars have argued that privacy is not an appropriate ground for anchoring the right to abortion, and that a stronger constitutional base could have more firmly

---

[11]   Ibid., at 153.
[12]   *Cassey v. Planned Parenthood*, 505 US 833 (1992).
[13]   Ibid., at 851.
[14]   See, e.g. *State v. Bair*, No. 1997 CA 00232, 1999 WL 99032 (Ohio Ct. App., 1 Feb. 1999) (holding that the right to privacy does not apply in the context of harm to reputation caused by registering sexual predators).

secured the right.[15] I will explain why I disagree with this criticism and believe that privacy was precisely the right frame for protecting abortion and the other personal self-defining choices it captures. I will do this by considering alternative frames for grounding the right to abortion, thereby sharpening the scope and particular attributes of the right to privacy and clarifying the importance of this right.

Some argue that the right to abortion should have been based on the right to bodily integrity.[16] However, the right to abortion under the banner of privacy reaches further than merely the right to privacy of the body, which includes freedom from unjustified search and seizure,[17] the need for informed consent,[18] the protection of genetic information,[19] and the right to ingest what one wants,[20] among other protections of bodily integrity. For instance, the right to privacy is not constrained by issues impacting the body, and thus may include the right to determine what to do with gametes or frozen embryos, even when they have been separated from the body.[21] Basing the right to abortion on bodily integrity, although also implicated, narrows the scope and import of that right. The right to abortion is not just about the body; it is about the protected nature of the decision.

---

[15] See R. West, 'From Choice to Reproductive Justice: De-Constitutionalizing Abortion Rights' (2009) 118 *Yale L.J.* 1394; L.R. BeVier, 'What Privacy is Not' (1989) 12 *Harv. J. L. & Pub. Pol'y* 99, 101–102.

[16] See, e.g. *Preterm Cleveland v. Voinovich*, 89 Ohio App. 684, 627 N.E.2d 570 (1993) ('regulation of abortion inherently impacts on a right to bodily integrity. A state's effort to compel birth, for instance, subjects females to the tremendous demands and the innate risks of reproduction, an unquestionably indelible event for any living organism, and especially for a woman in our society.'); E. McDonagh, *Breaking the Abortion Deadlock: From Choice to Consent*, Oxford University Press, 1996, p. 6.

[17] See, e.g. *John M. v. Paula T.*, 524 Pa. 306 (1990) (right to bodily integrity includes right to be free of searches and seizures in the context of compelled DNA test); In re *Proceeding under Article 10 of Fam. Ct. Act Nassau Cnty. Dep't of Soc. Servs. ex rel. C.R.*, 873 N.Y.S.2d 513, at 2 (Fam. Ct. 2008) ('when the government seeks to discover evidence by means which intrude upon a person's bodily integrity, the government action implicates the Fourth Amendment prohibition against unreasonable searches and seizures, and should be justified by probable cause that the evidence is reasonably related to establishing the allegations in the petition.').

[18] See, e.g. *Matter of Conroy*, 98 N.J. 321, 486 A.2d 1209, 1222 (1985) (stating that '[t]he doctrine of informed consent is a primary means developed in the law to protect [the] personal interest in the integrity of one's body.'); See *Johnson v. Kokemor*, 199 Wis.2d 615, 628 (1996) (The doctrine of informed consent 'arose from and reflected the fundamental notion of the right to bodily integrity.').

[19] See, e.g. *State v. Surge*, 160 Wash. 2d 65, 72 (2007) (linking DNA with rights to bodily integrity).

[20] See, e.g. *Minnesota State Bd. of Health by Lawson v. City of Brainerd*, 308 Minn. 24, 36–37 (1976).

[21] See *Davis v. Davis*, 842 S.W.2d 588 (Tenn. 1992), on rehearing in part, No. 34, 1992 WL 341632 (Tenn., 23 Nov. 1992) (discussing the extension of the right to privacy to the right to determine what to do with frozen embryos).

Others argue that the right to abortion should have been grounded in the right to make autonomous choices more specifically than the general amorphous 'right to privacy'.[22] However, the right to abortion is not just about the right to ultimately decide, or to assert one's will; it is about the right to be left alone from uncomfortable interactions with the State – to be given liberty to decide without State interference. It is about privacy in decision-making. Urging that *Roe* protects the privacy of reproductive decision-making, and not just 'privacy', Chemerinsky and Goodwin argue that: 'The best approach to the abortion issue is for the Court to declare that the decision whether to have an abortion is a private judgment which the state may not encourage, discourage, or prohibit.'[23] One can still have the right to choose but be besieged by pressures and interference from the State, which undermines that right. Thus, in *Cassey*, informed consent policies that flooded women with potentially unwanted information were allowed to infringe privacy only because of foetal interests. And in *Gonzales*, the Court directly interfered with such privacy by paternalistically presuming to make the choice for the woman, indicating that she would regret the abortion.[24] The right to privacy involves freedom from State coercion, imposition, interrogation and influence that can squelch individual identity.[25] This does not mean that the State should not enable or inform persons in making private choices; however, such assistance cannot be coercively imposed or reflect biases, harassment or threats, without infringing the right to privacy.[26]

Moreover, privacy is most concerned when issues of identity are at stake, as opposed to other choices where autonomy alone may be at stake.[27] For instance, the right to make health care decisions involving a person's medical preferences may have more to do with the right to autonomy than the right to privacy – it

---

[22] See A. ALLEN, 'Taking Liberties: Privacy, Private Choice, and Social Contract Theory' (1987) 56 *U. Cin. L. Rev.* 461, 467 (stating that abortion is about autonomy not privacy).

[23] E. CHEMERINSKY and M. GOODWIN, 'Abortion: A Woman's Private Choice' (2017) 95 *Tex. L. Rev.* 1189, 1202–1203 (discussing the lack of mention of reproductive autonomy in *Griswold*).

[24] *Gonzalez v. Carhart*, 550 US 124, 133, 141, 159 (2007) ('Respect for human life finds an ultimate expression in the bond of love the mother has for her child ... While we find no reliable data to measure the phenomenon, it seems unexceptionable to conclude some women come to regret their choice to abort the infant life they once created and sustained. Severe depression and loss of esteem can follow.').

[25] See *Olmstead v. United States*, 277 US 438, 478 (characterising 'the right to be left alone' as 'the right most valued by civilized men'); *Bellotti v. Baird*, 443 US 622, 634 (1979) (parental autonomy is basic to the structure of our society because the family is 'the institution by which we inculcate and pass down many of our most cherished values, morals and cultural'.); See L. HENKIN, 'Privacy and Autonomy' (1974) 34 *Colum. L. Rev.* 1410, 1425.

[26] P. LAUFER-UKELES, 'Reproductive Choices and Informed Consent: Fetal Interests, Women's Identity and Relational Autonomy' (2011) 31 *American Journal of Law and Medicine*, 567, 607–620 (discussing how reproductive choices need affirmative support in order to be truly informed and consensual).

[27] See *Eisesenstadt v. Baird*, 405 US, at 453 (privacy applies to only those 'matters ... fundamentally affecting a person').

can be based on stated desires, a living will or substituted judgement.[28] On the other hand, the cases of incompetent patients or infant children, who do not have their own desires to assert, may have more to do with the right to privacy, as parents or guardians must define that persons' very identity free of State imposition of values. The difference between the two situations is important. In the first scenario, the person has a will that has either been clearly expressed or can be inferred, and what is important is that their will be implemented with the assistance of the State; that is, autonomy. In the second situation, there is no will to be asserted; rather, there is a right of the guardian or parent to shape the identity of the person without State interference; that is, the right to privacy. There is overlap between autonomy and privacy, but they are distinct.

Finally, some argue that the right to an abortion should have been based on the right to equality.[29] However, the precedent of *Aiello v. Geduldig*[30] holds that legislation regarding pregnancy does not discriminate on the basis of sex, but rather on the basis of pregnant status. While separating pregnancy from gender may seem artificial, this precedent keeps restrictions on pregnancy separate from sex discrimination. Moreover, although they are linked, privacy has a different scope from equality. Admittedly, equality is undermined when privacy is lacking, because privacy is first invaded for those who have fewer funds and are more dependent on State assistance. Those who can use money to evade the need for State-regulated processes, such as abortion, health benefits, socio-economic benefits, etc., can retain privacy when more dependent persons cannot.[31] And such dependence will lead to interference in personal decision-making, including the possibility of the threat of punishment and shaming. Ultimately, privacy involves freedom from State involvement in personal decision-making that may involve shaming and the threat of punishment for individuals who do not conform to societal world views, and who are, therefore, treated unequally.[32] Still, equality does not capture the scope of the problem of

---

[28]   But see B.A. RICH, 'The Assault on Privacy on Healthcare Decisionmaking' (1991) 68 *Denv. U. L. Rev.* 1 (arguing that privacy is what is at stake in basic decisions of health care).

[29]   See, e.g. S.A. LAW, 'Rethinking Sex and the Constitution' (1984) 132 *U. Pa L. Rev.* 955; C.R. SUNSTEIN, 'Neutrality in Constitutional Law' (1992) 92 *Colum. L. Rev.* 1, 29–44, 27; A.L. ALLEN, 'The Proposed Equal Protection Fix for Abortion Law: Reflections on Citizenship, Gender and the Constitution' (1994–1995) 18 *Harv. J.L. & Pub. Pol'y* 419.

[30]   *Aiello v. Geduldig*, 417 US 484 (1974).

[31]   J. CARBONE and N. CAHN, 'The Triple System for Regulation Women's Reproduction' (2015) *J.L. Med. and Ethics* 275, 279–280 ('The result has little impact on the elite who, with enough money, can easily circumvent the restrictions. Instead, the restrictions make it that much harder for the poor to escape the circumstances that lock successive generations into poverty.').

[32]   See, e.g. *John Doe v. Poritz*, 142 N.J. 1, 89 (the right to privacy encompasses 'the right of an individual to be … protected from any wrongful suffering, shame or humiliation to a person of ordinary sensibilities').

State interference in individual identity involved in immoderate abortion bans; it only captures part of the problem.

Indeed, it is my contention that the fundamental right to privacy was precisely the right basis upon which to grant the right to abortion. Abortion is not just an expression of will, but an intimate, identity-forming decision, and women making such choices have a right to be free from State interference. Interference with abortion is more than an infraction on the body, and it is more than a violation of equality – it is a violation of a more fundamental kind into the private lives of women. And it is this right to privacy – the right to be free of State interference – that most reflects the distinct system of government in the US, in which the principle that unenumerated rights are retained for the people was put forth in the Ninth Amendment. Thus, I argue, the significant curtailment of the right to privacy in *Dobbs* undermines something fundamental about the exceptional focus on freedom and liberty from the State grounding the US constitutional system.

2. SHARPENING THE RIGHT TO PRIVACY BY CONTRASTING ACCESS TO ABORTION IN THE US AND ISRAEL

To sharpen the centrality of the right to privacy and its importance in the context of abortion, insight and perspective can be gained from considering what a legal system looks like in which privacy is not central to access to abortion. The regulation of abortion in Israel is governed by the Criminal Law, sections 312–321, situated after the discussion of murder.[33] Regulations further clarify that, in order to legally have an abortion in Israel, a specially appointed committee must approve such a request, and without such permission, an abortion is illegal.[34] Performing illegal abortions is considered a criminal violation punishable by up to five years in prison.[35]

Until a few months ago, according to abortion regulations governing the committee procedure, a woman had to list one of five potential reasons – age, illegitimacy, defect, physical or emotional harm, rape or incest – and then appear

---

[33] Penal Law (Isr.) 5737-1977.

[34] Penal Amendment (Termination of Pregnancy) of 1977, 5737-1977, SH No. 842 p. 70 (Isr.) (as amended); N. MORAG-LEVINE, 'Abortion in Israel: Community, Rights, and the Context of Compromise' (1994) 19 *Law & Soc. Inquiry* 313, 322; M. ZONSZEIN, 'Israel's Abortion Committees', *New York Times*, 12 June 2015, available at https://www.nytimes.com/2015/06/14/opinion/sunday/israels-abortion-committees.html [https://perma.cc/JD5S-TZZJ].

[35] Ibid.

before a committee, in order to receive permission to have an abortion.[36] In discussions with social workers, and in hearings, in order to justify her request for an abortion, a woman may be forced to reveal embarrassing information and answer questions about relationships with multiple partners, sexual behaviours and decisions about marriage.[37] While there are tricks of the trade (casting doubt about whether the husband is the father, or getting a psychological report about the emotional impact of another child), and about 98 per cent of such requests are permitted,[38] it is approximated that 50 per cent of abortions each year are performed illegally by paying a private doctor.[39] And this is the case even though legal abortions are funded by the State. Why?

It is the lack of privacy! Women do not want to appear in front of committees and be shamed for sexual acts that may include compromised circumstances, mistakes, improper behaviours, or just deep regret. The process in general, and the committee hearing in particular, was enacted as a form of oversight and even chastisement, to curb what were perceived as women's irresponsible behaviours.[40] These committees often took upon themselves the task of educating and shaming women for their 'problematic' choices.[41] For women, the choice to abort is incredibly difficult, and being faced with a committee which has the power to determine whether your decision is necessary and reasonable is humiliating and shame-inducing. Such a system of oversight has since been suggested, at least in part, by some politicians in the US, as a way to allow some instances of abortion.[42] Like in Israel, allowing exceptions to a ban means that someone will have to consider whether such exceptions apply. While exceptions may seem more moderate than full bans, they also come with invasive inquiries in basic tension with privacy. What was so sacred about the right to abort in the US was the way the federal constitution was understood to preserve the private decision-making rights of women – or, more precisely, the right not to be examined and overseen by the State while making such decisions. That is what

---

36   Ibid.
37   See D. AMIR and O. BENJAMIN, 'Defining Encounters: Who are the Women Entitled to Join the Israeli Collective?' (1997) 20 *Women's Stud. Int'l F.* 639, 644–645.
38   See N. RIMALT, 'When Rights Don't Talk: Abortion Law and the Politics of Compromise' (2017) 28 *Yale J. L. & Feminism* 327, 368–369.
39   See Y. YISHAI, 'Public Ideas and Public Policy: Abortion Politics in Four Democracies' (1993) 25 *Comp. Pol.* 207, 214–215; see also R. GHERT-ZAND, 'Black Market Abortions in Israel', *Forward*, 5 February 2013, http://forward.com/sisterhood/170506/black-market-abortions-in-israel/ [https://perma.cc/WR5P-A2CL].
40   See D. AMIR and O. BINIAMIN, 'Abortion Approval as a Ritual of Symbolic Control' in C. FEINMAN (ed.), *The Criminalization of a Woman's Body*, Routledge, 1992, pp. 5, 18.
41   See ibid., pp. 5–25.
42   See, e.g. K. BREUNINGER, 'Lindsey Graham's abortion ban bill baffles some Republicans as Democrats sharpen attacks in key midterm races', *Politics*, 16 September 2022 (Senator Graham proposes federal bill that would ban abortions after 15 weeks except for cases of rape, incest or threat to a mother's health).

the US had got right when treating abortion as an issue of the fundamental right to 'privacy', but has since abandoned.

Ironically, since the decision in *Dobbs*, Israel has decided to expand privacy in abortion decision-making.[43] New regulations were passed in June 2022 that altered somewhat the process for obtaining permission to receive an abortion.[44] During initial requests, women no longer need to indicate a reason, and unless the committee asks for a reason or an appearance, they can receive permission without standing before the committee. However, abortion is still not a constitutional right in Israel, but is governed by liberal and permissive legislation. Access to abortion is highly dependent on the discretion of these committees, which are still required, according to the primary criminal law, which has not been altered. Still, in practice, the changes instil more privacy into the system, after seeing in the US how privacy can be undermined, in *Dobbs*.

The privacy protected by the US is both exceptional and critical. In Israel, and in other Western democracies, reference to the right to privacy involves the right to bodily privacy – closer to bodily integrity and privacy of information.[45] The broad, self-defining concept of privacy entrenched in constitutional case law is distinct. Ultimately, the right to privacy protects human identity and individualism in areas of the law which, by definition, concern the most intimate of human activities and relationships. Decisions about whether to accomplish or prevent contraception, how to create a family, and how to raise children, are considered the most personal and self-defining in US constitutional jurisprudence.[46] There is an inherent right, in the US tradition, to keep personal identity and the family we build free of State intrusion. It is in these kinds of choices that State interference and control are most threatening to liberty, individuality and diversity. In this way, the US system of government has been distinct in its protection of liberty – the negative right to be kept free of State interference – in a manner different from other legal systems that are more focused on positively protecting human rights or human dignity, as is the case in Israel.[47]

---

[43] See S. Rubin, 'Israel Loosens Abortion Law Restrictions After *Roe v. Wade* Decision', *Washington Post*, 28 June 2022.

[44] Penal Amendment (Termination of Pregnancy) of 1977, 5737-1977, SH No (Amended on 04.07.2022).

[45] Basic Law: Human Dignity and Liberty, (Isr.) Arts. 4 and 7; Privacy Protection Law (Isr.) 5741–1981; E. Gross, 'The Struggle of a Democracy against Terrorism – Protection of Human Rights: The Right to Privacy versus the National Interest – the Proper Balance' (2004) 37 *Cornell Int'l L.J.* 27, 46–47 (describing the Israeli right to privacy as one reflecting restrictions on searching the person or belongings on a person).

[46] *Trammell v. State*, 751 N.E. 2d 283 (Ind. Ct. App. 2001) (prohibiting women convicted of neglect and abuse from becoming pregnant, as a condition for probation).

[47] D.S. Law and M. Versteeg, 'The Declining Influence of the United States Constitution' (2012) 87 *NYU L Rev.* 762, 779–808; M. Versteeg, 'Unpopular Constitutionalism' (2014) 89 *Ind. L.J.* 1133, 1176.

However, *Dobbs* puts forward a new proposition: that, because of State interest in potential life, the right to privacy does not adhere. Indeed, unlike in previous cases, where the interests of the State were balanced against the right to privacy, and thereby limits on women's right to privacy were justified by State's interest in potential life, in *Dobbs* the Court says that because abortion is distinct from all other cases where the right to privacy is relevant – due to the existence of potential life – the right to privacy is not relevant at all in the context of abortion.[48] The Court explains,

> [n]one of the other decisions cited by *Roe* and *Casey* involved the critical moral question posed by abortion. They are therefore inapposite. They do not support the right to obtain an abortion, and by the same token, our conclusion that the Constitution does not confer such a right does not undermine them in any way.[49]

That is a huge change in our understanding of the right to privacy – that, due to potential life being at issue, the right to privacy does not adhere? Yet, women's self-defining choices in reproducing and having a family still appear to be at stake, so the impact of such a limitation is significant. What are the implications?

3. THE POTENTIAL IMPACT OF *DOBBS* BEYOND ABORTION

Beyond abortion, *Dobbs* most directly undermines the right to other actions that can impact potential life – usually, but not always, women's actions. The right to birth control, first announced in *Griswold* and *Eisenstadt*, may be limited by state law if it can be shown that potential life may be harmed by certain methods. For example, in some instances, depending on when the pill is taken, the morning-after pill can cause a fertilised egg to detach from the lining of the uterus, and has thus been deemed murder by certain segments of society.[50] This can be considered to undermine potential life – as can any birth control that prevents life from taking form. Certainly, it is a problem for medication/chemical abortions as a class, which are already subject to state law restrictions in some states.[51] Medication abortion, which is self-administered through pills, involves terminating a pregnancy through the ingestion of mifepristone and misoprostol. It can be safely administered up to ten weeks of pregnancy, according to the

---

48   *Dobbs*, 597 US ___ (2002), at 32.
49   Ibid.
50   See, e.g. *Stormans, Inc. v. Selecky*, 854 F. Supp. 2d 925, 934 (W.D. Wash. 2012).
51   See C.D. Forsythe and D. Harrison, M.D., 'State Regulation of Chemical Abortion After *Dobbs*' (2022) 16 *Liberty U. L. Rev.* 377.

US Food and Drug Administration, and up to twelve weeks of pregnancy, according to the World Health Organization.[52]

Moreover, women's other choices during pregnancy may face increasing challenges and control by the State. If potential life obviates a woman's right to privacy, the State can potentially exert more control over a woman's body during pregnancy, including determining how she births,[53] what medical treatment she seeks,[54] and controlling her actions to ensure she is promoting a healthy pregnancy – like taking prenatal vitamins and eating an appropriate diet.[55] Perhaps committees could be used to force women to undergo certain procedures or be given treatments, even if they refuse. Neonatal operations might be forced upon women despite risks to their lives, and a range of choices during pregnancy may not be considered private, but a matter of State interest. While forced treatment is different from illegalising an abortion, as forcing medical involvement is different from refusing to perform a medical procedure, there are already precedents on the books for coercing medical treatment during pregnancy, when the interests of the unborn are at stake. Forced treatment may more firmly violate the right to bodily integrity and autonomy, but as these rights are derivative, and narrower, than the constitutionally entrenched right to privacy that does not adhere when potential life is involved, after *Dobbs*, attempts to resist such coercion may be weakened. Criminally, a woman may be prosecuted for potentially endangering a foetus, whether through drug or alcohol abuse, or other actions during pregnancy, a trend which has already begun in many states in the US.[56]

Control over any woman during pregnancy might become more like the way surrogate pregnancies are controlled. Surrogate pregnancies are more controlled

---

[52]   KFF, Women's Health Policy, 'The Availability and Use of Medication Abortion' (1 June 2023) (available at https://www.kff.org/womens-health-policy/fact-sheet/the-availability-and-use-of-medication-abortion/). Such pills are not in stock in retail pharmacies, limiting access, but can be obtained, with a prescription, from online pharmacies.

[53]   See *Pemberton v. Tallahassee Mem'l Reg'l Med. Ctr., Inc.*, 66 F. Supp. 2d 1247 (N.D. Fla. 1999); *Almerico v. Denney*, 378 F. Supp. 3d 920 (D. Idaho 2019); C. MALACRIDA and T. BOULTON, 'The Best Laid Plans? Women's Choices, Expectations and Experiences in Childbirth' (2014) 18 *Health* 41, 42–57 (studying women's birth experiences which suggest that institutional and medical pressures push woman towards C-sections and medical interventions in their births, despite plans to birth naturally and vaginally).

[54]   See, e.g. *In re Brown*, 689 N.E.2d 397 (1997) (forcing blood transfusion on pregnant woman).

[55]   B.R. CLARK, 'Centering Black Pregnancy: A Response to Medical Paternalism, Stillbirth, & Blindsided Mothers' (2021) 106 *Iowa L. Rev. Online* 85, 95–96 (discussing State actions to control women's prenatal care); L.C. Ikemoto, 'The Code of Perfect Pregnancy: At the Intersection of the Ideology of Motherhood, the Practice of Defaulting to Science, and the Interventionist Mindset of Law' (1992) 53 *Ohio St. L.J.* 1205, 1248.

[56]   See *Whitner v. State*, 328 S.C. 1, 492 S.E.2d 777 (1997); *Ex parte Ankrom*, 152 So. 3d 397 (Ala. 2013); G. HOWARD, 'The Pregnancy Police: Surveillance, Regulation, and Control' (2020) 14 *Harv. L. & Pol'y Rev.* 347; D.F. CHAVKIN, '"For Their Own Good": Civil Commitment of Alcohol and Drug-Dependent Pregnant Women' (1992) 37 *S.D. L. Rev.* 224.

because intended parents have a strong interest in the welfare of the foetus the surrogate is carrying.[57] Thus, contract terms can restrict the surrogate's actions, and control her diet and medical care.[58] Surrogates in India have been known to live in hostels and be tightly monitored.[59] Taking away privacy makes the pregnancy and the foetus a matter of public concern. Thus, while surrogacy itself may not have resulted in dystopian nightmares of control of women's bodies, as the control is private and regulated by contracts and mutual relations, State involvement in any women's pregnancy should sound the alarm bells more clearly.

In the field of fertility treatments, in vitro fertilisation (IVF), surrogate motherhood, and other technologies that assist a woman, man or couple in bearing children, the elevated status of potential life can curtail access to treatment options. If a woman becomes pregnant with multiples foetuses, due in part to the use of IVF, the ability to limit the number of foetuses could be forbidden by abortion restrictions. In a state without abortion, a surrogate mother, more than ever, becomes a prisoner to her own body, despite complications that might occur or intended parents' desires not to have a baby with certain disabilities. This will make surrogate motherhood, an already difficult and life-altering process for all involved, in which informed consent is limited by contract and autonomy curtailed, an even more harrowing process.[60] Indeed, I would urge that, despite the benefits surrogacy can provide, the process needs to be reconsidered entirely in states where abortion is now illegal, due to the greater hardships and potential complications such laws could pose.

The complex determination of what can be done with frozen embryos could also be implicated. Perhaps, as potential life, such embryos can no longer be destroyed, even with consent of genetic contributors, as such choices would not be considered privately protected? This only exacerbates an already overwhelming problem of how to contend with the cost and space needed to keep millions of unused frozen embryos frozen, where there is no consent to destroy them.[61]

---

[57]   P. LAUFER-UKELES, 'The Disembodied Womb: Pregnancy, Informed Consent, and Surrogate Motherhood' (2018) 43 *N.C.J. Int'l L.* 96, 127–135.

[58]   See T.W. MAYO, 'Medical Decision Making During a Surrogate Pregnancy' (1988) 25 *Hous. L. Rev.* 599, 623–624; In re Baby M., 537 A.2d 1227, 1249 (N.J. 1988).

[59]   P. LAUFER-UKELES, 'Mothering for Money: Regulating Commercial Intimacy' (2013) 88 *Ind. L.J.* 1223, 1267–1269.

[60]   See K. DRABIAK-SYED, 'Waiving Informed Consent to Prenatal Screening and Diagnosis? Problems with Paradoxical Negotiation in Surrogacy Contracts' (2011) 39 *J.L. Medicine & Ethics* 559, 561–562 ('additional interested parties – the intended parents – are involved in the medical decision-making relationship.'); LAUFER-UKELES, 'The Disembodied Womb', above n. 57, at 134–139.

[61]   See, e.g. J.L. DOLGIN, 'Surrounding Embryos: Biology, Ideology, and Politics' (2006) 16 *Health Matrix* 27; M. DAVIS, 'Indefinite Freeze? The Obligations A Cryopreservation Bank Has to Abandoned Frozen Embryos in the Wake of the Maryland Stem Cell Research Act of 2006' (2012) 15 *J. Health Care L. & Pol'y* 379.

Finally, tort cases such as wrongful life and wrongful birth cannot be brought in states where abortion is not allowed, as there would be no causation – if there is no option to abort, it is not possible to sue for wrongful life or birth.[62] Such tort cases are available against doctors for negligence in failing to sterilise, failing to screen for embryonic defects, and failing to diagnose embryonic disease or disabilities. This kind of limit on torts will further narrow the recourse available for people who suffer negligence at the hands of doctors during fertility treatments and the reproductive process, curtailing autonomy and access to justice. The medical system is already heavily weighted towards protecting a foetus and delivering a live baby, as opposed to respecting the medical decision of the woman.[63] The lack of torts for negligence in prebirth care will further limit recourse for parents, and increase doctors' control over pregnant patients.

But these implications of curtailing privacy are just the beginning. If the interests in potential life can cancel the relevance of the right to privacy for a pregnant woman, what about the interests of actual, living, born children? The US has established a strong line of cases protecting parental privacy.[64] Indeed, that is seen as one significant reason that the US has not signed the Convention on the Rights of the Children, which has been widely adopted by nearly all other countries.[65] In the US, a parent's rights to raise children as they see fit – according to personal world views, and without interference by the State to determine how a child is educated or medically treated – is considered protected and fundamental. Yet, if a woman's privacy can be overwhelmed to such an extent that privacy does not adhere, due to the interest of the State in potential life, why would parents' privacy not be overwhelmed by State's interest in actual children's lives? Are they worth less than potential life? This could have a monumental impact on parental privacy, especially in the areas of education, healthcare, vaccinations and religion, in which US parents have traditionally enjoyed a large amount of discretion, based on the right to privacy.

Again, to understand what is at stake, it is worth contrasting the US constitutional system, which gives parents tremendous discretion when it comes to children's health care decisions, with the system in Israel, which allows much more State involvement in the private lives of its citizens. On the whole, in the US, unless a health care decision implicates a potential conflict of interest (sibling

---

62   See, e.g. E.T. Ramey, 'Wrongful Birth after *Dobbs*' (31 October 2022), available at SSRN: https://ssrn.com/abstract=4263215 or http://dx.doi.org/10.2139/ssrn.4263215 (discussing how pre-*Dobbs* courts resisted wrongful birth and wrongful life actions, due to the lack of access to abortion).

63   Laufer-Ukeles, above n. 26, at 621–623.

64   See, e.g. *Pierce v. Society of Sisters*, 268 US 510 (1925); *Meyer v. Nebraska*, 262 US 390 (1923).

65   See, e.g. M. Albertson Fineman, 'What Is Right for Children?' in M. Albertson Fineman and K. Worthington (eds.), *What Is Right for Children? The Competing Paradigms of Religion and Human Rights*, Routledge, 2009, pp. 1, 1–4.

donors),[66] or involves a non-reversible medical decision (sex changes),[67] or, at times, refusal to accept life-preserving non-invasive medical care (usually for religious reasons),[68] parents retain full discretion in making medical decisions for their children.[69] Only if parental behaviour is so extreme as to be considered medical neglect will the State initiate a legal proceeding, and courts override parental decision-making.[70]

In Israel, on the other hand, State involvement in overriding parental health care choices for children is more common, the State is more paternalistic, less concerned with 'privacy', and therefore decisional autonomy in issues of child-rearing has not been so thoroughly protected in its case law. For instance, in Israel, in the Legal Capacity and Guardianship Law, there is a section that gives the State the power to 'take temporary or permanent measures which seem to it appropriate for protecting the interests of the minor'.[71] On this basis, the Israeli judicial system has allowed children to be given vaccines and other medications coercively, including tetanus shots and other basic treatments.[72] Moreover, even in extreme circumstances where treatment is highly invasive and may not be effective, courts have overridden parental decisions in favour of medical advice to provide chemotherapy,[73] dialysis,[74] and even surgery for child patients who enjoy a very low quality of life – living on life support – regardless of treatment.[75]

---

[66] D. HAWKES, 'Elective Surgery – When Parental and Medical Opinion Supersedes a Child's Right to Choose' (2009) *Utah L Rev.* 613, 617.

[67] E.D. THORN, 'Drop the Knife! Instituting Policies of Nonsurgical Intervention for Intersex Infants' (2014) 52 *Fam. Ct. Rev.* 610, 616–617. Intersex operations on minors have been banned in Malta and Portugal: R. SAVAGE, 'Intersex surgery "abuses" condemned by 34 states at U.N. rights forum', *Reuters*, 1 October 2020, https://www.reuters.com/article/un-lgbt-health-idUSL8N2GS5NQ [https://perma.cc/CND7-WFBE].

[68] In *re D.L.E.*, 645 P.2d 271, 276 (Colo. 1982); *In re J.J.*, 582 N.E.2d 1138, 1141 (Ohio Ct. App. 1990); but see *Newmark v. Williams*, 588 A.2d 1108, 1109 (Del. 1991) (allowing parents to refuse chemotherapy for child due to religious reasons); E.M. CHIU, 'The Culture Differential in Parental Autonomy' (2008) 41 *U.C. Davis L. Rev.* 1773, 1825; HAWKES, above n. 66, at 619.

[69] *Wisconsin v. Yoder* 406 US 205 (1972); *Pierce v. Soc'y of Sisters* 268 US 510 (1925); *Meyer v. Nebraska* 262 US 390 (1923); D. DIAZ, 'Minors and Cosmetic Surgery: An Argument for State Intervention' (2012) 14 *DePaul J. Health Care L.* 235, 246, 251.

[70] R. POVENMIRE, 'Do Parents Have the Legal Authority to Consent to the Surgical Amputation of Normal, Healthy Tissue from their Infant Children?: The Practice of Circumcision in the United States' (1998) 7 *Am. U. J. Gender Soc. Pol'y & L.* 87, 104–106; S.D. HAWKINS, 'Protecting the Rights and Interests of Competent Minors in Litigated Medical Treatment Disputes' (1996) 64 *Fordham L. Rev.* 2075, 2083–2084.

[71] Legal Capacity and Guardianship Law Sec. 68 (Isr.) 5722-1962.

[72] FamA 71141-02-20 *Plonit v. Attorney General of the State of Israel*, Nevo Legal Database (29 November 2020).

[73] GU 16397-04-14 *A-G v. Ch.K.*, Nevo Legal Database (27 May 2014).

[74] CA 5587/97 *Ben Icar*, Nevo Legal Database (24 September 1997).

[75] FamC 24638-02-14 *RE A*, Nevo Legal Database (19 February 2014) (14-month-old with congenitalmuscular dystrophy on ventilator forced to undergo surgery and remain on ventilator despite parental objections); CA 506/88 *Yael Shefer v. State of Israel*, Neval Legal

While parental privacy is often mentioned in the case law as a factor, such autonomy is regularly overridden because it is held not to be in the best interests of the children, which courts regularly hold to be to follow medical advice. This Israeli line of cases is vastly different from US case law, which has traditionally presumed that parents' decisions are in the best interests of their children, and that their privacy must be respected.[76] Parental privacy is traditionally thought of as a conservative value, whereas liberals were more inclined to want to allow State interference to protect children's rights. However, in *Dobbs*, the conservative courts' words would threaten parental privacy.

State involvement in personal, identity-forming reproductive choices and family decisions, more common in other countries, goes against traditional American values focused on liberty – values of conservatives and liberals alike. It also threatens diversity and autonomy. Whether the courts and the states will stop at just abortion is unknown; however, it is clear that many other areas of individual rights, torts and criminal law may be impacted.

Indeed, *Dobbs* could impact those unenumerated rights 'not mentioned'. Although not relating directly to potential life, and thus not immediately threatened by the language of *Dobbs*, weakening substantive due process, and the unenumerated rights that have been held to 'emanate' from the Constitution regardless of what is written, could threaten same-sex marriage, the right to gender identity, and other individual and personal rights that were not recognised as fundamental at the time of the writing of the Constitution, despite how dearly they are held today.

4. CONCLUSION: WHY *DOBBS* IS THE BEGINNING OF THE END OF US LEGAL EXCEPTIONALISM

Ultimately, advocates of overturning *Roe v. Wade* argue that *Dobbs* is about respecting states' rights,[77] and that it will not impact on most women who are in serious need of an abortion.[78] This is likely true for those who are financially secure, well-connected, or can travel independently.[79] But for young girls in unstable households, or in foster care or the child welfare system; migrants and

---

Database (24 November 1993) (2-year-old in state of PVS with Tay-Sachs forced to undergo continuous treatment despite objection of the mother).

[76] *Troxel v. Granville*, 530 US 57 (2000).

[77] See R. JOHNSON, '*Dobbs v. Jackson* and the Revival of the States' Rights Constitution' 93/4 *The Political Quarterly*, October/December 2022.

[78] See, e.g. R. PONNURU, 'In Defense of *Dobbs*', *National Review*, 14 July 2022 (arguing that when women's lives are at stake, abortion is unlikely to be prohibited).

[79] CARBONE and CAHN, above n. 31, at 279–280 ('Wealthier women have always, even when abortion was illegal, been able to buy reproductive ability for themselves.').

illegal residents; victims of rape, incest and domestic abuse; for the disabled and mentally impaired – the absolute weakest and most vulnerable amongst us in society – access to abortion, and to privacy, has been undermined in an alarming manner.

When the Court says that a pregnant woman's privacy does not apply because of the existence of potential life, the State is separating between woman and foetus in a clear and binary fashion. If the foetus exists, the woman does not have privacy. But such separation – between woman and foetus, or between caregiving parent and child – is dangerous, and must be done cautiously. The codependence and intertwined nature of woman and foetus in pregnancy is unique, and must be accounted for.[80] The emotional and physical state of the parent will impact on the child.[81] If a woman desperately does not want a child, but also cannot bear to give the child up for adoption (or abandon the child at a hospital, as has been suggested by some lawmakers post-*Dobbs*),[82] she is likely to have extreme difficulties in a parental role, at least in the beginning, and these difficulties are likely to have ripple effects on her children, and her family, community and society. Moreover, once a child is born, providing protection in the form of health care, education, or financial security directly to children without considering the needs of parents is likely to fall short of helping those children – parents need to feel secure, and children rely on them for sustenance.[83] For instance, attempts to support breastfeeding for the health benefits for babies will not be sufficiently successful unless maternity leave and pumping breaks are also provided.[84] Policy initiatives that focus on children without also taking care to protect caregivers are weak and face many hurdles. Indeed, the *Dobbs* decision reflects a world in which the innocent child is saved, while the naughty adults (mothers) are punished and shamed.[85] The US does not provide sufficient social welfare benefits to help economically unstable mothers, and thus the primary recourse is adoption. But child removal, foster care and adoption all suffer from

---

[80]   R. WEST, *Caring for Justice*, New York University Press, 1997, p. 102; B. KATZ ROTHMAN, *Recreating Motherhood*, Rutgers University Press, 2000, pp. 35–36 (describing maternal rights based on gestation as a uniquely nurturing social and physical relationship); see also *In re Union Pac. R.R. Emp't Practices Litig.*, 378 F. Supp. 2d 1139, 1147–1148 (D. Neb. 2005).

[81]   P. LAUFER-UKELES, 'Separating Care from Caregiver' (2014) 15 *Nevada Law Journal* 236, 260–276.

[82]   D. GOLDSTEIN, 'Drop Boxes for Babies: Conservatives Promote a Way to Give Up Newborns Anonymously', *New York Times*, 13 August 2022, available at https://www.nytimes.com/2022/08/06/us/roe-safe-haven-laws-newborns.html.

[83]   LAUFER-UKELES, 'Separating Care from Caregiver', above n. 81, at 276–281.

[84]   P. LAUFER-UKELES and A. RENAN-BARZILAY, 'The Health/Care Divide' (2018) 35 *Columbia J. Law & Gender* 264, 272–282 (describing the health push to breastfeed, and the difficulties women face in complying with such recommendations).

[85]   J. CARBONE and N.R. CAHN, 'The Court's Morality Play: The Punishment Lens, Sex, and Abortion', *Southern Cal. L. Rev* (forthcoming) (available at SSRN: https://ssrn.com/abstract=4319373).

criticism that the system underserves adults in need, transferring children to more white, more upper-class and more stable homes, without even attempting to help those in need – those who are most vulnerable.[86]

The US focus on negative rights – the right to privacy interpreted as the right to be left alone – has provided an exceptional undergirding to the US constitutional tradition, in comparison with other developed countries, such as Israel, where committees and State evaluations regarding children overwhelm citizen choices.[87] This privacy has kept at bay paternalism, interference, and a heavy-handed State. While a more robust system of social welfare benefits, common to states that endorse positive understandings of constitutional rights that require the State to ensure basic levels of dignity, would certainly help the poor and the vulnerable,[88] a robust protection of privacy has, at the least, supported diversity and freedom. Arguably, more social welfare benefits may also come with more State involvement and control, as it does in Israel, although this is not necessarily true, and balance can be achieved.[89] Still, the US focus on privacy has promoted autonomy, diversity and freedom, even while, perhaps, doing too little to help the vulnerable.

But *Dobbs* takes the American constitutional system to new places. After *Dobbs*, not only does the US fail to use more positive conceptions of constitutional rights to help the vulnerable obtain basic needs and dignities through social benefits, but punishes the vulnerable by preventing access to abortion and protecting, in their stead, their potential offspring. Breaking privacy allows tyranny of the majoritarian, normative, established culture, and it is the disenfranchised who suffer from the interference and disapproval of the State. Respecting privacy regardless of who you are, or what you can pay for, has been exceptional and cherished in the US system, and its erosion marks the end of such exceptionalism in new and disheartening ways.

---

[86] See D.E. ROBERTS, 'Prison, Foster Care, and the Systemic Punishment of Black Mothers' (2012) 59 *UCLA L. Rev.* 1474; R. WEXLER, 'Take the Child and Run: Tales from the Age of ASFA' (2001) 36 *New Eng. L. Rev.* 129 (describing in detail the connection of poverty, foster care and termination of parental rights). See, generally, D. ROBERTS, *Shattered Bonds: The Color of Child Welfare*, Basic Books, 2002.

[87] See above n. 47.

[88] See, e.g. M. FINEMAN, *Neutered Mother, The Sexual Family and Other Twentieth Century Tragedies*, Routledge, 1995, p. 228; C.J. Ross and N. CAHN, 'Subsidy for Caretaking in Families: Lessons from Foster Care' (1999) 8 *Am. U. J. Gender. Soc. Pol'y & L.* 55, 70–71 (describing the Temporary Assistance for Needy Families programme, and child welfare policy as focused on the child and not the caregiving unit).

[89] See, e.g. B. STARK, 'Rhetoric, Divorce and International Human Rights: The Limits of Divorce Reform for the Protection of Children' (2005) 65 *La. L. Rev.* 1433, 1442 (describing the difference between positive and negative rights).

ARTIFICIAL INTELLIGENCE AND FAMILY LAW

ARTIFICIAL INTELLIGENCE AND ALGORITHMS IN FAMILY (PATRIMONIAL) LAW*

Nishat Hyder-Rahman,** Elisabeth Alofs***
and Marco Giacalone****

* Co-funded by the European Union (under grant agreement no. 101046629). Views and opinions expressed are, however, those of the authors only, and do not necessarily reflect those of the European Union or the European Commission. Neither the European Union nor the granting authority can be held responsible for them.

** Corresponding author: nishat.hyder-rahman@vub.be. Postdoctoral Researcher, Department of Private & Economic Law, Vrije Universiteit Brussel; Lecturer, Department of Private, Business & Labour Law, Tilburg University.

*** Corresponding author: elisabeth.alofs@vub.be. Professor of Family (Property) Law, Head of the Department of Private & Economic Law and Director of the Master in Notarial Studies, Vrije Universiteit Brussel.

**** Corresponding author: marco.giacalone@vub.be. Postdoctoral Researcher, Department of Private & Economic Law, Vrije Universiteit Brussel.

Résumé

Au cours des trois dernières décennies, l'utilisation de l'intelligence artificielle (IA) et des algorithmes a gagné du terrain dans la pratique du droit de la famille. Les litiges « classiques » de droit de la famille, tels que le divorce, les pensions alimentaires et la liquidation des régimes matrimoniaux et des successions, sont encore représentés par des images de salles d'audience, où les parties au litige et leurs avocats comparaissent devant un juge. Pourtant, de l'obtention d'un divorce à la liquidation du régime matrimonial des époux, en passant par l'organisation des modalités d'exercice de l'autorité parentale et de résidence des enfants, le règlement des contentieux familiaux s'effectue de plus en plus souvent en ligne, par le biais d'une application ou d'un site web. Dans le présent article, nous donnons un aperçu de l'utilisation de l'IA dans la pratique du droit de la famille aujourd'hui, spécialement dans sa dimension patrimoniale. Nous retraçons l'émergence des outils d'IA dans les contentieux traditionnels, ainsi que dans les processus de règlement extrajudiciaire des litiges (ADR), et en particulier dans le règlement des litiges en ligne (ODR).

Les présents développements s'attachent d'abord à expliquer les technologies d'IA utilisées et à explorer leur application dans la pratique juridique en général et en droit (patrimonial) de la famille en particulier. À l'aide d'exemples concrets, nous examinons l'utilisation actuelle de l'IA dans la pratique du droit de la famille à travers le monde. Ensuite, les avantages et les inconvénients de ces outils technologiques sont étudiés. Une réflexion sur l'utilisation de l'IA dans la pratique du droit de la famille est menée afin d'en analyser, de manière critique, les succès et les échecs et d'en tirer les leçons qui s'imposent. Enfin, nous nous interrogeons sur la valeur ajoutée que l'IA et les algorithmes peuvent apporter à la pratique du droit de la famille, aujourd'hui et à l'avenir, en nous concentrant particulièrement sur l'Europe.

1. INTRODUCTION

When you hear the word 'divorce', what image comes to your mind? Adam Driver and Scarlett Johansson's characters in the Netflix movie, *Marriage Story*, exchanging snarky barbs across conference tables and courthouse corridors? Perhaps you think of the public dramas of celebrity divorces that have graced the pages of broadsheet and tabloid newspapers? Or perhaps you think of the mindful 'conscious uncoupling' of Gwyneth Paltrow and Chris Martin? The image that comes to mind is probably not an app, a swipe and a tap, on a mobile phone. Yet, despite the lasting (and realistic) association of divorces with proceedings before a judge in mahogany-panelled courtrooms, divorces today are increasingly conducted on an app or website.

The introduction of a parallel process – one that shifts legal proceedings from courtroom to computer, or integrates traditional and computer-based processes – is part of a broader, long-term trend towards the so-called 'technologisation' of legal practice in all areas of law, including family law. Today, a number of artificial intelligence (AI)-powered tools are available to assist the parties in, for example, dividing assets, calculating maintenance, and arranging child custody schedules. Moreover, the infrastructure for divorce and ancillary proceedings can also be found online, via online dispute resolution (ODR) platforms. AI tools can be embedded within an ODR platform or available separately.

This chapter provides an overview of the use of AI in (the practice of) family (property) law today. It begins by briefly explaining and defining the technology, in section 2. Section 3 explores the application of these technologies in general legal practice and family (patrimonial) law practice, and analyses the advantages of these technological tools – what can this technology bring to legal practice? – and the shortcomings – what do we need to be aware of in the future? Section 4 gives an overview of the (most famous) existing AI tools and AI-based ODR platforms used in family (patrimonial) law practice around the world. Subsequently, the chapter examines one success story (amica, in Australia) and one failure (Rechtwijzer, in the Netherlands) in depth, in section 5, drawing out lessons learned from the application of AI and algorithms in family law practice to date. Finally, section 6 offers concluding thoughts on how AI and algorithms are shaping the practice of contemporary family (property) law, focusing particularly on Europe.

2. TERMS AND DEFINITIONS

Before proceeding further, it is helpful to set out some brief working definitions of the technologies referred to throughout this chapter. While the precise technical details of these definitions might vary amongst academic and industry experts – in large part because the technological fields (artificial intelligence and computer science) are relatively young, and are currently in a phase of rapid advancement – the general layperson's definitions are consistent, and sufficient for our purposes.

2.1. ARTIFICIAL INTELLIGENCE (AI)

Coined in 1956 by the American scientist John McCarthy, the term 'artificial intelligence' was defined, at its inception, as 'the science and engineering of making intelligent machines, especially intelligent computer programs'.[1] Within this rather broad definition, AI can be distinguished by type, as per the table below.[2]

Table 1. Types of AI by strength

Type	Definition	Applications
Weak/narrow	The AI performs a single task, or at most, a series of interlinked tasks.[3]	Weather apps, digital assistants (e.g. Siri, Alexa, etc.), Google search function, chatbots, data processing.
Strong/general	The AI can comprehend, think, learn and act (make decisions) as a human would, strategically and creatively, while managing complexity, and without relying on human preprogramming to do so.	Not yet in existence.
Super	Surpasses human intelligence and ability.	Not yet in existence.

Source: Compiled by the authors.

The AI applications that we have encountered in our daily lives so far would fall into the category of weak/narrow. The terminology is somewhat misleading, as the words 'weak/narrow' refer to the scope of the AI itself, which is limited to the specific task that it was programmed to perform, and which it does in a highly

---

[1]   http://jmc.stanford.edu/artificial-intelligence/what-is-ai/index.html, last accessed 14.02 2023.
[2]   https://builtin.com/artificial-intelligence/strong-ai-weak-ai, last accessed 14.02.2023.
[3]   https://www.accenture.com/us-en/insights/artificial-intelligence-summary-index, last accessed 14.02.2023.

efficient manner. The impact of this can be incredibly powerful. The aim of this type of AI is to maximise or optimise efficiencies, replicating human behaviour rather than human intelligence. Strong/general AI remains, as yet, a theoretical possibility. This type of AI would exhibit intelligence indistinguishable from, and on a par with, human intelligence. In strong/general AI, the goal is to emulate human intelligence. Finally, some experts refer to super AI, an intelligence that exceeds human intelligence, and which, for now at least, is well and truly in the realm of science fiction.

Alternatively, AI can be split into four categories according to its capability, as per the table below, which also correspond roughly to the weak/strong/super division.[4]

Table 2. Types of AI by category

Category	Definition	Corresponding Type
Reactive machines	The AI performs a single task; it has no memory.	Weak
Limited memory	The AI has a memory, and uses past experiences to guide decision-making.	Weak
Theory of mind	The AI has social intelligence; it understands emotions, motives and intentions.	Strong
Self-awareness	The AI is aware of itself; it has consciousness.	Strong/Super

Source: Compiled by the authors.

The types of AI discussed in the next sections of this chapter all fall into the weak/narrow or reactive machine and limited memory categories.

AI is a broad field, comprising many subfields and technologies. It is not possible to define every element of AI here; however, the main technologies relevant to the application of AI in legal practice are defined below.

2.2. MACHINE LEARNING[5]

Machine learning is the process by which a computer or AI system extracts knowledge from data,[6] in order to make a prediction or decision. Through

---

[4] https://theconversation.com/understanding-the-four-types-of-ai-from-reactive-robots-to-self-aware-beings-67616; https://www.techtarget.com/searchenterpriseai/definition/AI-Artificial-Intelligence; https://builtin.com/artificial-intelligence/types-of-artificial-intelligence, all last accessed 14.02.2023.

[5] https://www.techtarget.com/searchenterpriseai/definition/machine-learning-ML; https://hai.stanford.edu/sites/default/files/2020-09/AI-Definitions-HAI.pdf, both last accessed 14.02.2023.

[6] In computing, data is information that has been translated into a form that is efficient for processing.

processing large amounts of data, the system learns to detect patterns without needing to be specifically programmed. There are three types of machine learning:

1. Supervised learning: data sets put through the system are labelled (by a human), so that the system can learn the patterns and label future data.
2. Unsupervised learning: here, the data sets are not labelled, and the system organises the data according to patterns that can be distilled.
3. Reinforcement learning: here also, the data sets are not labelled; however the system is given feedback (by a human) on its decisions.

Machine learning is now ubiquitous: examples include email spam filters and online recommender systems.

2.3. ALGORITHMS[7]

An algorithm is a very precise set of step-by-step rules or instructions for transforming or computing input data (data sets) into output data (a prediction or decision). Machine learning, for instance, relies on algorithms in order to process data sets; it is the algorithm that determines, or even learns, how to process data, based on its past experiences, and delivers a result.

2.4. NATURAL LANGUAGE PROCESSING (NLP)[8]

NLP enables human–computer communication. The language of computing is code, as opposed to a human or 'natural' language, such as English, French, Dutch, etc. NLP is the process through which a computer understands human speech and/or writing, interprets it, and delivers a response; it is what allows us to communicate with a digital assistant such as Siri, or a chatbot, in our own human language, rather than typing out the command in code.

2.5. ONLINE DISPUTE RESOLUTION (ODR)

It is worth taking a moment here to consider the definition of ODR, for it is a concept that is evolving as our technological capabilities evolve. At its

---

[7]   https://hai.stanford.edu/sites/default/files/2020-09/AI-Definitions-HAI.pdf; https://www.thinkautomation.com/eli5/what-is-an-algorithm-an-in-a-nutshell-explanation/; https://theconversation.com/what-is-an-algorithm-how-computers-know-what-to-do-with-data-146665, all last accessed 14.02.2023.

[8]   https://www.techtarget.com/searchenterpriseai/definition/natural-language-processing-NLP, last accessed 14.02.2023.

inception, ODR was the synthesis of alternative dispute resolution (ADR) and information and communication technology (ICT), developed in order to resolve disputes that arose within the online environment.[9] The definition of ODR and what it encompasses have both expanded since then: for example, ODR can be used to settle offline as well as online disputes. Furthermore, the term is contemporaneously used to refer to the transfer of traditional in-person ADR processes to online forums – a shift propelled by the COVID-19 pandemic. Finally, ODR is now also used as an umbrella term to capture all dispute resolution processes – non-judicial, and judicial – that take place online.[10]

In terms of what ODR can deliver, this too has expanded over time, from a dedicated online space (platform) for meeting and information exchange, to services enhanced through the inclusion of AI tools. ODR marks a fundamental change in the conceptual framework of dispute resolution. In an archetypal dispute, there are three parties involved: the two disputing parties, and a third party tasked with facilitating the resolution of the dispute, in the form of a judge, adjudicator, mediator or arbitrator, etc. Reflecting on the interparty relationships in ODR, Katsh, Katsh and Rifkin refer to the fourth party[11] – the technology itself – and Lodder to a fifth party[12] – the provider of the technology – and even a sixth party[13] – the administrative body that provides the technology (for example, the implementation of an ODR system by a government authority who has, for instance, outsourced the building and provision of the technological platform). Reframing the interparty relationships within ODR thus highlights the distinct role of technology in actively shaping the dispute resolution processes and outcomes. For Lodder, and for Katsh, Katsh and Rifkin, the technology is more than just a tool subject to human manipulation; it is a party within the process and framework of dispute resolution.[14] Notwithstanding the influence that these technologies have on the processes within which they are used, and thus on the eventual outcomes, this chapter will continue to refer to these technologies as 'tools' rather than 'parties'.

ODR is a natural home for AI tools, and these tools can easily be embedded within the online platforms and processes. But it is important to highlight that

---

9   E.E. Katsh, M.E. Katsh and J. Rifkin, *Online Dispute Resolution: Resolving Conflicts in Cyberspace*, John Wiley & Sons, Inc., 2001.
10 https://search.coe.int/cm/Pages/result_details.aspx?ObjectId=0900001680a2cf96; https://rm.coe.int/publication-guidelines-and-explanatory-memoreandum-odr-mechanisms-in-c/1680a4214e, both last accessed 14.02.2023; D. Reiling, 'Beyond Court Digitalization with Online Dispute Resolution' (2017) 8(2) *International Journal for Court Administration* 2.
11 Katsh, Katsh and Rifkin, above n. 9.
12 A.R. Lodder, 'The Third Party and Beyond. An analysis of the different parties, in particular The Fifth, involved in online dispute resolution' (2006) 15(2) *Information & Communications Technology Law* 143–155.
13 Ibid.
14 Ibid., 145.

AI tools need not only be used in the context of ODR; they are also available as stand-alone tools that can be used by the parties themselves, their lawyers, ADR facilitators, and even judges, to complement offline as well as online legal procedures. In that context, these tools are sometimes referred to as negotiation support systems (NSSs) or decision support systems.

3. THE USE, ADVANTAGES AND CHALLENGES OF AI TOOLS IN LAW AND LEGAL PRACTICE

This section explores the use, advantages and challenges of AI tools and AI-based ODR in general legal practice, and in the practice of family law.

3.1. AI TOOLS IN GENERAL LEGAL PRACTICE

The technologies described in section 2 above are currently applied in legal practice in a variety of different ways:[15]

1. Legal research: databases such as LexisNexis[16] and Westlaw[17] both incorporate machine learning algorithms into their search engines, to deliver better results for the user.
2. Document review: AI tools such as eBrevia[18] combine natural language processing and machine learning algorithms, in order to read and review legal documents, such as contracts. The algorithm can be trained to classify data, as well as to extract and/or flag certain data points, according to the users' needs.
3. Document drafting: software is available to facilitate automated document drafting, taking the user through an interactive set of questions to extract data and fill in a form, or to create a draft document.[19]
4. Case prediction: software using AI-based predictive modelling can help determine probable case outcomes, based on past cases, by analysing and detecting patterns. This information can, in turn, help lawyers guide their

---

[15] https://www.lexisnexis.co.uk/blog/future-of-law/artificial-intelligence-trends-their-impact-on-the-legal-sector, last accessed 14.02.2023.

[16] https://www.lexisnexis.com/community/insights/legal/b/thought-leadership/posts/the-power-of-artificial-intelligence-in-legal-research, last accessed 14.02.2023.

[17] https://legal.thomsonreuters.com/en/products/westlaw-edgehttps://legal.thomsonreuters.com/en/products/westlaw-edge, last accessed 14.02.2023.

[18] https://www.dfinsolutions.com/products/ebrevia, last accessed 14.02.2023.

[19] J. BENNETT et al, 'Current State of Automated Legal Advice Tools' (Discussion Paper No 1, Networked Society Institute, University of Melbourne, April 2018), 22–25.

clients' courses of action, for example whether to litigate or to settle – and, if so, for how much.

5. Advisory services: legal web advisors are based on AI that follows a decision-tree method; the AI takes the user through a series of questions, in order to extract data, sort and analyse it, and offer a result.

6. Chatbots: law firm websites often use live chatbots to take down a potential client's preliminary information, and either answer their question or direct them to the relevant department or personnel.

These applications, in line with the weak/narrow function of AI, are focused on automation and data processing – essentially, the hyperefficient performance of a single programmed task. In the context of time-consuming and repetitive tasks, such as document review, or tasks that require the processing of large amounts of data, such as search engine optimisation or case prediction, it is easy to see the use for AI. The AI can perform such tasks significantly faster and more accurately than a human can, given human constraints (time, concentration) and proneness to 'human error', and frees up practitioners' time for other, more creative, cerebral and person-facing tasks that the AI cannot perform. Notably, these tasks are, to a large extent, depersonalised rote work, and are, therefore, easier to accept as being performed by an AI rather than human.

Sourdin separates the impact of AI in legal practice into three categories: supporting practitioners and users of the legal system, supplementing work previously undertaken by humans within the system, and disrupting or fundamentally transforming the legal system.[20] To date, AI applications largely fall within the supporting and supplementing categories, although automated decision-making (particularly by public bodies) falls into the third category.[21]

3.2. AI TOOLS IN THE PRACTICE OF FAMILY LAW

How does AI fit into the practice of family (property) law, where matters are more personal and intimate? Family law practice is typically, and accurately, characterised as one of the more 'person-facing' areas of legal practice.

---

[20] T. SOURDIN, 'Justice and Technological Innovation' (2015) 25(2) *Journal of Judicial Administration* 96; see also J. ZELEZNIKOW, 'Using Artificial Intelligence to provide Intelligent Dispute Resolution Support' (2021) 30(4) *Group Decision and Negotiation* 789–812; J. ZELEZNIKOW, 'Can Artificial Intelligence and Online Dispute Resolution Enhance Efficiency and Effectiveness in Courts' (2017), 8(2) *International Journal for Court Administration* 30–45.

[21] See, further, D. HOGAN-DORAN, 'Computer Says "No": Automation, Algorithms and Artificial Intelligence in Government Decision-Making' (2017) 13(3) *The Judicial Review* 345; M. ZALNIERIUTE, L. BENNETT MOSES and G. WILLIAMS, 'The Rule of Law and Automation of Government Decision-Making' (2019) 82(3) *Modern Law Review* 425, 426–427.

It is associated with a requirement for strong interpersonal skills and a certain understanding of human relations, as it deals with the intimate elements of private life. It is also, in large part due to ADR, associated with a less litigious style of practice, in which conciliation and mediation are preferred to all-out adversarial litigation; modern family lawyers look for constructive solutions, rather than all-or-nothing wins for their clients.[22] The necessity for these skills in good family lawyering has led to some to argue that the field is relatively sheltered from the so-called technological takeover that other lawyers have predicted.[23] Semple, for instance, emphasises the importance of the human side of family law practice, and an 'an enduring need for a local human touch' in 'personal plight legal practice'.[24] However, as Bell argues, human lawyers are not without flaws and criticisms, and given the systemic issues that plague family law practice – costs, delays, backlogs – the technology, and what it can offer, should not be dismissed out of hand, even in an area of law as personal and sensitive as family law.[25]

There is plenty of evidence demonstrating that family law is not isolated from technological advances in AI. It is certainly true that an AI cannot offer empathy, contextualise the law for the client, offer perspective when weighing options, or explain the ramifications for the client, as a lawyer would, and moreover that an AI judge cannot apply discretion in the interests of justice[26] (a woolly concept in itself) or manage a case. However, not every client or case will demand this. In the cost–benefit analysis between time-limited, expensive human practitioners versus accessible, cheaper AI's, there is certainly room for the latter. Perhaps surprisingly, family property law has proven to be an ideal testing ground for AI (for example, asset division tools), and some jurisdictions have a lengthier history than others of embracing these tools. It is the present authors' opinion that family law practice will evolve to become a hybrid or integrated human–technology practice, in which human practitioners are supported and supplemented – and, indeed, in some instances altogether displaced – by the technology.

Notwithstanding the fact that AI tools can be, and are, used as stand-alone tools within ADR and the traditional adversarial process, it is also possible to trace a progression in family law from court-based litigation to ADR, to ODR,

---

[22] F. Bell, 'Family law, access to justice, and automation' (2019) 19 *Macquarie Law Journal* 103, 111.

[23] D. Ben-Ari et al, '"Danger, Will Robinson?" Artificial Intelligence in the Practice of Law: An Analysis and Proof of Concept Experiment' (2017) 23(2) *Richmond Journal of Law & Technology* 2.

[24] N. Semple, 'Personal Plight Legal Practice and Tomorrow's Lawyers' (2014) 39(1) *Journal of the Legal Profession* 25.

[25] Bell, above n. 22.

[26] T. Sourdin, 'Judge v Robot? Artificial Intelligence and Judicial Decision-Making' (2018) 41(4) *University of New South Wales Law Journal* 1114.

and to an AI-enhanced ODR experience.[27] The mainstream adoption of ADR (the use of arbitration, negotiation and mediation to settle disputes out of court) in family law in some (but certainly not all) jurisdictions around the world, throughout the 1970s, 1980s and 1990s, demonstrates the sector's willingness to look beyond traditional dispute resolution methods (i.e. litigation in the courts) to serve clients.[28] This was driven by two main factors. The first factor was to facilitate a shift away from acrimonious divorce proceedings, towards proceedings and processes that encouraged the parties to reach agreements. The second purpose was necessity – specifically, the length, slow pace and high cost of litigation in an overwhelmed court system.[29] Throughout the 2000s, and continuing today, the same factors have urged the sector, in some jurisdictions, towards ODR.

The following sections reflect on the advantages and drawbacks of these technologies, in comparison with the traditional processes of going to court, and explore the technologies currently in operation in family (property) law.

3.3. ADVANTAGES AND CHALLENGES

AI tools and AI-based ODR offer a number of clear advantages over both traditional court process and ADR, as well having their own set of challenges.

3.3.1. Advantages of AI Tools and AI-Based ODR

One of the primary advantages of AI tools is that they are, or at least should be, neutral, and free from the cognitive biases that plague human beings, and also that they operate without the risk of human error. In theory, AI-based decisions should be more accurate and objective than human decision-making. Clients often ask their lawyers, 'how likely am I to win?'. Competent, experienced lawyers will have a sound enough understanding of the relevant jurisprudence, and the practical experience, to have a realistic idea of the likely outcome, though they would be unlikely to pinpoint chances to an exact percentage. An AI tool – for example, a machine-learning algorithm – will be able to analyse every single

---

27 M. GIACALONE and S. SALEHI, 'CREA – An Introduction to Conflict Resolution with Equitative Algorithm' in F. ROMEO, M. DALL'AGLIO and M. GIACALONE, (eds.), *Algorithmic Conflict Resolution*, Giappichelli Torino, 2019, available at SSRN: https://ssrn.com/abstract=3782322; E. WILSON-EVERED and J. ZELEZNIKOW, *Online Family Dispute Resolution*, Springer, 2021, ch. 2, pp. 17–35.

28 WILSON-EVERED and ZELEZNIKOW, above n. 27, ch. 1, pp. 1–16; M. MACLEAN and B. DIJKSTERHUIS (eds.), *Digital Family Justice: From Alternative Dispute Resolution to Online Dispute Resolution?*, Bloomsbury Publishing, 2019.

29 GIACALONE and SALEHI, above n. 27.

case on the issue at hand, and offer a response based on statistical analysis, within a matter of minutes, if not seconds. Likewise, clients want to know, 'how much will this cost me?'. An AI tool with access to a law firm's data points on billing will be able to analyse the data and deduce the exact average cost of cases similar to the client's one. For these types of simple, calculable questions, AI is undoubtedly superior.

Furthermore, AI tools themselves can be used to build broader, AI-based ODR platforms with particular advantages. The court system, including the family courts, are notoriously slow at delivering justice; they are overburdened, and constrained by limited time, resources, processes and personnel. Litigation is costly, lengthy and stressful for all involved. Moreover, the adversarial process encourages acrimony, positioning the parties against each other, both metaphorically, and physically in the court room, each hoping to win at the other's expense. This is exacerbated in jurisdictions where divorce is fault-based, or where there is no option for divorce by mutual consent. In the context of a family breakdown, particularly where children are involved and shared custody is likely, the parties will have future interactions with each other regarding their children, and the adversarial approach is unhelpful. ADR attempted to address some of these issues by taking the process out of the formal courtroom and into an informal setting to encourage open communication, developing procedures based on negotiation rather than argumentation, and eliminating the adversarial approach, in order to focus on reaching an agreement. AI-based ODR not only incorporates all these advantages of ADR, but adds several further practical benefits. AI-based ODR are available 24 hours a day, seven days a week, removing the constraints of business hours and personnel availability. Court schedules, law firms, and even ADR services, operate according to fixed business hours, at a fixed place of business. Given that the divorcing parties may also have work or other commitments (for example, childcare) during those hours, arranging a physical or live digital meeting or hearing at a time convenient for all the parties concerned can prove challenging. Online platforms and tools operated by AI remove these inconveniences – AI does not need a lunch break, coffee break or work-life balance! ODR can be accessed at any time of day, via a smartphone, device or computer. These factors – speed, cost and ease of accessibility – together significantly increase access to justice for citizens.[30] In particular, AI will help

---

[30]   See L.R. Lupica, T.A. Franklin and S.M. Friedman, 'The Apps for Justice Project: Employing Design Thinking to Narrow the Access to Justice Gap' (2017) 44(5) *Fordham Urban Law Journal* 1363; J. Frank, 'A2J Author, Legal Aid Organizations, and Courts: Bridging the Civil Justice Gap Using Document Assembly' (2017) 39(2) *Western New England Law Review* 251; D. Luban, 'Optimism, Skepticism and Access to Justice' (2016) 3(3) *Texas A&M Law Review* 495, 502; Sourdin, 'Judge v Robot?' above n. 26, 1118; M. Legg and J. Corker, 'Unbundling for Access to Justice and for Commercial Law', Presentation to Future of Law and Innovation in the Profession (FLIP) Conference, Sydney, 14 September 2018.

the so-called 'missing middle': those who are not poor enough to qualify for legal aid, but not wealthy enough to retain a lawyer.[31] From the perspective of public services, having a viable alternative method for citizens to settle their disputes reduces the burden on the courts.

Finally, AI tools can help streamline cross-border divorce processes, which are currently complicated, and costly in terms of both time and money. In the context of the European Union (EU) and the fundamental freedoms which guarantee, inter alia, all EU citizens and their families the right to move and reside freely within the EU,[32] this is a significant advantage. Although family law, including divorce, remains a matter of national law within the EU, the private international law dimension of divorce must be addressed, particularly in light of citizen mobility throughout the Union. Here, AI tools can help: a multi-language NLP eliminates the need for separate translation services, and a digital platform (whether part of a broader ODR, or stand-alone) enables the storing, sharing and tracing of documents. This advantage applies not only to inter-EU divorces, but also to international divorces.

Finally, the key advantages of AI tools mentioned above – neutrality, accuracy, speed, low cost, and accessibility – are incorporated into AI-based ODR as well.

3.3.2. Challenges of AI Tools and AI-Based ODR

However, AI tools and AI-based ODR come with several challenges. Firstly, the algorithms are written by humans.[33] This introduces the possibility of a poorly written algorithm returning poor-quality results. More concerningly, it introduces the possibility of coded bias: a situation where the biases of the human programmer are written into the algorithm, compromising its neutrality and accuracy. An example of coded bias is the Dutch child benefits scandal, where the algorithm targeted citizens with dual nationality or a non-Dutch name for fraud investigation.[34] Secondly, an AI tool, such as a machine learning algorithm, will only be as good as the dataset it was trained on, and is continuing

---

[31]   G. CANNY, 'Online dispute resolution: A marriage of law and AI technology' (2019) 41(5) *Bulletin (Law Society of South Australia)* 14–15.

[32]   Art. 21, Consolidated version of Treaty on the Functioning of the European Union, 26 October 2012, OJ L.326/47-326/390; Art. 45, Charter of Fundamental Rights of the European Union, 26 October 2012, 2012/C 326/02.

[33]   D. LEHR and P. OHM, 'Playing with the Data: What Legal Scholars Should Learn about Machine Learning' (2017) 51(2) *University of California, Davis Law Review* 653; L. BENNETT MOSES and J. CHAN, 'Using Big Data for Legal and Law Enforcement Decisions: Testing the New Tools' (2014) 37(2) *University of New South Wales Law Journal* 643, 668.

[34]   https://www.amnesty.org/en/latest/news/2021/10/xenophobic-machines-dutch-child-benefit-scandal/; https://www.europarl.europa.eu/doceo/document/O-9-2022-000028_EN.html, both last accessed 14.02.2023.

to learn from: the better the quality of the data, and the more of it the algorithm is fed, the better the results will be.

However, what constitutes quality data is difficult to ascertain. In the context of family law, historical data, albeit accurate and detailed, is likely to reflect historical attitudes and conventions that do not reflect our contemporary understanding of how families and family law operate. For example, social attitudes towards gender, and particularly the division of labour based on gender, will be reflected in the division of assets in past divorce agreements.[35] It is not clear that an algorithm can 'read' social change over time within the data set, thus risking results based on outdated attitudes and norms. Limiting the dataset only to recent divorce agreements is not ideal, as Bell points out, because this means working from a significantly smaller dataset.[36] More generally, datafication carries the risk that focusing attention on seemingly objective data, and adapting legal systems to incorporate this information, might undesirably influence the operation of legal systems.

In terms of reaping the benefits of these tools, the inherent structure and design of AI tools and AI-based ODR means that there are some barriers to accessing this technology: it is limited to those who have access to an internet-enabled smartphone, device or computer. Furthermore, as divorcing parties can use the technology to lead their own negotiations, it is limited to those who are literate and numerate. Arguably, some of these factors create obstacles to access for the members of the population who need it most, namely those in deprived socio-economic circumstances.

Moreover, both AI tools and AI-based ODR can be limited in their applicability – the latter to parties who are willing to communicate reasonably with one another. Certain AI tools or AI-based ODR will only work between willing and rational parties. For those facing a complex or contested divorce, matters such as division of assets and/or the child custody situation will likely still be required to follow traditional court or ADR processes, in whole or part.

3.3.3. Challenges of AI in Legal Practice

AI and digitalisation are forcing the legal profession to evolve,[37] but not without challenges. For practitioners, the possibility that AI could function in ways that are difficult for humans to comprehend is problematic, as the information ultimately needs to be relayed and explained to a client. Furthermore, in order to guide clients through these tools, legal professionals must adapt to new

---

[35]   L. BENNETT MOSES and N. PELEG, 'Why have a lawyer when you can have a robot?' (Presentation to National Family Law Conference, Brisbane, 5 October 2018).

[36]   BELL, above n. 22, 118.

[37]   R. KOULU and L. KONTIAINEN (eds.), *How will AI shape the future of law?*, University of Helsinki Legal Tech Lab Publications, 2019.

systems and develop new skills. Research on the growth of electronic delivery of services emphasises that prospective users may range from those who have 'no willingness to engage with online services … to those who exhibit willingness but lack ability … to those who might be considered "expert" users'.[38] However, scholars like Barton have argued that self-help technology remains the best way to expand access to justice.[39] In terms of legal adaptation to technologies like AI, there will always be some degree of latency as the legal system recalibrates to the new technology. One method of addressing the issue of legal adaptation and uncertainty is to involve the field from an early developmental stage, and encourage exploration through a policy of controlled experimentation – so-called 'sandboxing'.[40]

4. AI TOOLS IN FAMILY (PROPERTY) LAW

4.1. ONLINE DIVORCE PLATFORMS

Online divorce platforms are a good example of AI tools being embedded within a broader structure. These platforms offer a comprehensive divorce service, guiding users through planning a divorce, the divorce process itself (i.e. the legal severance of a marriage or civil partnership), and the separate processes for ancillary relief and child custody, as well as post-divorce matters – all entirely online. They have, for the most part, been developed privately across common law jurisdictions, particularly Australia and the US. The development and use of online divorce platforms and AI tools outside common law countries is limited to a few examples.

Specific online divorce platforms are available, and notable examples include Wevorce.com, HelloDivorce.com, ItsOverEasy.com, 3stepdivorce.com and divorcewriter.com (all US-based), CommonSenseDivorce.ca (from Canada),[41] and Amicable (UK-based).[42] Interestingly, It'sOverEasy (launched in 2018), and HelloDivorce (launched in 2017), are both initiatives of experienced family lawyers: Laura Wasser and Erin Levine, respectively. These platforms include tools, for example, to assess 'divorce readiness', gather data and

---

38   C. Denvir, Civil Justice Council, 'Assisted Digital Support for Civil Justice System Users: Demand, Design, & Implementation' 4 (2018).

39   B.H. Barton, 'Technology Can Solve Much of America's Access to Justice Problem, If We Let It' in S. Estreicher and J Radice (eds.), *Beyond Elite Law: Access to Civil Justice in America*, Cambridge University Press, 2016, pp. 444–445.

40   M. Richard and A. Solow-Niederman, 'Developing Artificially Intelligent Justice' (2019) 22 *Stanford Technology Law Review* 242.

41   There are many more examples, as well as general online legal services that also offer an online divorce service, such as rocketlawyer.com and legalzoom.com.

42   https://amicable.io, last accessed 14.02.2023.

generate documents (such as the forms to be filed with the court, to facilitate the court process), divide assets, calculate maintenance costs, and develop a co-parenting plan. Automation software is integrated into the platform, to create a streamlined, step-by-step 'do-it-yourself' process for negotiating an agreement and filing for divorce. Visitors to the Wevorce platform (launched in 2013) are guided by a chatbot, Carter, 'the peace-provoking robot'. Section 5 below will closely examine the Australian platform amica, which is currently in operation; the story of amica will be compared with that of Rechtwijzer, a now defunct Dutch platform.

Additionally, online divorce services are offered by a number of general online legal service providers, such as lawgeex.com and rocketlawyer.com (both American sites).

Finally, tools to assist in specific matters, such as child maintenance calculators,[43] spousal maintenance,[44] and divorce settlement calculators,[45] are also available, often via law firm websites.

4.2. CO-PARENTING TOOLS

Specific apps have also been developed that are dedicated to managing (post-divorce) co-parenting, such as OurFamilyWizard.com and CoParenter.com. The former offers a platform for divorced parents 'to communicate, share calendars and journals, track expenses, and transmit payments', and is available in America, Canada, the UK, New Zealand and Australia. The app seeks to promote clear, amicable communication by sometimes limiting available responses to yes/no, as well as offering users a clear, time-stamped record of the parenting plan, calendar, and all communication and documentation, in the interests of accountability and transparency. The aim is to enable a smooth co-parenting journey post-divorce, and to help former spouses avoid returning to court to settle co-parenting disputes.

CoParenter.com offers a similar service in the US and Canada, but goes one step further. Its web page reads, '[s]ay goodbye to expensive lawyers, messy spreadsheets and confusing court forms. Use artificial intelligence and live mediators to help you and your ex create the perfect parenting plan.' This app uses what it calls 'intelligent dispute resolution' (IDR) – essentially a machine learning algorithm – to predict and prevent conflicts. The algorithm learns to detect the kind of language and patterns that can lead to conflict between

---

[43]   https://www.divorcefinancetoolkit.co.uk/child-maintenance-calculator/, last accessed 14.02.2023.
[44]   https://austinkemp.co.uk/spousal-maintenance-calculator/, last accessed 15.05.2023.
[45]   https://iflg.uk.com/tools, last accessed 15.05.2023.

co-parents, and attempts to diffuse brewing conflicts.[46] The website shows an example of the algorithm interrupting an expletive-filled message with the question: 'Hey, this message sounds hostile. Do you want to send it?' The AI also actively offers suggestions, based on the users' communications. For example, it might suggest creating an informal agreement between co-parents in certain situations, and then take the users through the steps to do so, based on what it has (machine-)learned works for other co-parents.

4.3. ASSET DIVISION TOOLS (BASED ON GAME THEORY)

Australia is a leading jurisdiction in successfully integrating AI and algorithmic technology into the practice of family law, via online divorce platforms, asset division tools and negotiation tools. Much of this work has been undertaken by John Zeleznikow and his collaborators from the field of management and information systems. In 2005, Zeleznikow and Bellucci launched Family Winner, a software that combines AI, game theory and an electronic or human mediator, to help divorcing couples divide assets.[47] This was swiftly followed by Family Mediator, a sister programme, to help couples reach settlements on issues relating to children, again with the guidance of an electronic or human mediator.[48] These tools pre-date the online divorce platforms discussed above, and are designed to support legal professionals guide their clients on- or offline.

Family Winner itself is an adaptation of Brams and Taylor's Adjusted Winner procedure.[49] This process draws on game theory, and aims to deliver an equitable allocation of assets between the parties. The parties, i.e. the divorcing couple, are asked to rank each asset within the pool of matrimonial property according to

---

[46] https://www.marketplace.org/2022/02/18/whats-it-like-when-an-algorithm-moderates-your-divorce/, last accessed 14.02.2023.

[47] E. BELLUCCI and J. ZELEZNIKOW, 'Developing Negotiation Decision Support Systems That Support Mediators: A Case Study of The Family Winner System' (2005) 13 *Artificial Intelligence and Law* 233–271; J. ZELEZNIKOW and E. BELLUCCI 'Family Winner: Integrating Game Theory and Heuristics to Provide Negotiation Support', JURIX 2003, *Proceedings of Sixteenth International Conference on Legal Knowledge Based System* (2003), pp. 21–30.

[48] J. ZELEZNIKOW and E. BELLUCCI, 'Family_Mediator–Adding Notions of Fairness to Those of Interests', in T.M. VAN ENGERS (ed.) *Legal Knowledge and Information Systems. Jurix 2006: the Nineteenth Annual Conference*, IOS Press, 2006, pp. 121–130. Family Negotiator, created by the same team, was an earlier tool to help determine child custody, and determine and split the common pool of assets: E. BELLUCCI and J. ZELEZNIKOW, 'Family-Negotiator: an intelligent decision support system for negotiation in Australian Family Law' in Proceedings of the Fourth Conference of the International Society for Decision Support Systems, Lausanne, 1997, pp. 359–373.

[49] S.J. BRAMS and A.D. TAYLOR, *Fair Division: from cake-cutting to dispute resolution*, Cambridge University Press, 1996; http://www.nyu.edu/projects/adjustedwinner/, last accessed 14.02.2023.

preference. Here, preference refers to utility, which will be subjective to each party, rather than value. The assets are then split (by the algorithm) between the parties, based on their own rankings. In theory, this should lead to a 'win-win' situation, where each party believes they have 'won' because they have been allocated assets that align with their own preferences – in other words, an 'envy-free' outcome.[50] The process is best demonstrated by a simple example. Suppose that, amongst the matrimonial assets of a fictional divorcing couple, Anne and Eliot, there is a Steinway grand piano, and a restored racing car. Anne is an amateur pianist, who plays every day purely for her own enjoyment, and occasionally with a local quartet. Eliot cannot read a note of music and is tone-deaf. He has spent the better part of each weekend for the last ten years restoring the racing car as a hobby, and enjoys taking it out for country drives. Anne does not have a driving licence, preferring to cycle, walk or take public transport. The Steinway, which is commercially valued at more than the restored car, is of more utility to Anne, whereas the car is of more utility to Eliot. Following the Adjusted Winner procedure, the Steinway would likely be allocated to Anne, and the car to Eliot. Eliot is also more likely to accept an outcome of lower financial value if it includes assets that are of utility to him. Thus, each party will walk away with their preferred assets, each having 'won'. However, this approach to asset division only works if both parties are willing to participate honestly and rationally. If Anne, in a fit of vindictiveness, chooses to rank the car above the piano, ignoring her own preferences in order to spoil Eliot's, the outcome will not be equitable, fair or 'win-win'.

The appeal of a game theory approach to asset division in the context of divorce is understandable. Unravelling the joint finances of a couple and splitting their property is a time-consuming, stressful and contentious task, even in the most amicable mutual consent divorces. Ascertaining a method of fair division, given the unique socio-economic history of each couple, remains a worthwhile pursuit; to find a method that is both time-efficient and which minimises conflict would, indeed, be 'win-win'.

Game theory-based asset divider algorithms offer a number of advantages. Firstly, the split is based on the users' own preferences, not external ones, so the result is more likely to be acceptable. Secondly, ranking assets in order of preference is a far quicker and logistically simpler task than negotiations. Thirdly, the entity performing the split, namely the algorithm, is neutral, or at least 'personality-free', as opposed to a human, and therefore unlikely to be swayed by its own biases.

However, this method is limited to rational, willing users. Furthermore, it does not necessarily take into account the interests of those who are not party to the property division, but are nevertheless impacted by it (for example, children).

---

[50]   GIACALONE and SALEHI, above n. 27.

Therefore, a follow-up step might be required to take account of the parties' other legal obligations. Nonetheless, the game theory approach, packaged as an AI tool, is hugely advantageous and transformative to the practice of family law.

A number of asset division tools based on this approach are currently available. In Australia, Split-Up[51] (developed by Zeleznikow, Stranieri and Grawler) and AssetDivider[52] (developed by Zeleznikow and Bellucci) are notable examples. The latter builds on Family Winner by including principles of fairness into the system. Realising that Family Winner divided assets between the divorcing parties according to parties' own interests, and without paying heed to any existing legal obligations, such as maintaining the best interests of children, Bellucci and Zeleznikow integrated principles of fairness into the AssetDivider tool.[53] In the US, Adjusted Winner has been commercialised as Fair Outcomes, and other tools such as Spliddit[54] are also available. In Canada, Smart Settle[55] offers a suite of negotiation support system tools, including a successful tool for asset division. To the best of the present authors' knowledge, no similar tools have been launched for use within European civil law jurisdictions.[56] The ongoing EU/JUST-CREA projects,[57] in which a legal framework and applicable game theory-based algorithm is being developed, will fill this gap.

From a close dialogue with Prof. Steven J. Brams (creator of Adjusted Winner), the 'Conflict Resolution with Equitative Algorithms' project (CREA,[58] followed by CREA2[59]) was founded as an interdisciplinary European effort towards

---

[51] J. Zeleznikow, A. Stranieri and M. Gawler, 'Project report: Split-Up – A Legal Expert System which determines property division upon divorce' (1995) 3 *Artificial Intelligence and Law* 267–275.

[52] E. Bellucci, 'AssetDivider: a new mediation tool in Australian family law' in *Proceedings of the 1st International Working Conference on Human Factors and Computational Models in Negotiation*, Delft, Netherlands, ACM 8–9 December 2008, pp. 11–18.

[53] J. Zeleznikow, 'Comparing the Israel–Palestinian dispute to Australian family mediation' (2014) 23 *Group Decision and Negotiation* 1301–1317.

[54] http://www.spliddit.org, last accessed 14.02.2023.

[55] https://www.smartsettle.com, last accessed 14.02.2023.

[56] Sondier.ai, based in Berlin, looked promising, however the project does not appear to have launched as a product: https://medium.com/blockchain-for-law/could-an-algorithm-make-divorce-and-custody-disputes-simpler-and-less-stressful-f959a31931d6, last accessed 14.02.2023.

[57] The three authors of this chapter are involved as post-doctoral researchers, project coordinators and/or project deputy coordinators in CREA and/or CREA2.

[58] European project co-funded by the Justice Programme 2014–2020, Call: JUST-AG-2016-05, under grant agreement no. 766463. The CREA project is written by M. Giacalone, putting in practice the concepts discussed and studied in his PhD thesis on 'Dispute Resolution and New IT Realities' (2016, joint PhD, Universita degli Studi di Napoli Federico II and Vrije Universiteit Brussel). For more information on CREA, see http://www.crea-project.eu, last accessed 14.02.2023.

[59] European project co-funded by the Justice Programme 2021–2027, Call: JUST-2021-EJUSTICE, under grant agreement no. 101046629 (M. Giacalone is Project Coordinator and E. Alofs is Project Deputy Coordinator).

developing an AI-powered algorithm to assist parties in asset division. The project was funded by the European Commission from 2017 to 2019 (CREA), and from 2022 to 2024 (CREA2), for the innovation it brings to the area of civil dispute resolution in the EU. CREA was conceived as a dispute resolution model based on game theoretical algorithms, and was proposed as a decision support system for parties engaged in settlement negotiations concerning the division of assets after divorce, separation or death. Importantly, the CREA approach towards civil dispute resolution tackles the existing disparities amongst the national legal systems of the EU Member States involved in the project, by establishing a 'European Common Ground of Available Rights' (ECGAR), i.e. putting aside all the mandatory rules of each EU Member State and operating on the remaining 'rights available'.[60] This is an innovative theoretical approach that allows for a broader application of the CREA algorithmic decision support tool across the civil law jurisdictions within the EU, in national and cross-border matters. The CREA2 project builds on the results of its predecessor, and aims to introduce, within the existing CREA platform, innovative features based on AI and blockchain technology, aimed at facilitating the use of ODR in cases specifically related to asset division. In CREA2's platform, an AI chatbot will be created to guide the parties through the process; it will suggest possible outcomes based on previous cases, and will directly attribute certain values (based on the parties' own answers with regard to the preferential ranking of assets) into the algorithm. Then, the game theoretical algorithm will provide a possible solution to the parties, which they are free to accept or reject. In addition, CREA2 will implement blockchain technology, which has extensive use in ODR procedures, by enabling the development of transactions of digital assets to facilitate the property settlement.[61] For example, if the parties accept the solution offered by the algorithm, or reach an agreement themselves, they have the possibility to record the agreement on the electronic medium (the blockchain system), which can improve data quality and long-term sustainability, and ensure trust in, and the reliability of, the system.

---

[60]   The ECGAR focuses mostly on distinguishing available rights *(droits disponibles)* from national mandatory rules *(loi de police)* in force in the different EU Member States. The concept of a European Common Ground of Available Rights (ECGAR) was first mentioned by MARCO GIACALONE, in his PhD thesis on 'Dispute Resolution and New IT Realities', above n. 58, freely accessible. See also M. GIACALONE and S. SALEHI, 'Conflict Resolution with Equitative Algorithms – A tool to establish a European Common Ground of Available Rights' in F. ROMEO, S. MARTUCCELLI and M. GIACALONE (eds.), *The European Common Ground of Available Rights*, Ed. Scientifica Napoli, 2019.

[61]   The White Paper on the Ethereum platform provides further technical information about applications of the block chain infrastructure: C. CHENG LIANG, 'A Next-Generation Smart Contract and Decentralized Application Platform' (2016), available at https://github.com/ethereum/wiki/wiki/White-Paper, last accessed 14.02.2023.

5. SUCCESSES AND FAILURES OF AI AND ODR: A TALE OF TWO PLATFORMS

This section takes a closer look at two online divorce platforms, the success story of amica in Australia, and the failed Rechtwijzer platform in the Netherlands, to gain insight into how these platforms and the tools used within them have fared. These two platforms were selected for a number of reasons: they were both developed with government backing and actively publicised to citizens as an option, and they are both recent examples from within the last decade.

5.1. AMICA (AUSTRALIA)

Amica, Australia's national divorce platform, is possibly the biggest success story of AI-based technology in family law to date. Launched in 2020, amica is an independently developed but government-backed online platform to assist divorcing/separating couples in dividing their assets and making co-parenting arrangements.[62] It was developed by the Legal Services Commission of South Australia (an independent statutory authority for the purpose of providing legal assistance services to the public), in partnership with the design and technology company, Portable,[63] on behalf of Australia's National Legal Aid (the body representing all eight Australian state and territory legal aid commissions), with funding from the Attorney-General's Department of the Australian government.[64] This, in itself, is significant, as few (if any) nations have successfully introduced a federally endorsed platform of this kind.[65] Importantly, amica itself does not allow the parties to obtain a divorce: that process must be undertaken separately, in the family courts, although it can also be done online.[66] Rather, amica guides users through the negotiation process for dividing property and developing a co-parenting plan, thus facilitating the broader divorce process.

Within the platform, AI-based technology is used in a number of ways. Amica is only suitable for divorces between parties who are on relatively amicable terms. The parties do not need to agree on all points – after all, these tools are designed to help the parties to reach an agreement if possible – but they must be willing to communicate and work with the tools. It is not a suitable platform for complex

---

[62]   https://amica.gov.au., last accessed 14.02.2023.

[63]   https://portable.com.au/work/amica, last accessed 14.09.2023.

[64]   https://www.ag.gov.au/families-and-marriage/families/family-law-system/amica-online-dispute-resolution-tool, last accessed 14.02.2023.

[65]   MyLawBC is an example of a successful state-based system (British Columbia in Canada) – see section 5.3. below.

[66]   See 'How Do I Apply for a Divorce?', Federal Circuit Court of Australia, http://www.federalcircuitcourt.gov.au//wps/wcm/connect/fccweb/how-doi/divorce/apply-for-a-divorce/apply-for-divorce., last accessed 14.02.2023.

or acrimonious separations, and users are screened during the sign-up process (for example, domestic violence situations are unsuitable). Communication between the parties is monitored via sentiment analysis technology that filters out inappropriate language and remarks, detects coercion, and sends a warning message to the sender. A machine learning algorithm is used to suggest a division of assets, based on: (1) the divorcing couple's assets and the circumstances; (2) the types of agreements reached by other couples in similar circumstances; and (3) how the courts have approached similar situations. The AI guides the divorcing parties through a negotiation until an agreement is reached. If amica is used, the agreement reached by the couple must be within a 20 per cent margin of amica's original suggested division; if the agreement is outside the 20 per cent margin, the amica platform cannot be used to proceed. A separate tool assists parents in reaching and implementing a co-parenting agreement. Once an agreement has been reached, amica also generates the formal agreement documents, including applications for consent orders, ready to submit to court.

What are the reasons behind amica's success? What makes amica different to many, but not all, of the tools and services available is that it was developed by family lawyers, led by Gabrielle Canny, current director of the Legal Services Commission of South Australia, as well as technology experts. For instance, neither Zeleznikow nor Bellucci, who have shaped the field considerably, are family lawyers, and nor are the teams behind the ODR platforms developed by Modria, one of which is discussed later in this chapter. In contrast, as noted above, It's Over Easy and Hello Divorce are both initiatives of experienced family lawyers, and appear to be quite successful and popular too.[67]

Furthermore, amica was actively explained and promoted to Australian citizens via a nationwide media campaign on television and radio, and in newspapers and journals.[68] The initial reactions to, and uptake of, amica are promising: within its first six months, approximately 2,000 matters were initiated, more than 500 asset division suggestions offered, more than 200 property agreements and 120 parent agreements finalised, and around 75 consent orders generated.[69] The platform has won a number of prestigious industry awards.[70]

---

[67] https://www.forbes.com/advisor/legal/divorce/best-online-divorce-services/; https://www.newyorker.com/culture/the-new-yorker-interview/life-lessons-from-laura-wasser-divorce-lawyer-to-the-stars; https://fintech.global/2022/10/20/hello-divorce-rakes-in-3-25m-in-oversubscribed-seed/#:~:text=Hello%20Divorce%2C%20the%20legal%20FinTech,CEO%20of%20Clio%20Jack%20Newton., all last accessed 14 February 2023.

[68] See, e.g. this interview: https://www.google.com/url?sa=t&rct=j&q=&esrc=s&source=web&cd=&ved=2ahUKEwiRkYXj4On7AhWa_7sIHeNSAuQQtwJ6BAgmEAI&url=https%3A%2F%2Fwww.youtube.com%2Fwatch%3Fv%3DxlBjmDh7EwY&usg=AOvVaw1dUm_gNU9xq8ptBvnO7tf3; this news article: https://www.theaustralian.com.au/nation/diy-divorce-website-saves-those-at-breaking-point/news-story/339cdd7cf3bc5c133f702b8ee2f30e31, both last accessed 14.02.2023.

[69] G. CANNY, 'Can AI help resolve family law disputes?: Computer says yes.' (2021) 43(1) *Bulletin (Law Society of South Australia)* 18–20.

[70] Ibid.

Significantly, amica was launched during the COVID-19 lockdown, at a time when many aspects of life were being transferred to online forums. Hence, public acceptance of using online and AI tools in family law matters was, arguably, not as difficult to garner as it might otherwise have been.

5.2. RECHTWIJZER (THE NETHERLANDS)

Whereas AI tools have been well-received in Australia (and also in Canada),[71] not all countries that have attempted to introduce these tools as public-private initiatives have enjoyed a similar level of success. The Netherlands was an early adopter of ODR and technology in family law. The Rechtwijzer (which translates as 'roadmap to justice')[72] platform was developed as a partnership between the not-for-profit institution the Hague Institute for Innovation of Law (HiiL); Modria (now part of Tyler Tech), the American software development company behind the ODR platforms for the e-commerce giants PayPal and eBay; and the Dutch Legal Aid Board. The project began in 2007 with Rechtwijzer 1.0, itself an innovative platform that delivered advice via guided pathways, to create an interactive tailored experience for the user. The project operated in contrast to traditional advice platforms, which present a wall of static information that the user has to read, distil and apply for themselves.

In 2014, Rechtwijzer 2.0 was introduced. Lauded internationally as a revolutionary partnership of law and technology,[73] version 2.0 was a comprehensive ODR service, offering an algorithm-facilitated negotiation process for divorcing and separating parties on all issues at stake in a family break-up (dividing property, child support, parental plans and visiting rights, alimony), as well as access to personalised counselling, mediation and legal support if required. However, by 2017, it had been scaled back to near-oblivion,[74] and it was eventually replaced with a much-modified version of its former self, Uit Elkaar,[75] which supports rather than replaces traditional divorce negotiation processes, and offers a hybrid online/offline service. Uit Elkaar is operated by Justice42, which includes some of the team members involved in Rechtwijzer, notably Laura Kistemaker, the chief operating officer for the project. Justice42 is

---

71 https://mylawbc.com/, last accessed 14.02.2023.
72 B. DIJKSTERHUIS, 'The online divorce resolution tool "Rechtwijzer uit Elkaar" examined' in M. MacLean and B. DIJKSTERHUIS (eds.), *Digital Family Justice: From Alternative Dispute Resolution to Online Dispute Resolution?*, Bloomsbury Publishing, 2019, pp. 193–214.
73 https://law-tech-a2j.org/odr/rechtwijzer-why-online-supported-dispute-resolution-is-hard-to-implement/, last accessed 14.02.2023.
74 https://www.hiil.org/news/rechtwijzer-why-online-supported-dispute-resolution-is-hard-to-implement/ last accessed 14.02.2023. Ibid.
75 https://law-tech-a2j.org/advice/goodbye-rechtwijzer-hello-justice42/; https://law-tech-a2j.org/odr/the-rechtwijzer-rises-from-the-ashes-an-interview-with-laura-kistemaker-of-justice42/, both last accessed 14.02.2023 (sites no longer available); https://www.legalfutures.co.uk/

working on a new platform with new commercial partners, trying to incorporate the lessons from the Rechtwijzer.[76]

Relate, formerly the National Marriage Guidance Council (of England and Wales), had followed on the heels of Rechtwijzer 2.0's launch with a similar ODR platform for England and Wales, also developed in partnership with HiiL and Modria. By 2017, this platform too had been suspended.[77] There are now a number of privately developed options available in the UK for negotiating divorce matters, as enumerated above, but at the time of writing there is no full-service ODR platform available for negotiating the divorce agreement.

So, what went wrong with the Rechtwijzer model? The Dutch model was supposed to demonstrate the proof of concept that would revolutionise divorce negotiation proceedings around the world. Engaging in a critical self-reflection on the project, HiiL programme director, Maurits Barendrecht,[78] writes that there were three possible causes:

1. Citizens do not want online resolution services.
2. Legal aid boards, ministries, courts and law firms are not ready for online dispute resolution services.
3. The market can resolve the access to justice problem, so government is not needed, and the Rechtwijzer model failed to deliver.

According to Barendrecht, extensive social research and user feedback during the testing of Rechtwijzer, and in the period of six months post-launch, indicated that not only was there demand from citizens for self-help tools, but that the platform itself was user-friendly and had a positive impact on the divorce process. However, Barendrecht cites a combination of not enough time or money (this is a problem that legal aid boards, in particular, face) and lack of infrastructure within the legal system to support and develop innovative tech solutions. Part of the issue is that, typically, government funded projects are 'one-shot deals'. Whereas entrepreneurs and private investors have some freedom to learn and grow stronger from their experiments, governments and foundations, with a constituency or board to answer to, do not tend to provide second chances. Law firms and mediation centres are too small to invest in new technology; moreover, there are regulations limiting

---

76 latest-news/pioneering-odr-platform-to-rein-in-ambitions-after-commercial-setback, last accessed 14.09.2023. L. KISTEMAKER, 'Rechtwijzer and Uitelkaar. NL. Dutch experiences with ODR for divorce' (2021) 59(2) *Family Court Review* 232–243.
76 Ibid.
77 https://law-tech-a2j.org/odr/rechtwijzers-english-daughter-relate-suspends-online-family-dispute-resolution-project/, last accessed 14.02.2023 (site no longer available); https://www.legalfutures.co.uk/latest-news/relate-puts-pioneering-online-divorce-project-hold, last accessed 14.09.2023.
78 https://law-tech-a2j.org/odr/rechtwijzer-why-online-supported-dispute-resolution-is-hard-to-implement/, last accessed 14.02.2023 (site no longer available); https://www.hiil.org/news/rechtwijzer-why-online-supported-dispute-resolution-is-hard-to-implement/, last accessed 14.09.2023.

where they can direct their resources, and bringing in outside investment is proscribed. Thus, these types of business models, relying on private and/or public investment, are tricky to implement. Overall, for the government ministries in charge, aligning politicians, courts and the legal profession towards a clear vision for facilitating and funding this technology proved too tall an order.

Moreover, Barendrecht writes:

> There are certainly things we could have done better. The Dutch legal aid board and Ministry of Justice did not actively market the platform, but perhaps we could have raised money for this and have done this ourselves. We could perhaps have made the platform more attractive for lawyers working on it. Perhaps we focused too much on the satisfaction of users, as well as offering them an affordable platform in the spirit of legal aid.[79]

Marketing the product to the end user, to the legal profession, and to the public institutions involved is, therefore, key. Rechtwijzer may have received positive feedback from its users, but overall user uptake was low (2 to 3 per cent, with spikes of up to 5 per cent following media coverage).[80] The legal profession were never fully engaged: even during the initial post-launch excitement, 'criticism came from the Dutch Bar [who] wanted more safeguards for security and informed consent, and also lobbied for having lawyers do the intake instead of doing this online.'[81] Dijksterhuis[82] points out that the Dutch Bar's critical outlook, though some of the criticisms were valid, might also have come from a fear of competition, losing work, and ultimately being replaced by a computer. Furthermore, Rechtwijzer was a voluntary 'new kid on the block', trying to enter a very old and established club – it was not a formal part of civil or judicial procedure, and was, therefore, difficult for professionals to incorporate into their practice.

In her extensive analysis, Dijksterhuis points to two further possible reasons for Rechtwijzer's failure. Firstly, there was a lack of understanding, amongst the creators, of the nature of divorce, not only legally but also psychologically. Arguably, the team focused on the technology, innovation and interactive user experience at the expense of understanding the harsh realities of divorce – even the most amicable divorces are unpleasant. The present authors suggest that involving legal experts to a greater extent could have enabled and improved the communication and collaboration with, and therefore the acceptance of, Rechtwijzer by the legal profession. Secondly, Dijksterhuis points out that Rechtwijzer only has a

---

[79]   Ibid.

[80]   Ibid. See also https://lawyerwatch.wordpress.com/2017/03/31/after-the-rechtwijzer-energizer/, last accessed 14.02.2023.

[81]   https://law-tech-a2j.org/odr/rechtwijzer-why-online-supported-dispute-resolution-is-hard-to-implement/, last accessed 14.02.2023 (site no longer available); https://www.hiil.org/news/rechtwijzer-why-online-supported-dispute-resolution-is-hard-to-implement/, last accessed 14.09.2023; DIJKSTERHUIS above n. 72.

[82]   DIJKSTERHUIS, above n. 72.

use case for parties who are mutually consenting to divorce, are willing to use the self-help platform, and – crucially – have equal bargaining power. Complex cases and situations involving domestic violence are not suited to this type of negotiation and dispute resolution. The correct procedures to follow in situations where an inequality of bargain power was evident in the final agreement (i.e. one party was clearly favoured at the expense of the other) were also unclear.

Ultimately, Rechtwijzer and Relate both pointed to financial reasons for their closure. While a lack of funding will certainly foreshadow the end of a technology-enabled platform that costs money to build and maintain, there are clearly other reasons, not related to finance, that played a role in their demise.

5.3. LESSONS LEARNED

What can be learned from the contrasting experiences of amica and Rechtwijzer? First, it is important to point out that the founders and developers of amica likely benefited from the Rechtwijzer experience. Despite its failure as a platform, the Rechtwijzer project was a pioneer in developing the incorporation of algorithmic tools into the divorce negotiation process. Rechtwijzer remains an important and influential development in technology-enabled family dispute resolution. The successful Canadian platforms MyLawBC and MyLawBC Family Resolution Centre are derivates of Rechtwijzer 1.0 and 2.0, respectively.[83]

Two inter-related points can be made. Firstly, the experience with the two systems underscores the importance of engagement and cooperation between the technology experts, the relevant government agencies and institutions, the legal profession, and the end users (citizens). What the makers of amica did – and Rechtwijzer failed to do – was to involve all stakeholders in a meaningful way. Family lawyers were involved in amica from the outset, bringing crucial practical and academic expertise. Thus, the platform is designed in a way that is cognisant of the realities of divorce, from the client's perspective. Technical experts are, obviously, essential in building the platform and translating the legal principles and processes into sensible working algorithms. Government agencies and ministries were involved in the development of the platform, and were, therefore, well placed to offer financial support and endorsement. Finally, amica was actively marketed to the public, explaining its application within the legal process and demystifying the technology behind the platform.[84] Much of the marketing was undertaken by the leading family lawyer on the amica project,

---

[83] https://law-tech-a2j.org/odr/classical-lessons-from-the-rechtwijzer-a-conversation-with-professor-barendrecht/, last accessed 14.02.2023 (site no longer available); R. SMITH, 'Two Steps Forward' (15 April 2016) New Law Journal Issue 7694, https://www.newlawjournal.co.uk/content/two-steps-forward, last accessed 14.09.2023.

[84] See above n. 68.

Gabrielle Canny, lending clear epistemic authority to the case in favour of using amica. Secondly, 'soft' factors – collaboration and communication between stakeholders, particularly cooperation with the legal profession, whose function the AI will, in some part, assume, and engaging in a public marketing and information campaign – help to build trust between all stakeholders, and in the product itself, which is essential to the success of the platform or tool. As those involved with Rechtwijzer found out, the legal profession is unlikely to endorse a product that overlaps with its own functions, without adequate consultation, for they have no basis for trust in the product. Likewise, citizens are unlikely to be comfortable using a tool that has not been fully explained to them, and which does not have the support of the existing experts, namely family lawyers and governmental institutions.

Trust is key – a sentiment subsequently acknowledged by Laura Kistemaker, who was part of the Rechtwijzer project, and now leads Uit Elkaar.[85] When it comes to implementing AI-based solutions, and particularly elements such as machine learning algorithms, with the associations – however misplaced – of cold, programmatic robots replacing human empathy and reasoning, it is imperative that: (1) stakeholders and experts are consulted in the design of the technology; and (2) that its purpose and capabilities are clearly communicated, in order to build trust and public acceptance. The latter step is especially important when the technology is being used in the context of extremely sensitive and difficult personal life events, such as relationship breakdown.

Finally, incentives are needed to bring the parties and professionals to an ODR platform. Governments could stimulate both lawyers and clients to use ODR platforms (for example, by funding lower court costs for the ODR track for clients, and by providing free or subsided training and certification for lawyers as part of continuing professional development programmes).

6.   CONCLUSION

It is the present authors' opinion that there is a clear use case for AI tools in family (patrimonial) law. Many aspects of human life are manifesting themselves online, and in technology, including life as a legal subject. AI tools increase access to justice for citizens, enabling them to better manage their own legal affairs, and simultaneously relieving strain on overburdened court systems. This chapter has focused on tools and platforms within family law practice, from

---

[85]   https://law-tech-a2j.org/odr/the-rechtwijzer-rises-from-the-ashes-an-interview-with-laura-kistemaker-of-justice42/, last accessed 14.02.2023 (site no longer available); https://www.legalfutures.co.uk/latest-news/pioneering-odr-platform-to-rein-in-ambitions-after-commercial-setback, last accessed 14.09.2023; KISTEMAKER, above n. 75.

AI tools that assist, for example, with asset division, alimony and childcare arrangements, to the integration of those tools in AI-based ODR and online divorce platforms. It is contended here that these tools are helpful, both within and outside the traditional processes for divorce. AI tools that offer solutions for ancillary and childcare arrangements can be used by lawyers, as part of the negotiation process, or at the direction of a judge, as part of the litigation process. Likewise, post-divorce co-parenting tools can be integrated into the legal process, and have the advantage of maintaining secure records of the custody agenda and communications, should a dispute arise. When used in the right context (straightforward divorce situations; willing and rational parties), these tools offer a significantly faster and cheaper method of reaching fair agreements, compared with traditional processes that take place at the negotiation table or in the courtroom.

Given the trend in Europe towards non-judicial divorce[86] (i.e. legal divorce by mutual consent, conducted outside the judicial procedure, usually before a notary or registrar), the authors foresee a strong use case for AI-based asset division tools in this context too. In a non-judicial divorce, the couple is asked to draw up their own divorce agreement (including property division, maintenance, and child custody and child support arrangements), which is brought before a notary, who will formalise it. Although requirements differ from country to country, independent legal representation for each party is not usually required, and there is a clear role here for asset division tools in aiding the divorcing parties to manage the complex task of property division fairly. As non-judicial divorces are usually by mutual consent (as opposed to contested divorces), the parties are in a good position to approach property divisions with the requisite rationality and willingness to settle. A further use case for these tools is in relation to couples who are splitting, and who need to divide jointly accumulated assets, but have not been in a legally recognised and regulated relationship, i.e. they are not married, in a civil union, or similar. Finally, AI tools can help streamline cross-border divorces, too, which are currently complicated and costly, in terms of both time and money.

Further work is undoubtedly needed as we rethink and rework the justice system with a view to harnessing the benefits of AI and algorithmic innovations. Two key conclusions can be derived from the present study.

Firstly, the public justice system and the plethora of AI tools and AI-based ODR processes currently have very different starting points and underlying principles, which need to be understood and used in the appropriate context. In ODR systems, the parties together are the initiators, and the procedure is both

---

[86]   See, e.g. E. D'ALESSANDRO, 'The Impact of Private Divorces on EU Private International Law' in J.M. SCHERPE and E. BARGELLI (eds.), *Interaction between Family Law, Succession Law and Private International Law: Adapting to Change*, Intersentia, 2021; M. RYZNAR and A. DEVAUX, 'Voila: Taking the Judge out of Divorce' (2018) 42 *Seattle University Law Review* 161.

based on, and geared towards, reaching an agreement. On the other hand, the respondent may be compelled by the applicant to go to court. Here, AI tools can be used as part of the litigation process, on the initiative of the judge, or by the parties themselves or their lawyers, in an effort to negotiate the divorce settlement, either out-of-court or as part of the arguments presented to the court. These systems should operate in concert. The mechanisms of AI tools and AI-based ODR – whether utilised inside or outside the judicial process – should be compatible, and integrated with the broader substantive and procedural framework of a legal system, to maximise fair and full access to justice. Courts – including online courts – can be positioned as an end solution and forum for defending citizen rights', once all forms of private agreement have been exhausted.

Secondly, as can be seen from the contrasting histories of Rechtwijzer and amica, it is uncertain whether any ODR system – and, indeed, any AI tool within the domain of family dispute resolution – will succeed without some form of government support (financial, structural or ideological), throughout the developmental, implementation and operational stages.[87]

The nature of family law is changing. AI tools can help lawyers, judges and citizens apply the law in a more efficient, and often more accurate, cheaper and faster manner. The present authors foresee the future of family law practice as a thoughtful integration of AI and human intelligence. To reach this goal, meaningful conversations between stakeholders across the field must take place, in order to garner the trust and secure the participation required to successfully implement these technologies.

---

[87] This is a sentiment echoed by Sir Terence Etherton, senior judge, Master of the Rolls in England and Wales: https://www.judiciary.uk/wp-content/uploads/2017/06/slynn-lecture-mr-civil-court-of-the-future-20170615.pdf; https://law-tech-a2j.org/odr/we-can-see-clearly-now-online-courts-and-disruption, both last accessed 14.02.2023 (site no longer available); R. SMITH, 'Make Haste Slowly' (11 August 2017) *New Law Journal Issue* 7758, available at https://www.newlawjournal.co.uk/content/make-haste-slowly, last accessed 14.09.2023.

INDEX

Milton Keynes UK
Ingram Content Group UK Ltd.
UKHW031013151123
432615UK00010B/488